Diana Kennel

SECRETS OF THE GREAT PYRAMID

Other books by Peter Tompkins

To a Young Actress
Shaw and Molly Tompkins
The Eunuch & the Virgin
A Spy in Rome
The Murder of Admiral Darlan
Italy Betrayed

Diana Kennedy's copy

PETER TOMPKINS

SECRETS OF THE GREAT PYRAMID

with an appendix by Livio Catullo Stecchini

Harper & Row, Publishers
New York • Evanston
San Francisco • London

First Edition
Standard Book Number: 06-014327-4
Library of Congress Catalog Card Number: 74-88639

To Henry B. Tompkins, whose avuncular support made possible a quarter century of cosmopolitan research; to my friends Alan C. Collins, John Newhouse and Carlo and Nicola Caracciolo, in whose hospitable houses this book was largely written; to my wife, who, though she would rather it had been a novel, was a constant help.

CONTENTS

Acknowledgments xi

Introduction xiii

I   Ancient Background 1

II   Medieval Exploration 5

III   Renaissance and Revival of Interest 21

IV   The Age of Enlightenment 35

V   Exploring with Chisel and Gunpowder 56

VI   First Scientific Theories 70

VII   First Confirmation of Scientific Theories 77

VIII First Refutation of Scientific Theories 96

IX   Scientific Theory Developed 108

X   A Theodolite for Surveyors 117

XI   Almanac of the Ages 121

XII   Astronomical Observatory 147

XIII Astronomical Temples of Egypt 159

XIV Geodetic and Geographic Landmark 176

XV   The Golden Section 189

XVI Scientific Survey Gives Geographical Proof 201

XVII Decline of Ancient Knowledge 214

XVIII Who Built the Pyramid? When? And How? 217

XIX Why Were the Pyramid Passages Plugged? When? And How? 236

XX   Temple of Secret Initiation 256

XXI More Secret Passages and Chambers 268

XXII Astrological Observatory 281

Appendix: Notes on the Relation of Ancient Measures to the Great
       Pyramid 287
       Glossary 383
       Bibliography 393
       Index 405

ACKNOWLEDGMENTS

My first debt is to the courteous and efficient staff of the
Library of Congress, whose institution—along with those of
other helpful librarians round the world—made the research
for this book a delight instead of an ordeal; they are a better
and cheaper investment for our future than more weapons
of destruction.

To Geraldine Dent, of Hopewell, New Jersey, and to
Edward O. Mitchell, of McLean, Virginia, I wish to express
my gratitude for painstaking help in reproducing the pictures
which adorn this volume; to Diagram Ltd. of London for the
streamlined drawings which illustrate the text.

Father Francis J. Heyden, S.J., Director of Georgetown
College Observatory, I wish to thank for his cheerful
encouragement in the face of monumental problems: and
Monsignor Patrick W. Skehan for his kind assistance with the
weighty tomes of the Semitics Library of Catholic University.

For a careful checking of the mathematical properties
incorporated in the Great Pyramid I am indebted to Philippe
Dennery, author of *Mathematics for Physicists.* His
mathematical analysis of the secret geometric structure of
the Great Pyramid as discovered by the Danish engineer
Tons Brunés, made it possible to resolve the problem of the
geodetic and geographic functions of the pyramid.

Most grateful I am to Livio Catullo Stecchini, Professor of
the History of Science (characterized by Professor Giorgio
de Santillana of MIT as "a Copernicus of the twentieth
century"), for permission to quote from numerous
unpublished monographs, the fruit of thirty years research into
the advanced science of geography, geodesy and astronomy
developed by the ancient Egyptians and Sumerians, several
of which appear for the first time in the appendix to this
volume.

This is indeed a cumulative effort, and I hope that my
successors in pyramidal quests will be as lively and
entertaining as have been my predecessors.

I have taken the book's 350 illustrations from the most
disparate Medieval, Renaissance, Romantic, and Modern
sources, from the 400 engravers of Napoleon's 20-volume
Description de l'Egypte to the most recent archeological
journals.

I am indebted to the Royal Society of Edinburgh for the
original plates of the first photographs ever taken inside the
Great Pyramid, by Professor Piazzi Smyth in 1865.

In particular I wish to thank Manly P. Hall for permission to reproduce the illustrations on pages 4 and 257 from his *Encyclopedic Outline of Masonic, Hermetic, Qabalistic and Rosicrucian Symbolical Philosophy;* Mlle. Lucy Lamy for permission to reproduce from the works of R. A. Schwaller de Lubicz, published in Paris by Flammarion and Caractères; Charles E. Jeanneret-Gris, better known as Le Corbusier, for the illustrations on page 192, from his *The Modulor,* published by Harvard University Press; Albert Champdor for the illustration on page 259, from his *Le Livre des Morts,* published by Albin Michel; C. Funk-Hellet for illustrations from his *La Bible et la Grande Pyramide,* published by Vincent Fréal; David Davidson for several plates from his *The Great Pyramid: Its Divine Message,* published by Williams & Norgate; Morton Edgar for plates from his *The Great Pyramid, Its Scientific Features,* published by Bone & Hulley; Howard B. Rand for the intricate interior of the Pyramid on page 28, from his *The Challenge of the Great Pyramid,* published by Destiny Publishers; Ludwig Borchardt for line drawings from his various works listed in the bibliography; Georges Goyon for the illustrations on pages 252 and 254 from *Revue Archéologique;* Leonard Cottrell for the portrait of Flinders Petrie from his book *The Mountains of Pharaoh,* published by J. Hale; and Sir Flinders Petrie for the illustrations on pages 98 and 99 from his *70 Years in Archeology,* published by S. Low, Marston in London. The jacket and the extraordinary interiors of the Grand Gallery and the King's Chamber on pages 14 and 16 are from Ludwig Mayer's *Views of Egypt from the Original Drawings in the Possession of Sir Robert Ainsley During his Embassy in Constantinople,* published in London in 1804.

INTRODUCTION

Does the Great Pyramid of Cheops enshrine a lost science? Was this last remaining of the Seven Wonders of the World, often described as the most sublime landmark in history, designed by mysterious architects who had a deeper knowledge of the secrets of this universe than those who followed them?

For centuries a debate has been waged between supporters of such a theory and its opponents, with eminent scientists and academicians lining up on either side. Though all agree that the Great Pyramid is at least four thousand years old, none can say for certain just when it was built, by whom, or why.

Till recently there was no proof that the inhabitants of Egypt of five thousand years ago were capable of the precise astronomical calculations and mathematical solutions required to locate, orient and build the pyramid where it stands.

It was attributed to chance that the foundations were almost perfectly oriented to true north, that its structure incorporated a value for π (the constant by which the diameter of a circle may be multiplied to give its true circumference) accurate to several decimals and in several distinct and unmistakable ways; that its main chamber incorporated the "sacred" 3–4–5 and 2–$\sqrt{5}$–3 triangles ($a^2 + b^2 = c^2$) which were to make Pythagoras famous, and which Plato in his *Timaeus* claimed as the building blocks of the cosmos. Chance was said to be responsible for the fact that the Pyramid's angles and slopes display an advanced understanding of trigonometric values, that its shape quite precisely incorporates the fundamental proportions of the "Golden Section," known today by the Greek letter φ (pronounced *phi*), revered equally by masters of the *cinquecento* and luminaries of modern architecture.

According to modern academicians the first rough use of π in Egypt was not till about 1700 B.C.—at least a millennium after the Pyramid; Pythagoras' theorem is attributed to the fifth century B.C.; and the development of trigonometry to Hipparchus in the second century before Christ. That is what the Egyptologists say, and that is what they put in their textbooks.

Now the whole subject has had to be reviewed.

Recent studies of ancient Egyptian hieroglyphs and the cuneiform mathematical tablets of the Babylonians and Sumerians have established that an advanced science did flourish in the Middle East at least three thousand years before Christ, and that Pythagoras, Eratosthenes, Hipparchus and other Greeks reputed to have originated mathematics on this planet merely picked up fragments of an ancient science evolved by remote and unknown predecessors.

The Great Pyramid, like most of the great temples of antiquity, was designed on the basis of a hermetic geometry known only to a restricted group of initiates, mere traces of which percolated to the Classical and Alexandrian Greeks.

These and other recent discoveries have made it possible to reanalyze the entire history of the Great Pyramid with a whole new set of references: the results are explosive. The common—and indeed authoritative—assumption that the Pyramid was just another tomb built to memorialize some vainglorious Pharaoh is proved to be false.

For a thousand years men from many occupations and many stations have labored to establish the true purpose of the Pyramid. Each in his own way has discovered some facet, each in its own way valid. Like Stonehenge and other megalithic calendars, the Pyramid has been shown to be an almanac by means of which the length of the year including its awkward .2422 fraction of a day could be measured as accurately as with a modern telescope. It has been shown to be a theodolite, or instrument for the surveyor, of great precision and simplicity, virtually indestructible. It is still a compass so finely oriented that modern compasses are adjusted to it, not vice versa.

It has also been established that the Great Pyramid is a carefully located geodetic marker, or fixed landmark, on which the geography of the ancient world was brilliantly constructed; that it served as a celestial observatory from which maps and tables of the stellar hemisphere could be accurately drawn; and that it incorporates in its sides and angles the means for creating a highly sophisticated map projection of the northern hemisphere. It is, in fact, a scale model of the hemisphere, correctly incorporating the geographical degrees of latitude and longitude.

The Pyramid may well be the repository of an ancient and possibly universal system of weights and measures, the model for the most sensible system of linear and temporal measurements available on earth, based on the polar axis of rotation, a system first postulated in modern times a century ago by the British astronomer Sir John Herschel, whose accuracy is now confirmed by the mensuration of orbiting satellites.

Whoever built the Great Pyramid, it is now quite clear, knew the precise circumference of the planet, and the length of the year to several decimals—data which were not rediscovered till the seventeenth century. Its architects may well have known the mean length of the earth's orbit round the sun, the specific density of the planet, the 26,000-year cycle of the equinoxes, the acceleration of gravity and the speed of light.

But to disentangle the authentic from the phony in what has been attributed to the builders of the Great Pyramid has required the technique of a Sherlock Holmes. To climax the story there is a mystery of detection to match the classic style of Sax Rohmer's Abu Hassan, complete with radiography by cosmic rays.

I. ANCIENT BACKGROUND

Ten miles west of the modern city of Cairo at the end of an acacia, tamarind and eucalyptus avenue stands a rocky plateau. A mile square, it dominates the luxuriant palm groves of the Nile Valley from a height of 130 feet. On this man-leveled plateau, called Giza* by the Arabs, stands the Great Pyramid of Cheops. To the west stretch the vast wastes of the Libyan desert.

The Pyramid's base covers 13 acres, or 7 midtown blocks of the city of New York. From this broad area, leveled to within a fraction of an inch, more than two-and-a-half *million* blocks of limestone and granite—weighing from 2 to 70 tons apiece—rise in 201 stepped tiers to the height of a modern forty-story building, etched against the cloudless blue of the Egyptian skies.

In terms of solid masonry, the structure contains more stone than all the cathedrals, churches and chapels built in England since the time of Christ; as a feat in masonry it was not to be matched till the construction of Boulder Dam. Modern engineers are astounded by both the enormity of the problems involved in the construction of the Pyramid and the optician's precision with which these problems were resolved. As originally designed, with its full mantle of polished limestone, the Pyramid must have been a dazzling sight. Unlike marble, which tends to become eroded with time and the weather, limestone becomes harder and more polished.

Near the Pyramid of Cheops stand two more pyramids, one, slightly smaller, attributed to Cheops' successor, Kephren, and another, smaller still, partly sheathed in red granite, attributed to Kephren's successor, Mykerinos. Together with six diminutive pyramids, supposedly built for Cheops' wives and daughters, they form what is known as the Giza complex. About a hundred more pyramidal structures of various sizes and in various stages of dilapidation follow the western bank of the Nile southward toward the Sudan, mostly within one degree of latitude, or 70 miles; but it is the Great Pyramid, unique in size and proportion, which is of paramount interest in this story.

The three large pyramids on the Giza plateau seen from across the Nile. The nearest of the three large pyramids is that of Cheops. Kephren's appears to be higher because it stands on higher ground. The third is that of Mykerinos. The two smallest pyramids are attributed to Cheops' wife and daughter.

* Most often spelt Giza, but transliterated by various authors as Djiseh or Jeeseh, the *G* is pronounced hard by the Egyptians and soft by other Arabs—as in *J* or *Dj*.

Reconstruction of a pyramid, showing the original polished limestone mantle which covered the entire structure.

What the Great Pyramid looked like when it was completed, or even for the first one or two millennia thereafter, is not recorded in history. No description of the Pyramid has survived in the Egyptian texts. Legends have it painted in various colors, marked with designs and inscribed with symbols. The thirteenth-century Arab historian, Abd-al-Latif, says the Pyramid was once inscribed with unintelligible characters in inscriptions so numerous they would fill ten thousand pages: his colleagues assumed them to be the graffiti of myriads of ancient tourists.

The first eyewitness descriptions from classical authors are pitifully sparse. Thales, the father of Greek geometry, who visited the Pyramid sometime in the sixth century B.C., is reputed to have astounded its Egyptian guardians with a correct computation of its height by measuring its shadow at the time of day when his own shadow was equal to his height. Unfortunately he left no detailed description of his visit.

The works of other classical authors known to have written about the Pyramid, such as Euhemerus, Duris of Samoa, Aristagoras, Antisthenes, Demetrius of Phaleron, Demoteles, Artemidorus of Ephesus, Dionysius of Halicarnassus, Alexander Polyhistor, Butoridas, and Apion are all lost, and survive only in fragmented quotation.

Herodotus, who saw the Pyramid about 440 B.C.—by which time it was as ancient to him as his period is to us—says that each of the structure's four perfectly triangular faces was still covered with a mantle of highly polished limestone, the joints so fine they could scarcely be seen. In his *History,* which contains the first comprehensive account of Egypt to have survived intact, Herodotus

2

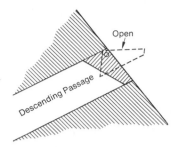

Open

Descending Passage

Though no remains of a swivel door have been found at the Great Pyramid, Strabo's description fits the conditions; and a similar swivel door was found at the south pyramid of Dashur.

From the original entrance a long passage descends into the heart of the Great Pyramid at an angle of 26 1/2°, or a slope of about 1 in 2. The passage is 3 feet 5 inches wide and 3 feet 11 1/2 inches high.

For the first 130 feet down, the passage is built into the masonry with beautifully finished sides of white limestone, perfectly straight and smooth. Thereafter it is cut equally smoothly through the bedrock of limestone on which the Pyramid is founded.

At 345 feet from the entrance, the passage levels out for 25 feet, then enters a roughly cut pit.

deals with other aspects of the Pyramid, but not all his information can be taken at face value.

Diodorus Siculus, the Greek historian who lived soon after the time of Christ, described the Great Pyramid's 22 acres of polished casing stones as being "complete and without the least decay." The Roman naturalist Pliny gives a report of natives gamboling up the polished sides to the delight of Roman tourists.

A man who may have had a lot to say about the Pyramids, in the forty-seven books of his *History,* was Strabo, the Pontine geographer who took a trip up the Nile in 24 B.C., but his history is lost: in the geographical appendix which survives he does little more than describe an entrance on the north face of the Great Pyramid made of a hinged stone which could be raised but which was indistinguishable from the surrounding masonry when it lay flush.

Strabo reports that this small opening gave onto a narrow and low passage, less than 4 feet by 4, which descended 374 feet into a damp, vermin-infested pit dug from the live bedrock 150 feet below the base of the Pyramid. That this pit was visited in Roman times was deduced from initials supposedly written with smoking torches on the rough ceilings by wealthy Greek and Roman tourists.

Sometime during the early centuries of the Christian era, the precise location of the movable door was lost. It was a period when information of all sorts began to grow scarce, when worldly learning came to be despised and denigrated. Christianized Egyptians were forbidden access to the ancient temples, which were either seized or razed by the Catholics; thousands of statues and inscriptions were disfigured; the hieroglyphs, whose meaning was already lost to most, became dead letters to the world to remain so for the next fifteen hundred years.

The great library of Alexandria, accidentally damaged by Julius Caesar and restored by Mark Anthony, was intentionally destroyed by a Christian mob on orders of the Christian emperor Theodosius in A.D. 389. All that was

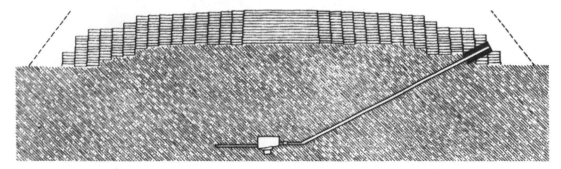

ancient was pagan, and therefore sinful. Those interested in mathematics and astronomy were persecuted and put to death for their inquisitiveness. Even women weren't spared, as with the lovely Hypatia, who was seized by an angry mob (incited by the monks under the control of St. Cyril, then Bishop of Alexandria), dragged into a church, stripped naked, and scraped to death with oyster shells. Her crime was to have been the daughter of the celebrated Alexandrian mathematician Theon, to have edited her father's works, taught mathematics, and become a leading philosopher in her own right, renowned for her beauty, modesty and learning.*

As the Dark Ages continued, little or nothing more was heard of the Great Pyramid of Cheops.

* Though her writings perished with the burning of the library of Alexandria, Hypatia is known from contemporary writings to have produced a commentary on the *Arithmetic* of Diophantus, one on the *Astronomical Canon* of Ptolemy, and one on the *Comics* of Appolonius of Perga. Synesius, Bishop of Ptolemais requested her assistance in the construction of an astrolabe and a hydroscope.

4

II. MEDIEVAL
EXPLORATION

The first dawn of a renaissance came with the Arabs.
When the followers of Mohammed swept into power in the
Near East in the seventh century and captured Alexandria
in A.D. 640, they found no library of any importance, but
a city of four thousand palaces, four thousand baths and
four hundred theaters. Impressed by the opulence of the
city and the size of the Christian fleet, they decided to
emulate both.

The Mohammedans' delight in navigation engendered
a need for geography, which required astronomy and
mathematics. The search for such data was to lead them
to the secrets of the Pyramid. To broaden their knowledge,
the Arabs set about translating into Arabic all they could
lay hands on of ancient Greek and Sanskrit material,
ransacking monasteries for rare copies of Euclid, Galen,
Plato, Aristotle, and the Hindu sages. In the midst of otherwise Dark Ages, Mohammed's religious successors, the
caliphs of Baghdad, were soon the most enlightened as
well as the most powerful potentates. Under caliph Harun
Al-Rashid, whose feats were to be celebrated in the
Arabian Nights, translators were paid in gold by the weight
of each manuscript.

Harun's young son Abdullah Al Mamun, who came to
the throne in A.D. 813, founded universities, patronized
literature and science, and turned Baghdad—known as
Dar-al-Salam, or City of Peace—into a seal of academic
learning, with its own library and astronomical observatory.

Described by Gibbon as "a prince of rare learning who
could assist with pleasure and modesty at the assemblies
and disputations of the learned," young Al Mamun was
responsible for the translation into Arabic of Ptolemy's
great astronomical treatise, the *Almagest.* This work contained astronomical and geographical data, including
the earliest star catalogue which has survived, all of
which knowledge had been lost to the West for centuries
but was of great value to the Arabs in their growing empire.

Claiming that Aristotle had appeared to him in a dream,
Al Mamun commissioned seventy scholars to produce
an "image of the earth" and the first "stellar map in the
world of Islam." (Though they have since disappeared,
these maps were consulted by the Arab historian Al Masudi
in the first half of the tenth century.) To check Ptolemy's

In the *Arabian Nights* the Great Pyramid was reputed to have magical qualities and to contain extraordinary treasures. E. W. Lane's picture illustrates his nineteenth-century translation of *The Thousand and One Nights*.

statement that the circumference of the earth was 18,000 miles, Al Mamun ordered his astronomers to measure the actual overland length of a degree of latitude across the adjacent plain of Palmyra, north of the Euphrates. From a central point the observers moved north and south till they noted by astronomical observation that the latitude had changed 1°; with wooden rods they measured across the sandy plain and obtained a degree of 56 2/3 Arabic miles, the equivalent of 64.39 English statute miles. This figure, which gave a circumference of 23,180 miles, was more precise than Ptolemy's, but the Arabs had no way of checking it: no one had yet circumnavigated the globe; indeed, most still argued that the world was flat!

Al Mamun, who ran an up-to-date intelligence service under the direction of his postmaster-general employing as many as seventeen hundred old women as intelligence agents in Baghdad alone, was informed that the Great Pyramid was reputed to contain a secret chamber with maps and tables of the celestial and terrestrial spheres. Although they were said to have been made in the remote past, they were supposed to be of great accuracy. The chamber was also reported to contain vast treasures and such strange articles as "arms which would not rust" and "glass which might be bended and not break."

Arab historians, including one with the imposing name of Abu Abd Allah Mohammed ben Abdurakin Alkaisi, have recounted the tale of Al Mamun's attempts to enter the Pyramid. In 820 the young caliph collected a vast conglomeration of engineers, architects, builders and stonemasons to attack the Pyramid; for days they searched the steep polished surface of the northern slope for its secret entrance, but could find no trace of it.

Not to be thwarted, so the story goes, Al Mamun decided to burrow straight into the solid rock of the structure in the hope of running across some passage within the interior. Hammer and chisel would not dent the huge blocks of limestone, no matter how many blacksmiths stood ready to sharpen them; so a more primitive but effective system was used: fires were built close to the blocks of masonry, and when these became red hot they were doused with cold vinegar until they cracked. Battering rams knocked out the fragmented stone.

Al Mamun forced his way into the Pyramid to the west of the main axis of the northern face, at the level of the seventh course of masonry. He misjudged the level of the original entrance by starting ten courses too low, and too far to the west.

7

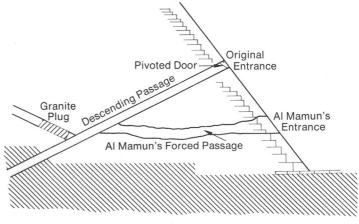

Pivoted Door

Original Entrance

Granite Plug

Descending Passage

Al Mamun's Entrance

Al Mamun's Forced Passage

8

Entrance to Descending Passage.

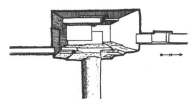

The subterranean pit cut deep into the bedrock is almost 600 feet directly below the apex of the Pyramid. It is 31 feet in the east-west direction but only 27 feet north-south.

Though its ceiling is relatively smooth, its floor is cut in several rough levels, the lowest being 11 feet 6 inches from the ceiling.

In the south wall, opposite the entrance, is a low passage which runs another 53 feet southward before coming to a blind end.

In the center of the floor is a square hole, which was 12 feet deep in 1838, but was dug deeper by the English explorer Howard-Vyse in the vain hope of finding an outlet for a further hidden chamber.

For over 100 feet Al Mamun's men tunneled into the solid core of the Pyramid, excavating a narrow passage that became hotter, dustier and more constricted. Illumination by candle or flare consumed oxygen and poisoned the air.

Al Mamun was on the point of giving up when a workman heard a muffled sound of something heavy falling somewhere within the Pyramid, east of the tunnel. Renewing their efforts and altering the direction of the bore, the workers broke into a hollow way "exceeding dark, dreadful to look at, and difficult to pass." It was a passage 3 1/2 feet wide by 3 feet 11 inches high, which sloped at a steep angle of 26°. On the floor lay a large prismatic stone which had been dislodged from the ceiling of the passage.

Struggling up the passage on all fours, the Arabs discovered the original secret entrance about 90 feet to the north. It had been placed 49 feet above the base of the Pyramid, ten courses higher than Al Mamun had guessed, and 24 feet east of the main axis of the north face of the Pyramid.

Retracing their steps, Al Mamun and his men groped down the low, slippery, Descending Passage, cut deep into the rock of the plateau. At the bottom they were disappointed to find nothing but the unfinished, roughly hewn chamber, or "pit," with an uneven floor, containing nothing but debris and dust. On the far side of it, an even narrower horizontal passage led 50 feet to a blank wall; in the floor a well shaft appeared to have been carved to a depth of 30 feet, leading nowhere.

From the torch marks on the ceiling, the Arabs deduced that the "pit" had been visited in classical times and that anything of interest it may have contained had long since been removed.

What now intrigued the Arabs was the large prismatic stone that had fallen from the ceiling of the Descending Passage. It had evidently covered the end of a large rectangular red-and-black granite plug which completely filled what looked like another passage sloping *up* into the body of the Pyramid. Of such a passage there had been no mention in the writings of Strabo or other classical authors; Al Mamun figured he might have stumbled onto a secret which had been kept since the original construction of the building.

The Arabs tried to chip or dislodge the granite plug, but it was tightly wedged, of indeterminate length, and it evidently weighed several tons. Spurred by the prospect of a new passage leading to some hidden treasure chamber, Al Mamun ordered his men to cut around the plug through

9

The granite plug in the ceiling, halfway down the descending passage, was of very hard quartz, mica and feldspar, which blunted the Arabs' chisels.

The Arabs dug a large cavity into the softer limestone blocks of the body of the Great Pyramid to the west of the Descending Passage. By means of this hole Al Mamun was able to circumvent the three impenetrable granite monoliths which barred his way to what appeared to be a passage leading upward into the Pyramid.

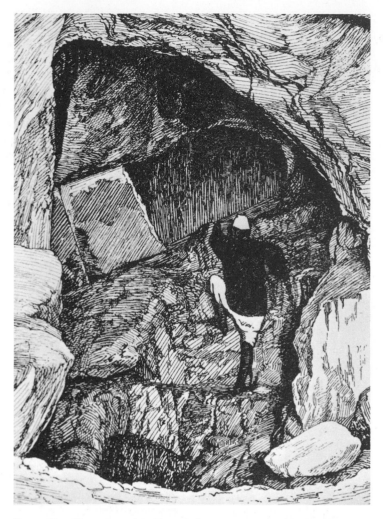

the softer limestone blocks of the surrounding walls. Even this turned out to be more of a job than expected. When the Arabs had bored beyond the first granite plug for over 6 feet, they encountered another granite plug, equally hard and equally tightly wedged. Beyond it lay yet a third. By now the Arabs had tunneled more than 16 feet. Beyond the third granite plug they came upon a passage filled with a limestone plug which could be cracked with chisels and removed piece by piece.

It is not recorded how many such plugs the Arabs encountered, but they may have had to clear a score or more before they could force their way into a narrow ascending passage, again less than 4 feet high and equally narrow. On their hands and knees, holding their torches low, Al Mamun and his men were obliged to scramble up 150 feet of dark, slippery passageway, at the same steep

10

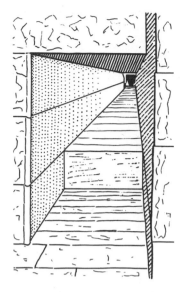

The first-level passage, at the top of the first long incline, is 127 feet long, 3 feet 9 inches high, and 3 feet 5 inches wide.

A sudden drop of 2 feet mysteriously appears in the passage.

Queen's Chamber, with niche, excavated by Arabs.

slope of 26°, before they could raise their heads and stand on a level spot.

In front of them stretched another low horizontal passage, no higher than the one they had painfully ascended.

Inching their way to the end of this passage, they found themselves in a rectangular limestone room with a rough floor and a gabled limestone roof. Because of the custom among the Arabs of placing their women in tombs with gabled ceilings (as opposed to flat ones for men), this room came to be known as the "Queen's Chamber."

The bare room, 18 feet long, and almost square, had an empty niche in the east wall large enough to have contained an overlifesize statue. Thinking the niche might conceal the entrance to a second chamber, the Arabs hacked their way into its solid masonry for another yard before giving up.

11

The name "Queen's Chamber" is considered a misnomer by Egyptologists, who claim that the Egyptians placed no queens in the pyramids of the Pharaohs.

The walls of the chamber are unblemished limestone blocks, beautifully finished, but early explorers found them mysteriously encrusted with salt as much as 1/2 inch thick.

Originally the niche was 3 feet 5 inches deep, but treasure seekers have hacked a passage through the back for several yards. The niche is just over 16 feet high. The sides have four corbeled courses, and are 61 3/4 inches (3 cubits) apart at the base and 20 1/4 inches (1 cubit) apart at the top.

The chamber, placed directly beneath the apex of the Pyramid, is almost square: 18 feet 10 inches from east to west and 17 feet 2 inches from north to south. It has a double-pitched ceiling, 20 feet 5 inches at its highest, formed by huge blocks of polished limestone at a slope of 30° 26', which extend 10 feet beyond the supporting walls; there is no pressure, or arch thrust, at the apex, the center of gravity of each block being well behind the wall face.

The floor of the chamber is of roughly dressed stones, and appears never to have been finished, as if another layer of polished stones were to be laid.

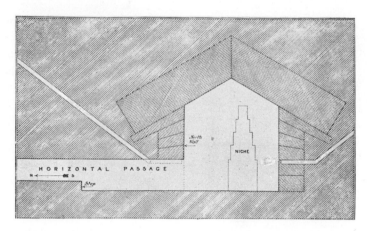

Retracing their steps to where they had left the low Ascending Passage, the Arabs raised their torches into an ominous void above them. In the side walls joist holes indicated that the floor of the Ascending Passage had once continued upwards, blocking and hiding the low passage to the Queen's Chamber.

Climbing on each others' shoulders and raising their torches, the Arabs now saw that they were at the bottom of a narrow but grand gallery, about 28 feet high, which appeared to stretch upward at the same steep slope as the Ascending Passage into the black and mysterious heart of the Pyramid.

The center of this new passage was very slippery, but to either side of it were two narrow ramps slotted at regular intervals; they afforded a better foothold.

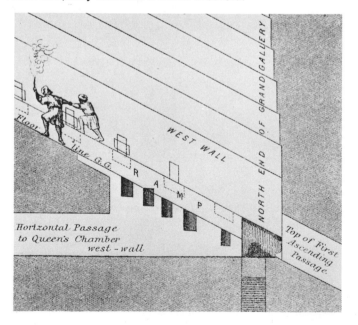

Holding their torches high, the Arabs proceeded to escalade these ramps. At the end of another 150-foot climb, they came upon a huge solid stone, raised 3 feet from the floor, which they had to clamber up in order to stand at the top of the gallery on a 6 × 8 foot platform.

Beyond this platform the floor continued level, but the

The overall length of the Grand Gallery, shown here, is 157 feet. It is inclined 26°, as is the Ascending Passage.

The walls are 28 feet high, rising vertically in seven courses of polished limestone, each corbeled 3 inches toward the center, making the gallery narrow from 62 inches at the base to 41 inches at the top. The first corbeling is 7 feet high.

On either side of the central 2-foot passage are two ramps 18 inches wide and 2 feet high; along the walls is a series of notches.

The gallery is considered an architectural masterpiece. Egyptologists have differed as to its function, and that of its ramps and notched holes.

13

At the top of the Grand Gallery lies a huge stone step, 6 feet wide, 3 feet high, which blocks the Ascending Passage and forms a platform 8 feet deep, now badly chipped and worn.

Beyond the Great Step there stretches another low, level passage 41 inches (or 2 cubits) square. A third of the way along this passage, it rises and widens into a sort of antechamber, the south, east and west walls of which are no longer of polished limestone but of polished red granite.

ceiling fell to a mere 41 inches, forming a sort of portcullis entrance to a small antechamber.

Past the portcullis, Al Mamun's men were again obliged to stoop along a short passage which led to yet another chamber.

Their torches revealed a great and well-proportioned room; the walls, floor and ceiling were all of beautifully wrought and polished red-granite blocks, squared and extremely finely jointed: "a right noble apartment, thirty-four feet long, seventeen broad, and nineteen high." Because of its flat ceiling, the Arabs named it the "King's Chamber."

Al Mamun's men frantically searched every cranny of the chamber but could find nothing of interest or value— there was no sign of any treasure, only a large lidless "sarcophagus" of highly polished, dark chocolate-colored granite.

Some Arabian authors have reported that Al Mamun found in the sarcophagus a stone statue in the shape of a man. They say that within the statue lay a body wearing a breastplate of gold set with precious stones, an invaluable sword on his chest, and a carbuncle ruby on his head the size of an egg, which shone as with the light of day. According to the storytellers the statue was inscribed with a mysterious writing that no one could decipher; but there is no historical evidence to support the tale.

To Al Mamun it appeared that either the vast mausoleum had been built about nothing but a single empty chest, or the whole place had previously been looted; though how and by whom it was hard to imagine, considering the enormous number of stone plugs the Arabs had been obliged to break up in order to make their entrance.

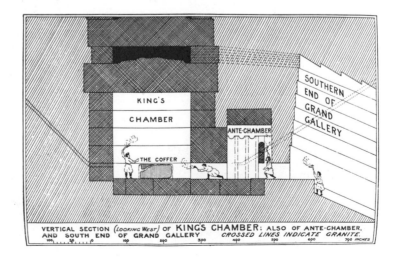

VERTICAL SECTION (LOOKING WEST) OF KINGS CHAMBER: ALSO OF ANTE-CHAMBER, AND SOUTH END OF GRAND GALLERY   CROSSED LINES INDICATE GRANITE.

15

The sole item within the King's Chamber is a lidless coffer cut from a solid block of chocolate-colored granite, whose granules of feldspar, quartz and mica are even harder than those of the chamber walls. They were fabled to have come not from the Egyptian quarries up the Nile at Syene but from the mythical Atlantis or even from America.

Because the coffer is 6 feet 6 inches long, 2 feet 3 inches wide and 3 feet deep and could comfortably accommodate a human body, it has been called a sarcophagus and is believed by Egyptologists to have been the tomb of the Pharaoh Cheops.

A ridge along the top edge of the coffer indicates it may have once had a sliding lid, though no trace of the lid has been found.

As the Arabs removed 22 acres of 100-inch-thick pure-limestone covering from the Great Pyramid, vast mounds of chips and refuse built up as high as 50 feet around the base.

In a fury of disappointment, the Arabs ripped up part of the floor and hacked at the beautiful granite walls, even burrowing a short tunnel into a corner of the room, all to no avail.

Legend has it that to pacify his disappointed men Al Mamun had a treasure of gold secreted in the Pyramid at night, amounting to just the wages due his men, and palmed off the coincidence on the wisdom and prescience of Allah.

For another four centuries the great pile lay undisturbed on the desert's edge, its outer casing virtually intact, its geometric shadows lengthening and shortening with the revolutions of each year. An Arab historian who saw the Pyramid in the early thirteenth century compared it to a great female breast rising from the bosom of Egypt. He remarked that it was still perfect except for the entrance carved in it by Al Mamun.

Subsequently a series of earthquakes demolished large parts of northern Egypt, and the descendents of Al Mamun's workers wreaked their revenge on the treasureless Pyramid by stripping it of its precious limestone casing to rebuild their new capital city El Kaherah, "The Victorious." In the course of several generations they managed to remove the entire 22 acres of 100-inch-thick covering of the Pyramid, and even built two bridges especially to drag the heavier stones across the river on camel trains to Cairo for the construction of a series of mosques and palaces.

17

The Mosque of Sultun Hasan in Cairo, built in 1356 with limestone blocks removed from the covering of the Great Pyramid.

One of the more renowned of the several hundred minareted mosques in what came to be known as "Grand" Cairo was built in 1356 by Sultan Hasan almost entirely with stones removed from the Pyramid. Forty years later, in the reign of his successor Barluk, when the French Baron d'Anglure traveled to Egypt, he was able to see and report on the continued dismantling of casing stones by Arab stonemasons. D'Anglure was naïve enough to fall for the historical canard that the pyramids had been built as granaries by the biblical Joseph to store Pharaoh's grain in years of plenty; but his old French gives a vivid picture of the despoilers tumbling the massive blocks from the summit: ". . . *certain ouvriers massons qui à force desmuroient les grosses pierres taillés qui font la couverture de desdits greniers, et les laissoient devaller à val.*" ("Certain masons demolished the course of great casing stones which covered these granaries, and tumbled them into the valley.")

The stripping of the limestone left the core masonry exposed in a series of gradually ascending and receding steps to be weathered and worn by wind, sand and rain. Some of the underlying core blocks proved to be of pure limestone, others of nummulitic limestone containing large quantities of fossil shells resembling coins.

Around the stripped Pyramid, fragments of limestone and rubble were piled so high that they finally obliterated the entrance which Al Mamun had forced in the north face.

18

But the removal of the outer casing brought to light
two huge transoms embedded in the masonry which formed
a protective gable over the tiny gaping original entrance
to the Descending Passage.

Only now, no one cared to reenter the Pyramid.

III. RENAISSANCE
AND REVIVAL
OF INTEREST

Superstition shrouded the ancient structure. It was said to be haunted by ghosts and to be alive with venomous vermin. According to the Arabs the Great Pyramid was haunted at noon and sunset by a naked woman with large teeth who seduced people into her power and then drove them insane.

When Rabbi Benjamin ben Jonah of Navarre, an adventurous twelfth-century traveler, reached the Giza plateau from Abyssinia he noted that "the Pyramids which are seen here are constructed by witchcraft."

Abd-al-Latif, who taught medicine as well as history in Baghdad, summoned the courage to enter the Great Pyramid shortly after Benjamin's visit but admitted that within its stifling interior he fainted from fear and came out more dead than alive.

The Pyramid's bad reputation spread so far afield that when the fabulous English explorer Sir John Mandeville is supposed to have visited Egypt in the fourteenth century, he is said to have complained he dared not enter the Pyramid because it was filled with serpents: but the serpents turned out to be as fabulous as his *Travels* which were produced by a notary in Liège who had never even left his native country.

Not till the Renaissance had swept away some of the cobwebs of medieval obscurantism, and revived man's interest in science, was there enough motive for Europeans to enter the Pyramid and rationally examine its interior.

In 1638 John Greaves, a 36-year-old mathematician and astronomer who had studied at Oxford and taught geometry in London, decided to set off for Egypt. His was no idle curiosity: like Al Mamun, he hoped to find in the Great Pyramid a datum that might help to establish the dimensions of the planet. Although the preceding century had spawned the great voyages of exploration, and Magellan's crew had circumnavigated the earth, the sciences of geography and astronomy were still so much in their infancy—to all appearances—that no one had improved on Ptolemy's or Al Mamun's geographical degree and hence no one knew the true circumference of the earth.

The Giza pyramids and Sphinx as depicted in 1610, showing European travelers.

A clue to a possible solution had been postulated by Girolamo Cardano, an astonishing Milanese physician and mathematician of the early sixteenth century and a close friend of Leonardo da Vinci's, who maintained that a body of exact science must have preexisted the Greeks. Cardano suspected that a degree of meridian (far more exact than that of Eratosthenes, Ptolemy or Al Mamum) must have been in existence hundreds if not thousands of years before the Alexandrians and that to find it one must search in Egypt. Pythagoras was said to have claimed that the measures of antiquity were derived from Egyptian standards, themselves copied from an invariable prototype taken from nature. It followed that the pyramids might have been built to record the dimensions of the earth and furnish an imperishable standard of linear measure.

Greaves had already traveled to Italy to measure its ancient buildings and statues in an attempt to establish the original standard of measure used by the Romans—which he concluded to be a foot somewhat shorter than a British foot by 28 thousandths.

22

John Greaves.

Statue of young Roman architect, Statilius Aper, in Vatican gardens, from which Greaves measured a Roman foot which was related to the circumference of the earth.

In the Vatican gardens Greaves found a statue commemorating a young architect of the first century A.D., T. Statilius Vol Aper, who had died in his twenty-third year. Portrayed in relief were Aper's architectural instruments, including a Roman foot. Greaves copied this foot and compared it to an English foot made of brass which he had divided in 2,000 parts. "I spent at least two hours," wrote

23

Greaves, explaining the diligence with which he performed the operation, "so often comparing the several divisions and digits of it respectively one with another, that I think more circumspection could not have been used."

Greaves found that the Roman foot contained "1,944 such parts as the English foot contains 2,000." The interesting result of this measurement was the fact that it confirmed a Roman foot to be exactly 24/25ths of the Greek foot derived from the Parthenon—a foot of which there are 100 in the width and 225 in the length of the building.

Greaves's next problem was to establish the basic unit on which the Pyramid had been built—whether foot, pace, cubit (an arm's length), or palm.

To help defray his expenses, Greaves applied for the patronage and assistance of the magistrates of the City of London, but they turned him down. Luckily the Archbishop of Canterbury thought enough of Greaves, and was sufficiently interested in rare Arabic and Persian manuscripts which might be discovered in the East, to patronize him. Greaves was able to equip himself with instruments for measuring the inside and the outside of the Pyramid and for obtaining the declination and right ascension of the stars above it, and have enough money left over to spend a few weeks in Cairo.

Though a bookish mathematician and an ingrained antiquarian, Greaves was not without courage as an explorer. At the Pyramid he climbed onto the mound of rubbish 38 feet high which surrounded it and gingerly let himself into the Descending Passage, "creeping like a serpent," horrified to

The outside of the first Pyramid

Entrance to the Great Pyramid as depicted by John Greaves.

find himself in a storm of bats "so ugly and so large, exceeding a foot in length," such as he had never imagined.

To scare off the bats and clear the air, Greaves resorted to firing his pistols; the explosions reverberated like cannon shots in the restricted passage of the Pyramid.

Working his way downward, Greaves reached the point where Al Mamun's original tunnel joined the Descending Passage, but was unable to proceed in a downward direction because of the debris left behind by Al Mamun's men when they had broken up the series of limestone plugs that had filled the upper passage.

Following in the Arabs' footsteps, Greaves climbed around the massive granite plugs and up into the low Ascending Passage. Having scrambled to the top, Greaves retraced Al Mamun's course along the short Horizontal Passage to the Queen's Chamber, where he found the stench of vermin so offensive he could not linger.

Everything Greaves came across was a puzzle to him. The steepness of the Grand Gallery seemed to preclude its having been designed as a chamber: the difficulty of scaling its polished slope made it impractical as a stairway. Also, it was accessible only through the preceding very low passage.

He admitted nevertheless that the Pyramid was "a very stately piece of work, and not inferior, either in respect of the curiosity of art or richness of materials, to the most sumptuous and magnificent buildings." He noted that it was built of polished limestone "very evenly cut in spacious

25

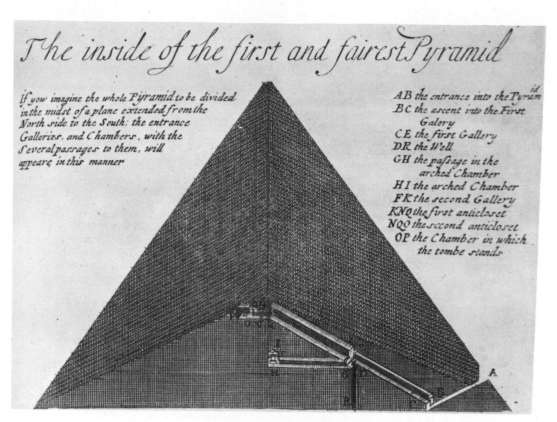

If you imagine the whole Pyramid to be divided in the midst of a plane extended from the North side to the South; the entrance Galleries, and Chambers, with the Several passages to them, will appeare in this manner

AB the entrance into the Tyramid
BC the ascent into the First Galery
CE the first Gallery
DR the Well
GH the passage in the arched Chamber
HI the arched Chamber
FK the second Gallery
KNQ the first anticloset
NQO the second anticloset
OP the Chamber in which the tombe stands

squares or tables"; and he found that the "coagmentation or knitting" of the joints was so close it was scarcely discernible with the naked eye.

Making his way to the King's Chamber, Greaves was puzzled that so incredibly imposing a structure as the Pyramid should be built around a single chamber with a single empty coffer. He could see no apparent reason for its portcullis entrance or for the complexity of its antechamber where the walls changed mysteriously from limestone to granite. But being a scientist by nature, Greaves set to collecting and noting data about the building.

How the King's Chamber and its Antechamber with its portcullis are entirely cased by granite blocks within the limestone body of the Pyramid.

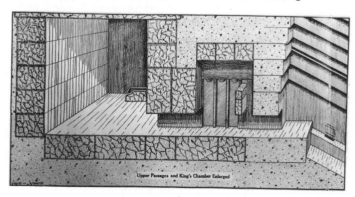

Upper Passages and King's Chamber Enlarged

26

Entrance to the "well."

In the west wall of the Grand Gallery, not far from the north wall, a small part of the ramp is missing, allowing entry into a shallow pit. At the bottom of this pit a short passage leads westward to an opening in the floor which becomes a shaft.

This shaft descends through the nucleus masonry of the Pyramid and penetrates a rocky core which was left by the builders as an anchor for the Pyramid *above* the level of the foundation pavement.

A grotto opens off the shaft and the shaft passes through several natural fissures in the bedrock.

For many centuries the shaft's terminus was a mystery, as was its purpose.

Shaft entrance to the grotto.

In London Greaves had furnished himself with a special 10-foot measuring rod based on a standard English foot deposited in Guild Hall, finely divided into 10,000 equal parts. With great care he measured the length, breadth and width of the King's Chamber, commenting that "the structure of it hath been the labour of an exquisite hand." He counted its tiers of granite, measured their length and breadth, and did likewise to the empty coffer, "even to the thousandth part of a foot," finding it to be 6.488 English feet.

Picking his way back to the foot of the Grand Gallery, Greaves made a new and startling discovery. From the ramp at one side, a stone block had been forcibly removed and a passage appeared to have been dug straight down into the bowels of the Pyramid.

The aperture was a little over 3 feet wide; but as notches had been carved opposite one another on the sides of this "well," Greaves lowered himself into it and descended about 60 feet, to where the shaft had been enlarged into a small chamber, or "grotto." Below him the shaft continued into the murky darkness, but the air was so foul, and the bats so thick, that Greaves decided to climb back up the way he had entered, puzzled by this strange feature of the Pyramid.

That the well shaft was not bottomless he established by dropping a lighted flare which continued to flicker from its depths.

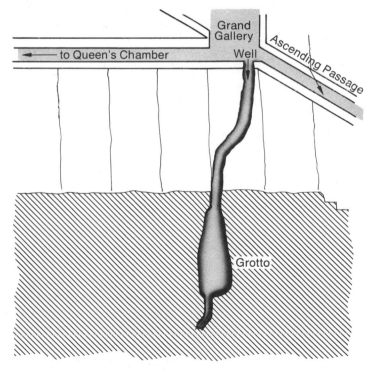

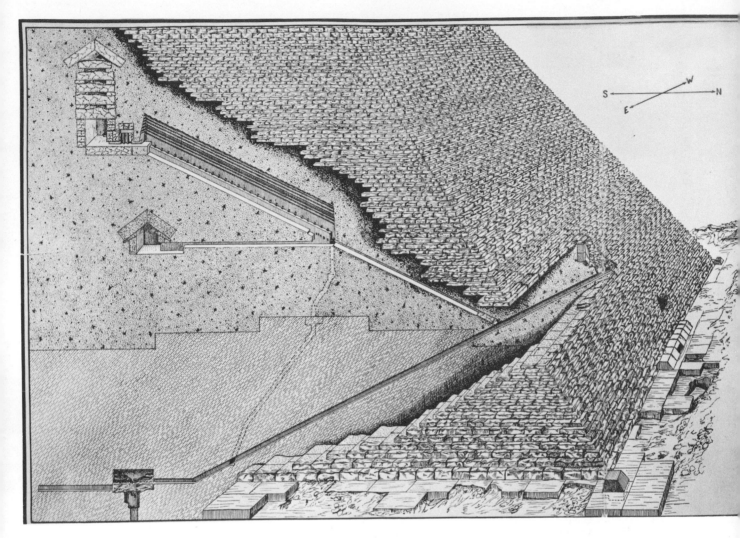

Chambers and passages in
the Great Pyramid.

Outside, Greaves climbed to the top of the Pyramid. From
this high point he could admire the minarets of Cairo, the
range of Mokattam hills across the Nile, and the silhouettes
of the pyramids of Abusir, Saqqara and Dashur to the south.

On his way down Greaves was the first to make a
reasonable count of the Pyramid's visible tiers of chiseled
blocks, which he figured to be 207, estimating the total
height of the structure to be 481 feet, or 499 with the missing
capstone. This was within a dozen feet of being correct.

As a length for the base, Greaves estimated 693 feet,
which was short of the mark by some 70 feet: but the base
was so littered with rubbish that he had no way of telling
where the first tier might rise from the hidden base.

Back in England Greaves was rewarded for his efforts at
the Pyramid by being appointed Savilian Professor of

Astronomy at Oxford. All the facts and figures Greaves had accumulated he meticulously wrote up in a scholarly booklet entitled *Pyramidographia.*

His conclusions led to a very lively discussion—with as much con as pro—in which even the celebrated Dr. William Harvey, discoverer of the circulation of blood, took part. Harvey was surprised that Greaves had not described, or apparently even discovered, any conduits by means of which the central chambers in the Pyramid could be ventilated from the exterior. According to Harvey such conduits were bound to have existed, or the air in the King's Chamber would have become extremely foul—"Seeing we never breathe the same air twice, but still new air is required to a new inspiration (the succus alibilis of it being spent in every expiration)." Harvey's surmise turned out to be true, but was not established for another two generations.

Greaves had indeed noted "two inlets or spaces, in the south and north sides of the chamber, just opposite from one another," but attributed the blackness within them to their being receptacles for burning lamps.

Before returning to England, Greaves had left his instruments, including the special 10-foot rod, to a young Venetian whom he had met in Egypt and who had accompanied him to the Pyramid, Tito Livio Burattini, who who was as anxious as Greaves to find out not only the exact measurements of the Pyramid, but the unit—whether cubit, foot or palm—on which it had originally been designed.

Burattini's trip to Egypt had been subsidized by the Jesuit Father Athanasius Kircher of Cracow, Poland, who had moved to Rome and entered into correspondence with Galileo Galilei on the subject of a universal standard of measure.

At that time Galileo was living in seclusion near Florence, having been tried and imprisoned by the Inquisition for supporting the Copernican belief that the earth and the planets revolved round the sun, and the equally heretical conceit that the earth and the sun spun on their own axes.

As a young man Galileo had timed the oscillations of a lamp swinging in the Duomo of Pisa by means of his pulse beats and found the time for each swing to be the same, no matter what the amplitude of the oscillation, thus discovering what is known as the isochronism of the pendulum.

Developing Galileo's idea, Burattini had tried to obtain a universal standard of measure by using the length of a pendulum that would vibrate exactly 3600 times in one hour, or once every second, but the gold-ball pendulum he devised proved impractical because it was found that its swing varied with temperature, location, and altitude above sea level.

Burattini lingered four years in Egypt taking careful measurements with Greaves's instruments, and he sent reports of the results to Father Kircher by letter, which was lucky for the scientific world: on Burattini's journey through the Balkans back to his adopted Poland he was set upon by bandits and deprived of not only his cash but all his notes on the Pyramid which he intended to have printed as a book in Italy.

There remained the data which he had sent to Father Kircher; but it was from Greaves's data that Sir Isaac Newton deduced that the Great Pyramid had been built on the basis of two different cubits, one of which he called "profane" and the other which he called "sacred." From Greaves's and Burattini's measurements of the King's

Sir Isaac Newton is described by Giorgio de Santillana, of MIT, as "the last of the magicians, the last of the Babylonians and Sumerians, the last great mind which looked on the visible world with the same eyes as those who began to build our intellectual world rather less than 10,000 years ago."

Chamber, Newton computed that a cubit of 20.63 British inches produced a room with an even length of cubits: 20 × 10. This cubit Newton called the "profane," or Memphis, cubit; whereas a longer, more arcane cubit appeared to measure about 25 British inches.

This longer, or "sacred," cubit Newton derived from the Jewish historian Josephus's description of the circumference of the pillars of the Temple at Jerusalem. Newton estimated this cubit to be between 24.80 and 25.02 English inches, but believed the figure could be refined through further measurement of the Great Pyramid and other ancient buildings.

All of this Newton wrote up in a small and now hard-to-find paper called *A Dissertation upon the Sacred Cubit of the Jews and the Cubits of several Nations: in which, from the Dimensions of the Greatest Pyramid, as taken by Mr. John Greaves, the ancient Cubit of Memphis is determined.*

Newton's preoccupation with establishing the cubit of the ancient Egyptians was no idle curiosity, nor just a desire to find a universal standard of measure; his general theory of gravitation, which he had not yet announced, was dependent on an accurate knowledge of the circumference of the earth. All he had to go on were the old figures of Eratosthenes and his followers, and on their figures his theory did not work out accurately.

By establishing the cubit of the ancient Egyptians, Newton hoped to find the exact length of their stadium, reputed by classical authors to bear a relation to a geographical degree, and this he believed to be somehow enshrined in the proportions of the Great Pyramid.

Unfortunately Greaves's and Burattini's measurements of the *base* of the Pyramid were incorrect because of the accumulated debris, and though Newton's figure for the cubit was very close to perfect, the false measurements of the base failed to give him the answer he was searching.

To resolve Newton's problem, Burattini suggested taking the actual measure of two or three degrees of latitude across the flat countryside of Poland; but the operation proved too costly. Unfortunately, neither Newton nor Burattini knew that in 1635 Richard Norwood, author of *Sea-Man's Practice,* had made an observation of the sun at noon at York using a sextant more than 5 feet in radius, and a similar observation in London near the Tower; the distance between the two points was 9149 chains, and he thus obtained a figure of 69.5 English statute miles for 1° of latitude. This figure would have solved Newton's problem, but because of the political unrest in Cromwellian England he did not hear of it; so he put away his theory of gravitation for several more years, or until the French astronomer Jean Picard repeated Norwood's feat with rather more fanfare.

In 1671 Picard measured a degree of latitude between Amiens and Malvoisine. His method was to measure a base line at Amiens very meticulously with wooden rods, then measure the angles formed by this base line with a point on the horizon and deduce its distance by trigonometry. Selecting a series of points on hilltops easily distinguished with a telescope and measuring only the angles between their sides, he was able to string out a series of thirteen large triangles across the countryside and obtain a very accurate degree of 69.1 English statute miles.

On the basis of this computation Newton was able to announce his general theory of gravitation—that all bodies in the universe attract each other in proportion to the product of their mass and inversely as the square of their distance apart—and so launch a new era of physics.

As the English poet Alfred Noyes summed up the event:

> . . . Newton withheld his hope
> Until that day when light was brought from France,
> New light, new hope, in one small glistening fact . . .
> Picard in France—all glory to her name—
> Had measured earth's diameter once more
> With exquisite precision . . .

But all this Anglo-Gallic dalliance was short-lived because an argument developed between Newton and a French family of astronomers, map makers, and surveyors called Cassini. Newton figured that the centrifugal force of the globe spinning on its north-south axis would cause the earth to bulge at the equator and be slightly flattened at the poles.

In his *Principia* Newton estimated that this would have the effect of making a degree of latitude longer nearer the poles and shorter nearer the equator.

The theory was heatedly opposed by the Cassinis, who had extended Picard's triangulation survey north to Dunkirk and south to Perpignan on the Spanish border, and maintained that the earth was elongated like an egg, as depicted in Ptolemaic Egypt: that the degree of latitude was *shorter* north of Paris.

To settle the argument the French Academy of Sciences sent out two expeditions, one to Lapland to measure an actual degree near the Arctic Circle and another to Peru to measure a degree near the equator.

After 18 months of being frozen in winter and devoured by mosquitoes in summer, the expedition to Lapland returned with a figure that showed a degree of latitude was *longer* near the flattened Pole. The Peruvian expedition suffered

The Great Sphinx lies about twelve hundred feet southeast of the Pyramid of Cheops near the valley building of Kephren. Carved from a single sandstone knoll, the colossus is 240 feet long, 66 feet high, and 13 feet 8 inches at its widest.

The headdress and the cobra on the forehead are said to have been symbols of royalty; the features are thought to resemble those of Kephren.

At one time the Sphinx may have been coated with plaster and painted in various colors.

A rational explanation of the mystery of the Sphinx was produced by the British astronomer Sir Norman Lockyer, who said that its being half lion, half virgin symbolizes the junction of the constellations Leo and Virgo which occurred at a summer solstice in the fourth millennium B.C.

even worse conditions, measuring from mountaintop to mountaintop in the Andean highlands, but after ten years of misery, came back with a similar conclusion that the degree was shorter at the equator, vindicating Newton: the Peruvian degree measured 56,734 French *toises,* the Paris degree was 226 *toises* longer, and the Lapland degree 362 *toises* longer still.*

Cassini, who very sensibly proposed the adoption of a geodetic foot representing 1/6000th part of a terrestrial minute of arc, would have been astounded had he known that just such a foot had been in existence for several millennia and that the Sphinx, which could be used as a geodetic marker to indicate the equinox, also once had an obelisk between its paws whose shadow could be used to compute not only the correct circumference of the earth but the variance in the degree of latitude.

But in all this geodetic enterprise the Pyramid's geodetic values were forgotten; its secrets remained as enigmatic as those of its neighbor the Sphinx, which by this time was almost obliterated in the accumulation of wind-blown sand from the Libyan desert.

* The *toise,* or double arm's length, was the standard of measure used by the French before the development of the meter.

33

IV. THE AGE OF ENLIGHTENMENT

Travel to the Giza plateau became a dangerous undertaking in the eighteenth century. Though Egypt was still nominally under the suzerainty of the Ottoman Turks, the traveler was likely to be robbed or killed by gangs of bandit Arabs unless protected by a bodyguard of friendly Janissaries such as had accompanied Greaves.

Not until the time of the American Revolution was any further discovery of importance made at the Pyramid. In 1765, Nathaniel Davison, who was later British Consul General in Algeria, was able to spend a vacation in Egypt in the company of Edward Wortley Montagu, former British ambassador to the Sublime Porte, and carefully explore the Pyramid.

More intrepid than Greaves, Davison lowered a lamp into the "well," tied a rope round his waist, and had himself carefully lowered into its ominous darkness, about a hundred feet farther than Greaves, only to find the bottom blocked with sand and rubbish. To Davison it appeared strange that anyone should go to such an enormous amount of effort to dig a shaft almost 200 feet into the heart of the Pyramid and simply come to a dead end. But there was nothing more he could do. It was extremely close and filthy at the bottom of the "well," and his candle soon burnt up what little air was available. Also, an immense number of huge bats made it difficult for Davison to keep his candle alight; so he laboriously made his way back to the surface.

Abandoning this quest, Davison set about finding any other secret features within the interior of the Pyramid. At the top of the Grand Gallery he noted that his voice was answered in a curious way by repeated echoes which appeared to resonate from somewhere above him.

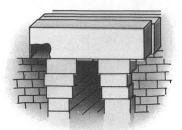

Davison's hole at the top of the Grand Gallery.

Placing a candle at the end of two long canes, Davison was able to spot a small rectangular hole about 2 feet wide at the very top of the Grand Gallery, where its wall joined the ceiling.

To reach this hole was a precarious ordeal: the walls of the gallery were polished and slippery; the perch upon which he had to place his ladder was extremely small and stood high above a yawning drop of 150 feet, all the way down the Grand Gallery. Nevertheless Davison managed to raise seven short ladders till the topmost reached the small rectangular hole.

Davison climbed this rickety echeloning with difficulty. At the top he found that he was prevented from entering the 2-foot hole by some 16 inches of bat dung, which had accumulated through the centuries.

Masking his face with a kerchief, Davison managed to wedge himself into the stifling passage and crawl 25 feet to a chamber not high enough to stand in, but every bit as wide and as long as the King's Chamber below it.

Beneath the bat dung Davison was able to make out a floor consisting of the tops of nine rough-hewn monolithic granite slabs, each weighing up to 70 tons, or as much as a modern railway engine. The under sides of these slabs formed the ceiling of the King's Chamber. To Davison's amazement, the low flat ceiling of the chamber was also constructed of another similar row of granite monoliths.

Otherwise, Davison could find nothing of either historical or architectural interest: no treasure, no inscription, no sign of any further passage. His sole reward was to carve his

36

Three distinct types of Egyptian bats as depicted in the eighteenth century. The bats found by Greaves in the Great Pyramid were over a foot long, with an even greater wingspread. Of the more than a thousand known varieties of these curious nocturnal mammals the "flying foxes" of Australia have a wingspread of up to 5 feet.

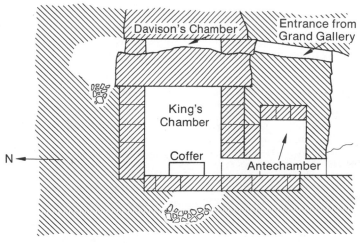

Davison's Chamber above the King's Chamber.

37

Davison's and other graffiti in the Great Pyramid, including that of Mercator, the Flemish cartographer.

Reverse of the seal of the United States of America. According to Manly P. Hall, an expert on Masonic lore, not only were many of the founders of the U.S. government Masons, but they received aid from a secret and august body existing in Europe, which helped them to establish the United States for "a peculiar and particular purpose known only to the initiated few." The Great Seal, says Hall, was the signature of this exalted body, and the unfinished pyramid on its reverse side "is a trestleboard setting forth symbolically the task to the accomplishment of which the U.S. Government was dedicated from the day of its inception." The eagle was apparently intended to represent a phoenix, or symbol of the immortality of the human soul. Great currency has been given to the pyramid and phoenix symbols by placing them upon a one dollar bill.

graffito on the wall and to have the newly discovered chamber named Davison's Chamber in his honor.

When the American Revolution was followed by the French, and Napoleon set out to spread his political doctrines of Free Masonry, interest was rekindled in the Pyramid.

The American revolutionaries had already gone so far as to adopt the ancient Masonic symbol of the Pyramid for the reverse of the Great Seal of the United States.

In their own revolutionary housecleaning, the French outlawed the biblical seven-day week and reverted to the decades of the ancient Egyptians. The *sans-culottes* replaced the old holidays with feast days celebrating Nature and the Supreme Being, the Human Race, the Martyrs of Liberty, Truth, Justice, Paternal Tenderness, Conjugal Faith and even Misfortune. To replace the archaic *toise* made up of six *pied de roi,* the new academicians remeasured the arc from Dunkirk to Perpignan and adopted as a decimal unit the meter, which they computed to be exactly one ten-millionth of the Paris meridian from pole to equator.

On the last day of the month of Floreal in the IXth year of the revolution—our May 19, 1798—General Bonaparte, a sallow little man of 29, set sail from Toulon with a force of 35,000 soldiers crammed into 328 vessels, to conquer Egypt as a steppingstone to India and world domination. Bored by the company of his fellow officers, Napoleon spent most of his time with an extraordinary collection of erudite French civilians classified as "savants." He had brought them along because they were reputed to have acquired a profound knowledge of Egyptian antiquities despite the fact that no one had yet deciphered Egyptian hieroglyphics, so that very little was known of Egypt's remote antiquity.

These savants, a hundred and seventy-five of whom were scattered throughout the fleet, were treated with something less than respect by Napoleon's lower ranks, who were convinced that the "graybeards" had been brought along solely to help locate and dig up hidden treasure. Once the learned gentlemen had landed in Egypt, where their function was to "civilize the natives," they were issued no rations or billets, and whenever the French came under attack from the Mameluke forces of Murad Bey, Napoleon's soldiers would form their famous squares and shout "savants and asses to the center."

Not that the savants ran any real risk. When the French reached the Great Pyramid and were attacked by 10,000 Mameluke horsemen armed with glittering yagatans under the command of Murad himself, in a brilliant green turban astride a snow-white charger, the slaughter consisted entirely of the intrepid Mamelukes. Renowned for having withstood the hordes of Genghis Khan, they were no match for the French sharpshooters and cannoneers.

In two hours two thousand Mamelukes were killed for two score Frenchmen.

Mameluke Beys and their horsemen were mostly converted Christian slaves like the Janissaries and Pages of the Sublime Porte, trained to police, tax, and control Egypt under the nominal suzerainty of the Ottoman Sultan.

In 1811 the Mamelukes were destroyed in one of the foulest but most successful ambushes in history. May 1 they were invited to a feast by Mohammed Ali, the Greek-born adventurer who governed Egypt for the Turks. Dressed in their finery, on richly caparisoned horses, 420 Mameluke Beys arrived at the citadel. Once they were crowded into the narrow street, Mohammed Ali's Albanian mercenaries opened fire from rooftops and windows with rifle and cannon. The Mamelukes screamed, their horses neighed, the street ran with blood. In half an hour all the Mamelukes were dead with the exception of Amir-bey whose horse is reputed to have leapt from the battlements and carried him safely to Syria.

Bonaparte's general staff
arriving at the Great Pyramid.

Napoleon Bonaparte before
the Battle of the Pyramids.

Murad Bey, whose Mameluke forces were defeated.

July 12, 1798, in the shadow of the pyramids of Giza, some 25,000 Frenchmen, demoralized, hungry, and sleepy from a ten-hour march, were ordered by Napoleon to face what he overestimated to be 78,000 Egyptians, including 12,000 mounted Mamelukes in multi-colored turbans and gold-embroidered caftans that floated like gauze. The French formed into squares, ten soldiers deep, their cannons (and savants) in the center. With remarkable discipline the French held their fire till Murad Bey's cavalry were upon them. The Mamelukes outdid themselves in bravery, slashing through the barrels of the Frenchmen's rifles with their scimitars, but in vain. In two hours the squares were surrounded by corpses, the Battle of the Pyramids was over, and Napoleon was master of Egypt. As the flames from the Egyptian fleet illumined Cairo's minarets, Napoleon's men feasted on hoards of captured sweetmeats and looted the gold-laden bodies of the Mamelukes, dumping them into the Nile to float seaward the news of the Egyptian defeat.

42

43

Jomard, Coutelle and Le Père exploring the Grand Gallery.

The discoveries of the savants within the Pyramid were not sensational, mostly because of the hindrance of bats, which had greatly increased since the time of Davison.

Edmé-François Jomard, one of the younger but more astute of the savants, described the painful process of moving through the passages bent double, seared by the heat of the torches, stifled by lack of air, and sweating profusely from the effort.

Colonel Jean Marie Joseph Coutelle, a military member of the expedition, made another exploration of the well, but complained of being attacked by clouds of infuriated bats, "who scratched with their claws and stifled with the acrid stench of their bodies."

Discharging their pistols at the top of the Grand Gallery, the French were astonished at the repeated echo which sounded like thunder moving away into the distance.

In Davison's Chamber the accumulation of bat dung had risen to 28 centimeters. The savants retired without further contribution to the problem of the Pyramid's interior.

Outside, the savants were more successful. Jomard dogtrotted round the Pyramid, appalled by the amount of sand and debris which had accumulated on its flanks.

With the help of 150 Ottoman Turks, the French were able to clear the northeast and northwest corners of the building and make an important discovery.

They found the "esplanade" on which the Pyramid had originally been established, as well as two shallow rectangular "encastrements," or sockets, 10 feet by 12, hollowed some 20 inches into the base rock, quite level with each other, where the original cornerstones had once been laid.

These gave the savants two firm points from which to measure the base of the Pyramid. Though the huge mounds of debris all along the north face of the structure still impeded their efforts, Jomard was able to make a series of measurements up and down and around. These gave a length for the base of 230.902 meters, or 757.5 English feet. The French now needed to know the height.

Jomard took almost an hour to climb the Pyramid, stopping on the way for breath. Once he reached the summit, his imagination was exalted by the view of the green Delta to the north, the black strip of fertile earth along the Nile, the wavelike dunes to the west. Arab villages looked like anthills on the horizon; men at the base of the Pyramid were barely distinguishable.

With a slingshot Jomard tried to hurl a stone far enough to clear the base, but in vain. Not even the Arabs had been able to shoot an arrow from the summit that would clear the footing.

44

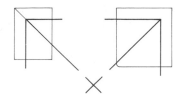

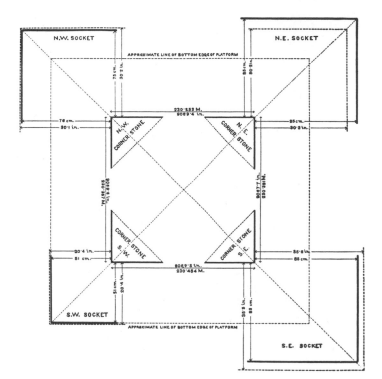

The positions of the sockets.

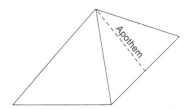

To obtain a height of the Pyramid, Jomard measured down each step, for a total of 144 meters, or 481 feet. By elemental trigonometry this gave him an angle for the slope of 51° 19′ 14″ and an apothem of 184.722 meters.

The apothem is the slant height of the Pyramid, or line from apex to center of each base, down which a raindrop would run as the shortest distance to the ground.

Because the outer casing was entirely missing there was no way to know just how thick it had been: so the measure for the apothem had to be an estimate; but the figure of 184.722 meters was to open up a whole new vista for Jomard, who was a very well-read young man.

Jomard remembered that according to Diodorus Siculus and Strabo, the apothem of the Pyramid was supposed to be one stadium long. He also knew that an Olympic stadium of 600 Greek feet—from which our modern stadium is derived —was a basic unit of land measure in the ancient world, one which was said to be related to the size of the earth.

Searching further through the trunks full of classics which the savants had brought to Egypt, Jomard found that the stadium of the Alexandrine Greeks (of Eratosthenes and Hipparchus) had been the equivalent of 185.5 meters—which was within a meter of what he had found for the apothem.

To reinforce the point, Jomard discovered that the

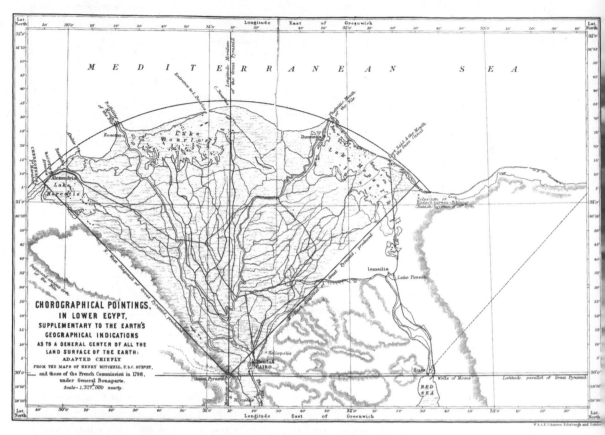

CHOROGRAPHICAL POINTINGS,
IN LOWER EGYPT,
SUPPLEMENTARY TO THE EARTH'S
GEOGRAPHICAL INDICATIONS
AS TO A GENERAL CENTER OF ALL THE
LAND SURFACE OF THE EARTH:
ADAPTED CHIEFLY
FROM THE MAPS OF HENRY MITCHELL, U.S.C. SURVEY,
and those of the French Commission in 1798,
under General Bonaparte.
Scale - 1,327,000 nearly.

Bonaparte's surveyors found that the Pyramid was accurately oriented to the four cardinal points of the compass and therefore used the meridian running through its apex as the base line for their measurements.

Having mapped Lower Egypt, they were surprised to find that this meridian neatly cut the Delta region into two equal portions, and were even more surprised when they found that the diagonals drawn through the Pyramid, at right angles to each other, completely enclosed the entire Delta.

Evidently a structure which could serve as such a perfect geodetic benchmark could not have been located at random, and without considerable proficiency in astronomy, as well as a developed understanding of the configuration of the planet.

distance between the Egyptian localities as measured by Napoleon's surveyors also coincided with the classical distances between these localities computed in stadia, if the stadium was taken to be 185 meters.

Finally, Jomard learnt from his perusal of the classics that a stadium of 600 feet was considered to be 1/600 of a geographical degree.

Jomard calculated that a geographical degree at the mean latitude of Egypt was 110,827.68 meters. Dividing this figure by 600 resulted in a measure of 184.712 meters. This was within 10 centimeters of his value for the apothem.*

Could the Egyptians, Jomard wondered, have been capable of working out their basic units of measure—such as the stadium, the cubit, and the foot—from the size of the earth and then built this knowledge into the Pyramid?

To reinforce this exciting hypothesis Jomard found that several Greek authors reported that the perimeter of the base

---

* At Seyne the degree of longitude is 110,791.11. At Alexandria it is 110,892.66. The mean for the whole planet is 111,111.9. Jomard took the mean for Egypt.

of the Pyramid was intended to measure half a minute of longitude. In other words, 480 times the base of the Pyramid was equal to a geographical degree.

Jomard took the 110,827-meter degree and divided it by 480. The result was 230.8 meters, or again within 10 centimeters of his measured length of the base.

To find the length of the cubit that would fit these measures, Jomard again consulted the classics. According to Herodotus 400 cubits made a stadium of 600 ft. Jomard divided the apothem of the Pyramid by 400 and obtained a cubit of .4618 meter. To his surprise this turned out to be the common cubit of the modern Egyptians.

According to other Greek sources the base of the Pyramid was said to be 500 cubits. Multiplying his .4618 meter cubit by 500, Jomard got 230.90 meters—which was just what he had measured for the base.

Jomard's theory was impressive to his colleagues; but when Gratien Le Père and Colonel Coutelle re-measured the base of the Pyramid, they found it to be 2 meters longer. They also re-measured the height with a specially designed instrument, step by step, and the results showed Jomard's angle of incline to have been too low, and his apothem consequently too short.

In vain Jomard argued that he had found an even more surprising coincidence in that the four-hundredth part of his base of the Pyramid gave a figure of .5773 meter, which was exactly the length of a longer modern Egyptian cubit called the *pyk belady*.

Jomard's colleagues insisted there was no evidence in any other ancient Egyptian building of the use of such odd cubits and that the only adequate cubit they had found was the one marked on the nilometer of Elephantine, which was nearly the same as the "royal" cubit of Memphis of .524 meter, or 20.63 inches, which Newton had derived from the dimensions of the King's Chamber.

Unperturbed, Jomard continued his observations. It seemed to him that from the bottom of the Descending Passage, the ancients might have been able to see the transit across the meridian of some circumpolar star, and thus have previously established true north and correctly oriented the building. Because of the length and narrowness of the passage, he said, they might even have been able to see such a star by daylight. His colleagues argued that the trap door would have prevented any such observation.

Jomard suggested that the King's Chamber, with its empty sarcophagus, might not necessarily have been a tomb but a metric monument, designed to embody, and perpetuate, a system of measures.

47

Nilometer discovered by the French at Elephantine, near Syene, used by the Egyptians for measuring the rise of the Nile at flood time, and marked in cubits very close to the royal cubit of Memphis.

To the end, Jomard remained convinced that the builders of the Pyramid had the necessary astronomical know-how to measure a geographical degree and thus the true circumference of the earth, and had developed an advanced science of geography and geodesy which they had immortalized in the geometry of the Great Pyramid.

Jomard pointed out that Herodotus, Plato, Diodorus and many others had all named Egypt as the birthplace of geometry, that Solon as well as Plato had come to Egypt to study geometry, and that Pythagoras had learnt from the Egyptians his theorems of geometry, his art of calculation, and his doctrine of metempsychosis.

Jomard's classically indoctrinated colleagues could not stomach the idea that their cherished Greeks might not be the founders of geometry; so the pursuit was dropped.

One last boost to Jomard's theory was given by one of Napoleon's favorite generals, Louis Charles Antoine Desaix: on his way up the Nile to conquer Upper Egypt, the 29-year-old general found a gorgeous temple near Thebes half

Edmé-François Jomard.

buried in the sand. On its ceiling was a circular zodiac. Because the zodiac clearly depicted the skies over Egypt and showed the recognizable constellations in quite different positions, the savants deduced that it must have represented the skies many centuries in the past and that the ancient Egyptians must have been acquainted with the zodiacal constellations in remote antiquity.

Unfortunately, an inscription also found in the temple appeared to date it from Ptolemaic times, shortly before our era; so another of Jomard's balloons was pricked.

Meanwhile Napoleon, whose logistical mind enabled him to figure that the Great Pyramid and its Giza neighbors contained enough stone to build a wall 3 meters high and one meter thick all around France, had become attracted by the arcane qualities of the King's Chamber.

On the twenty-fifth of Thermidor (the Revolutionaries' August 12, 1799) the General-in-Chief visited the Pyramid with the Imam Muhammed as his guide; at a certain point Bonaparte asked to be left alone in the King's Chamber,

Napoleon in the King's Chamber.

as Alexander the Great was reported to have done before him.

Coming out, the general is said to have been very pale and impressed. When an aide asked him in a jocular tone if he had witnessed anything mysterious, Bonaparte replied abruptly that he had no comment, adding in a gentler voice that he never wanted the incident mentioned again.

Many years later, when he was emperor, Napoleon continued to refuse to speak of this strange occurrence in the Pyramid, merely hinting that he had received some presage of his destiny. At St. Helena, just before the end, he seems to have been on the point of confiding to Las Cases, but instead shook his head, saying, "No. What's the use. You'd never believe me."

When military and political priorities obliged Napoleon to pull out of Egypt, he abandoned his savants to be captured by the British. Chivalrously treated as civilians, they were allowed to return to France with their notes and drawings. By the time they got home Napoleon had gained sufficient power as First Consul to order them to produce a truly monumental work on all they had discovered about the sites, buildings, inscriptions, life, language and manners of the ancient and modern Egyptians. With the help of an army of painters, typographers and four hundred engravers, the study was completed and published over a period of 25 years

50

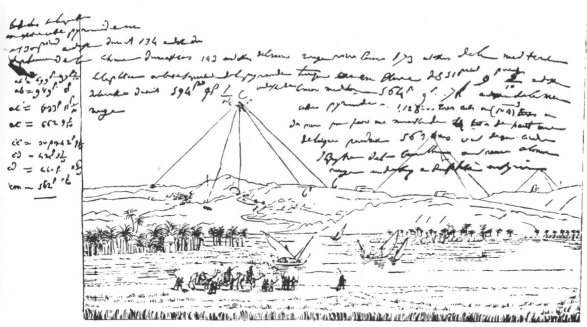

Napoleon's notes on his sketch of the Pyramid.

with the title, *Description de l'Egypte ou Recueil des observations et des recherches qui ont été faites en Egypte pendant l'expédition de l'armée française.*

The work ran to nine folio volumes of text and twelve of plates, and was described as "the most immortal conception and glorious performance of a book ever realized by man." Jomard contributed to it brilliantly, but his perspicacious thesis received little credit.

The savants were scooped by the wily Baron Vivant Denon, who brought out two volumes of the etchings he had made during the campaign in Egypt. His *Voyage dans la basse et la haute Egypte* became an instant best seller, stunning Europe with incredible sights of an unknown world of Egypt both ancient and modern, and launching a great vogue for the style known as *Empire.*

Denon's publication and the *Description de l'Egypte* which followed it piecemeal were to turn what had been a French military disaster into a cultural triumph. They also shattered once and for all the figment that before the Homeric Greeks there had been nothing but primitive barbarism.

Scientifically the most sensational discovery made by the French in Egypt proved to be a 3-foot diorite slab engraved with hieroglyphics found by a Captain Bouchard in a branch of the Delta near Rosetta. Hijacked by the British, the

51

Frontispiece for the twenty-one volume *Description de l'Egypte,* bearing Napoleon's imperial crown, and showing a composite picture of the principal monuments described by the French.

DESCRIPTION
DE L'ÉGYPTE,
ou
RECUEIL
DES OBSERVATIONS ET DES RECHERCHES
QUI ONT ÉTÉ FAITES EN ÉGYPTE
PENDANT L'EXPÉDITION DE L'ARMÉE FRANÇAISE,
PUBLIÉ
PAR LES ORDRES DE SA MAJESTÉ L'EMPEREUR
NAPOLÉON LE GRAND.

ANTIQUITÉS. PLANCHES.
TOME PREMIER.

A PARIS,
DE L'IMPRIMERIE IMPÉRIALE.
M. DCCC. IX.

Dominique Vivant Denon accompanied Napoleon on his expedition to Egypt and produced a series of drawings and etchings of the land of the Pharaohs which revealed a whole new world to an amazed Europe.

Born an aristocrat and renowned mostly for a series of pornographic etchings, Denon managed to ingratiate himself with the revolutionaries and escape execution. Hypnotically attractive to women, Denon was befriended by such notables as Madame de Pompadour and Catherine II of Russia. He was introduced to Napoleon by his wife Josephine.

In Egypt Denon would ride ahead of the French columns, sometimes under fire, to catch the vivid scenes of action. Sketching directly from the saddle, in which he had been for as many as sixteen hours, his eyelids ripped by the windblown sand, and seeing through a veil of blood, Denon managed to reproduce the most evocative scenes of Egypt, ancient and modern, full of verve and an exquisite sense of composition.

Brought up to think that Greek architecture of the best period was *the* standard of beauty, he was seized by the extraordinary beauty of the Egyptian works "with no extraneous ornaments or superfluity of lines." His two-volume illustrated description of Bonaparte's campaign in Egypt was an instant bestseller in Europe.

Denon was made a baron by his emperor and became superintendent of the Louvre and director of the Beaux Arts.

53

Nubians drawn by Denon in 1799.

Denon making a sketch in Upper Egypt.

Napoleon reviewing the French troops at Rosetta.

J. F. Champollion.

The Rosetta Stone, found in 1799, was ordered by Napoleon to be placed in the French Institute in Cairo. By an article of the treaty of capitulation it was surrendered to the British in 1801. Major General Turner sailed with it to Portsmouth in 1802 and deposited it with the Society of Antiquarians in London who turned it over to the British Museum.

A plaster of paris cast of its inscription in hieroglyphs, demotic Egyptian, and Greek, enabled Champollion to decipher the hieroglyphic language of the ancient Egyptians and formulate a system for their grammar; this made it possible for archeologists and Egyptologists to read the millennial inscriptions found throughout Egypt.

trophy ended up in the Egyptian Gallery of the British Museum. It lay there undeciphered for twenty years, until another young Frenchman, Jean-François Champollion, was to crack the mystery of its ancient hieroglyphs and throw the first real light on several millennia of Egypt's mysterious past.

As Napoleon had somewhat pompously remarked when elected a member of the National Institute, "the only true conquests are those gained by knowledge over ignorance."

V. EXPLORING WITH CHISEL AND GUNPOWDER

After Wellington's victory at Waterloo, the efforts of the French savants at the Pyramid were forgotten and the sockets they had cleaned were covered once more with the sands of the desert.

It remained for an obscure Italian to make the next impressive discovery within the Pyramid. While Napoleon was languishing on St. Helena, an exophthalmic Genoese merchant, Captain G. B. Caviglia, arrived in Egypt as the master of a Maltese vessel flying the British flag. Seized by the mystery of the Great Pyramid, he gave up the sea and settled down to exploring the Pyramid and its neighbors on the Giza plateau, financing himself by helping rich Europeans scavenge the surrounding tombs to assuage their taste for original Egyptian antiquities—a taste which ran to anything from scarab rings to thousand-ton obelisks.

Described by a contemporary as an "enthusiastic devotee at the shrine of antiquarian learning, who sacrificed country, home, friends and fortune for the indulgence of the refined though eccentric taste of exploring the hidden mysteries of the Pyramids and Tombs of Egypt," Caviglia cleared out the bat excrement from Davison's Chamber and set up housekeeping within it, turning "the gloomy recess into a residential apartment"—though how this was accomplished under a 3-foot ceiling is not explained.

Alexander William Crawford (later Lord Lindsay), who encountered Caviglia in Cairo, found the Italian to be a deeply religious man, well versed in the Bible, which he constantly quoted, but also a man with some pretty strange ideas about what he would find in the Pyramid. To England Crawford wrote: "Caviglia told me that he had pushed his studies in magic, animal magnetism, etc., to an extent which nearly killed him . . . to the very verge, he said, of what is forbidden man to know, and it was only the purity of his intentions which saved him."

Caviglia was convinced that if he dug into the Pyramid he would eventually encounter a secret room. To find it he hired a gang of Arab workmen to dig a tunnel leading off from Davison's Chamber. But no matter how far they dug, they found nothing but solid masonry.

Caviglia cleared the sand from the base of the Sphinx and revealed the footing for a missing obelisk between its paws.

At last Caviglia was obliged to give up the job; to console himself he set about analyzing the mystery of the "well." Lowering himself down the shaft, Caviglia got as far as 125 feet below the grotto only to find, as Davison had before him, that the bottom was completely stopped, and that the air was so scarce his candle spluttered, making it difficult for him to breathe.

However, as the bottom appeared to be mostly sand and loose rocks, Caviglia was determined to unplug it and see where it led. For a while he managed to impress a gang of Arabs into raising basketfuls of the sand all the way up to the top of the well; but the shaft was so tight, the air so fetid with bat dung, and the dust so suffocating, that the Arabs began to faint and refused to work further. Caviglia attempted to clear the air at the bottom of the well by burning chunks of sulfur, but it was still impossible to breathe that far down for any length of time, and the Arabs would not resume their digging.

57

Lower end of the well shaft.

Caviglia decided to attack the problem from a different angle. He would attempt to clear the main Descending Passage to the subterranean pit which had been filled since Al Mamun's time with the refuse of the plugs they had broken out of the Ascending Passage. Caviglia had the refuse carried up and out of the Pyramid, and was able to push his way on hands and knees down the passage for 150 feet; then the air became so impure and the heat so great that he started to spit up blood. Still, he would not give up. At the end of another 50 feet he made a discovery which seemed to indicate he might be on the right track. On the west side of the passage he found a low doorway leading into a hole. As the Arabs began to dig upward into this hole, Caviglia noted a strong smell of sulfur. It occurred to him that he might have hit upon the solution to his previous problem: the smell of sulfur might be coming from the bottom of the well, which must therefore be very close.

Digging harder, the Arab workmen dislodged some loose earth. A pile of dust and rubbish fell onto them, including a basket and ropes which had been left at the bottom of the well. There was also a sudden gush of air up the tunnel, and those in the passage were able to breathe with ease. Caviglia had discovered the end of the well. But a greater mystery remained. Why had it been dug there, when, and by whom?

As Caviglia set about resolving this mystery, another

58

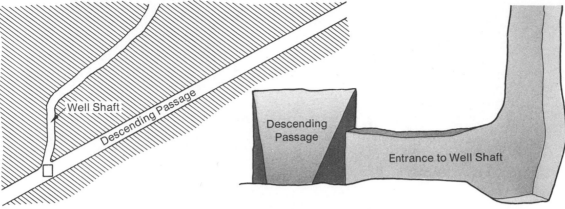

Where the well joins the Descending Passage.

Colonel (afterward General) Howard-Vyse in 1830.

strange figure joined in the Pyramid research, one quite the opposite of the romantic, uncommunicative Caviglia. Richard Howard-Vyse, a British Guards officer, at first collaborated heartily with Caviglia, but they soon grew angry at each other and came to a heated parting.

Colonel Howard-Vyse, son of General Richard Vyse and grandson of the Earl of Stafford, was a martinet with little humor who had been equerry to the Duke of Cumberland (later first king of Hanover) and had stood unsuccessfully for Parliament in the borough of Windsor. He has been described as thoroughgoing and as artless as Wellington, under whom he served.

A trial to his family, who were pleased to have him away from the county seat in Buckinghamshire, even if it cost them some of the family patrimony, Howard-Vyse was to spend over 10,000 pounds sterling on exploration of the Pyramid site.

Howard-Vyse first saw the pyramids on a moonlit ride from across the Nile at Turah in November of 1836, during a trip to Egypt as "a fashionable amusement seeker." In his own words he was attracted by "the remote antiquity and uncertainty of their origin, and . . . the peculiarity of their mysterious construction." He was curious about "the purpose for which the passages and chambers already discovered were originally intended, but in much greater degree respecting any other passage or apartments which might reasonably be supposed to exist in the enormous structures."

Impressed by Caviglia's theories about the mysterious and hermetic purposes for which the Great Pyramid had originally been constructed, Howard-Vyse hired the services of a professional civil engineer, John Shae Perring, who had been an assistant to Mohammed Ali, the khedive of Egypt. Perring was to take measurements of all the pyramids and tombs which had thus far been discovered on the Giza plateau, as well as many of those farther south.

59

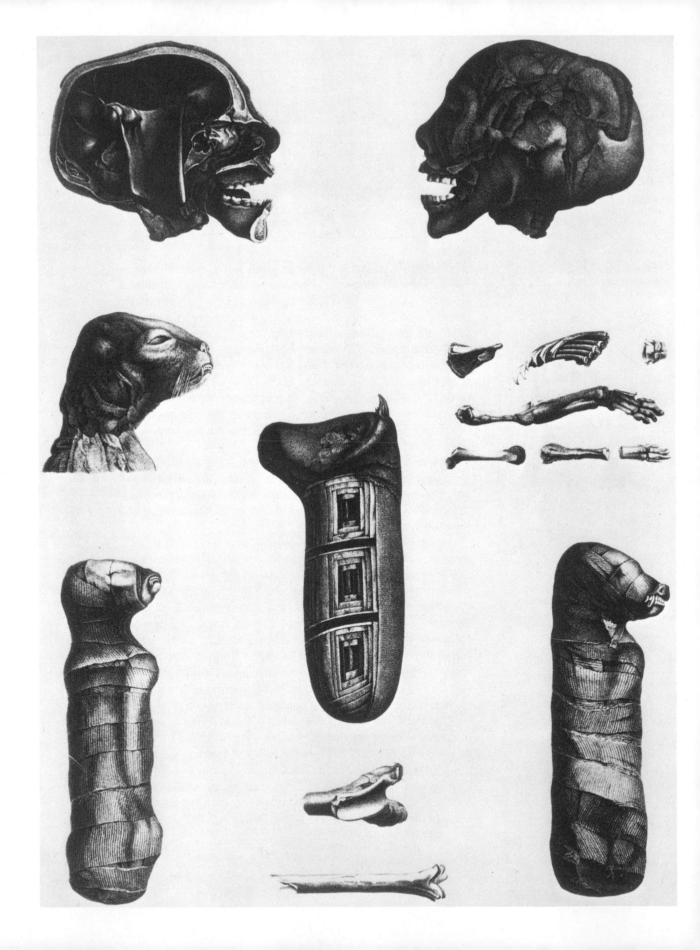

In his *La Pyramide de Cheops ât-elle livré son secret* Fernand Ihek says that the shape of the Great Pyramid was such that it enabled bodies (either animal or vegetable) to become naturally mummified when placed within the King's Chamber. He says the end result was a desiccation or dehydration of the body with no sign of putrefaction. Experiments revealed that an uncleaned trout became mummified in thirteen days, a radish in fifteen days, and the heart of a sheep in forty days.

Ancient Egyptians removed the brain and entrails of a body to be mummified without scarring it by pulling the brain out through the nose and the viscera through the anal aperture.

The body was then soaked in brine for a month; aromatic plugs, often perfumed with onion, were placed in the nostrils and other orifices.

According to Manly P. Hall, there is every reason to suppose that originally only those who had received some grade of hermetic initiation were mummified; for "it is certain that, in the eyes of the Egyptians, mummification effectually prevented reincarnation."

Reincarnation was considered necessary to imperfect souls, or those who had failed to pass the tests of initiation. "The body of the Initiate," says Hall, "was preserved after death as a species of Talisman or material basis for the manifestation of the soul upon earth." When the body of a "god-like" Pharaoh was mummified it could serve as a medium through which survivors could communicate and plead their cause with "the beyond." At first only Pharaohs appear to have been mummified; later it was done to persons of royal rank, and to anyone who could afford it; eventually even animals were mummified.

Howard-Vyse set up his headquarters in an empty tomb near the Great Pyramid and was soon employing a larger number of workmen than anyone since the time of Al Mamun, often as many as seven hundred, using Captain Caviglia as superintendent of works.

All went well till the colonel chose to take an extended tour up the Nile to inspect a further series of pyramids. When he returned he was outraged to find that Captain Caviglia had almost entirely neglected the Great Pyramid and was using the men hired by Howard-Vyse to search for mummies and little green idols in the neighboring burial pits.*

Caviglia became equally outraged at the colonel's reprimands, and gesticulated abusively declaring that "he alone had the head to conduct excavations and to understand the value of 'curios' and '*anticos*,' the colonel having nothing but money."

When the colonel asked for the return of his money, Caviglia disdainfully appeared at breakfast in the colonel's tent and threw on the table the money wrapped in an old stocking.

It was the end of Caviglia's exploring in Egypt. He retired to Paris, where he was sporadically supported by another great scavenger of antiquities, the former British ambassador to the Sublime Porte, Lord Elgin.

Howard-Vyse took over Caviglia's duties. In the words of a Victorian lady admirer, the colonel "sat down before the Great Pyramid as a fortress to be besieged, and through winter and spring and the burning summer of Egypt, long after all travelers had left the country, became the sole director of operations, clerk of the works and paymaster of his hundreds of workmen, day after day, month after month, until they had wrought out his own ideas of pyramidical exploration to the full. For not only was he one of those men who was never known to turn back after having put his hand to the plow, but he was a religiously [*sic*] minded man, a devout Christian, who felt that he was in this case called to a certain work for the Master, and though in the first instance he had distrusted himself in a new field of labor

---

* Mummy flesh was in great demand in Europe during the sixteenth and seventeenth centuries as a medicinal; it was a common drug to be found in all apothecaries. Mistaken for Persian *moma,* or pitch, which was used to heal cuts and bruises, mummy flesh was believed to make fractures unite in a few minutes and to be good for all kinds of internal ailments. When mummies became scarce traders used the bodies of executed Christians, or the bodies removed from hospitals, many of which had died of loathsome diseases. The bodies were stuffed with bitumen, wrapped in bandages and baked.

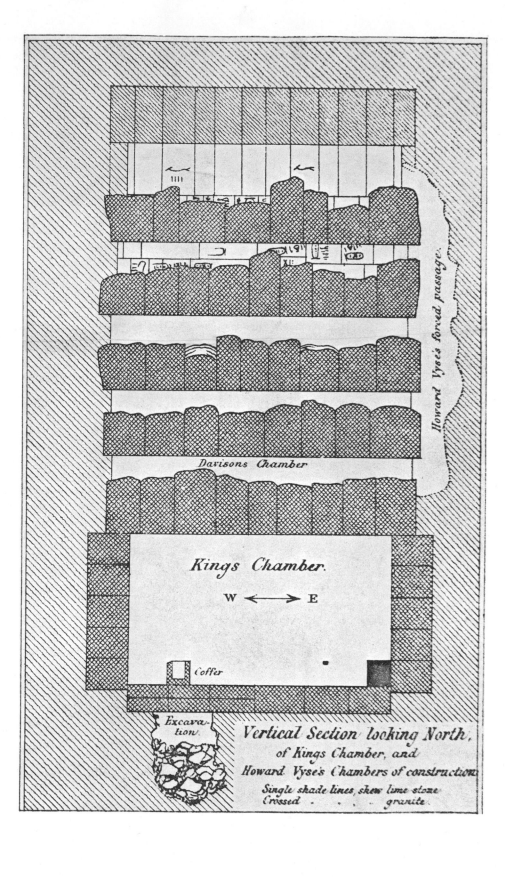

Howard Vyse's forced passage.

Davisons Chamber

Kings Chamber.

W ← → E

Coffer

Excavation.

Vertical Section looking North,
of Kings Chamber, and
Howard Vyse's Chambers of construction.
Single shade lines, skew lime stone
Crossed . . . , granite.

so that he had thought it better to use the purchased help of the Italian professional, yet when that failed he became a most admirable example to all kinds of men, rich and poor alike, of giving himself to the work, putting his own shoulder to the wheel, and never quitting it until the end was gained, during all the time, too, preserving the utmost urbanity, but dealing out the strictest justice in a manner that made a most honorable and lasting impression on the tawny Arabs around him."

In the Queen's Chamber Colonel Howard-Vyse had relays of men work day and night digging up the floor in front of the niche, but all they found was an old basket: so they refilled the hole.

In Davison's Chamber they found a crack in the ceiling through which they could run a reed about 3 feet long. Believing this to be an indication of a similar chamber above, Howard-Vyse had the workmen chisel their way into the granite over their heads. But the stone was too hard, and again the Arabs could not stand the heat in the restricted space of Davison's low-ceilinged chamber.

Special quarrymen were imported from the Mokattam hills across the valley. When even they could not manage the job, the colonel resorted to gunpowder to blast his way upward. To handle the charges he found a workman called Daued who lived mostly on hashish and alcohol. Daued successfully set off the blasts—a job that was particularly dangerous as the splintered granite flew about like shrapnel.

When the dust subsided Howard-Vyse found that they had indeed broken through to another chamber, which he chauvinistically named after Wellington. Its floor was the top of the nine monolithic blocks of granite which formed the rough-hewn ceiling of Davison's Chamber, each block weighing over 50 tons. About a yard above them lay another flat ceiling made of eight blocks of granite.

The new chamber had a strange effect on those who entered; it turned them black. Instead of bat dung, the floor was covered with a thin black powder which when analyzed turned out to be exuviae, or the cast-off shells and skins of insects. Of living insects there were none to be found.

Convinced that the monoliths of the ceiling were in turn the floor of a third chamber, Howard-Vyse ordered the blasting resumed. The colonel's excavations above the King's Chamber became more and more difficult as they rose vertically to a height of 40 feet and took three and a half months to accomplish.

One by one, three more chambers were found above the two already discovered, the uppermost being gabled with huge blocks of sloping limestone. These chambers

Construction chambers above the King's Chamber.

63

As some of the quarry marks found in the chambers are hieroglyphs signifying "year 17," Egyptologists deduced that the building had reached that stage in the seventeenth year of the king's reign. Most of the marks were roughly daubed in red paint and appeared upside down, indicating they were quarry marks and not decorations.

Similar marks, mostly red, but occasionally black, were also found on the first five or six courses of the Pyramid, behind the casing blocks.

Howard-Vyse sent copies of the crayon marks to Samuel Birch of the British Museum who identified one of the ovals as belonging to King Suphis, or Shofo, or Khufu.

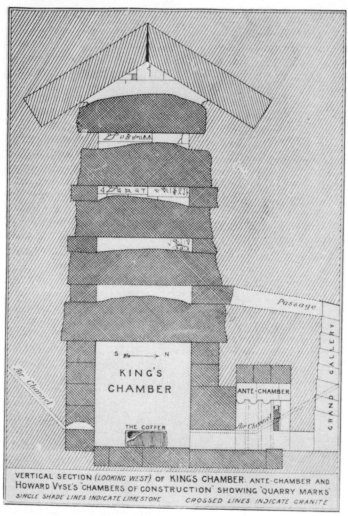

VERTICAL SECTION (*LOOKING WEST*) OF KINGS CHAMBER, ANTE-CHAMBER AND HOWARD VYSE'S CHAMBERS OF CONSTRUCTION SHOWING 'QUARRY MARKS'. SINGLE SHADE LINES INDICATE LIMESTONE   CROSSED LINES INDICATE GRANITE

Sectional drawing of the King's Chamber, looking west, showing all four chambers discovered by Howard-Vyse.

Lady Arbuthnot's Chamber, discovered by Howard-Vyse.

Ceiling construction above
Campbell's Chamber.

Howard-Vyse named in turn for Admiral Nelson, for Lady
Ann Arbuthnot, wife of Lt. General Sir Robert Arbuthnot,
who happened to visit the Pyramid shortly after the room
was discovered, and for Colonel Campbell, Her Brittanic
Majesty's Consul in Cairo.

The most interesting discovery was not so much the
chambers themselves but some red-paint cartouches
daubed on the inner walls of the upper chambers. Thanks to
the Rosetta Stone and Champollion's successors, one of
these cartouches was recognized by Egyptologists as
belonging to Khufu, believed to be the second Pharaoh of
the Fourth Dynasty, called Cheops by the Greeks, whose
reign was thought to have occurred in the third millennium
before our era.

There was, of course, no way to prove that this Khufu
was indeed the Cheops who had reigned in Egypt. But the
fact that similar cartouches had been found in the quarries
of the Wadi Magharah hills, from which much of the stone
for the Pyramid was derived, added weight to the assumption.

One thing seemed clear. Whoever had daubed the
cartouches on the inner walls of the upper chambers must
have done so *before* the chamber was sealed and the
Pyramid completed; there appeared to be no entrance or
exit other than the one blasted by the colonel.

Doubt still lingered that there might have been a far
earlier king with a similar cartouche, quite unknown to
Egyptologists; but until further evidence could be adduced,
it seemed hard to go against the theory of the Pyramid
having been built in the reign of the historic Cheops, as
reported by Herodotus and other classic authors.

As for the reason for the five superimposed chambers, it
was the conclusion of Howard-Vyse, and many who came
after him, that they had been designed to relieve the flat

65

Air vent in the north wall of the King's Chamber.

Casing stones and pavement as exposed by Howard-Vyse. Both entrances can be seen, Al Mamun's on the sixth course, and the original entrance ten courses higher.

ceiling of the King's Chamber from the pressure of the 200 more feet of solid masonry piled above it.

Another remarkable discovery made by the colonel in the walls of the King's Chamber was to vindicate the hypothesis of Dr. Harvey. Greaves had found the two 9-inch-wide openings in the side walls of the King's Chamber, but it was not till Mr. Hill, one of Howard-Vyse's assistants, who ran a hotel in Cairo, climbed high up on the outer surface of the Pyramid and found two similar outlets that it was established they were connected for over 200 feet right through the solid masonry to the holes in the King's Chamber. The colonel's engineer, Perring, was nearly decapitated when a stone dislodged by Hill came crashing all the way down one of these conduits.

When the conduit was cleared, an immediate rush of cool air entered the King's Chamber. Thus ventilated, the temperature of this chamber in the center of the Pyramid was to remain at an even and pleasant 68 degrees, irrespective of the weather or season outside, a prehistoric system of air conditioning. This added substance to Jomard's theory that the chamber might have been the repository for weights and measures which require an even temperature and constant barometric pressure, such as the Paris observatory for measurements of standards 85 feet below ground.

Even more sensational for those who were bent on unraveling the secrets of the Pyramid was the next discovery of Howard-Vyse. Ever since the Middle Ages, when the Arabs had despoiled the outer casing, the whole perimeter of the base of the Pyramid had been heaped high with fragments of limestone, and sand and debris, often in piles as high as 50 feet. The two northern corners uncovered several years earlier by the French had already been buried again. This time Howard-Vyse decided to clear away a patch of debris in the center of the north façade to see if he could get down to the very base and bedrock of the Pyramid. In doing so, he was to make a great discovery: two of the original polished-limestone casing stones on the lowest level of the Pyramid were still in the spot where they had been originally placed.

This ended the argument about the casing; it silenced forever those who had continued to consider it a fiction that the whole of the Pyramid had once been covered with a fine mantle of limestone. The original limestone was there, and so finely carved that it was now possible to correctly measure the angle of the slope on which the Pyramid had originally been constructed. The blocks, 5 feet high, 12 feet long, and 8 wide, showed an angle of about 51° 51', a little sharper than the one estimated by the French.

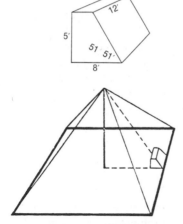

Relation of the casing stones to the slope of the Pyramid.

The base circuit of the Pyramid rests on a platform of finely finished limestone blocks which project beyond the end of the casing stones for an average of 2 feet on the south, east and west sides, and are still in place some 33 feet from the north edge.

This platform is so finely leveled that the official survey of the Egyptian government found it does not exceed 7/8 inch from dead level, and this variation may be due to subsidence.

At present it is not possible to say how far the platform extends under the building; but where the platform stones have been removed, the bedrock is found to have been cut and leveled to receive each individual stone, sometimes as deep as 2 inches.

On the north side the platform stones have been deliberately laid at irregular angles, each corner being carefully cut out to receive the next irregularly angled stone.

Hewn to the correct angle and polished to a uniform surface, they were quite perfect, in the words of Howard-Vyse, "in a sloping plane as correct and true almost as modern work by optical instrument makers. The joints were scarcely perceptible, not wider than the thickness of silver paper."

The colonel also managed to uncover part of the original pavement on which the building rested, and which appeared to stretch away to the north. "It was well laid and beautifully finished," noted Howard-Vyse, "but beneath the edifice it was worked with even greater exactness, and to the most perfect level."

Though the reason for this astounding accuracy on the northern side was not to become apparent for some years, Howard-Vyse summed up his discoveries thus: "I consider the workmanship displayed in the King's Chamber, in the pavement and the casing stones, is perfectly unrivaled."

The colonel had the casing stones quickly covered up pending permission to take them to the British Museum, but he was not able to prevent the infuriated local Moslems from uncovering them again and smashing the fine edges with hammers, jealous that Christians might obtain and dispose of something of value in their country.

With the angle of 51° 51′ of the casing stones and the base length of 763.62 feet measured by the Frenchmen Coutelle and Le Père, it was now possible to obtain by trigonometry a new dimension of the Pyramid. Its perpendicular height to where the missing capstone was presumed to have come to a point was figured to be 485.5 feet, or 147.9 meters, above the center of the base.

Stone sarcophagus found by Howard-Vyse in the pyramid of Mykerinos, which was lost at sea en route to the British Museum.

In 1840 Colonel Howard-Vyse sailed for England with his accumulated notes. Back home, at his own expense, or his family's, he produced two elegant volumes crammed with detailed but patronizingly Victorian descriptions of his exploits in Egypt, called *Operations Carried on at the Pyramids of Gizeh in 1837*. The book had the merit of including quotations from the works of 71 Europeans and 32 Asiatic authors who had written about the Pyramid from the fifth century B.C. to the nineteenth century.

The colonel's assistant John Perring also produced a handsome volume with some lovely copperplate etchings, *The Pyramids of Gizeh from Actual Survey and Measurement on the Spot.*

Unfortunately, Howard-Vyse was to lose his best trophy, the sarcophagus of Mykerinos, which he had found in the subterranean chamber of the Third Pyramid; the ship carrying it foundered in a storm off the coast of Spain and was sunk in deep water.

But the general measurements taken by Howard-Vyse and Perring were to open a whole new phase in the study of the Great Pyramid, now to be ennobled by the appellative "pyramidology."

69

VI. FIRST SCIENTIFIC THEORIES

A poet and essayist who had never set eyes on the Pyramid was to take the measurements of Howard-Vyse and those of the French savants and draw from them a set of conclusions, the most far-reaching thus far about the origin and purpose of the Pyramid.

John Taylor, the son of a London bookseller, whose regular job was editing the *London Observer,* already in his fifties when Howard-Vyse returned from Egypt, was to spend the next thirty years collecting and comparing accounts of travelers who had visited the Pyramid.

A gifted mathematician and amateur astronomer, Taylor made models to scale of the Pyramid and began to analyze the results from a mathematician's point of view. To account for the discrepancies in the length of the base reported by successive travelers—which increased progressively from the 693 feet of Greaves to the 763.62 feet of the French—it occurred to Taylor that as each measurer had arrived on the scene, more sand and rubble had been cleared from the base. Each had measured accurately, but at a constantly deeper layer of masonry.

Taylor set about drawing and redrawing every feature of the Pyramid on the basis of the measurements reported by Howard-Vyse, so as to see what geometrical or mathematical formulas might be derived from the structure.

Taylor was puzzled as to why the builders of the Pyramid should have chosen the particular angle of 51° 51′ for the Pyramid's faces instead of the regular equilateral triangle of 60°.

Analyzing Herodotus' report of what the Egyptian priests had told him about the surface of each face of the Pyramid, Taylor concluded they had been designed to be equal in area to the square of the Pyramid's height. If so, this meant the building was of a particular if not unique geometric construction; no other pyramid has these proportions.

Taylor then discovered that if he divided the perimeter of the Pyramid by twice its height, it gave him a quotient of 3.144, remarkably close to the value of π, which is computed as 3.14159+. In other words, the height of the Pyramid appeared to be in relation to the perimeter of its base as the radius of a circle is to its circumference.

John Taylor.

This seemed to Taylor far too extraordinary to attribute to chance, and he deduced that the Pyramid might have been specifically intended by its builders to incorporate the incommensurable value of π. If so, this was a demonstration of the advanced knowledge of the builders.* Still today the oldest known document which indicates that the Egyp-

* Not till the sixth century was π correctly worked out to the fourth decimal point by the Hindu sage Arya-Bhata. It took another thousand years before the Dutchman Pierre Metius calculated π to six decimals by means of the fraction 335/113. In 1593 François Viete carried the computation to eleven figures, and a generation later Rudolph Van Ceulin, just before he died, took π to 127 figures by postulating a circle with 36,893,488,147,419,103,232 sides. In 1813 the English mathematician William Shanks developed π to 707 decimals. Modern computers have carried the operation to 10,000 points of decimal, but with no solution to this apparently incommensurable number.

71

tians had a knowledge of the value of π is the Rhind Papyrus, dated about 1700 B.C., and therefore much later than the Pyramid. Found in the wrappings of a mummy in 1855 by a young Scottish archeologist, Henry Alexander Rhind, the rare papyrus is now in the British Museum. It gives a very rough value for π of 3.16.

Searching for a reason for such a π proportion in the Pyramid, Taylor concluded that the perimeter might have been intended to represent the circumference of the earth at the equator while the height represented the distance from the earth's center to the pole.

Perhaps Jomard had been right: perhaps the ancient designers *had* measured the length of a geographical degree, multiplied it by 360° for the circumference of the globe, and by the π relation had deduced the polar radius of the earth, immortalizing their knowledge by making the circumference to scale with the perimeter and the radius to scale with the height of the Pyramid.

Taylor underlined his thesis: "It was *to make a record of the measure of the Earth* that it was built." He then elaborated: "They knew the Earth was a sphere; and by observing the motion of the heavenly bodies over the earth's surface, had ascertained its circumference, and were desirous of leaving behind them a record of the circumference as correct and imperishable as it was possible for them to construct."

But it was evident to Taylor that the builders of the Pyramid could not have used for their calculations such a unit as the British foot, which fitted neither the height nor the base exactly; he therefore looked for a unit that would retain the π proportion and fit the Pyramid in whole numbers.

When he came to 366:116.5 he was struck by the similarity of 366 to the number of days in the year and wondered if the Egyptians might have intentionally divided the perimeter of the Pyramid into units of the solar year.

He then noticed that if he converted the perimeter into inches, it came to very nearly 100 times 366. Also he was surprised to see that if he divided the base by 25 inches, he obtained the same 366 result. Could the ancient Egyptians have used a unit so close to the British inch? And a cubit of 25 such inches?

By coincidence, Sir John Herschel, one of Britain's most eminent astronomers at the beginning of the nineteenth century, had just postulated a unit half a human hair's breadth longer than a British inch as the only sensible earth-commensurable unit, or unit based on the actual size of the earth.

72

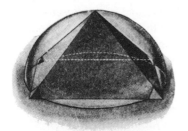

Relation of a hemisphere to the Pyramid.

Sir John F. W. Herschel.

Herschel criticized the French meter derived from a curved meridian of the earth as being erratic and variable from country to country because the earth is not a true sphere, and each meridian of longitude would therefore be different. (What's more the French had erred, and produced a meter that was .0002 too short.)

According to Herschel the only really reliable basis for a standard of measure was the polar axis of the earth— the straight line from pole to pole—which a recent British Ordnance Survey had fixed at 7898.78 miles (by taking the mean of all the available meridians measured). This translated into 500,500,000 British inches, or an even five hundred million inches if the British inch were half a human hair's breadth longer.

Herschel suggested that the regular British inch— which was officially computed as the length of three grains of barley taken from the middle ear and placed end to end— be arbitrarily lengthened by a mere one-thousandth part in order to obtain a truly scientific, earth-commensurable unit exactly one fifty-millionth part of the polar axis of the earth.

73

Fifty such inches, said Herschel, would make a yard that was exactly one ten-millionth of the polar axis, and half that measure, or 25 inches, would make a very useful cubit.

By coincidence these were the cubit and the inch which Taylor had found to fit the Great Pyramid in multiples of 366.*

Another unexpected piece of evidence astounded Taylor. He discovered that recent maps produced by the British Ordnance, the largest and most expensive yet undertaken, had been done on a scale of 1:2500. This scale turned out to bear no relation to the standard British mile of 5280 feet, which had varied through the ages, but almost miraculously fitted the "sacred" cubit as postulated by Newton, as well as the British acre, one side of which was equal to 100 cubits of 25 inches. It appeared that the British inch must have been an ancient unit of measure which had lost a thousandth part as it was handed down from generation to generation.†

To Taylor the inference was clear: the ancient Egyptians must have had a system of measurements based on the true spherical dimensions of the planet, which used a unit which was within a thousandth part of being equal to a British inch.

Fired by what he considered a stunning discovery, Taylor launched into a monumental study of the cubits, feet, spans, inches and stadia, not only of the ancient Egyptians, but of the Babylonians, Hebrews, Greeks and Romans. He found that all kinds of cubits had been used in the past, some of which appeared to have mathematical relations to each other. He also analyzed the ancient measures of cubic capacity along with the modern gallons, firkins, kilderkins,

N

10,000,000 meters

10,000,000 Pyramid sacred cubits

S

* That this figuring was not arbitrary was confirmed by the International Geophysical Year 1957–58 geodetic research with orbiting vehicles, which obtained a figure of 3949.89 miles for the polar radius of the earth. Divided by 10,000,000 British inches, this gives 25.02614284, or the length of Taylor's and Newton's "sacred cubit" correct to the third point of decimal.

† Corroborative evidence for Taylor's conclusion was recently produced by Algernon E. Berriman in his *Historical Metrology,* published by E. P. Dutton in New York in 1953. "The English acre," writes Berriman, who is an engineer and an architect, "is the most intriguing of ancient measures because it is virtually equal to a hypothetical geodetic acre defined as one myriad-millionth of the square on the terrestrial radius." Berriman noted that the geodetic acre could also be defined as measuring one myriad square cubits of a hypothetical cubit equal to one ten-millionth of the terrestrial radius. Berriman gave a value to this cubit of 25.064 inches, saying "its former existence is as plausible (or as incredible) as a cubit derived from the sexagesimal division of the Earth's circumference." Berriman also noted that the slightly larger Scottish and Irish acres are related to each other and to the basic English acre as a square to an inscribed circle.

74

hogsheads, butts, barrels, gills, pecks, faggots, and chaldrons—all in the hope of finding an ancient unit of measure that could be used as a standard, and from which others could have been derived or corrupted.

Pursuing Jomard's theory that the King's Chamber and its sarcophagus might have been designed not so much as a tomb as to monumentalize a system of weights and measure, Taylor was amazed to find that the cubic capacity of the granite coffer was almost precisely four times what the British farmer still used as a standard measure for grain: the *quarter,* or eight bushels.

From all his studies, Taylor concluded that the proportions of the Pyramid had definitely been intended to incorporate geometric and astronomical laws simply and easily expressed, and that its purpose had been to preserve and pass on this knowledge to future generations.

However, as there was nothing in Taylor's philosophy to indicate the existence in such remote antiquity of any civilization which could have had a knowledge of the true shape of the planet, its actual size, and its motion in the solar system; and as the conceit was not then current that this planet might have been visited by superior beings from some other part of the universe, Taylor was hard put to explain the sources of science he found incorporated in the Pyramid. More than a scholar and a mathematician, Taylor was also a profoundly religious man, thoroughly steeped in the Old Testament which he believed to be literally true. To Taylor the creation of Adam had occurred in 4000 B.C. and the Flood in 2400 B.C. It seemed to him hard to believe that in a mere 300 years man could have redeveloped to the point of building so complex a structure as the Great Pyramid. Taylor could come to but one conclusion: whoever had built the Pyramid must have done so under the direct influence of Divine Revelation as Noah had built the Ark. In his own words: "It is probable that to some human beings in the earliest ages of society, a degree of intellectual power was given by the Creator, which raised them far above the level of those succeeding inhabitants of the earth."

Taylor even ventured the hypothesis that the builders of the Pyramid were of "the *chosen race* in the line of, though preceding Abraham; so early indeed as to be closer to Noah than to Abraham."

Because of the close similarity of the British inch to the "Pyramid inch," his idea was to give impetus to the theory that the British were related to the Lost Tribes of Israel, "which during their captivity and wanderings preserved a knowledge of the wisdom of the Egyptians."

As might have been expected, Taylor, who had been

75

known as a benign and dignified old gentleman, had a hard time convincing his quiet Victorian contemporaries of such wild and revolutionary theories, especially as they were just then being rocked by Darwin's theory of the descent of man.

A paper on the Pyramid which he presented to the prestigious Royal Society was rejected with the suggestion that such a paper might be more appropriate for the Society of Antiquarians.

Growing older and more infirm, Taylor was afraid he would die without developing any audience for his theories which by 1859 he had formulated into a volume entitled *The Great Pyramid: Why Was It Built & Who Built It?*

Nearing his death, he had the luck to find the support of an eminent academician with the reputation of having an excellent and sober mathematical mind: Professor Charles Piazzi Smyth, the Astronomer Royal of Scotland.

VII. FIRST CONFIRMATION OF SCIENTIFIC THEORIES

Piazzi Smyth, who was born in Naples to Admiral William Henry Smyth (and named for his godfather, the renowned Sicilian astronomer, Father Giuseppe Piazzi, discoverer of the first known asteroid), was enough of a mathematician not to mock at Taylor's reasoning. Carefully studying Taylor's figures, Piazzi Smyth decided to support them with a paper which he presented to the Royal Society of Edinburgh, of which he had become a member because of his important contribution to the new science of spectroscopy.

It was Smyth's conclusion that the sacred cubit used by the builders of the Great Pyramid was the same length (25.025 British inches) as the one used by Moses to construct the tabernacle and by Noah when he built his Ark, and because the twenty-fifth part of this cubit was within a thousandth part of being the same as a British inch, Smyth also concluded that the British had inherited this "sacred" inch down through the ages.*

Smyth's fellow academicians treated him no better than they had treated Taylor.

During the last few weeks of Taylor's life, there was an animated correspondence between Smyth and Taylor. When Taylor died in 1864 Piazzi Smyth decided that the only way definitely to confirm or refute Taylor's theories about the π relation, and the Pyramid cubit, would be to go to Egypt and carefully measure the Pyramid.

In "utmost straits for funds," Smyth asked his fellows of the Royal Society in London for help; though the Society

---

* Attributing to Newton the original discovery of the presence of the sacred cubit in the Pyramid, Smyth wrote: "How thankful should we be that it pleased God to raise up the spirit of Newton amongst us; and enable him to make one of the most important discoveries of his riper years—though the opposition of the Church of England has caused it to remain unread almost to the present day—that while there undoubtedly was in ancient times a cubit of 20.7 inches nearly . . . and which Newton calls "the profane cubit" there was another which he equally unhesitatingly speaks of as the *sacred* cubit, decidedly longer."

C. Piazzi Smyth, Astronomer Royal for Scotland.

was "in receipt of a large annual grant from the government for the assistance of precisely such special efforts in science, it not only gave nothing to my semi-pauperized expedition, but actually sent back part of that year's grant to the government on the plea that there was nothing going on that needed it."

That same December, Piazzi Smyth and his wife—then in their early forties—set sail for Egypt with a vast number of boxes containing scientific instruments more accurate than any yet taken to the Pyramid, and with stores and equipment enough for several months.

Despite a series of mishaps, and the almost ruinous expense of everything in Egypt—which was in the midst of a cotton boom engendered by the American Civil War—the Smyths eventually arrived in Cairo, where they were obliged to hang around waiting for permits and local supplies. In his diary Smyth morosely entered exotic descriptions of "the abominations of the worst city in the world," where the food reeked of garlic, lard and African macaroni, the air was fetid from mounds of desiccated human excrement, where he was infested with flies by day and mosquitoes by night, and woken up by a predawn cacophany of howling cats and dogs which roused the pigs which roused the geese and turkeys "just before the disk of the sun comes up like a ball of liquid fire."

Poignantly he described little girls "diving between the hind feet of colossal camels to pick up its hideous droppings, pat them into nicely shaped cakes . . . to make high-scented ammonia-filled fuel for the cooks . . . of the resplendent city."

Smyth was so well received by Ismail Pasha (who a few years later was to commission Verdi's opera *Aïda* which opened in Cairo in 1871) that he tried to buttonhole the viceroy into providing men and funds to remove the great mounds of debris around the base of the Pyramid, to have a 3-inch hole carved through the center of the granite plugs in the Ascending Passage (so as to ascertain its true meridian), to have the ventilating ducts to the King's Chamber cleared, and to sink a shaft through the hole in the pit down to the level of the Nile.

The pasha shook his head, promising to provide twenty men for two weeks to clean and wash the main chambers of the Pyramid so that Piazzi Smyth might take some measurements. The pasha also kindly agreed to provide the Smyths with donkeys and a camel train to bear them and their luggage to the Great Pyramid.

Leaving "the purse-proud modern Muslim city with its tulip-clothed individuals struggling for wealth," the Piazzi

Traveling from Cairo to the Great Pyramid in the mid-nineteenth century.

79

Sandstorm in the desert.

Smyths set off for the Pyramid. On the way they stopped to eat buns "from Mrs. Smyth's commissary" and refresh themselves with Nile water "muddy and opaque as milk with suspended clay" but celebrated, says Smyth, for its health-giving qualities, the best cure for "the windy melancholy arising from the shorter ribs."

The pyramids, tinted by the golden rays of the setting sun "embalmed in the intense azure of the western heaven," appeared to grow no larger as the caravan approached. Only in the immediate vicinity did they suddenly tower so completely as "to take possession of the mind."

Looking up at the vast stepped sides toward the "dizzy apex 480 feet above in perpendicular height, the mind slowly and almost painfully began to realize the enormous size of the mountainous buildings."

80

Descending Passage blocked
by Arab guides below the
level of the granite plug.

As a place to live within reach of the Pyramid, the Smyths selected an abandoned tomb in the eastern cliff of the Giza hill which had previously been used as a storeroom by Howard-Vyse. It proved to be an agreeable residence: the solid rock was the best possible protection against the midday heat, and the orientation of the cave protected it from the sandstorms and the clouds of multicolored locusts that otherwise made life in the desert a misery.

To assist Smyth in his measurements, and to help with the general chores, he found a whiskered Arab called Ali Gabri who had carried baskets for Colonel Howard-Vyse a generation earlier.

At twilight Professor and Mrs. Smyth sat on campstools and watched with amazement as flock after flock of bats flew out of the Pyramid, "for almost twenty minutes without any cessation," to be pounced on by hawks or owls.

Several days were wasted while Ali Gabri impressed a gang of Arabs to clean the chambers of the Great Pyramid, but at last, in late January, the day came for Smyth to enter what he called "the largest building in the world by the smallest of all doorways."

As Smyth picked his way down the Descending Passage, partly on his seat and partly on hands and knees, he was relieved to find that shallow notches had been dug by Howard-Vyse every 2 or 3 feet so as to keep from slipping on the steep incline. However, each step raised a cloud of fine white dust that made it almost impossible to breathe. To his distress, Smyth also found that the passage leading down to the "pit," which had been cleared by Caviglia, was once more blocked with sand and stones, and barred by a grill just below Al Mamun's hole to the Ascending Passage.

It was explained to Smyth that it cost the Arab guides too much time and candle grease to accompany tourists all the way down to the "pit" before making the long climb back up to the King's Chamber, so they had blocked the passage and informed gullible tourists there was nothing but sand beyond the barrier.

Bent on finding proof that the Great Pyramid had been built on units of his "sacred cubit," Smyth had brought from England a 105-inch metal bar with built-in thermometers at either end to indicate the slightest variation in temperature with which to measure the available passages. A mere change of .01 degree Fahrenheit was enough to produce a sensible change in the length of the standard bars.

To obtain the exact angle of the Descending Passage, Smyth had a specially designed clinometer equipped with a gunmetal circle 8 inches in diameter, divided into units of

The Grand Gallery as Piazzi Smyth saw it in 1865.

Brass-tipped mahogany measuring rod.

Piazzi Smyth's special apparatus for measuring the Grand Gallery.

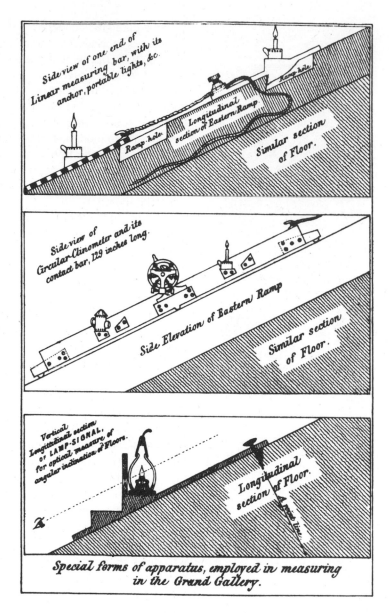

Special forms of apparatus, employed in measuring in the Grand Gallery.

10 seconds, and fitted with three pairs of verniers. The slope he calculated was the most precise to date: 26° 27′.

For measuring the individual stones of the floors, walls and ceilings, Smyth had mahogany and teak rods tipped with brass, carefully painted or waxed to prevent variation from humidity or temperature. One special ruler, remarkable for its straight, fine grain, had been obtained from an antique musical organ dating from the reign of Queen Anne. To fashion these measuring instruments, Smyth had obtained the services of an expert optician.

Each rod was checked daily for atmospheric shrinkage

"Miniature" camera, 8 inches long, used by Piazzi Smyth to photograph the interior and exterior of the Great Pyramid. On the right is a tiny container for the vulcanite nitrate bath which held the exposed wet-collodion plates which measured an inch square. Some two hundred microscope negatives, packed in a storage box, are still missing, but 48 lantern slides, 24 transparencies and 23 stereotypes are in the possession of the Royal Society of Edinburgh, examples of which are reproduced with their permission.

The camera is in the possession of the present Astronomer Royal for Scotland, Prof. H. A. Brück, and is here reproduced by kind permission.

or enlargement against a basic fine-grained clinkstone which could be measured with a magnifying glass to 1/100 inch.*

Thus began the first really systematic analysis of the Pyramid with modern measuring equipment. For weeks on end Smyth measured and remeasured whatever he could reach in the interior of the Pyramid, counting the stones in passages and chambers, computing angles and declinations.

Measuring the coffer in the King's Chamber, Smyth concluded that Taylor had been correct in recognizing it as a standard of linear and cubic measure. Unlike the European standards, such as the yardstick kept at Whitehall, which vary with temperature and barometric pressure, shrink, decompose, tarnish or oxidize with time, the coffer appeared to be designed to remain at a constant temperature and barometric pressure, its polished sides unaffected by decomposition over a period of thousands of years, subject only to the vandalism of man.†

* A clinkstone is a compact grayish-blue felspathic rock little subject to atmospheric changes which makes a clink sound when struck.

† Smyth echoed Herschel's complaint about the standard yard at Whitehall. Herschel had called it "a purely individual object, multiplied and perpetuated by careful copying, from which all reference to a natural origin is studiously excluded, as much as if it had dropped from the clouds."

Today our yard is related to the meter, which is determined by a finite number of wavelengths per second in vacuum of an atom of Krypton 86—measured by means of light waves. A second is no longer defined as the 3600th part of an hour but as the duration of cycles of radiation in a cesium atom.

Photograph of Mrs. Piazzi
Smyth taken by her husband
outside their tomb apartment
in the Giza Hill, which Piazzi
Smyth characterized as "a
quiet nook, looking out over
the green Egyptian plain."

For outside measurements Smyth used a 500-inch
cord, and for elevations he had theodolites, sextants and
telescopes, which were laboriously carted from spot to spot,
up and around the Pyramid, to measure all that could be
measured, despite the mounds of debris.

With his long and varied experience in observational
astronomy, Smyth had brought the requisite apparatus for
obtaining astronomical observations with a high degree of
precision.

To obtain the correct latitude of the Great Pyramid
without having his plumb line diverted from the perpendicular

Photograph of Ali Gabri (sometimes spelt Alee Dobree) seated outside the tomb in the east bank of Pyramid Hill where Piazzi Smyth, who is handling the camera, had his quarters.

by the attraction of the huge bulk of the Pyramid, Smyth made his observations from the very summit; there the Pyramid's pull of gravity would be directly downward.

Smyth and his wife spent several nights on the circumscribed platform, close to the stars, along with Ali Gabri, who complained he could not sleep because of indigestion. Smyth described the first night as eerie but wonderful, with the ghostlike summit of Kephren's pyramid lurking in the misty darkness. At daybreak he saw "a broad pinioned eagle floating serenely along looking downwards on other things, as we were looking down on him."

From the vantage of the summit Smyth figured the latitude of the Pyramid to be 29° 58′ 51″. From this he concluded that the designers might have purposely not placed the Pyramid directly on the thirtieth parallel because of the atmospheric refraction, which would have caused an error in their observations of about that much. Later he attributed the displacement to a gradual shifting of latitude, registered at Greenwich as 1.38″ per century.*

As for the extraordinarily precise orientation of the Pyramid—which Smyth found to be far superior to that of the world-renowned observatory of the sixteenth-century Danish astronomer Tycho Brahe—the Scottish astronomer concluded that for such refinement a meridian must have been obtained by observing a polar star along the Descending Passage.

When Caviglia had cleared this passage of the rubble left by Al Mamun, he noticed one night that the North Star was observable in the small patch of sky—about 1° square—of the opening. Intrigued by this phenomenon, Howard-Vyse had asked Sir John Herschel whether the direction of the passage could have been determined by the polestar. Herschel replied that 4000 years earlier Ursa Minor could *not* have been seen from the passage at any time throughout the twenty-four hours. He added, however, that alpha Draconis, the leading star in the constellation of Drago, would have been near the pole, and that though a comparatively insignificant star of less than the third magnitude, it could nevertheless have been clearly seen by an observer at the bottom of the passage at the moment of its inferior culmination, when its circumpolar orbit was at its lowest.

Smyth proceeded to subtract the 26° 17′ angle he had found for the Descending Passage from the Pyramid's latitude of 30° (or height of a true North Star above the horizon as seen from 30° of latitude) and obtained an angle of 3° 43′. Calculating that alpha Draconis would have been 3°43′ from the pole at its lower culmination in 2123 B.C. and again in 3440 B.C., Smyth concluded that either date might be taken as the one when the Great Pyramid had been laid out.

---

* Other pyramid experts have attributed the slight displacement to the fact that the Pyramid needed the solid basis of the Giza plateau for a foundation, and could not have been built any farther north, in the soft sand of the Nile valley. The astronomer Richard A. Proctor suggests that the emplacement was the result of the mean latitude obtained from observing sun shadows and star elevations, which are affected in opposite directions by the atmospheric refraction. An interesting explanation was produced by Dr. Everett W. Fish of Chicago who suggested at the turn of the century that the deviation of the Pyramid's latitude from 30° is neither an error in instrumentation, nor in polar axis, or latitude, but compensates for the spheroidal shape of the earth as postulated by Newton.

This photograph was taken by Piazzi Smyth and sold at auction after his death. It shows Mrs. Smyth sitting on the edge of what Smyth calls Shafre's burial chamber north of the Great Sphinx. It was taken at high noon to show that the tomb was correctly oriented along the meridian so that with the sun at its zenith, no light would fall on either the east or the west wall.

To ascertain the correct moment for noon Piazzi Smyth spent the previous night observing the stars with his telescope.

Piazzi Smyth photographed the Great Pyramid with the same scientific thoroughness with which he measured it, despite the difficulties of developing in the desert. He brought all his own chemicals, and used a special 1-inch plate "as small as an ordinary microscopic slide," which gave results that could be blown up with almost the detail of the larger photographic plate. To light the interiors of the Pyramid he used magnesium flares, experimenting with varying amounts so as to obtain the best exposure and the clearest detail. He had to wait hours between exposures in the King's Chamber, which filled up with smoke from each magnesium flare.

Smyth also achieved some remarkable stereoscopic effects by shooting with two cameras, and is responsible for the innovation of placing his cameras much farther apart than the standard 2 inches.

For lack of funds Smyth was unable to publish some fourscore photographs thus obtained at the Great Pyramid. The positive prints which he made were lent to scientific exhibitions or donated to friends interested in pyramidology, and gradually became lost, with the exception of this rather poor reproduction.

In support of the later date Smyth worked out that if the foundation of the Pyramid had occurred at midnight of the equinox in 2170 B.C., when alpha Draconis was at meridian below the pole, another very important star would have been crossing the meridian above the pole: n-Tauri, or Alcyone, of the Pleiades. In other words, when alpha Draconis was visible down the Descending Passage, the chief star of the Pleiades, n-Tauri, would have been crossing the meridian in the vertical plane of the Grand Gallery, at the moment of the autumn equinox.

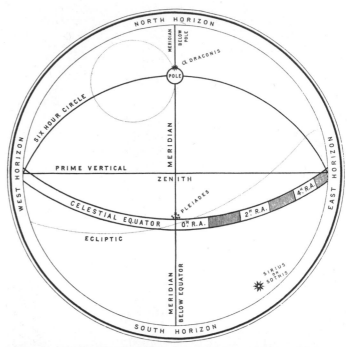

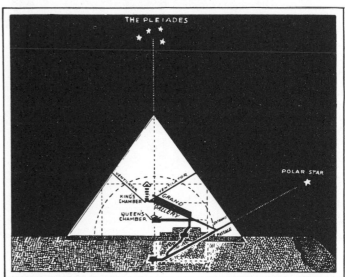

Piazzi Smyth's ground plan of the circles of the heavens above the Great Pyramid, at the epoch when he believed it was founded: midnight of the autumnal equinox 2170 B.C. Smyth noted that *alpha* Draconis was on the meridian below the pole while the Pleiades were on the meridian above the pole, coincidentally with the vernal equinox.

Piazzi Smyth figured that the Great Pyramid might have been built so its Descending Passage was aligned with the polestar and at a time when the Pleiades were at the zenith at midnight.

88

Casing stones donated by Smyth to the Edinburgh Museum, showing the angle of the slope of the Great Pyramid.

Smyth considered this a very important date in history, as many ancient peoples dated the beginning of their year at Halloween, when the Pleiades and the equinoctial point were on the meridian together at midnight.

But Smyth's prime preoccupation was still with establishing whether Taylor's π proportion was really incorporated in the structure.

Along the face of the Pyramid, Smyth checked the angle of the casing stones discovered by Howard-Vyse. Unfortunately the sharp lines had already been almost obliterated by the Arabs and by the chipping away of souvenir hunters. But searching through the debris piled high round the base, Smyth was able to find fragments of casing stones with the angles still intact.

Invariably the angle checked out at about 52°, or its complement of 128°, confirming Taylor's theory that the height of the Pyramid was designed to be in relation to the perimeter of its base as the radius of a circle is to its circumference.

To see if he could refine this angle, Smyth observed the silhouette of all the backing stones against the sky by means of a very accurate altitude azimuth circle which had been donated to his friend and mentor Professor Lyon Playfair by his students in 1806 and in turn lent to Smyth.

By this method Smyth obtained an angle of 51° 49′. Meanwhile Sir John Herschel had obtained a figure of 51° 52′ 15.5″ from the dimensions of the casing stones as reported by Howard-Vyse. Smyth chose to take the mean of these available measures as 51° 51′ 14.3″—a difference of less than a minute from either figure. He also chose to take the mean of the 763.62-foot base line measured by the

89

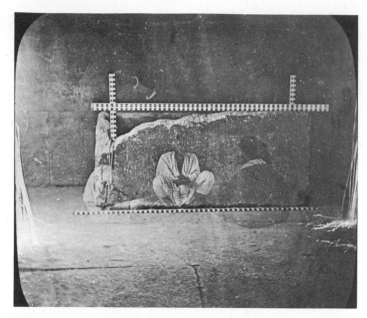

Magnesium-light photography had been developed only a few months before Piazzi Smyth took this double exposure of the coffer in the King's Chamber. The apparent reflections are those of Ali Gabri and another Arab. Mrs. Smyth's head appears beyond the coffer. Smyth's method of burning magnesium powder in a spirit-lamp flame was an innovation in photography.

French and the 764 feet measured by Howard-Vyse, and got 763.81—a difference of barely 2 inches on a length of 763 feet.

This was an arbitrary act, but the result produced an astounding value for π in the Great Pyramid proportions of 3.14159+.

Searching for a reason for the incorporation in the Pyramid of this relation of the radius of a circle to its circumference, Smyth pursued Taylor's theory of the base being divided into 366 units to coincide with the number of days in the year.

To have been absolutely precise, the perimeter should have measured 365,24.2 Pyramid inches. This would require that each side be 9140.18 British inches. The measure obtained by Howard-Vyse and the French savants, though within 6 inches of each other, were both about 2 feet too long.

The only solution appeared to be to dig up the sockets and remeasure the base line more accurately; but time and money were running short. Fortunately two engineers from Glasgow, Messrs. Inglis and Aiton, happened to pass through Egypt on their way from a tour of the Holy Land. Cajoled by their fellow Scot, they agreed to help him uncover the sockets originally found by the French (which had once more become covered with debris in the intervening half century) and make a truly accurate survey.

Following Smyth's complex computations, the engineers were able to uncover not only the sockets but a perfectly leveled stretch of pavement at the perimeter of the base.

Stereographic photo taken by Piazzi Smyth of Mr. Inglis and Arab workers in the northeast socket cleared in April of 1865. The Royal Engineer surveyor went all over the floor of the socket with a spirit level and found it absolutely level.

To measure the distance between the sockets, up and around the debris, required a great deal of digging and moving of rocks. But Smyth could not tarry. His own instruments were already packed and his passage had been booked by the British consul. When the engineers promised to take great care in their measurements and forward the results to Scotland, Smyth disconsolately agreed to depart as scheduled.

All that remained to be done was to dispense the customary baksheesh to the neighboring Arabs who had helped during four months' stay. The Smyths gave each man a gold sovereign plus a present depending on the willingness with which he had served his Scottish employers: the best got globe lamps mounted in copper; the middling got frying pans; and the worst got mousetraps.

When the ancient Arab who guarded their cave by night appeared for his just reward, Piazzi Smyth puritanically noted that the old man "seized on the money with such an agony of clutch, and his eyes brightened with so strange a fire, that alas for perverted human nature! we feared we had done more harm to his soul than good to his body."

As the camel train was prepared for departure, the faithful Ali Gabri stood silent for a time, "then suddenly putting his fingers to his eyes" rushed into the desert to conceal his crying.

Back in Scotland, Piazzi Smyth received the results of the engineers' survey; these gave a much shorter length of 9110 inches for a side of the Pyramid. Smyth concluded that the true length must be the mean between this figure and the

longer one of 9168 inches obtained by Howard-Vyse, or
9140 inches, which was just 1 inch less than was required for
Smyth's theory, resulting in a year of 365.2 days instead of
the precise 365.24 required by theory.

A great deal now hung on the exactness of these figures.
If Smyth's theory could be proved correct, it could mean that
the ancient Egyptians had produced a structure whose basic
unit, the Pyramid inch, incorporated not only a system for
linear measurement—with the cubit and the inch—but also
for temporal measurement, with a year of 365.24 days, both
based on the most sensible foundation: the polar axis of the
planet around which it rotates once in a day.

In Smyth's opinion "the linear measure of the base of this
colossal monument, viewed in the light of the philosophical
connexion between time and space, has yielded a standard
measure of length which is more admirably and learnedly
earth-commensurable than anything which has ever yet
entered into the mind of man to conceive. . . ."

Smyth summed up his work: the Pyramid "revealed a
most surprisingly accurate knowledge of high astronomical
and geographical physics . . . nearly 1500 years earlier than
the extremely infantine beginning of such things among the
ancient Greeks."

From the Royal Society of Edinburgh, Smyth received
a gold medal for the careful measurements he had taken
in Egypt; these he published in monographs, and in a

92

three-volume opus running to 1600 pages entitled *Life and Work at the Great Pyramid of Jeezeh during the Months of January, February, March and April, A.D. 1865.*

The work was not well received. As much of a religious zealot as had been his predecessor Taylor, Smyth was unable to account for the mathematics displayed by the ancient Egyptians. Like Taylor he was obliged to attribute this science to Divine Wisdom, somehow imparted to an earthly architect who had constructed the Pyramid under the direct influence of revelation. "The Bible," said Smyth, "tells us that in very early historic days, wisdom, and metrical instructions for buildings, were occasionally imparted perfect and complete, for some special and unknown purpose, to chosen men, by the Author of all wisdom."

The idea was received by some with derision, by others with acrimonious opposition. One reviewer remarked that Smyth's book contained "more extraordinary hallucinations than had appeared in any other three volumes published during the past or present century." A friendly reviewer summed up reaction to the book saying "it evoked numerous illustrations of envy, hatred, malice, and much uncharitableness from vain, flippant, and unqualified writers, the author being scoffed at, traduced, worried and all but *argued* with, by opponents who only succeeded in proving their egotistic inefficiency to apprehend the truth."

To make things worse another Scot, a religious enthusiast called Robert Menzies, advanced the theory that the passage system in the Great Pyramid was nothing less than a chronological representation of prophecy, corroborating the Bible, built on a scale of one pyramid inch to the solar year.*

As Menzies' theory was formulated before anything was known of ancient Egyptian messianic prophecy, such as *The Book of the Dead,* the texts of which had not yet been deciphered, this new contribution merely added to Smyth's problems. Smyth was further derided and lampooned by his

---

* Menzies, knowing that Smyth had made an approximate calculation of the date at which alpha Draconis shone exactly down the Descending Passage, put forward the theory that the date of this important astronomical phenomenon should be clearly marked some way in the Descending Passage itself, at the place representing the said date on the chronological scale. To Menzies' delight, Smyth replied that he had discovered two scored lines on each side of the passage at the very spot indicated. Although the joints in the walls of the Descending Passage were perpendicular to the floor, said Smyth, there were two joints on each wall, immediately to the north of the scored lines, that were not so: these were peculiarly vertical joints, as if intended to draw attention to something of importance: in Smyth's and Menzies' opinion, evidently the scored lines.

fellow academicians. Sir James Y. Simpson, an eminent member of the Royal Society of Edinburgh, publicly ridiculed Smyth before his fellow members, saying, "the whole of Professor Smyth's theory about the Great Pyramid is a series of strange hallucinations, which only a few weak women believe, and perhaps a few womenly men, but no more." Simpson added that he had "talked about it to a great many engineers, mathematicians, and others, and found them scoffing at and despising it."

Smyth's mixing of religious and prophetic conclusions with sound scientific discoveries caused his entire theory to be discarded by skeptics. To this day, the lampooning persists. One modern writer on pyramidology still refers to Smyth as the world's "pyramidiot," and laments that "such a first-class mathematical brain should have wasted its energies in so unprofitable a field."

But Piazzi Smyth was far from being quashed. He continued to produce even more fantastic theories from the results of his measurements of the Pyramid. Recomputing the height of the Pyramid, Smyth found it to be about 6 inches longer than Taylor's figure of 5813 inches from base rock to apex. The new measurement revealed that the Pyramid rose from its base in a proportion of 10:9, that is, for every 10 units of height, the Pyramid extended 9 units in width. To Smyth this was an indication that the proportions were intended to symbolize in yet another way the earth's circuit round the sun. Multiplying the height by 10^9, he obtained an astonishing result. Reduced to British miles, the answer was 91,840.000—or a very good figure for the mean radius of the earth's orbit round the sun. The present figure varies between 91 and 92 million miles. Was this mere coincidence? The argument between the supporters of Smyth's theories and the entrenched academicians who opposed them became intensely heated.

Basic to the whole argument was the fact that no one had a series of absolutely reliable measurements for the *exterior* of the building, especially beneath its debris where the base line must actually be measured. Even a new survey by the Ordnance surveyors made in 1869, which gave a length of 9130 inches, was made on the basis of cumulative measurements up and down and around the piles of debris that still clogged part of the base of the Pyramid between the exposed sockets. Results which varied by even 3 or 4 inches could not be considered accurate enough to prove or disprove the theories of Taylor and Smyth. So long as the *actual* dimensions of the Pyramid, both interior and exterior, were not obtained, correct to a fraction of an inch, there would be no real way of *knowing* if Smyth had a point or not.

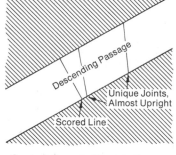

Scored lines in Descending Passage.

VIII. FIRST REFUTATION OF SCIENTIFIC THEORIES

To resolve the problem of the dimensions of the Pyramid once and for all, a mechanical engineer by the name of William Petrie, who had become fascinated by the theories of both Taylor and Smyth, set about designing and constructing even more specialized sextants, theodolites, and verniers with which to tackle the technical problems encountered by Smyth. It was no easy job. Smyth had gone a long way in perfecting his own equipment, and it was to take William Petrie all of twenty years to accomplish the task to his own satisfaction. Petrie stressed the importance of further exploration of the Pyramid because of its "paleologic, chronologic, metrologic, geodetic, geologic and astronomic interest to mankind," and above all "for its symbolic interest relating to the higher ideas intentionally embodied therein by its originator." Yet Petrie kept tinkering with the new instruments and postponing his departure for Egypt.

His young son, William Flinders Petrie, perhaps because of a spirit of adventure inherited from his maternal grandfather, the great explorer Matthew Flinders, became so impatient he finally decided to prime the pump by leaving ahead of his father, convinced that his father would quickly follow.

Fascinated by the varied standards of measure used in different parts of the world, young Petrie had read all he could on the subject; instead of going to school, he tramped around England, becoming proficient as a surveyor by measuring churches, buildings and ancient megalithic ruins such as Stonehenge, about which he was to write the first of his several score books.

At the age of thirteen, young Petrie had read Piazzi Smyth's *Our Inheritance in the Great Pyramid.* It had not only revived in him the ideas of Greaves and Burattini, but convinced him that a real history of measures might be deduced from a careful measurement of surviving monuments and objects. He was also determined to prove, one way or another, whether or not Taylor and Smyth had been correct in their theories regarding the Pyramid. To do so he would have to resurvey and measure the entire building.

96

William Flinders Petrie.

On a stormy day in November of 1880, Flinders Petrie, now a bearded professional surveyor of twenty-six, set off from Liverpool with a vast quantity of boxes containing the rare instruments designed by his father to eliminate the defects revealed by Smyth's experience. He also had with him the necessary supplies with which to survive for a long period in the inhospitable, bandit-infested desert. The gale blew so hard Petrie slept on the engine grating, too seasick to go below deck. Within a week of landing at Alexandria, Petrie had transported his equipment to Cairo, where he managed to get hold of Ali Gabri to help transport his food and instruments to the Giza plateau.

Ali Gabri was now a veteran of 40 years' service with Caviglia, Howard-Vyse and Piazzi Smyth. Reaching the Pyramid in December, Petrie followed the established practice of setting up house in an abandoned tomb.

Ali helped Petrie furnish his quarters with shelves and a hammock, helped him stock the larder with ship's biscuits,

97

Petrie standing before his living quarters in a tomb on the Giza plateau.

canned soups, tapioca and chocolate. To cook his evening meal Petrie had brought along a kerosene stove. Like his predecessors, Petrie found the solid rock of the tomb an extremely hospitable home, remarking that it seemed "as good as a fire in cold weather, and deliciously cool in the heat."

Petrie's day started with the lighting of his kerosene stove and the ritual boiling of tea water while he enjoyed a makeshift bath.

Breakfast was the time he accorded to reception. Men and women would look in at the door of his tomb, and if a special Arab friend paid a visit, Petrie would brew some coffee in his honor on the little stove by the door.

Petrie got along well with the Arabs, noting that "the smallest entering into their ways pleases them enormously; only sit squat, return the proper replies to salutations, catch their tricks of manner, and imitate their voice, and they will laugh heartily and treat you as a friend."

Petrie's first preoccupation was to accomplish what had been beyond the means of Smyth: a very precise triangulation all over the hill of Giza, including points around all three large pyramids, as well as the surrounding temples and walls which belonged to the complex. Though he couldn't remove the rubble, Petrie hoped to establish the dimensions of the pyramids by triangulation to within a fraction of an inch.

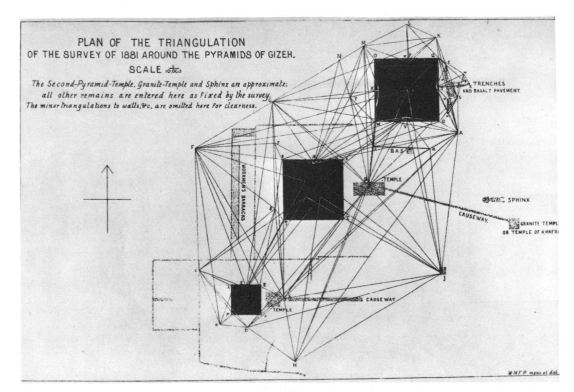

PLAN OF THE TRIANGULATION
OF THE SURVEY OF 1881 AROUND THE PYRAMIDS OF GIZEH.
SCALE 1/1000

The Second-Pyramid-Temple, Granite-Temple and Sphinx are approximate;
all other remains are entered here as fixed by the survey.
The minor triangulations to walls, &c, are omitted here for clearness.

Petrie accomplished his triangulation of the Great Pyramid over a period of months, by means of a ten-inch French theodolite, "a splendid theodolite by Gambay" with a ×35 telescope. Some of the angles were read as many as 14 times from as many as 50 fixed stations. Petrie estimated the probable error in his base measurement of the Pyramid to be ±.03 inch, or 1/260.000 of the whole. But because of the debris and the fact that the cornerstones were missing, Petrie could not establish where the original corners had actually been placed.

Using a highly accurate theodolite by means of which single seconds of angle could be read, Petrie repeated his observations so many times that it would take him from dawn till sunset to accomplish the work at a single station. A second of arc is so fine that it is commonly referred to as the angle subtended by a dime at the distance of a mile.

All the while Ali Gabri held a huge parasol over the theodolite to keep the sun from shining on the metal circle and expanding it unevenly. Once the sun had gone down Petrie would have a solitary meal, washing his own dishes—because he distrusted the Arab's idea of cleanliness—and then sit down to meticulously write up his figures, laying the groundwork for that scientific archeology of which he was to become the prime promoter. His sole entertainment was the "indescribable" tunes played on a reed flute by Ali Gabri's nephew, whose job was to guard him from a neighboring tomb through the night.

Choosing good days, with cool air but no wind, and working for ten hours at a stretch without food, Petrie was able to get a figure to within a quarter of an inch, and usually to within a tenth of an inch, for the actual layout of the three large pyramids at Giza. He was amazed to find the layout of the Great Pyramid "a triumph of skill. Its errors, both in length and in angles, could be covered by placing one's thumb on them."

99

Victorian tourist and her escort being helped up the Pyramid courses by Arab guides.

The Great Pyramid was so precisely aligned with the cardinal points of the compass that it surpassed in accuracy any human construction to date.

As the weeks wore on, Petrie realized he would not complete the exteriors before springtime and the arrival of the tourist season; so he had the way prepared for his indoor measurements by having a gang of Arab workmen clear the Descending Passage down to the lower "pit" which Smyth had been unable to reach because of the rubble. Armed with baskets, a chain of workers were able to carry the debris up and out of the main entrance.

When the tourists did begin to trickle toward the Pyramid, Petrie devised a system to avoid being bothered by going about outside the Pyramid in nothing but his pink underwear. At the sight of him, the good Victorian ladies kept a safe distance.

That the tourists were a formidable menace to the pursuit

of science had been made clear by Piazzi Smyth, who described "many and multitudinous scenes of lurid-lighted revelry, indulged in by many smoking, tobacco-stinking gentlemen and a few ladies, from some vulgar steamer" who performed "whirling dances over King Cheops' tombstone with ignorant cursing of his ancient name . . . and the painful thunder of the coffer being banged, to close upon breaking, with a big stone swung by their Arab helps."

For lack of salacious statues or pictorial attractions at the Pyramid, the more boisterous tourists would amuse themselves by removing loose blocks from the summit which they would send crashing down to the already vast heaps of rubble accumulated round the base.

At the end of the day, once the tourists had left, Petrie would work in the intense accumulated heat of the Pyramid, often till midnight and sometimes right through till morning, like "the Japanese carpenter who had nothing on but a pair of spectacles, except that I do not need the spectacles." The ventilating shafts in the King's Chamber, which had been opened by Howard-Vyse, had once more been clogged by vandals, making the air unwholesome. After the first few hours the dust which was raised at every move caused Petrie feverish headaches; but he persevered in his task.

With steel tapes and special chains 1200 inches long, as well as self-compensating accessory appliances, Petrie set about measuring with a far finer accuracy than Smyth could obtain all that was worth noting. Most of Petrie's instruments allowed him to measure to within 1/100 inch, and some, for really careful work, enabled him to do so to within 1/1000 inch.

To measure upright surfaces he used plumb lines; for horizontal surfaces a leveling instrument. Thus he could find the dimensions of a room at any level, and establish where any faults might lie.

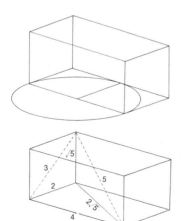

To measure the straightness of the sides of the Descending Passage Petrie used fine observations of Polaris at elongation—when it was farthest east and west from the pole. He was amazed to find that the average error in the part built of masonry was an infinitesimal 1/50 inch in 150 feet; and over the entire length of 350 feet the sides were within 1/4 inch of being absolutely straight.

In the King's Chamber, Petrie established to his satisfaction that the walls had been constructed on the basis of the same π proportion which ruled the exterior of the building. Its length was to the circuit of its side wall as 1 is to π.

This value was not immediately evident, because the floor of the chamber had been inserted between the walls so as to cut off a fraction at the bottom. But the cut was cunning in

President Ulysses S. Grant visited the Pyramid as part of a world tour.

In the archives of the Library of Congress lies a faded daguerreotype, with the unmistakable features of the general.

Piazzi Smyth describes the arrival of a party of enthusiastic Yankee tourists atop the Great Pyramid while Smyth was making early-morning observations. "In the short time they were there," writes Smyth, the Americans "arranged themselves into a meeting on constitutional principles of Anglo-Saxon derivation, with a chairman, secretary and audience; wherein a resolution was proposed, recorded and carried unanimously, to the effect—'that whereas this here pile whips everything in the way of building we've seen in all our grand tour through the used-up, worn-out world, yet we calculate King Cheops, its builder, must have been such a horrid old tyrant and cruel oppressor of the people, that it is hereby resolved by us free and independent citizens of the *Unyted* States that we *won't* give him a cheer.' "

After offering thanks to their "excellent chairman for his well-balanced conduct and impartial attitude on his very elevated seat," says Piazzi Smyth, "the gentlemen liquored up, the ladies, as they bashfully expressed it, consented to take a swallow, and the whole party disappeared down the steep slope of the pyramid . . . every man of them with little Confederate flags picked out on the soles of their boots, so that they might have pleasure in trampling on the hated ensign of the South wherever they went."

As an indication of how *tutto il mondo è paese,* Cheops is said (by Sir Gardiner Wilkinson) to have engraved the figures of the Gods of Egypt on the public roads "in order that they might be trodden under foot by man and beast."

that it thus incorporated in the chamber both the $2-\sqrt{5}-3$ and the 3–4–5 Pythagorean triangles.

Checking to see if the π proportion could also apply to the coffer, Petrie found that its dimensions appeared to be all multiples of a square fifth of a cubit. The difference between the requirements of the theory and the actual squares being a mere 1/1500.*

All of this tended to corroborate Smyth's theory that the builders of the Pyramid had been possessed of an advanced science of mathematics. But Petrie also found in the Pyramid an extraordinary mixture of brilliant workmanship and astonishing clumsiness. He was amazed to find that the granite in the antechamber had never been dressed: many of the stones had been left unfinished and some were even defective. From such indications Petrie concluded that "the original architect, a true master of accuracy and fine methods, must have ceased to superintend the work when it was but half done."

From a careful scrutiny of the coffer in the King's Chamber, Petrie established that the ancients had used saws with 9-foot blades, their teeth made of hard jewels, to cut the sides of the coffer out of a single solid block. To hollow it out they had used drills with fixed cutting points also made of hard jewels, probably diamond or corundum.

Petrie estimated that in order to cut through the hard granite a pressure of 2 tons would have had to be placed on the drill. How this could be done was a mystery to Petrie, who concluded: "Truth to tell, modern drill cores cannot hold a candle to the Egyptians . . . their fine work shows the marks of such tools as we have only now reinvented."

With such tools the ancient Egyptians were somehow able to cut sharp hieroglyphs into incredibly hard diorite, and also to turn stone bowls to paper-thin surfaces.

To measure the bottom of the coffer and to see if there were any secret opening beneath it, Petrie had its 3 tons raised about 8 inches, but found no sign of any opening. When raised and struck, the coffer produced a deep bell-like sound of extraordinary, eerie beauty.

Outside the building Petrie searched for more casing stones still in their original position such as had been

---

* Petrie also noted that the squares of the dimensions of the King's Chamber, Queen's Chamber, antechamber and subterranean chamber were all even numbers of cubits, nearly all multiples of ten. From this it followed that the squares of the diagonals were likewise multiples of 10 square cubits. And the King's and Queen's Chambers were so arranged that the cubic diagonals were in even hundreds of square cubits, or multiples of 10 square cubits.

Measuring the granite coffer
before it was vandalized.

The coffer showing corner
chipped away by tourists.

uncovered by Howard-Vyse at the base of the Pyramid. It was a painstaking and dangerous job to dig down through the accumulated debris. The rubble kept sliding back into the holes dug by the Arabs, and at one point Petrie nearly was killed.

Eventually he did manage to uncover more casing stones, as well as the base of the Pyramid. Petrie found the workmanship on the original casing stones, some of which weighed over 15 tons, quite as remarkable as Howard-Vyse had described it. The faces were so straight and so truly square that when the stones had been placed together the film of mortar left between them was on the average no thicker than a man's nail, or 1/50 inch over an area of 35 square feet.

Petrie found that the mean variation of the casings from a straight line and a true square was but 1/100 inch on a length of 75 inches. This staggering accuracy was equivalent to the most modern optician's straight edges.

As Petrie remarked, "Merely to place such stones in exact contact would be careful work, but to do so with cement In the joint seems almost impossible: it is to be compared to the finest opticians' work on a scale of acres."

So fine was the texture of the cement that after millennia of exposure to the elements, the stones shattered before the cement would yield.

The casing stones of the Great Pyramid (looking east), showing the platform on which they rest, the pavement in front, and the leveled natural rock.

Shallow sockets dug into the rock at the corners of the Pyramid were designed to hold the four cornerstones for the base, and were apparently cut through the pavement at these points. This has engendered an argument among pyramidologists as to whether the base circuit should be measured from the edge of the pavement or the edge or bottom of the sockets.

It was at first assumed that the bottom of the Pyramid cornerstones had been fitted into these sockets so as to counterbalance any eventual thrust produced by sliding away from the center of the structure, but modern archeologists discount the assumption because at the northeast corner, the depth of the socket is virtually zero; and the outer edge of the southwest socket is merely an incised line in the rock, more for measurement ·than for structural support.

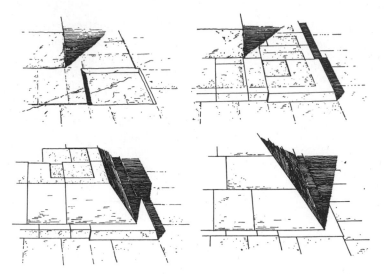

But the principal result of Petrie's survey was to prove a little abstruse. He considered the true base length of the Pyramid to be defined *not* by the limit of the sockets as measured by Smyth, but by the edge of the pavement 20 inches higher.

According to Petrie's measurements, the base of the Pyramid at the *pavement* was shorter than the distance between the outer corners of the sockets, as estimated by Smyth. Instead of measuring the 9140 British inches claimed by the Scottish astronomer, Petrie obtained a length of only 9069 inches for the base line.

Discarding Piazzi Smyth's theory that the Pyramid had been designed on an extra-long pyramidal cubit of 25.025 inches, Petrie showed by his own careful measurements that the builders of the Pyramid had used the royal cubit of 20.63 inches in order to produce a base line of 440 cubits and a height of 280 cubits. This confirmed Taylor's theory to the extent that the Pyramid was intended to symbolize the globe by giving a very effective π value of 22/7, or 3.14285, but apparently nullified Smyth's theories about the perimeter of the Pyramid giving the exact number of days in the year. The new product gave only 362.76 days.

Summing up the results of his measurements in a book entitled *The Pyramids and Temples of Gizeh* (which he was able to publish with a fortuitous grant of £100 from the Royal Society in London), Petrie remarked that he had never suspected, 15 years earlier, when he had first read Smyth's fascinating theory, that it would be he who "would reach the ugly little fact which killed the beautiful theory."

With success and recognition, Petrie turned from the romantic exploits of discovery to the prosaic minutiae of scientific archeology.

In the wake of Petrie's demolition of Smyth's basic contention about the length of the year being incorporated in the Pyramid's perimeter, soured academicians were happy to bury Smyth along with his theories. Foremost among such undertakers was Professor F. A. P. Barnard, president of Columbia College in New York, whose spadework in the 1890s consisted in arguing that the value of π was a modern discovery and therefore could *not* have been known to the ancients. In long-winded pieces for small periodicals, Barnard attacked Smyth for his "folly," and the builders of the Pyramid for the "stupidly idiotic task of heaping up a pile of massive rock a million-and-a-half cubic yards in volume."

In Barnard's opinion the Pyramids "originated before anything like intellectual culture existed; have been constructed without thought of scientific method, and have owed their earliest forms to accident and caprice."

Other academicians mocked the theory that the ancient Egyptians could have had an advanced knowledge of geometry, geodesy or astronomy. As recently as 1963 an eminent engineer in Baltimore, author of an expensive privately printed booklet, *Designing and Building the Great Pyramid,* was to write: "Because the sides of the Great Pyramid faced the four cardinal points almost precisely it is usually assumed that the designers intended they should, but it is unlikely that they had more than a vague idea, if any, of the four cardinal points. Like all peoples, the ancient Egyptians knew east and west from seeing the heavenly bodies rise in one and set in the other, but north and south were probably only known to them as general directions. There is no evidence in the Great Pyramid that they had any conception of true north or knew that a north-south line was perpendicular to an east-west line."

For years Smyth's painstaking measurements, carefully collected and illustrated in several large volumes (which went through several editions in his lifetime), were labeled by the academicians so much "trash and fancy."

In the conflict of opinions between biblical scholars and men of science, the true purpose of the Great Pyramid was buried in a rubble of verbiage.

Petrie had become Sir Flinders, and was on his way to becoming the dean of academic archeologists. Had it not been for the careful work of some conscientious scholars, Smyth and Taylor would have suffered the fate of Paracelsus and Mesmer, being relegated in the history books to the role of mountebanks.

IX. SCIENTIFIC THEORY DEVELOPED

Ironically, the next great investigator to throw light on the question of the Pyramid was a man whose object was to destroy and dispose of the theories of Robert Menzies, whose ideas about the prophetic revelations in the passage system had added to the difficulties of Piazzi Smyth.

An agnostic and a sober structural engineer from Leeds, in the north of England, David Davidson was determined to destroy Menzies' prophetic theory. But the more he attacked the data, the more he was obliged to assimilate it. In the end he was to produce an encyclopedic literature in support of Menzies' own idea, and to become convinced that the Pyramid was "an expression of the Truth in structural form" and that it "establishes the Bible as the inspired work of God."

From further analysis of the Pyramid, Davidson believed he could confirm Taylor's premise that the science of weights and measures of the ancients was founded upon two functions of the earth and its orbit, the standard time unit being the solar year, and the standard linear unit a decimal fraction of the polar axis about which the earth rotates.

On the question of the length of the Pyramid's base, Davidson was to vindicate Smyth, yet avoid harming Petrie. According to Davidson, not only was Petrie's survey correct, so was Smyth's theory that the Pyramid's base incorporated the length of the solar year.

Petrie, with his meticulously careful measurements, had managed to observe a definite hollowing of the core masonry on each side of the Pyramid. The accuracy of this observation, normally invisible to the human eye, was revealed in Petrie's lifetime in a dramatic aerial photograph taken accidentally at a specific time and angle by Brigadier P. R. C. Groves, the British prophet of air power. A similar line along the apothem, visible in an etching made by Napoleon's savants, had been ignored for a century.

Davidson noted that Petrie had failed to extend this hollowing feature of the core material to his measurement of the outside casing. If this were done, a base length was obtained which fitted Smyth's theoretical length to account for the solar year, to four points of decimal.

Sir Flinders Petrie noted a distinct hollowing of the core masonry in the central portion of each face of the Pyramid. Though the hollowing amounts to as much as 37 inches on the north face, it is not directly observable unless special lines of sight are taken.

Petrie found no evidence of hollowing along the lower-level casing stones, running along the base of the Pyramid, which have now been completely uncovered.

A recent survey by two Italian scholars, Maragioglio and Rinaldi, indicates the casing stones *above* the base line may have been slightly sloped toward a central line.

Davidson's plan of the base of the Pyramid, showing three different ways of measuring the year's length.

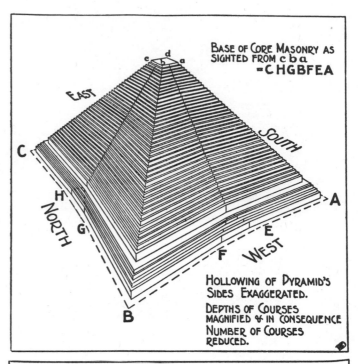

BASE OF CORE MASONRY AS SIGHTED FROM c b a =CHGBFEA

HOLLOWING OF PYRAMID'S SIDES EXAGGERATED.

DEPTHS OF COURSES MAGNIFIED & IN CONSEQUENCE NUMBER OF COURSES REDUCED.

CONSTRUCTION OF THE GREAT PYRAMID'S BASE.

(Hollowing-in of core masonry GREATLY EXAGGERATED to show effect.)

LMNO—Base as actually built.
SWXTYZUΠΔVQI—Base of core masonry.

110

As Davidson put it: "By reason of this unfortunate omission, scientists have been led to believe that the theory of the late Astronomer Royal of Scotland—Professor Piazzi Smyth—requiring a Great Pyramid base circuit of 36,524 inches, was nothing more than a delusion."

The ideal length postulated by Smyth for each side of the base in order to obtain the required length of 9131.5 Pyramid inches was 9141.1 British inches. Petrie's figure, revised by Davidson, came out to 9141.4, or about a third of an inch too long.

According to Davidson, the hollowing effect would give three basic lengths of the year as recorded in the base of the Pyramid: an outer or shortest length, from corner to corner, bypassing the hollowing, a second, slightly longer, which included part of the indentation of the four hollowed faces at the base; and a third, which included the entire angle within each hollowed face. These three measurements, which could have been performed by the ancients at their leisure, could have given the equivalents, according to Davidson, of the three lengths of the year as computed by modern science: the solar, the sidereal, and the anomalistic years, each of which is dependent on the system used for observation.*

The academicians rebutted that all this was purely attributable to chance. An American naval officer who dabbled in digging at Giza remarked that "if a suitable unit of measurement is found—say versts, hands or cables—an exact equivalent to the distance of Timbuctu is certain to be found in the roof girder work of the Crystal Palace, or in the number of street lamps in Bond Street, or the Specific Gravity of mud, or the mean weight of an adult goldfish."

But Davidson's conclusions were to reopen the entire subject of Pyramid measurements and breed a whole new school of pyramidologists.

* The solar year is obtained by observing the exact time between two successive vernal or autumnal equinoxes, when the day is exactly as long as the night. It is now 365 days, 5 hours, 8 minutes and 49.7 seconds, or in decimals: 365.2242. The sidereal year (from the Latin *sidus,* for star) is the time it takes a star to reappear in the same spot in the sky, as seen by an earth observer. It is about 20 minutes longer than the solar year, or 365.25636 days. This 20-minute lag causes what is known as the precession of the equinoxes, which come 20 minutes earlier each year in relation to the stars behind the equinoctial point. The anomalistic, or orbital, year is the time it takes the earth to return to the point in its elliptical orbit nearest the sun, or perihelion. This is about 4 3/4 minutes longer than the sidereal year. According to Davidson, not only does the Pyramid give this value, but it gives the number of solar years it takes for the perihelion to complete a full circle of 360°.

The president of the French College of Astrologers, D. Neroman, a mining engineer by profession, showed in his *La Clé Secrète de la Pyramide,* published shortly after World War I, that Smyth's sacred cubit and Petrie's royal cubit were mathematically related. Neroman revived Newton's conclusion that the Pyramid had been built with both basic cubits, Petrie's shorter cubit for the common workmen, and Smyth's longer cubit for the hermetic science of the designers. Neroman showed that the Pyramid was the precise height and width to contain a round number of each unit. As 33 sacred cubits are equal to 40 profane, or royal, ones, the base measured 440 royal cubits or 363 sacred cubits; the height 280 or 221.*

It was suggested that the priests measured the year's length with a sacred cubit so that they alone could make use of the Pyramid's hermetic science. But why this yielded a base of 363 days was not satisfactorily explained.

Another necromantic solution was provided by John B. Schmaltz in a small book entitled *Nuggets from King Solomon's Mines.* Schmaltz demonstrated that the modern deck of cards could be taken as a symbol of the Egyptian year incorporated in the Great Pyramid. According to Schmaltz the 52 cards represent the weeks, the 12 face cards the months, the 13 cards in a suit the lunations, the suits the seasons, the total face value of the cards (counting jack as 11, queen as 12 and king as 13) 364 days, plus the joker as the magic 1.234, for a total of 365.234 days in the year.

A more solid boost to the memory of Piazzi Smyth— quickly made much of by the pyramidologists—was the refined figure for the polar axis of the earth obtained in 1910 by the American geodesist John Fillmore Hayford, who computed it at 6,356,910 meters, the ten-millionth part of which gives a cubit of 635.69 millimeters, or Piazzi Smyth's sacred cubit, correct to .03 millimeter.

Another extraordinary figure found by the pyramidologists in the base of the Pyramid was the sum of its diagonals, which they computed as 25,826.68 pyramid inches. This gave a very close approximation of the number of solar years in what is known as the great year, which is determined by the precession of the equinoxes. The great year is the time it takes the earth to make a complete gyration in the wobble of its axis in relation to the plane of its orbit; this with the solar year, are the two prime standards for astronomical time.

Actually, the rate of precession is far from uniform, and

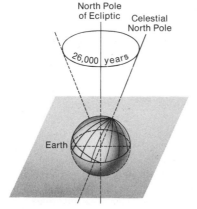

North Pole of Ecliptic   Celestial North Pole

26,000 years

Earth

The precession of the equinoxes.

* 33 × 25.025 = 825.72 and 40 × 20.643 = 825.72. It will be noticed from Neroman's figuring that to obtain this result he arbitrarily lengthened the royal cubit by about 1/100 of an inch.

is at present slowly increasing. According to Davidson, the Great Pyramid recognized this fact and provided a method of sums of diagonals at different levels of the monument to indicate the all-time mean, or average length of the precessional cycle.

To add to the coincidences, Morton Edgar, an ardent supporter of Davidson, who traveled to Egypt just prior to World War I and made extensive measurements and calculations, found that the perimeter of the thirty-fifth course, which is much thicker than any of the other courses, *also* gives a figure for the precession of the equinoxes.

Egyptologists and astronomers argued that if the Pyramid had been designed to incorporate the π proportion, and its base had been designed to be 365.2422 cubits long, the chances of its diagonals being intentionally designed to mark the length of the precession would be simply astronomical.

Davidson replied that to build the Pyramid its designer must have been deeply acquainted with the workings of natural law: that before such a design could be put into effect, the astronomical properties of the solar year would have to be reduced to a simple pyramidical expression.

Davidson claimed that—without getting into higher mathematics—it was evident that if you know the earth's distance from the sun and the length of the sidereal year in seconds, you can compute the rate at which the earth is falling toward the sun. This in turn would lead to finding the specific gravity of the earth, of the sun, of the earth and moon combined, the solar parallax, and even the speed of light.

To Davidson the mathematics of the Pyramid indicate that the former civilization was more highly skilled in the science of gravitational astronomy—and therefore in the mathematical basis of the mechanical arts and sciences—than modern civilization. It was his conclusion "that it has taken man thousands of years to discover by experiment what he knew originally by a surer and simpler method." In Davidson's words: "It means that the whole empirical basis of modern civilization is a makeshift collection of hypotheses compared with the Natural Law basis of the civilization of the past."

As to why the Pyramid was built and its passages carefully secreted, Davidson surmised that the builder intended to monumentalize the science of his time for another civilization far in the future, much as we go about burying time capsules. According to Davidson, the builder knew that the faculties by which he was able to handle the formulas of natural law could atrophy in man, and that by conveying his science to beings of a later civilization he might spur them to recover those powers.

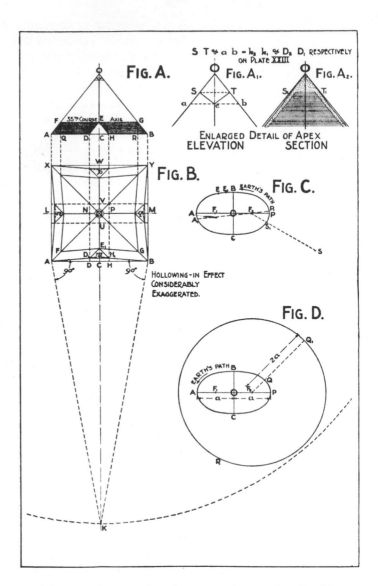

Davidson's computations to show that the Pyramid's base defines the earth and its orbit "in dimensions and motion."

Like Menzies and Smyth before him, all that Davidson managed to accomplish was to antagonize the scientific world with his insistence upon the record-preserving nature of the Pyramid while swamping the average pyramid enthusiast with the overwhelming bulk of his detailed mathematical analyses and computations.

Even worse were the efforts of a succession of pyramidologists who attempted to prove the Great Pyramid contained a six-thousand-year prophetic history of the world commencing in 4000 B.C. and going to A.D. 2045 which coincided with the prophecies of the Bible. They saw in the Pyramid an allegory in stone in which the Descending Passage represented humanity on its way down toward

114

Morton Edgar, supporter of the prophetic theories about the Pyramid, stooping to enter the King's Chamber. The picture shows how the floor was inserted between the walls so as to obtain both the π value and the 3–4–5 triangle.

THE GREAT PYRAMID

Its Scientific Features

(1914 A.D. AND THE GREAT PYRAMID – PART I)

By Morton Edgar

ignorance and evil. At the juncture of the Ascending Passage, evil spirits were to continue toward the pit, whereas the rest of humanity, benefiting by the Christian Dispensation, moved upward along the Ascending Passage toward the Light of the Grand Gallery. Having passed the Great Step, humanity must continue bent in submission through the Antechamber of Chaos—representing the modern age—before it could come out into the King's Chamber and the glory of the Second Coming.

The prophetic chronology was supposed to be marked out along the passages and chambers, with one year corresponding to one pyramid inch, commencing with "Adam," or the "first created man," and ending with the "Day of Judgement."

According to Morton Edgar: "By the year 2914, the end of the 1000-year 'Day of Judgement,' mankind will have experienced the full benefit of the sacrificial work of Christ, and will regain that perfect human nature which father Adam lost in the beginning of his disobedience 7040 years previously."

By general agreement the commencement of the Low Passage into the Antechamber was said to mark the beginning of the Great War in 1914. The end of the King's Chamber was supposed to be indicated by the year 1953.

Considering the wide popular acceptance of such medieval prophets as Nostradamus, and such modern prophets as Edgar Cayce and Jeane Dixon, it should not have been harder to believe that some ancient prophet could

115

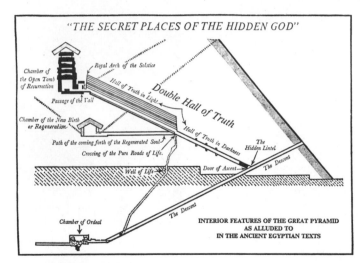

"THE SECRET PLACES OF THE HIDDEN GOD"

INTERIOR FEATURES OF THE GREAT PYRAMID
AS ALLUDED TO
IN THE ANCIENT EGYPTIAN TEXTS

Interior features in the Great Pyramid alluded to in the ancient Egyptian texts such as *The Book of the Dead,* according to the prophetic "pyramidologists."

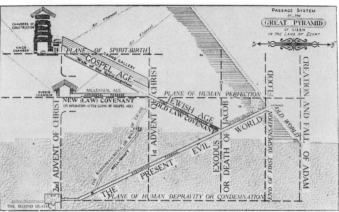

Chronology of the past 6000 years as indicated in the Great Pyramid passages according to Menzies and Piazzi Smyth.

have had prescience of the following 6000 years, and built his vision into the Pyramid passages; but as each prophetic date went by with no appearance of a Second Coming, the idea of the Pyramid as a prophetic calendar became largely discredited.

By 1920, when the waters of the Mediterranean failed to become thick and viscid, and the rivers and fountains of the world failed to turn into blood, as prophesied by Colonel J. Garnier on the basis of the Pyramid chronology, the whole subject became so unpleasant in the halls of academe that few professors dared mention the Pyramid as anything but the supposed resting place of the Pharaoh Cheops.

Nevertheless, a few intrepid investigators kept minds open enough to continue their research into the structure and purpose of the Pyramid, and to put forth some theories that in the end paved the way for a general vindication of much that Jomard, Taylor, Smyth, and even Davidson had propounded.

116

X. A THEODOLITE FOR SURVEYORS

One basic function of the pyramids on the Giza plateau was discovered by a chief engineer of the Australian railways, Robert T. Ballard, as he watched them from the window of a passing train in the 1880s.

From the constantly changing relative position of their clear-cut lines against the sky, Ballard realized that the pyramids could serve as excellent theodolites for a land surveyor, enabling him to triangulate the land anywhere within sight of the pyramids.

The land of ancient Egypt was parceled out in small lots to individual priests and soldiers, the boundaries of which would regularly vanish with the flooding of the Nile.*

By means of the pyramids, not only could the surrounding country be quickly resurveyed, but boundaries destroyed by the Nile could be readily restored.

From the silhouettes of the pyramids, the engineer realized that lines could be obtained as perfect as can be laid out nowadays with all of our modern instruments. With a string and a stone held in the hand and the clear-cut point of a pyramid 20 miles away against the ball of the sun 90 million miles away, the error in such a line would be trifling.

What's more, the same building could also be used with either moon or stars.

Knowing the latitude of the pyramids, survey lines could be shown all the way to the coast of the Delta—with nothing more than a string and a weight.

As the engineer's train steamed southward along the bank of the Nile, more pyramids appeared on the horizon, and the engineer realized that with a procession of such theodolites it would have been possible to adjust the boundaries of Egypt from one end of the country to the other.

Ballard figured that the simplest portable survey instrument would be a small scale model of the Pyramid of Cheops in the center of a circular graduated board marked like a compass. When the north end of the card was pointed toward the north, and the faces of the model turned to indicate the same light and shade displayed by the Great Pyramid, the

* Statisticians estimate that eight million people were crowded into a space of only 11,500 square miles, giving a density of 695 per square mile—which is more than modern Belgium, the most densely populated part of Europe.

117

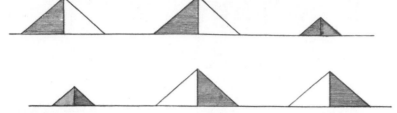

The pattern of shadows cast by the three large pyramids of the Giza plateau can serve to orient the viewer as accurately as a compass or theodolite. Ballard suggests that the smaller pyramid of Mykerinos was intentionally sheathed in red granite, in bold contrast to the other two pyramids, so as to facilitate the work of the surveyor.

Fig. 40.
From the North East
Bearing 45°
Sun in the East.

Fig. 41.
From the South West
Bearing 225°
Sun in the East.

Fig. 42.
South 21 West 20.
Bearing 223°.36'.10·15"

Fig. 43
South 4. West 3.
Bearing 216°.52'.11·65"

Fig. 44.
South 2. West 1.
Bearing 206°.33'.54·18"

Fig. 45.
South 96. West 55.
Bearing 209°.48'.32·81"

Fig. 46.
South 3. West 1.
Bearing 198°.26'.5·82

Fig. 47.
South 5, West 2.
Bearing 201°.48'.5"

Fig. 48.
South 7. West 3.
Bearing 203°.11'.55"

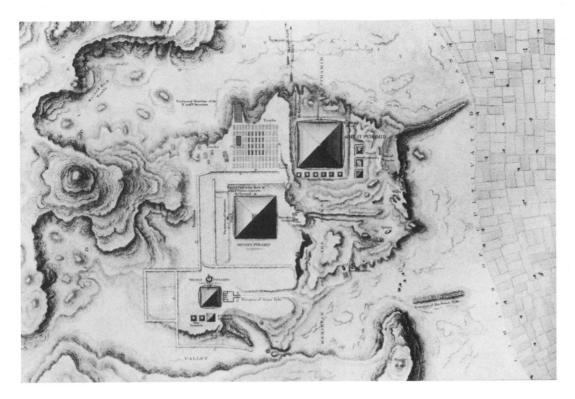

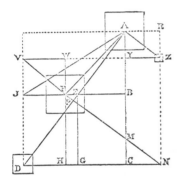

The Giza complex of pyramids, as depicted from the air, showing the north-south meridian through the center of the Great Pyramid.

According to Soviet space engineer Alexander Abramov the three large pyramids on the Giza plateau are arranged in a special geometric configuration known in ancient Egypt as an *abaka*. Ballard found that several Pythagorean triangles could be formed by the perimeters and centers of the pyramids.

surveyor could simply read off the angle of bearing. With a model of all three pyramids, the reading would be that much more exact. Furthermore, observation of the next pyramids farther to the south could be tied in with these readings.

The Australian engineer also worked out that the pyramids could be used for surveying by right-angled triangles with sides having whole numbers, such as the 3–4–5 triangle and the $2-\sqrt{5}-3$ triangle Petrie had found in the King's Chamber, both of which were fundamental to land surveying. Similarly incorporated in the ziggurat of the Babylonians, the triangles were conceived by the ancients to explain the secret order of the cosmos, a conceit which percolated to Plato. In the *Timaeus* he explains the cosmos as being constructed by the triangle 3–4–5 and the number $\sqrt{5}-1$ or 1.236068 (which in common practice was taken as 1.2345).

For right-angled trigonometry, the Australian engineer realized, true straight lines could be extended from the pyramids in given directions by direct observation, without aid of other instruments, and that with the simplest of instruments, angles could be exactly observed from any point.

In a short time *anyone* might construct a table for himself answering to every degree or so in the circumference of a circle for which only forty or fifty triangles are required.

119

Such primary triangulation would be useful to men of almost every trade and profession in which tools or instruments were used.

Having come to these conclusions, Ballard incorporated them in a small illustrated volume with the rather grand title of *The Solution of the Pyramid Problem*, published in 1882.

XI. ALMANAC OF THE AGES

Ballard's little booklet and one of Smyth's discoveries at the Pyramid brought another strange investigator to the scene. Smyth had been astonished that with the advent of spring, when the sun rose high enough to shine down the northern slope of the Pyramid, the structure appeared to swallow its own shadow at noon. Smyth deduced that the Pyramid had been designed as a huge sundial whose shadows could indicate the seasons and the length of the year.

By Smyth's reckoning the Pyramid had been intentionally located, oriented, and sloped for the phenomenon to occur in that latitude at the spring equinox, when at noon the sun is directly over the equator, although for some reason the phenomenon no longer occurred precisely at that particular date.

Unbeknownst to Smyth, the French astronomer Jean Baptiste Biot had been to Egypt in 1853 and noted that "with or without intention by the Egyptians who built the Great Pyramid, it has, since it existed, functioned as an immense sundial which has marked annually the periods of the equinoxes with an error less than one day, and those of the solstices with an error less than a day and three quarters."

The phenomenon had a great impact on an obscure Yorkshireman, Moses B. Cotsworth, a legislative enthusiast whose life's ambition was to reform our present barbarous almanac.*

* The present calendar derives from the early Romans, who had a 10-month year of 334 days: hence our September, October, November, December. In the seventh century B.C. Numa Pompilius is credited with adding January and February for a lunar year of 354 days. The shortage of 11 1/4 days caused the seasons and the calendar to diverge to the point where Julius Caesar was obliged to add 91 days to 46 B.C. and succumb to the suggestion of Cleopatra that he adopt the Egyptian civil calendar of 365 1/4 days. Even so, the difference between the civil calendar and the actual solar year of 365.2422 days added up to an extra day every 128 years, which obliged Pope Gregory XIII to drop 10 days from 1582. When Protestant England refused to go along, Christendom celebrated different Christmases in England and France, till the British finally relented in 1752, though there were street riots in London with shouts of "give us back our ten days." By skipping leap days in centuries which are multiples of 400 and 4000, our calendar is now good for the next 20,000 years, but anyone who troubles to read Cotsworth's impassioned plea for a more rational system than our calendar of floating holidays will find it hard to dispute his logic.

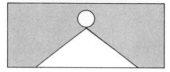

In early spring, when the sun rises just high enough above the apex of the Great Pyramid, the whole shadow on the north face vanishes at the stroke of noon.

Cones and pyramids designed by Moses B. Cotsworth to demonstrate how shadow patterns could be used to measure the length of the year.

Cotsworth's models show how a square-based pyramid oriented to true north will cast a pointed shadow on the meridan line. A cone, showing no orientation, will not serve the purpose.

Cotsworth was convinced that the designers of the Pyramid had intended their finished structure to serve as a perfect almanac for registering the seasons and the year. To prove his point Cotsworth went in search of further evidence.

Just before Piazzi Smyth died in 1900, Cotsworth managed to have several conversations with him, and after his death was able to get hold of Smyth's books and papers when they were put up for auction. Though Cotsworth refused to accept Smyth's prophetic theories, he was determined to vindicate the astronomical theories of the ancient Egyptians, so he set about reconstructing with models the sundial system on which he believed the Pyramid had originally been designed.

Cotsworth noted that at the latitude of the Pyramid, an ordinary obelisk would serve admirably for telling the time of day, or the general course of the seasons, but could not be built high enough to throw a shadow long enough to detect the length of a whole year of 365 days, let alone throw a shadow fine enough to distinguish the extra quarter of a day to four points of decimal. To obtain the difference in length of 1 foot per day would require an obelisk 450 feet tall, perfectly vertical and precisely oriented.

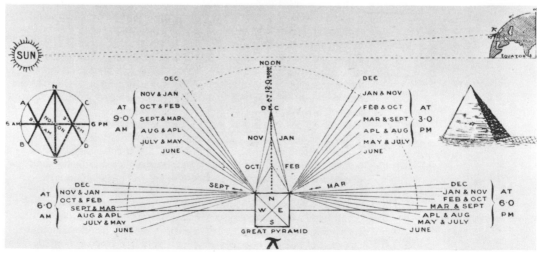

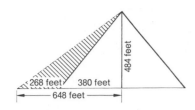

With the sun's winter solstice angle of 36° 45′, the Pyramid will throw a shadow of 648 feet. Deduct half the Pyramid's base length of 760 feet, or 380, and the maximum length of the Pyramid's winter shadow will be 268 feet.

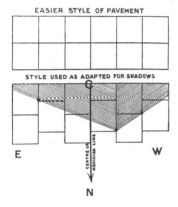

EASIER STYLE OF PAVEMENT

STYLE USED AS ADAPTED FOR SHADOWS

E   W

N

Cotsworth found that part of the pavement north of the Pyramid was paved with blocks whose widths were close to the 4 1/2-foot gradation of the sun's shadows on successive days just before the Pyramid consumed its own shadow in the spring.

Cotsworth figured that the dimensions of the Pyramid would be ideal for measuring the six winter months, when the northern slope of the Pyramid is constantly shaded and when the shadow cast at noon onto the northern pavement grows longer up the meridian to a maximum at the winter solstice, gradually decreasing to the point of disappearance at noon on a certain day in March.

To test his theory, Cotsworth made several model pyramids and cones and laid them out on carefully diagrammed paper. On these sheets he marked the outline of the shadow cast by the sun each half hour during a period of several months.

To his satisfaction Cotsworth was able to prove that the pyramid was the best shape for the purpose. The pyramid was more easily oriented to a perfect north, its flat slope was easier to angle, and its sharp edges cast a better shadow. Also, the actual structure would be easier to build to the required height in the form of a pyramid than a cone.

To measure the Pyramid's lengthening and shortening shadows, Cotsworth realized that a wide and perfectly level pavement, or "shadow-floor," should have been constructed on the northern side of the Great Pyramid, presumably with a meridian line running due north, and a pavement laid in some geometric pattern to facilitate the measuring of the shadows.

Cotsworth worked out that a structure 484 feet high, such as the Pyramid of Cheops, would require a "shadow-floor" stretching 268 feet northward of the base in order to include the full length of its shadow at its longest point, at the winter solstice in December.

To verify his theory, Cotsworth sailed for Port Said in November of 1900 aboard the P. & O. liner S.S. *Osiris*. At the Giza plateau he found the north side of the Pyramid of Cheops reasonably clear of rubble and the rocky plateau leveled to the required distance. At the level of the main platform on which the Pyramid rests, he found a pavement, or "shadow-floor," which extended as far as the remains of an old wall which had once surrounded the pyramid complex.

Instead of being paved in adjacent squares, Cotsworth found it laid in alternate half squares, which provided twice the number of junction points by which to measure the daily shadow of the Pyramid along the meridian at noon.

To support his observations, Cotsworth made a series of photographs of these shadows as they grew shorter toward the vernal equinox. To his delight he found that the paving blocks had been cut in widths very close to the 4.45-foot gradation by which each noonday shadow succeeded the former as they approached the vanishing point in March.

123

Photograph taken by Cotsworth showing shadow cast by the sun close to the base of Pyramid at noon of the last day before the intended equinox. The negative was stolen and the print has suffered in reproduction; but the pattern of shadow can be measured on the northern pavement.

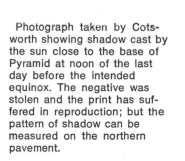

It was only thus, says Cotsworth, "that the ancient priests could have established by physical observation of the shadow on the flagstones, the precise length of a year to .24219 of a day."

William Kingsland, a professor of astronomy, commenting on Cotsworth's conclusions, pointed out that some of the paving stones are actually laid at all kinds of irregular angles and corners; but the corners of these stones are clearly cut out to fit into the adjoining stone—indicating, if anything, an even more sophisticated geometric pattern.*

To make up for the summer half of the year, when there

---

* According to Kingsland, Cotsworth's leveled rock area did not extend 268 feet north from the northern base of the Pyramid, but ended at a distance of only 33 1/2 feet, where there are the remains of a surrounding wall 9 1/2 feet thick; but there is no way of telling at what time this wall was built, or whether the pavement may not have once continued beyond it, and been dismantled by the Arabs for building blocks.

was no shadow on the northern slope of the Pyramid, Cotsworth figured that the priests could have subdivided and tabulated the intervening months.

In this he failed to realize that the southern face of the Pyramid, being highly polished, could throw a triangle, not of shadow, but of sunlight onto a southern pavement during the summer months, quite as definite as the winter shadows thrown on the northern side.

From May to August the south face would cast a triangular reflection of the sun onto the ground which would shorten as it approached the summer solstice, the shortest being at noon of the solstice, lengthening again till noon of the last day of summer.

Noon reflections would also be projected every day of the year from the east and west faces. But this was to remain for David Davidson to establish.

From a study of the sharper slopes of other pyramids, such as of Saqqara, Medûm and Dashur, Cotsworth deduced that their builders may have aimed these slopes not at the equinox, when the sun is midway, but at the summer solstice, when the sun is highest in the sky at noon. Sneferu's pyramid

Deliberately broken pattern of paving stones observed by William Kingsland on the north side of the Great Pyramid, apparently intended for finer mathematical measurement of the sun's shadow on successive days and years.

at Dashur, with its milder slope of 43°, may have been aimed at the winter solstice, when the sun is lowest at noon. From the gradually corrected slope of Saqqara and the change in angle in the bent pyramid at Dashur, Cotsworth concluded that the Egyptians may have progressed northward to the "truer" pyramid form, or π-shaped pyramid, at the thirtieth parallel, where morning and afternoon shadows form a series of perfectly straight lines.

In this, Cotsworth was supported by Joseph Norman Lockyer, the eminent British astronomer, who taught astronomical physics at the Royal College of Science. Lockyer noted that pyramids other than that of Cheops appeared to be oriented not to true north but to the rising sun at the solstice, which *changes with the latitude* of the place of construction.

According to Cotsworth the pyramids were originally developed from mastabas or raised terraces built to support an obelisk. To lengthen the shadow, the obelisk was successively raised on higher sloped platforms, which eventually turned into stepped pyramids.

Davidson's diagram of the reflections of sunlight cast by the Pyramid at noon of the summer solstice.

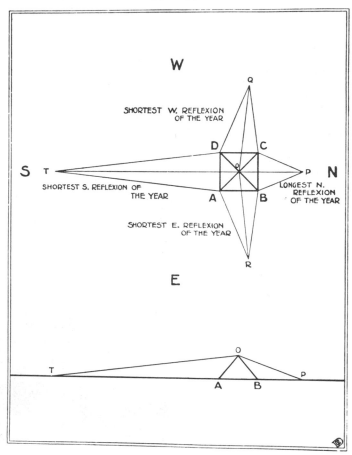

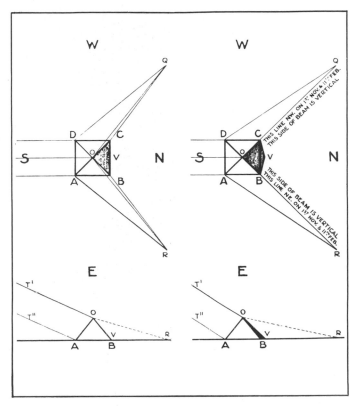

Davidson's diagram of winter shadows and reflections cast by the Great Pyramid. Left figure shows the noon shadow first appearing October 14–15. Other lines indicate reflected sunlight. Right figure shows the noon shadow first disappearing February 27–28. Other lines are pattern of reflected sunlight.

Cotsworth points out that the oldest true pyramid, that of Medûm, was constructed in several stages, as evidenced by the polished casings at each level.

The process, says Cotsworth, was developed to the point where the results no longer increased in proportion to the effort expended. A 60-foot platform which raised a 60-foot obelisk increased its shadow by 100 percent, but an added platform of 40 feet only increased the shadow by 19 percent; eventually the top platform became too small for raising an obelisk. According to Cotsworth, the optimum design turned out to be the solidified Pyramid of Cheops, with its slope set for a particular latitude to swallow the equinoctial shadow. Once this method of establishing the precise length of the year had been found, says Cotsworth, there was no further need for enormous pyramids.

Cotsworth obtained further confirmation of his theory from a comparison of the pyramids with the artificial hills built by ancient inhabitants of Britain who traced the year's end by the longest shadow of the year cast from vertical cones or artificial mounds such as Silbury Hill.

Later inhabitants of Britain, such as the Druids and Goths, continued to count the year's end from Yuletide, the December solstice.

127

Silbury Hill in Wiltshire, England, covers five acres and is built of over a million tons of hand-moved material. According to archeologists it is at least four thousand years old.

Cotsworth says that Silbury Hill was designed to have a Maypole on top to cast a shadow up and down the truncated hill and onto the level plain to the north, so as to mark the four seasons of the year.

The cone was truncated at a point where the shortest shadow thrown by the Maypole on the longest day of the year indicated the summer solstice. On the level plain north of the hill a stone was placed in the ground to mark the point of the longest shadow cast by the Maypole at the winter solstice, or shortest day of the year.

The juncture at the bottom of the hill, where it touched the plain, marked the spring and autumn equinoxes, when the day was exactly as long as the night.

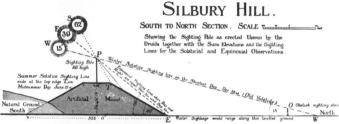

Aerial photograph of Silbury Hill, showing the footpath around the truncated top.

Druid in Old Irish meant "he who knows." Julius Caesar, our earliest source on the subject, considered the Druids highly educated and well organized. In *De Bello Gallico* he commented: "It is especially the object of the Druids to inculcate this—that souls do not perish, but after death pass into other bodies, and they consider that by this belief more than anything else men may be led to cast away the fear of death, and to become courageous. They discuss many points concerning the heavenly bodies and their motion, the extent of the universe and the world, the nature of things, the influence and ability of the immortal gods; and they instruct the youth in these things."

As Cotsworth reconstructed the system, the truncated cone of Silbury Hill enabled the ancient astronomers to measure the length of the seasons and the year by the length of shadow cast by a pine Maypole, which served as an obelisk, atop a hill intentionally truncated so that its edge would also mark the summer solstice, or the shortest shadow of the year.

Had these astronomers simply required a great height, says Cotsworth, they would have used the adjacent Abury Hill, with its wide top which could easily have been raised. But this, says Cotsworth, would not do; they required an absolutely level piece of ground on which to mark the progress of the shadow. Hence they had no alternative but to pile up an artificial hill above the level plain. Fortunately, in latitudes of 50° or 60°, such as Brittany or Stonehenge, low mounds would give shadows long enough for detailed measurement. A height of 225 feet in Wiltshire gives a

The main chamber in Maes-Howe, showing corbeled monoliths which could be closed at the top by a single movable slab. The jointing in this prehistoric masterpiece rivals that of the Great Pyramid.

The entrance passage to the Maes-Howe observatory is very similar to that of Egyptian pyramids.

Maes-Howe, near Stennes in the Orkney Islands, is a man-made cone-shaped pyramid 27 feet high and 115 feet across, with an outer circling ditch 45 feet wide and 700 feet in circumference.

It has a 54-foot observation passage aimed like a tele-scope at a megalithic stone to indicate the summer solstice.

Its central observation chamber, corbeled like the Great Pyramid's Grand Gallery, is built of megaliths weighing 3 tons, carefully leveled, plumbed and so finely jointed they will not admit the blade of a knife.

shadow almost equivalent to the shadow of the 484-foot Pyramid of Cheops.

One of the most remarkable of these prehistoric European mounds still exists at Maes-Howe, near Stennes, in the Orkney Islands. It is equipped with a 15-foot square observatory chamber and a 54-foot sighting tunnel. The tube is aimed at a conspicuous man-raised monolith 42 chains (2772 feet) from the entrance, which lines up with a spot on the horizon where the sun now rises 10 days before the winter solstice. Another monolith, to the west, called the Watchstone, indicates the equinoxes. Like the Great Pyramid of Cheops, the observatory chamber is built of huge megaliths and its ceiling is corbeled. There are also three "retiring rooms for the observers," somewhat like the Queen's Chamber in the Great Pyramid.

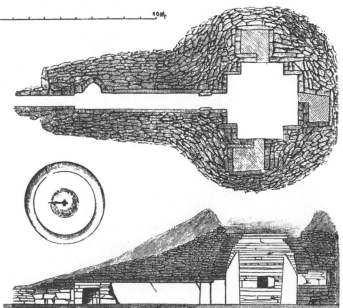

Circular monoliths similar to Stonehenge located at Stennes in the Orkneys near Maes-Howe.

In *Stonehenge, a British Temple Restored to the Druids,* which Piazzi Smyth considered a book "far before its age and perhaps not yet sufficiently appreciated," its author, Dr. William Stukely, attempted to show that such megalithic circles had always been arranged on even and round numbers of the "profane cubit of 20.7 inches nearly," and not in feet or any other known standard of length. Smyth remarked that although the idea "was pooh-poohed by more recent antiquarians, I have never heard of any of them having ascertained by actual measure at the place, that the Stukelian theory would not hold."

Professor Alexander Thom has recently shown they are built on a megalithic yard of 2.72 feet.

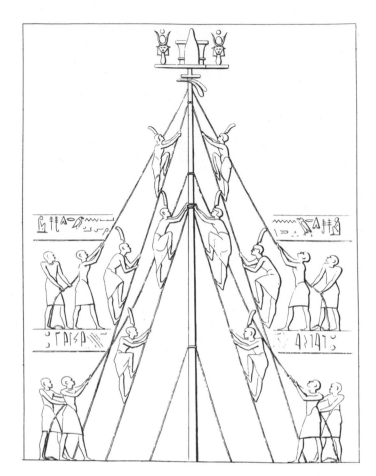

An Egyptian Maypole.

Various shaped mounds, or "barrows," were constructed in prehistoric Britain. Cotsworth considered them man-made instruments for observing the movements of heavenly bodies.

Alexander Thom considers Averbury Circle near Stonehenge the greatest and most remarkable circle in Britain, if not in the world. "Its greatness," says Thom, "does not lie in its size alone but in the remarkable manner in which its arcs are built up from a basic Pythagorean triangle so that each retains an integral character, and in the exceedingly high precision of the setting out, a precision only surpassed today in high-class surveying."

The Scottish lairds in residence at Maes-Howe—or Maiden's Mound—still plant a Maypole on the originally flat top, perpetuating the ceremony begun when observations were made of the shadows cast by the pole on the flat terrain to the north of the mound.

In England throughout the Middle Ages and the Renaissance, the Maypole with its tall garlanded and decorated shaft (stowed away for the rest of the year under the eave of a house) was set up on May Day. When Cromwell came to power he banned the Maypole. As the *National Encyclopedia* puts it: "The Puritans, to whom we owe the loss of so many of our public games, and so much of our merriment, ordered all Maypoles to be destroyed by Act of Parliament in 1644, as a 'heathenish vanity, abused to superstition and wickedness,' and fined the constables five shillings weekly as long as they stood."

The custom was revived with the Restoration, and the last Maypole erected in London—all of 100 feet high—stood on the spot where the church in the Strand now stands near Somerset House. It was taken down in 1717 and conveyed to Wanstead Park, in Essex, where it was fixed as part of the support of a large telescope set up by Sir Isaac Newton.

A glance at the outlines and cross sections of the pyramids of Saqqara, Dashur and Medûm will show that, like ancient British observatories, each had a sighting passage, pointed at a northern star. The passage ended in an

Remains of "Old Sarum," an ancient British stepped pyramid.

The original building of the stepped pyramid was a mastaba 63 meters square built of coarse rubble cased with fine white limestone, above a square pit.

The original entrance was through a hole in the roof directly into a 28-meter shaft lined with granite. The mastaba was subsequently heightened into a stepped pyramid by the superimposition of three more terraces. Extended eastward (ostensibly to include graves for Zoser's family!), the structure was then a rectangle 120 meters by 108. Two more stories were added, so that it became a six-step pyramid, cased with fine limestone, at a slope angle of 72° 30'. A second entrance was placed in the north face leading down a rock-cut flight of steps to a more restricted "sepulchral chamber."

The building was attributed to King Zoser (of the Third Dynasty) on the basis of his cartouche on some stones and is believed to have been erected by his fabulous architect Imhotep.

In 1929 Frith found a bas-relief in the pyramid depicting Zoser, and in the 1950s Prof. Lauer found a mummified foot which he believes to have been Zoser's.

Stepped pyramid of Saqqara, believed to be the oldest Egyptian pyramid.

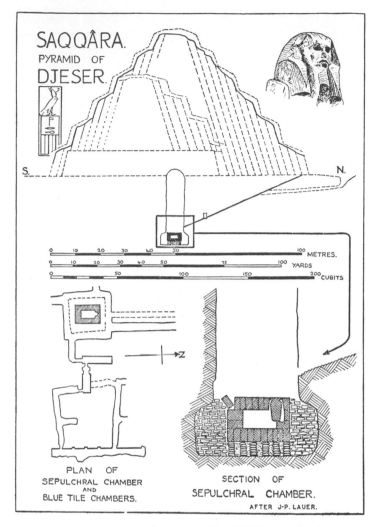

SAQQÂRA. PYRAMID OF DJESER

PLAN OF SEPULCHRAL CHAMBER AND BLUE TILE CHAMBERS.

SECTION OF SEPULCHRAL CHAMBER.

AFTER J-P. LAUER.

The pyramid of Medûm, on a square base of 144 meters, rises 92 meters high, and is so situated that it is a landmark for miles in all directions.

Most of the outside limestone casing, which sloped at 51° 52', has been removed, showing that the pyramid was built in several stages from an original mastaba about 20 meters long, with slopes of 75°.

The pyramid grew in seven steps by means of a series of accretion walls, each of which was cased in fine white limestone; eventually the spaces between the steps were filled in, and the entire pyramid cased with white limestone, most of which was removed at an early date (possibly during the reign of Rameses II) though portions remain. Three accretion faces are presently visible.

The base is still covered with sand and debris.

An entrance on the north side, 30 meters aboveground, leads down a ramp 57 meters long, sloping at 27° 30', to two antechambers and a vertical shaft in the center of the building. The shaft rises to the "sarcophagus chamber," which has a fine corbeled roof of limestone built in seven steps.

In 1891 Petrie found fragments of a wooden coffin believed to have belonged to Sneferu; so the pyramid has been attributed to Cheops' father.

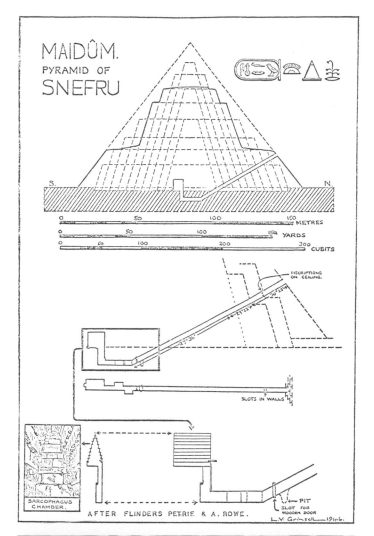

135

Sneferu's blunted or rhomboidal pyramid at Dashur is 190 meters square at the base and 100 meters high. The lower portion slopes 54° 41′, the upper portion 43°. The casing is of fine white limestone; the body is believed to be of coarser limestone.

There are two entrances, one on the north and one on the west side, leading to two main chambers.

The northern entrance is 11 meters aboveground in the center of the lower face and leads down a ramp inclined at 28° 38′ for the first 13 meters, then at 26° 10′ for the remaining 65 meters. A short horizontal passage 12 meters high leads to a fine chamber whose roof is corbeled on all four sides.

The western entrance, which is 29 meters above the base, leads to a ramp descending at 26° 36′ for 68 meters to a horizontal passage with two portcullis slabs and a chamber with a roughly corbeled roof.

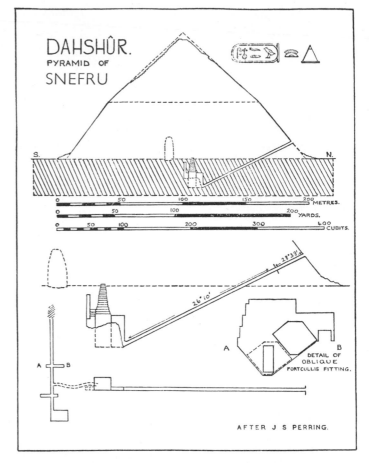

DAHSHÛR.
PYRAMID OF
SNEFRU

DETAIL OF OBLIQUE PORTCULLIS FITTING.

AFTER J S PERRING.

observation chamber with a corbeled roof with a small opening just at ground level, presumably for sighting a star directly overhead at the zenith, or for lowering a plumb line to coincide with a line sighted down the sloping passage. The similarity to the structure at Maes-Howe is indeed amazing. Yet Maes-Howe has also been considered as nothing but a burial chamber. A recent writer on Maes-Howe discarded the theory that the mound might have had astronomical significance, saying that the belief is accepted by no "serious students of archeology."

Scientists of other disciplines are in disagreement, and have produced interesting data on the orientation and purpose of megalithic monuments.

In his *Megalithic Sites in Britain,* published in 1967, Professor Alexander Thom, who for many years held the chair of Engineering Science at Oxford, shows how the stone and wood henges of Britain of the second millennium B.C. were aligned on certain stars, were planned on the basis of a geometry which anticipated Pythagoras, and were uniformly built on a unit of measure which he calls a megalithic yard of 2.72 feet or .829 meter.

According to Thom, megalithic sites in Britain served the purpose of calendars and clocks. During the long winter nights the only indicators of time were the stars. By observing the rising and setting of stars of the first magnitude, or their

Cotsworth's explanation of Druidical circles such as Stonehenge.

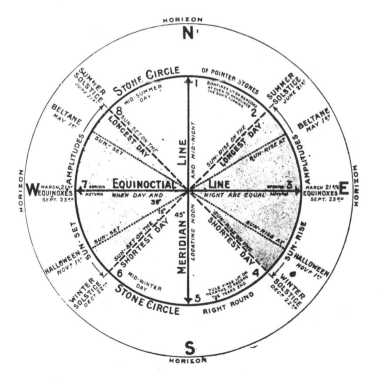

transit over the meridian, it was possible to tell the hour of night.

Thom says that in Britain between 2000 and 1600 B.C. there were about ten or twelve stars of the first magnitude whose rising and setting could be clearly observed. Thom also found a great number of stones set to indicate the point of rising and setting of first magnitude stars, and many slabs and alignments which accurately marked the meridian.

For such pointers to be accurate the observer also had to know the date. This was obtained from the sun calendar arrangement of the stones.

As for the accuracy of the alignments, Thom says the ancient engineers managed to raise perhaps ten thousand megaliths from one end of Britain to the other, and set them with an accuracy of 0.1. When they wanted to, says Thom, they could measure with an accuracy of 1 in 500.

R. J. C. Atkinson, professor of archeology at University College, Cardiff, an authority on Stonehenge, and a severe critic in this field, concludes from Thom's data that a high degree of competence in empirical astronomy existed in Britain 4000 years ago.

This supports the data of the contemporary Greek astronomer C. S. Chassapis, whose analysis of the Orphic Hymns indicates that the Greeks of the second millennium B.C., also had an advanced knowledge of astronomy.* These ancient Greeks, says Chassapis, knew that the seasons were caused by the earth's rotation around the sun along the ecliptic, and had determined the torrid, temperate and frigid zones. They had established the equinoxes and solstices, and knew that the apparent daily rotation of the stars in the heavens was due to the earth's rotation on its axis, which formed a northern pole in the sky. This knowledge, says Chassapis, was taught by the Orphics to the initiate who distinguished between the "fiery" stars and the seven planets which they called by today's names. The second millennium Greeks used a calendar of twelve conjuctive months from full moon to full moon, and accepted the presence of mountains on the moon. They believed that all phenomena were governed by a universal law, and conceived that space was filled with ether.

Lyle B. Borst, professor of astronomy and physics at New York State University in Buffalo, in an article in *Science* (November, 1969), notes that more than forty churches, mosques and temples have now been identified from Norway

---

* *Greek Astronomy in the Second Millennium B.C. according to the Orphic Hymns.* Athens, 1967.

Many churches in Europe continued to build with their towers oriented to the cardinal points, or to mark the solstices and equinoxes. Others were oriented to the sunrise of the saint for whom they were named.

St. Peter's Basilica in Rome is oriented due east so that at the vernal equinox the great doors can be thrown open at sunrise and the sun-rays passing through the nave will illuminate the high altar.

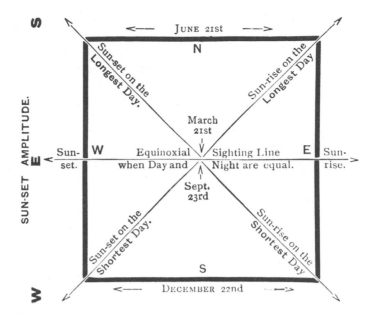

to Egypt, all laid out in megalithic yards of .829 to .840 meter.*

Professor Borst, who went to England to make a model of Stonehenge to demonstrate to his students how astronomy was practiced before there were telescopes, suggests that the axes of many early Christian churches in Britain are laid out on top of megalithic foundations originally determined by an alignment with stars; he suggests that Canterbury Cathedral was aligned with the equinoctial rising of Betelguese about 2300 B.C.

Borst also shows that the geometric plans of the megalithic monuments were obtained by means of 3–4–5 triangles and other right-angled triangles laid along the axis of stellar observations.

Alfred Watkins, in his *The Old Straight Track,* published in 1920, pointed out that many churches in England were situated on sight lines between beacon points and that ancient man was inclined to travel in a straight line from beacon to beacon. The churches served as relay points.

Watkins suggested that where topographical features were lacking, observation towers were built, and such geodetic points, initially guarded by the surveyor priesthood, remained hallowed spots even after the reason for them had been forgotten. Later arrivals built churches on these spots, as is indicated by Bede who reports that Pope Greg-

---

* If .840 meter is taken as a megalithic yard, there are exactly 275 such yards in a 231 meter base of the Great Pyramid of Cheops, 220 in the apothem and 175 in the height.

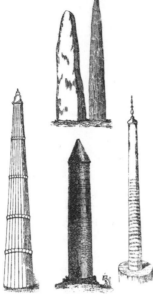

Examples of Irish and other round towers.

There are remains of some 120 observation towers in Ireland, twenty of them still in good condition, ranging in height from 60 to 132 feet. The tower at Killcullen is the highest.

Built near churches between the eighth and thirteenth centuries, the towers have door and window jambs that are narrow like the doors of ancient Egyptian temples, which served to measure the shadow of the sun in its daily and seasonal movements.

ory I explicitly ordered Bishop Miletus to build churches on pagan shrines.

In the Middle Ages in Ireland, Catholic monks still used tall conical towers with carefully oriented openings at the top to observe the skies and record the passage of the days, months and years by shadows on the walls and floors.

These "Round Towers," as they were called, were fitted for Polaris observations at the north window, for transit observations at the south window, and for noting the moment of the rising and setting of heavenly bodies at the east and west windows. H. G. Wood in his *Ideal Metrology* says that by threads drawn across the openings, like the spider lines in a telescope, the exact position of a star could be noted. The walls being two or three feet thick, the solar shadows of the jamb and lintel cast upon the floor within would show the hour of day and the time of the year. Every month could have its transit floor-mark.

Similar structures have been found in France. In a booklet oddly entitled *Falicon,* privately printed in 1970, the author Maurice Guignaud, a French artist and ceramist, describes a small pyramid in the south of France built in the thirteenth century by Knights Templar on their return from the Middle East.

Guignaud observed that at solar noon of the autumn equinox of September 21, 1969 (which in that region occurs at 12:53 P.M.) the pyramid projected no shadow on the ground around it. Guignaud also noted that a raised area in the doorway caused the sun to cast a shadow that precisely split the end of the entranceway.

At the equinox Guignaud measured the shadow of a meter stick held vertical at noon and found it to be exactly one meter long, whereas on June 21 it cast a shadow of .80 meter and on December 22 a shadow of 2.52 meters.

Guignaud found that this exotic truncated pyramid, which is known by the weird name of *Ratapignata* or "The Bat," was also built directly over two subterranean pits, one almost above the other, and that carved signs on its walls indicated it had been used for astronomical and astrological observation.

According to Cotsworth, the value of ancient astronomical observatories cannot be overestimated. The importance of establishing the exact length of the year so as to know when to plant and when to harvest crops could mean the difference between famine and plenty.

Far from being Professor Barnard's "stupendous monument of folly," the colossal effort employed by the ancients in building the Great Pyramid (or the million-ton mounds of the Britons) would have had a vital effect on the citizenry, redounding to the benefit not only of the builders, but of countless generations to come.

Cotsworth took several more photographs at the Great Pyramid to illustrate his thesis, but most of these were stolen from his carriage and irretrievably lost. This particular photograph, taken in 1900 by a third party, shows Cotsworth seated on a camel with the Sphinx and the Great Pyramid as a background. The white-whiskered Arab at the extreme right is none other than the indefatigable Ali Gabri, now over seventy, who added Cotsworth to the list of Great Pyramid explorers he guided round Giza since the time of Caviglia and Howard-Vyse in the 1830s.

Archeologists give varying opinions as to the age of the Sphinx. Petrie considered it possibly prehistoric. Budge refutes its being prehistoric. Most Egyptologists assign it to Kephren's reign in the Fourth Dynasty.

The Sphinx faces due east, which indicated to Cotsworth that it was used as a sighting device by priests who could stand on the flat platform of its rump and sight the rising sun in a direct line to the horizon marked by the point of the asp on the crown on the Sphinx. Cotsworth also found a series of ancient lines fanning out from the neck of the Sphinx which could have served to indicate the point of sunrise at different dates from solstice to equinox.

It has repeatedly taken several hundred men several years to clear the sand from its base and reveal a six-tiered obelisk against its chest (now missing), which Cotsworth believes was used for sighting the midday sun. Each time the base was cleared, windstorms filled it again with sand, indicating that when the Sphinx was originally built the Sahara was almost certainly not a desert.

Lancelot Hogben in *Science for the Citizen* says that "the continuity of careful observations which preceded, and the precision involved in settling the exact length of the year, entitle this achievement to be regarded as one of the half-dozen great cultural feats in the history of mankind."

With the present availability of cheap watches, radio signals and published almanacs, one is likely to underestimate the value to ancient people of a reliable system for telling the day, the season, the year, and, most important in Egypt, where the entire system of agriculture depended on the swamping of the arable land, the forthcoming flooding of the Nile.

For three-quarters of the year the Egyptian peasants would leave their protected villages on the hillsides and move into the flatland with their families, livestock and most of their belongings, to plow, seed and harvest the fields.

When the time came to move their families and belongings back to the hills, they required at least a fortnight's warning lest they linger too long and be cut off and drowned by the yearly rising of the waters.

According to Cotsworth, all efforts at tracing the number of days in the year by purely seasonal signs would have given imperfect and variable results.

In the early dynasties the flooding of the Nile was said to have been heralded by the annual heliacal rising of Sirius, known to us as the Dog Star. Once a year, with the first glimmer of dawn, Sirius, a bright star of the first magnitude, would appear in the eastern sky and dominate the heavens till its sparkle was eclipsed by the splendor of the risen sun. This stunning phenomenon was taken by the Egyptians as a sign that the Nile would be flooding in about twenty days.

But the flooding of the Nile is governed not by the stars but by the sun melting the snows and the rain falling in the Ethiopian highland sources of the Blue Nile. To have continued to date the flooding by the rising of Sirius would have gradually brought the phenomenon out of phase.

O. Muck, in his *Cheops and the Great Pyramid,* postulates that as a result of a series of disastrous inundations during the reign of Cheops, the Egyptians were obliged to change from a stellar calendar of 365.2563 days to a solar calendar of 365.2422 days, and that the historic Cheops introduced a new calendar by which an extra day was added every four years of 1460 days to account for the differing fraction.*

* According to Muck the new calendar was designed for Cheops not by an Egyptian but by a light-skinned European who brought to Egypt an older, more accurate calendar such as that of Dardanie. Muck says there is archeological evidence that Cheops married a light-eyed, white-skinned European with reddish-blond hair who bore him a blond, blue-eyed daughter whom Cheops gave in marriage to a European known as Didoufri who reformed the calendar and redesigned his pyramid. Other Egyptologists suggest that Cheops' wife, who is represented as a blonde in the Giza tomb of her daughter Meresank III, may be merely wearing a wig. Such divergencies give a slight idea of the general lack of concurrence among historians of Egypt. But there is no doubt that the Egyptians developed two basic calendars, a civil calendar of 365 days, and a sothic calendar one-quarter day longer. The extra quarter day caused the sothic New Year to fall back one full day every four years so that each and every day of the civil calendar coincided with the New Year over a period of 365 × 4, or 1460 years, until the New Year once more fell on its original July 19. Hence was generated what was known as the sothic cycle of 1460 years.

The double dating of sothic and civil years appears in many Egyptian documents, so that it has been possible to reconstruct the years in which the sothic new year coincided with the original new year and establish that sothic cycles began in A.D. 140, 1320 B.C., 2780 B.C., and 4240 B.C.

Muck and others believe the foundation of the sothic calendar occurred in the 2780 cycle, but Schwaller de Lubicz is convinced from his study of ancient texts and hieroglyphs that the year was 4240. He says that tradition always placed the heliacal rising of Sirius in the constellation of the Lion, and that this was so from 4240 on. The main objection to such an early date is the conviction of Egyptologists that the ancient Egyptians were not yet equipped for such careful astronomical observation.

That the Egyptians handled astronomical cycles of even greater duration is indicated by inscriptions recently found by Soviet archeologists in newly opened graves during the period of their work on the Aswan Dam. Here the cycles appear to cover periods of 35,525 years, which would be the equivalent of 25 cycles of 1461 years. The apparent discrepancy of one year in this recording of cycles is due to the sothic cycle of 1460 years being the equivalent of a civil cycle of 1461 years. According to Muck there were three main cycles: one of 365 × 4 = 1460; another of 1460 × 25 = 36,500; and a third of 36,500 × 5 = 182,500 years.

143

Dürer's woodcut of the zodiac.
In the course of a year the earth makes a 360° circle round the sun. Seen from the earth, the sun appears to move through a circular belt of constellations. These are the stars of the zodiac.
For convenience, the zodiac is divided into twelve constellations, so that every month at sunrise a new one appears to the earth viewer in the eastern sky; and every year the sequence is repeated, with a slight precession owing to the earth's wobble on its axis.

144

Schwaller de Lubicz in his *Le Temple de l'Homme* maintains the pharaonic Egyptians adopted neither the sidereal nor the solar tropical year, but a Sothic year based on the cycle of the fixed star Sirius, which is exactly 365.25 days. According to this archeologist and philosopher, who spent twelve years at Luxor measuring and studying its temples, tombs and hieroglyphs, the mere fact that the Egyptians were able to note that Sirius is the *only* fixed star with an unvaried cycle of 365.25 days denotes an extremely long period of previous careful observation.

From the texts it is clear, says Schwaller de Lubicz, that long after the heliacal rising of Sirius was no longer a visible phenomenon, it continued to be accurately computed by the priests of Heliopolis, who then broadcast their observations to the other temples of Egypt, there being a difference of as much as 4 days between the heliacal rising as noted at Thebes and at Memphis.

Muck suggests that to dramatize the importance of the 1460 cycle the figure was built into the pavement around the Pyramid of Cheops in such a way that a cortege of priests dressed in white could liturgically march round the pyramid rythmically counting out 1460 paces—which were subdivided into 25 inches, and again subdivided by 5.

By coincidence, Muck's pace of 25 inches is the same length as Newton's and Piazzi Smyth's sacred cubit, one hundred of which form the side of an English acre.

One incontestable deduction was drawn by Schwaller de Lubicz from the existence of the sothic calendar and the shifting of the annual festivals of the civil calendar: the ancient Egyptians must have been cognizant of and able to measure the phenomenon known as the precession of the equinoxes.

To obtain a simple picture of the precession, an earth observer in the northern hemisphere should be looking due east just before sunrise at the spring equinox. As the dawn tints the sky the observer will see a constellation on the eastern horizon: nowadays it is Pisces. In 2000 B.C. it was Aries. In 4000 B.C. it was Taurus. In A.D. 2300 it will be Aquarius.

The entire circle of the zodiac appears to be slipping back in relation to the sunrise at the equinox, at the slow rate of about 1 degree in 72 years; 30°, or one constellation, in 2160 years; and 360° in 25,920 years.

This *precession* of the equinox is said to have been discovered by Hipparchus in the second century. But a number of ancient representations of the zodiac bear the note: "The Bull marks the beginning of spring." This has been interpreted to indicate that astronomical observations of the constellations at the equinox were being made at least as early as 4000 B.C.

The phenomenon of the precession was not explained till Newton postulated that the earth's tilted axis was wobbling as it spun, causing the celestial pole of the earth's axis to draw a slow circle in the heavens around the fixed pole of the solar system, the pole of the ecliptic. To an observer on earth watching the sunrise at the equinox, this slow circling has the effect of making the equinoxes occur about 20 minutes earlier each year in relation to the zodiacal constellations then visible in the sky.

To have figured out the slow rate of the precession of the equinoxes, the ancient Egyptians must have had an appropriate system and equipment. According to Cotsworth, to devise an accurate *star* calendar to record the apparent movement of the stars around the heavens, someone first had to devise a structure that would provide a perfectly oriented meridian for the observation of stars in relation to a fixed point on earth.

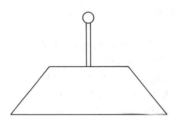

According to Muck, to have an accurate *sun* calendar, with which to establish the solstices and equinoxes, someone would have had to build an enormously high obelisk.

Sir Gaston Maspero, director of the Department of Antiquities of the Cairo Museum, found a curious hieroglyph in inscriptions around Saqqara for which he could find no explanation: an obelisk atop a truncated pyramid, with a solar disk balanced on top of it. For Cotsworth he kindly made a drawing of it.

To Cotsworth the similarity of Maes-Howe, the Silbury Hill Maypoles and the obelisks atop a mastaba or unfinished pyramid was inescapable. Only, how did this fit with the Pyramid of Cheops?

XII. ASTRONOMICAL OBSERVATORY

Richard Anthony Proctor.

That the Great Pyramid had originally been designed as an astronomical observatory and that it had contained reproductions of the celestial spheres was repeatedly reported by Arab historians; yet none could put forward a sensible solution as to how its steep polished sides could be climbed as an observatory, or its interior passages employed for observations; that is, until the appearance of a book shortly before the turn of the century by the British astronomer Richard A. Proctor, called *The Great Pyramid, Observatory, Tomb, and Temple.* Proctor found a reference in the works of the Roman neo-Platonic philosopher Proclus to the effect that the Pyramid had been used as an observatory *before* its completion. Analyzing the report, which appears in Proclus's commentary on Plato's *Timeaus,* Proctor theorized that the Pyramid might have made an excellent observatory at the time it had reached the summit of the Grand Gallery, which would have given onto a large square platform where the priests could observe and record the movements of the heavenly bodies.

Proctor's theory was so shockingly simple that it was quickly ignored by academic Egyptologists, who were as skeptical of its astronomical value as they were of the value of Stonehenge or the other megalithic observatories scattered about Europe.

In order to create a firm body of astronomical data, the ancients needed a true meridian on the solid earth from which to extrapolate a meridian across the heavenly vault, so as to detect the precise moment when stars, sun, planets and moon transited this meridian in their apparent rotation through the heavens.

In Proctor's analysis the builders of the Great Pyramid had accomplished such a feat by building what he, as a modern astronomer, considered the only sensible instrument short of a great modern telescope.

On the Giza plateau, in the heart of the Great Pyramid, they first built a huge graduated slot, perfectly aligned on the meridian. Through this slot they could observe the apparent movement of the panoply of stars, accurately noting their several transits.

Proctor describes in detail how the ancient architects would have gone about building such an observatory. To

147

Indian astronomical observatory erected at Delhi by the Maharajah of Jaipur consists of a 56-foot triangular structure which casts a shadow onto an arc of masonry calibrated in hours, minutes and seconds (top). Another Indian observatory at Benares, known as Yantra, provided fixed angles to check the position of the stars.

obtain a true north-south line for their terrestrial meridian, they would have observed across the tops of a couple of upright pillars whatever star was closest to the celestial north pole (the point around which the stars appear to wheel in their daily motion), then found the star's culmination, or the top and bottom of its circular path. A line through these two points, which could be measured with an ordinary plumb line, would be true north; and any such northern star would do, as all move in a small circle round the celestial pole.

Following the suggestion of Sir John Herschel, Proctor concluded that it might have been alpha Draconis, which was 3° 43′ from the pole in 2160 B.C. and again in 3440 B.C. The French astronomer A. Poge suggests that the ancients could have used Xi Mizar of the Great Bear any time before 1500; but alpha Draconis fits the rest of Proctor's theory quite adroitly.

The question of the method of orienting the pyramids has been the object of a detailed study by the Egyptologist Zbynek Zaba in a recent monograph for the Czechoslovakian Academy of Sciences entitled *L'orientation astronomique dans l'ancienne Egypte et la précision de l'axe du monde.* Far from considering the pyramids monuments to the

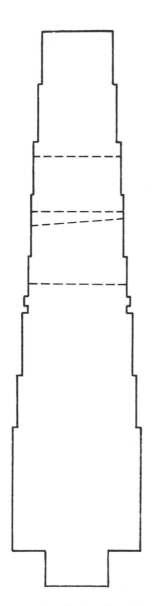

Meridian slot for observing the transit of the stars.

The stars appear to be carried around the pole of the heavens as if they were fixed points in the interior of a hollow revolving sphere. It is therefore possible to determine the position of the pole, even though no bright star actually occupies that point. Any bright star close to the pole revolves in a small circle whose center is the pole.

149

megalomaniac pride of some theocratic despot, Zaba considers them monuments incorporating the culture, science and technology of the times in which they were built.

The documents adduced by Zaba prove beyond question that the initial operation in erecting an important structure in Egypt was the ceremony of the "stretching of the cord," by which, through the observation of the culmination of some circumpolar star, the north-south direction was determined and marked out on the ground.

An inscription, translated by Johannes Dümichen, describes this royal ceremony: "Looking up at the sky at the course of the rising stars, recognizing the *āk* of the Bull's Thigh Constellation (our Great Bear), I establish the corners of the temple. . . ." "Dümichen says the word *āk* represents the star's culmination as it passes the meridian.*

Having transferred a true meridian from the sky to the ground, the ancient architects, says Proctor, could have begun to consolidate this line by digging it into a descending passage through the live rock, using their polar or circumpolar star to guide the tunnel downward at precisely the angle of its rays.

Such a cream-white tube, says Proctor, would have given perfect stability to this fundamental directional line, and the longer the passage the truer its orientation.†

For alpha Draconis, at 3° 43′ from the pole, to have shone directly down a passage at the thirtieth parallel, the passage would have had to be inclined at an angle of 26° 17′—just the angle of the Descending Passage beneath the base of the Great Pyramid.

Proctor points out that there would have been no question about the advantage of taking the lower culmination of such a star in preference to its upper one; using the bottom of its circular path as a fixed point would have required far less depth of boring to reach a point directly beneath the center

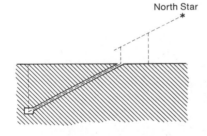

North Star

Proctor's design of how the North Star was sighted along the Descending Passage.

---

* The meridian, or great circle through the earth's celestial poles, is the plane in which all the heavenly bodies culminate, or obtain the highest point in their passage midway from the eastern to the western horizon as seen from the earth. Circumpolar stars have a high and a low culminating point on the meridian above and below the celestial pole.

† The advantage of digging such a tunnel is obvious when compared with what would have been needed to achieve the same result aboveground. Someone would have had to hold a plumb line 100 yards high standing at a distance of 200 yards from the observer, who in turn would have had to line up the top of the plumb line with the polar star by night at a slant distance of 260 yards—without benefit of a telescope.

150

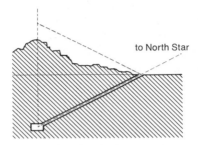

How the central point of the Pyramid base could be located by knowing the angle of the Descending Passage.

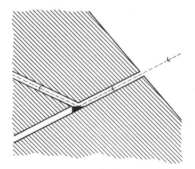

Reflecting pool at the juncture of the Descending and Ascending Passages.

of the proposed building, which was the next object of the operation.

The theory provides an explanation for the quite extraordinary straightness of the walls of the Descending Passage, as measured by Petrie, who was astounded to find a mean variation from a central axis along the entire length of 350 feet of less than 1/4 inch in azimuth—from side to side—and only .1 inch in altitude—up and down. In the part nearest the aperture, which was to be the most important, the exactness is even greater, the mean error amounting to less than 1/50 inch!

Once the ancients had measured the length of the Descending Passage and its angle of descent, it would have been simple, by elementary trigonometry, to locate a central spot immediately above the end of the Descending Passage as a center for the proposed pyramid—even if this were on roughly elevated ground.

With a central spot and a true meridian, the architects could set about laying the socket holes for a square base and begin to lay courses on a leveled platform. To obtain true levels, Proctor surmises that the ancient builders used water troughs in conjunction with the light rays from the star.

By continuing the tunneling up through the lower tiers of the growing pyramid, they could maintain a precise orientation for at least the first ten courses, or until the tunnel debouched from the narrowing side of the growing pyramid.

Thereafter their polar star would no longer serve directly, and a new system would be needed to continue the meridian alignment upward in the Pyramid. For this, says Proctor, the builders hit upon the idea of creating an Ascending Passage at precisely the reflecting angle of another 26° 17′. By plugging the Descending Passage and filling it with water, they could reflect the polar star back up an Ascending Passage and continue to keep the passage truly aligned and the building level as it rose another score or more of courses.

For the Descending Passage to have held water, says Proctor, its masonry at the point of juncture would have had to be of hard rock, carefully joined. For no other apparent reason, the stones at this particular point are quite different from the rest of the passage, much harder and smoother and more finely jointed. In fact, the feature escaped observation till 1865.

As Proctor expressed it in his Victorian style: "By using the known properties of liquids combined with the known property of light rays, the ancient builders were able to orient and level a building to a very great height."

But to what purpose? Of a sudden the constricted Ascending Passage changes to an overlapping gallery 28 feet high, in no way essential, or even desirable, to increase or maintain accuracy in orientation for the mounting courses. Yet so extraordinary an architectural design, so carefully executed, must, says Proctor, have served some definite purpose.

Analyzing the problem from the point of view of the astronomer rather than the architect, Proctor came up with an answer. Had an ancient astronomer wished for a large observation slot precisely bisected by a meridian through the north pole, so as to observe the transit of the heavenly bodies, what would he have requested of an architect? A very high slit with vertical walls, says Proctor, preferably narrower at the top, a gallery whose aperture, thanks to the reflected light of the polar star, could be designed so as to be exactly bisected by a true meridian.

Looking up through such a slot, an observer could watch the passage of the entire panoply of the zodiac, easily noting the transit of each star across a perfect meridian—precisely what is done today by the modern astronomer when he sets his transit circle to the vertical meridians. As Proctor points out, such a Grand Gallery might well be described as the *only* very accurate method available for preparing an accurate map of the sky and of the zodiacal cyclorama— before the invention of the telescope in the seventeenth century of our era.

With various observers in the Grand Gallery, placed one above the other on the slanted incline, the southing—or transit across the meridian—of every key star in an arc of about 80° could be observed with remarkable accuracy. As Proctor points out, the most important object of transit observation is to determine the exact moment at which the observed object crosses the meridian. This might have been best accomplished by noting the moment when the star was first seen on the eastern edge of the vertical sky space, and then when it disappeared past the western edge; the instant midway between these two would be the true time of transit.

Proctor surmises that someone in either the Queen's Chamber or on the flat platform of the truncated pyramid above the Grand Gallery could keep time by hourglass or water clock in coordination with the observers in the Gallery, who would signal the beginning or end of transit across the Gallery's field of view.*

Interior of the Grand Gallery (about one-quarter of its length) showing how it could have been used to observe the stars circling in the southern sky.

* A container with a small hole which drips one drop at regular intervals makes a satisfactory timer. Ancient Chinese astronomers had a system of three such containers in a series to minimize the effect of resistance.

152

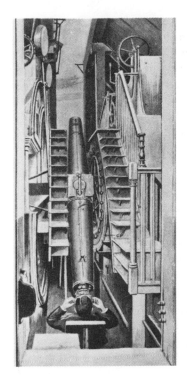

The Transit Circle, Royal Observatory, Greenwich.

By looking down the Descending Passage into a reflecting pool, an ancient astronomer could have noted the exact second of a star's transit, because only at that moment will its rays be reflected. The very same system is used today at the U.S. Naval Observatory in Washington, D.C., where the daily transit of stars is noted to a split second by their reflection in a pool of mercury.

The slope of the Gallery and the corbeling of its walls would also have made it remarkably easy to note the declination of a star—its distance above or below the celestial equator. By combining the observations made by several of what Proctor calls "watchmen of the night," stationed at different levels of the Grand Gallery, a very close approximation of true sidereal time could have been obtained. For such observers to function effectively, cross ramps or reclining benches of some sort would have had to be positioned at different levels of the Gallery.

In support of this theory, there is the series of 27 oblong holes cut vertically along the walls and into the ramps to a depth of 8 or 11 inches. They served to hold some sort of scaffolding across the Gallery. Proctor postulates that there were benches for observers at regular intervals up the Gallery.

The fact that the walls of the Gallery are corbeled like those of the earlier mastabas and of the megalithic observatories, whose top stones could be readily removed, and that each of the roofing stones of the Grand Gallery

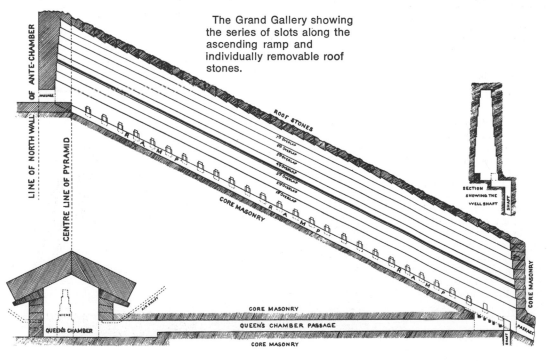

The Grand Gallery showing the series of slots along the ascending ramp and individually removable roof stones.

153

was independently removable (none presses down on its neighbor) may indicate that by the removal of these stones almost as much again of the northern arc of sky could be observed as was visible of the southern sky through the upper end of the Gallery. The movement of particular stars could be pinpointed by the removal of single stones.

Proctor surmises that the method used to determine the declination of a star involved a very practical use of the odd grooves that appear along the walls of the Gallery. At approximately half the height of the Gallery, just above the third overlap on each wall, a narrow groove runs the whole length of the gallery, 6 inches wide and 3/4 inch deep.

Proctor suggests that horizontal bars carrying vertical rods at suitable distances, perhaps with horizontal lines on them, were held between these grooves, and could be slid to any convenient position. The vertical rods could also have been adjustable.

To locate a star correctly, the transit observers would also have to determine what is called its "right ascension," or distance measured parallel to the equator from a certain assigned starting point on that circle. Knowing the time of transit, it is simple to position the celestial object in its "right ascension."

By placing observers not only in the Gallery but outside at the cardinal points of the great truncated pyramid, Proctor says that the entire visible sky could be accurately plotted. The ancient astronomers, says Proctor, would doubtless have made even more observations *off* the meridian, once they had established the meridian observations as their guide marks. They would certainly have made multitudinous observations of the risings and settings of stars at the

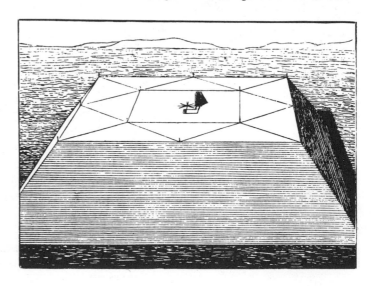

Ancient polar astrolabe.

The truncated pyramid, as depicted by Proctor, would have made an observation platform 142 feet high and 175 feet square.

The cardinal points, or compass rose, could have been marked by upright posts on the periphery of the platform. To locate the rising and setting of stars east and west, azimuth observers could occupy the center of the square from which they could command the entire compass.

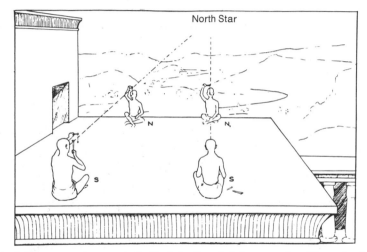

North Star

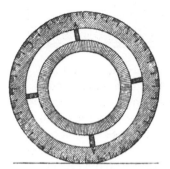

Ancient method of observing stars with rings and rods.

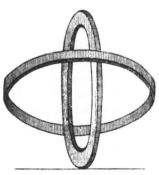

Late Egyptian armillary disk for measuring solstices.

Equinoctial armillary disk.

horizon, and especially their heliacal risings and settings just before dawn and just after sunset.

Proctor suggests that there were at least thirteen observers for azimuthal directions around the horizon, whose work could be combined with that of at least seven transit observers at different levels of the Grand Gallery.

The azimuthal observers would be supplied with astrolabes, armillary spheres of reference, direction tubes, or ring-carrying rods. Together with the transit watchers they would be able to make observations which, in Proctor's opinion, would be inferior only to those made in our own time with telescopic adjuncts.

George Sarton, professor of the history of science at Harvard, says the astronomical ability of the early Egyptians "is proved not only by their calendars, tables of star culminations, and tables of star risings, but also by some of their instruments such as ingenious sundials or the combination of a plumb line with a forked rod that enabled them to determine the azimuth of a star."

Proctor adds that for a greater knowledge of the sun's motion, the Grand Gallery slot could have been used to better effect than an obelisk or a sundial by noting the sun's shadow cast by the edges of the upper opening against the walls, sides and floor of the long Gallery. To make observations of the sun more exact, Proctor envisaged the use of screens: by placing an opaque screen at the upper end of the Gallery with a small aperture to receive the sun's light upon a smooth, white surface at right angles to the sun's direction, a much magnified image of the sun would be formed on which any sunspot could hardly have failed to appear. The movement of the spots would have indicated the sun's rotation on its axis.

The moon's monthly path and all its changes could have

155

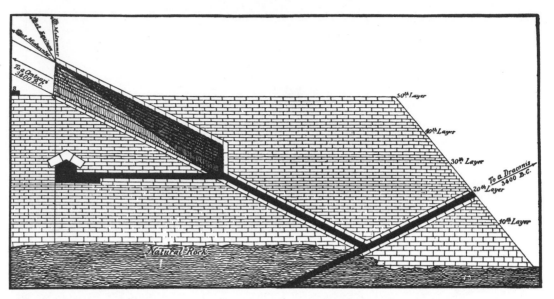

Proctor's direction lines show the midday sun at midsummer, midwinter, and the equinoxes as they would strike the Grand Gallery of the Great Pyramid, forming light and shadow marks even more effective than those of obelisks.

He also shows the alignment of alpha Draconis with the Descending Passage, as it was in 3400 B.C. and a line to alpha Centauri, which was then on the meridian, from the Grand Gallery. Proctor believes that through such a sighting tube as the Grand Gallery, alpha Centauri could have been seen transiting in broad daylight.

It is noteworthy that the Grand Gallery debouches at precisely the fiftieth course of masonry, and that at that level the square platform is exactly half the area of the base of the Pyramid.

been dealt with in the same effective way, as indeed the geocentric paths of the planets or their true orbits around the sun: these could have been determined very accurately by combining the use of tubes or ring-carrying rods with the direction lines determined from the Gallery's sides, floor, etc.

Once the diurnal pattern of the stars' apparent rotation past a fixed meridian had become clear to the observers, they could more easily plot the irregular and sometimes apparently retrogressive path of the planets and the moon in relation to the "fixed" stars. The heliocentric pattern of our solar system could well have been extrapolated from a study of the relative motions of these planetary satellites, anticipating Copernicus by several thousand years.

To Proctor, the Great Pyramid thus constructed would have been the greatest observatory and the most perfect till the art of the telescope could reveal a way to more exact observation without the need for such a massive structure.

That the flat top of the truncated pyramid served as the plan for mapping the zodiac is supported by the zodiacal maps of the early astrologers. Even Kepler and Galileo, when making a chart for someone's horoscope, used square charts for their zodiacs, which are the shape of the truncated pyramid.

The French mathematician Funk-Hellet even suggests that the 24 holes in the sides of the Grand Gallery once supported, two by two, movable panels with symbolic figurations of the zodiac.

At the end of a few years' observation it would have been obvious to the ancient astronomers at the moment of the

156

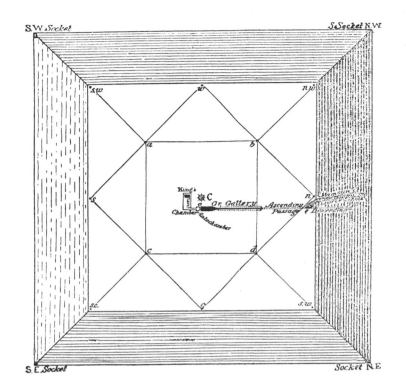

By placing the gallery slightly to the east of the north-south axis of the Pyramid, the ancient astronomers could make their observations from the center of the truncated square, and a gnomon, or shadow pole, could be raised in dead center. That such a square was the prototype for astrological as well as astronomical computations is strikingly illustrated by the format for horoscopes which persisted into the seventeenth century.

The twelve celestial houses of the zodiac according to astrological authors.

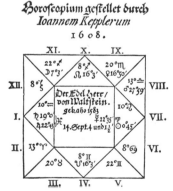

Horoscope prepared by Kepler.

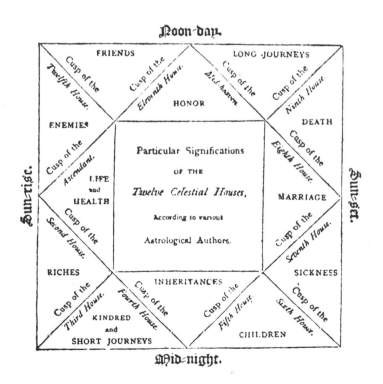

157

equinox that the whole stellar caravan was returning to its original position just a fraction later—hence each year the equinox itself appeared to move forward. By fine observation of the circumpolar stars, the ancient astronomers could have measured the angle of this precession and deduced its rate to be about 1° in 72 years, making a grand cycle of 25,920 years to cover a full circle of 360°.

Proctor's astronomical analysis of the Grand Gallery was discounted by Egyptologists on the grounds that they had no evidence the ancient Egyptians were capable of making accurate astronomical observations. But in 1934 Proctor received strong support from another professional astronomer, Eugene Michel Antoniadi, who was also an Egyptologist, attached to the Egyptian Observatory of Medûm, in a serious work dealing with the various branches of ancient Egyptian astronomy.* Antoniadi agreed that the Great Pyramid had been used as an observatory before the closing of its inner corridors. He also agreed with Proctor's theory of the alignment and use of the Grand Gallery.

Astronomer E. M. Antoniadi added a refinement to Proctor's theory, showing that the ancients might have used a temporary trestle to help start the alignment of the Descending Passage. However, such a trestle would have had to be 300 feet high and 600 feet long, with a slant height of 780 feet, merely to serve a function that could be better performed by digging the Descending Passage directly. It is more likely the builders avoided the scaffold.

Antoniadi figured that the Grand Gallery would have permitted priests to observe 80° of the sky. He says they should have been able to note the declination of all visible stars from −50° below the celestial equator to +30° above it, and that with the use of clepsydras (water clocks) they should have been able to measure hour angles and deduct the right ascension of stars and planets.

These two data are all that is required for constructing a star map or planisphere. "From a star map," says Lancelot Hogben, "it was a very short step to the recognition that the Earth itself could be divided into similar zones with simple relations to the fixed stars—hence the first world maps with latitude and longitude."

* L'Astronomie égyptienne depuis les temps les plus reculés, jusqu'à la fin de l'époque alexandrine (Paris, Gauthier-Villars, 1934).

158

XIII. ASTRONOMICAL TEMPLES OF EGYPT

In his avant-garde book *The Dawn of Astronomy,* written at the turn of the century, Sir Norman Lockyer minutely demonstrated how the Egyptians built and used their temples for astronomical observations from the very remotest antiquity. Lockyer showed how Egyptian solar temples were so arranged that at sunrise or sunset on the longest day of the year, a ray from the sun shot through a skillfully contrived passage into the dark interior of the inner sanctum of the temple. The illumination from the sun was cut off by means of pylon screens so that a concentrated shaft of light cut through the gloom.

Lockyer was the first English astronomer to conclude that Stonehenge had been accurately aligned in about 1680 B.C. to catch the first gleam of the midsummer sun at its solstice, a fact which was recently corroborated on the basis of computerized data by the astronomer Gerald S. Hawkins in *Stonehenge Decoded.*

Both of Lockyer's conclusions were ignored.

The difference between the megalithic and the Egyptian systems lies in the fact that anyone who can set up a circle of well-placed stones with a sighting avenue can note the farthest points north and south on the horizon where the sun rises at the summer and winter solstices; by taking the halfway mark along the semicircle of stones, the day of the equinox, when the sun is due east at the equator, can be geometrically fixed. To obtain a more precise length of the year—to within a matter of hours and minutes—requires a more sophisticated system.

Lockyer—whom Hawkins describes as "an extraordinary man whose true worth as an astronomer and theorizer concerning the history of astronomy has not yet been adequately appraised"—shows how the esthetically incomparable Egyptian temples scattered along the Nile were astronomical instruments designed like a modern telescope aimed at a specific point on the horizon.

Within the Egyptian temples the light of the sun, or other heavenly body, was funneled between two rows of delicately carved columns which ran through a chain of variously dimensioned halls, like the light of a heavenly body being funneled through the gradually narrowing diaphragms of a telescope.

Temple at Luxor (above) drawn by a member of Napoleon's expedition, showing a row of columns oriented as an astronomical observatory. Temples usually contained a pylon, forecourt, hypostyle hall, and sanctuary.

Astronomical temple at Edfu, later known as Appolonopolis Magna, half buried in the sand as it was found and drawn by Dominique Vivant, one of Napoleon's savants.

Sir Norman Lockyer.

(*Overleaf*)
  Colonnade to the temple of Amon-Ra at Karnak as it was discovered by members of Napoleon's expedition. Lockyer found that the temple's axis was accurately oriented to the summer solstice and considered it "beyond all question the most majestic ruin in the world."
  Reconstruction of the temple of Amon-Ra at Karnak showing how the colonnade was aimed like a telescope toward the sunset of the summer solstice. This romanticized etching was produced by the French savants for the *Description de l'Egypte.*

The longer the temple's axis, the longer and narrower the beam, and the greater the accuracy in measuring it. The darker the sanctuary, the more obvious the path of light on the end wall.

The purpose, says Lockyer, was to narrow the beam of light to the point where it could indicate the precise moment of the solstice.

According to Lockyer, a beam of light coming through a narrow passage some 500 yards all the way to a properly oriented sanctuary would remain there no more than a couple of minutes, then pass away. What's more, it would come in a crescendo and go in a diminuendo with an observable peak at the precise solstice.

This would enable the priests to determine the length of the year to within a minute, or four points of decimal—or 365.2422: an otherwise very difficult feat because the sun appears to linger several days around the point of solstice, and its movement of a mere 50″ a day is almost imperceptible without some refined instrumental aid.

Lockyer, who went to Egypt regularly in the summer holidays, found that the sun temple of Amen-Ra at Karnak was built in such a way that at sunset at the summer solstice —the longest day in the year—the sunlight entered the temple and penetrated along the axis to the sanctuary. In Lockyer's words it was "a scientific instrument of very high precision, as by it the length of the year could be determined with the greatest possible accuracy."

Extrapolating backward from the present orientation of the building, and taking into account the small but gradual shift in the tilt of the axis of the earth, Lockyer applied the

Rendering of the temple at Luxor by Schwaller de Lubicz, showing three successive changes in orientation.

Chiseled orientation line on subflooring of the temple at Luxor noted by Schwaller de Lubicz. The line was then hidden from view by superimposed finished flooring.

system he had used for Stonehenge and estimated the temple to have been originally laid out about 3700 B.C.

Lockyer found sun temples oriented to catch the sun at the solstice or equinox, and star temples oriented to frame a star rising on the horizon just before sunrise at the solstice or equinox, so as to give warning of the imminent solar event.

Herodotus describes two pillars of gold and green stone in the temple of Tyre which shone at midnight. According to Lockyer, "there can be little doubt that in the darkened sanctuary of an Egyptian temple the light of Alpha Lyrae, one of the brightest stars in the northern heavens, rising in the clear air of Egypt, would be quite strong enough to throw into an apparent glow such highly reflecting surfaces as those to which Herodotus refers."

Maspero suggests that the priests were not above "pious frauds" accomplished by means of statues which were animated, spoke, moved and acted. For those not in on the secret, the priests may have achieved quite stunning effects by having a large jewel in the breastplate of a statue suddenly and mysteriously sparkle with light.

Lockyer realized that temples oriented to the sun could provide a useful calendar for thousands of years because the tilt of the earth's axis shifts no more than a degree in six or seven thousand years. But temples oriented to stars could function only for a limited 200 or 300 years because each year the rising or setting of stars just before sunrise or after sunset at the solstice or equinox would occur a little later because of the precession of the equinoxes. The stars' lag behind the sun along the circle of the zodiac—a barely noticeable $1/72°$ each year—could become as much as $3°$ in 200 years, superannuating the usefulness of the temple. The temple would then need to have its axis reoriented, or another temple would have to be built. "This change of direction," says Lockyer, "is one of the most striking things which have been observed for years past in Egyptian temples."

Luxor, for instance, has four definite, well-marked changes in orientation. Lockyer measured temples at Karnak and found they were changed to match the precessional change of the stars' declination so that the priests could continue to observe it. Pylons were added, more courts were added, the sanctuary was moved eastward, the front of the temple westward.

As Maspero pointed out, "all the Ptolemaic temples and most of the Pharaonic temples have been reconstructed" during the period of their use.

Gunther Martiny, who tabulated the orientation of Assyrian temples for which the dates of foundation can be established

Small stones inserted in the regular masonry indicated a hidden line of orientation for the temple at Luxor.

(the oldest being about 1800 B.C.), found that the orientations also varied according to the angle of the precession of the equinoxes.

Nevertheless, says Lockyer, a temple once oriented to pick up the heliacal rising of a star could be *refitted* at a later time to mark the rising of some other heavenly body.

Lockyer drew up a stellar map with the positions of all the great stars along the sun's zodiacal path for the last 10,000 years, and he named a series of stars which could have been used to herald the solsticial dawn in different temples at different periods. In the course of centuries, according to

166

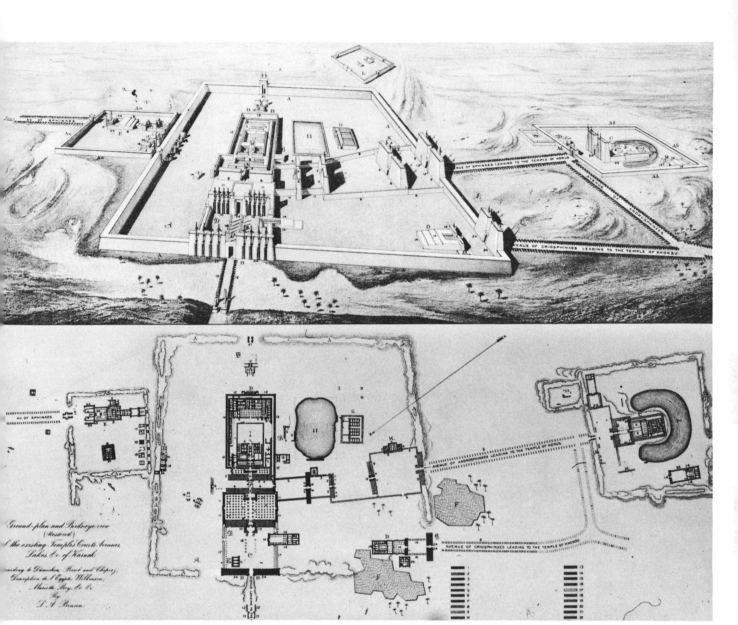

Reconstruction of the temple compound at Karnak showing the variation in axis of different buildings and colonnades.

Lockyer, the Egyptians oriented temples to alpha Ursa Major, Capella, Antares, Phact, and alpha Centauri. As early as 6000 B.C. they may have used Dubhe before it became a circumpolar star, and Canopus before 6400 B.C.

Professor Lockyer says that the earliest civilization in Egypt built temples at Annu or Heliopolis oriented to the heliacal rising of northern but noncircumpolar stars at the summer solstice. However, "the Great Pyramids were built by a new invading race representing an advance in astronomical thought" who used northern stars on the meridian and stars rising due east at the equinoxes.

167

The subsequent break in Egyptian history between the Sixth and the Eleventh Dynasties is associated by Lockyer with conflicts between these and two other races, which ended in a victory of the representatives of the old worship of Annu reinforced by supporters from the south, so that the north-star and south-star cults combined against the equinoctial cult.

Lockyer's deductions about the refurbishing of temples was to rekindle interest in the zodiac of Dendera found by Napoleon's General Desaix, and subsequently dynamited from the ceiling of the temple. It was purloined after a series of incredible adventures, to be sold to Louis XVIII for 150,000 francs and end up on display in the Louvre, where it resides today.

It was clear to Lockyer that there had been two temples of Dendera, one dedicated to Hathor and the other to Isis, both mythological personifications of heavenly bodies. Lockyer says the evidence is overwhelming that these two temples were also horizontal telescopes with the same number of pylons gradually getting narrower toward the holy of holies, so that a beam of horizontal light coming through the central door might pass uninterruptedly into the sanctuary to mark the rising of a celestial body. The columns, says Lockyer, shielded the eye from the sunrise light, so that the rising could be precisely indicated. According to Lockyer the present temples of Dendera were renovated in Ptolemaic times, but were built on much older sites.

The French astronomer Jean Baptiste Biot staked his academic reputation on his analysis of the circular zodiac. He said it represented the skies in Egypt in 700 B.C., and that it had probably been copied from older drawings made on papyrus or stone.

Lockyer confirmed that the Isis temple had been directed at Sirius in 700 B.C., when Sirius rose "cosmically," or in unison with the sun, at the Egyptian new year. But Lockyer quoted an old inscription which described a temple of Hathor at Dendera in the time of Khufu (Cheops) in the Fourth Dynasty (which he dated at 3733 B.C.) "when the star shone into the temple and mingled with the light of her father Ra."

Another inscription in a crypt of the temple indicated it had been built according to the plans of Imhotep, son of Ptah, who was the fabulous architect of the Third Dynasty King Zoser.

In Lockyer's opinion the temple of Dendera may have been rebuilt at least three times since then, once in the reign of King Pepi I (which Lockyer gives as 3233 B.C.), once again by Thothmes III in 1600 B.C., and finally by the Ptolemies about 100 B.C.

168

According to Lockyer the temple may previously have been directed at Dubhe, which ceased to be circumpolar about 4000 B.C., and before that at gamma Draconis, which ceased to be circumpolar in about 5000 B.C.

Egyptologists greeted Lockyer's astronomical theory about Egyptian temples with the same reserve they treated his theories about Stonehenge—which a computerized age has now shown to be correct. The Egyptologists objected to Lockyer's dragging in astronomy to straighten out the chronology of history, and dismissed his theory "with good-natured laughter, advising the cobbler to stick to his last"; so *The Dawn of Astronomy* dropped out of sight and became very hard to find, until reprinted in 1964 by Giorgio de Santillana at the Massachusetts Institute of Technology.

At the time of publication only Sir Gaston Maspero was impressed. He spent an Easter holiday at the sea studying Lockyer's theory, and he grudgingly agreed that "except for matters of detail I feel that on the whole your demonstration is conclusive, and in principle you must be correct."

Schwaller de Lubicz now supports Lockyer's conclusion, saying there can be no doubt about the orientation of temples or the fact that the ancient Egyptians understood the precession of the equinoxes, which brought a new constellation into position behind the rising sun at the vernal equinox every 2200 years. The mere fact that the cult of the Bull preceded the cult of the Ram in Egypt, and that the dates of these cults correspond with the equinoctial positions

Temple of Hathor at Dendera, as drawn by Denon, showing main axis possibly oriented to gamma Draconis before 5000 B.C., according to Sir Norman Lockyer.

Interior of the temple of
Hathor at Dendera as con-
ceived by the French savants.

The circular zodiac of
Dendera was on the ceiling
of an upper room of the
temple believed to have been
used as an observatory.

The outer circle of figures,
moving counterclockwise like
the stars, represent the
36 *decans,* or 10-day weeks
of the Egyptian year; the
twelve arms of the supporting
figures, the twelve months
of the year.

of their constellations at the appropriate time—approximately 4000 and 2000 B.C.—is conclusive in his opinion. Furthermore, says Schwaller, an emphasis on duality in the Predynastic Period indicates a cult of Gemini coincident with the dominance of that constellation at the vernal equinox.

Schwaller also agrees with Lockyer that the temple of Hathor at Dendera is built on the remains of much older temples. To prove his point he produced a solution to the arrangement of the constellations in the circular zodiac which has been such a problem to archeologists for well over a hundred years. Schwaller shows that the zodiac discovered by General Desaix was indeed carved in Ptolemaic times, but incorporates a palpable demonstration

Zodiac showing the overlap of the circuit of the earth's celestial pole around the pole of the ecliptic, indicating different dates in the past.

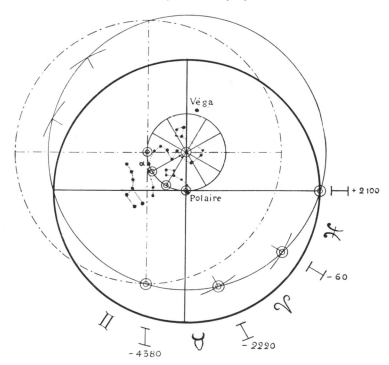

of the precession of the equinoxes as well as three important historical dates.

The zodiac is about 8 feet across, carved in relief on hard stone. The constellations are arranged in a spiral and the symbolic figures are marching counterclockwise in the diurnal direction of the stars as seen from the earth. Recognizable mythological figures for the constellations near the pole are a jackal for the Little Bear, an ox-leg for the Great Bear, and a hippopotamus for Drago. Sirius is depicted as a cow in a boat with a star between her horns.

The zodiac is in a circle at the center of which is our

172

The inner circle of spiraling figures shows the zodiacal constellations such as Gemini (the Twins hand in hand) and Taurus (the Bull) circling around our celestial north pole correctly situated in the Jackal (or Little Bear) which in turn circles around the celestial north pole of the ecliptic, situated in the breast of the Hippopotamus or Drago. Schwaller's lines show that the zodiac of Dendera correctly indicated earlier historical dates when different constellations appeared in the east at the equinox.

north pole. This circle is in a square oriented with the walls of the temple—or about 17° east of north. Our north pole is correctly located in the constellation of the jackal, or Little Bear, as it was at the time when the zodiac was carved, sometime about the first century B.C. But the zodiac also shows the pole of the ecliptic, located in the breast of the hippopotamus, or constellation of Drago.

To Schwaller this explains the spiral formation of the constellations. The mythological figures representing the constellations are entwined in two circles—one around the north pole and one around the pole of the ecliptic. Where these two circles intersect marks the point of the equinox, or due east. The zodiac thus becomes a calendar going back to remote antiquity.

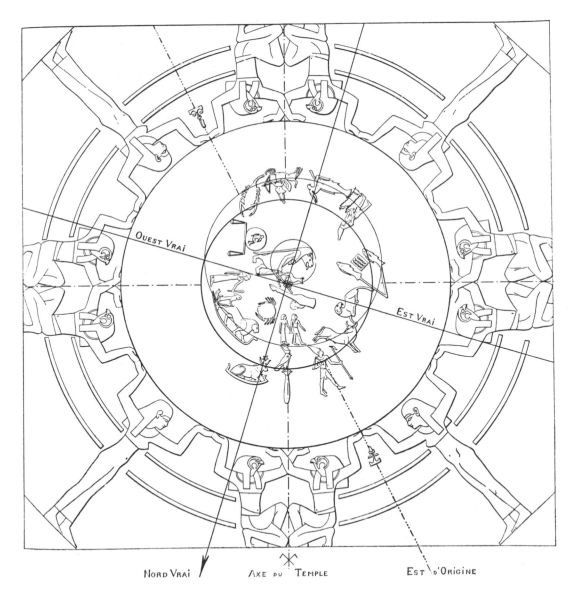

NORD VRAI   AXE DU TEMPLE   EST D'ORIGINE

A line due east, which runs between the end of the Ram and the beginning of Pisces, indicates the time when the temple was rebuilt, about 100 B.C. An earlier east line runs right through the Ram, indicating a date about 1600 B.C., at the height of the Amonian domination, during the Twelfth Dynasty.

A special hieroglyph on the ring of the zodiac indicates an equinoctial line running through the end of Gemini and the beginning of Taurus—the date of the founding of the empire of Menes and the beginning of the cult of the Bull and the adoption of the new calendar, sometime in the third or fourth millennium B.C.

In other Egyptian charts of the constellations there appears the figure of a hawk-headed man holding in his outstretched arms a line which ends against the figure of the ox-leg, representing the constellation of the Great Bear.

According to Zaba this line held by the hawk-headed man indicates the meridian through our north pole. But Professor Livio Stecchini points out that Zaba did not notice that this line always ends at a very specific position, at times with an arrow point, which divides the seven stars of the Great Bear into four and three. This line, says Stecchini, does not indicate the meridian passing through the north pole, but the meridian passing through the pole of the ecliptic. In Stecchini's opinion, the ancient Egyptians not only understood the precession of the axis of the earth but considered the true meridian the one passing through the pole of the ecliptic of the solar system. Lockyer added that the Babylonians had distinguished the pole of the equator from the pole of the ecliptic, naming the former Bil and the latter Anu.

The evidence leaves little doubt that the ancient Egyptians knew there were two poles in the sky, a north pole, which shifted round a fixed pole, or "open hole" in the heavens; they also knew that this slow circling brought about the precession of the equinoxes. That the phenomenon of the precession was the matrix from which a thousand myths were developed is abundantly illustrated by the work of Giorgio de Santillana and Hertha von Dechend in *Hamlet's Mill.**

There is no doubt in Santillana's mind that the ancient Egyptians were aware of the precession. In his preface to a recent reprint of *The Dawn of Astronomy,* Santillana, then professor of the history and philosophy of science at MIT, remarked that "when a stellar temple is oriented so accurately that it requires several reconstructions at intervals

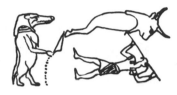
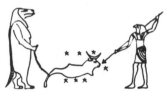

Hawk-headed man holding a spear (pointing at the Great Bear constellation) indicates the meridian through the pole of the ecliptic, according to Stecchini.

* Published by Gambit Inc., Boston, 1969.

of a few centuries, which involve each time the rebuilding of its narrow alignment on a star," and "when zodiacs, like that of Dendera, are deliberately depicted in the appearance they would have had centuries before, as if to date the changes," it is not reasonable to suppose the Egyptians were unaware of the precession of the equinoxes.

Santillana was even more forceful in his condemnation of modern archeological scholars who refuse to accept the idea that the phenomenon of the precession was known in Egypt thousands of years before it was *re*discovered by Hipparchus. In *Hamlet's Mill,* Santillana accuses the scholars of having "cultivated a pristine ignorance of astronomical thought, some of them actually ignorant of the precession itself."

The precession was considered the basic mechanism of the universe by the Egyptians, controlling not only astronomical phenomena but all human and biological development.

Since the beginning of history, the spring equinox has moved through Taurus, Aries and Pisces, or almost one-quarter of a whole cycle. Santillana points out that the Copernican system, which for us explains the precession as the wobble of the earth's axis, has stripped the phenomenon of its awesomeness:

"But *if,* as it appeared once, it was the mysteriously ordained behavior of the heavenly sphere, or the cosmos as a whole, then who could escape astrological emotion? For the precession took on an overpowering significance. It became the vast impenetrable pattern of fate itself, with one world-age succeeding another, as the invisible pointer of the equinox slid along the signs, each age bringing with it the rise and downfall of astral configurations and rulerships, with their earthly consequences."

XIV. GEODETIC AND GEOGRAPHIC LANDMARK

The strongest evidence that the ancient Egyptians were capable of accurate astronomical observations comes from the fields of geodesy and geography, sciences whose object is to determine the size and shape of the earth, and to locate landmarks upon it. Until the development of radio and laser beams, coordinates of latitude and longitude with which to locate a spot on this planet could only be obtained by means of accurate astronomical sightings. When a temple or observatory or the remains of a city are found in a geographical location, either of latitude or longitude, or both, specifically related to other established locations, it is clear that its founders must have been able to make the required astronomical observations.

Professor Stecchini—who obtained his doctorate at Harvard in the science of classical mensuration—has now established that the ancient Egyptians not only developed an advanced system of astronomy and mathematics, but an equally advanced system of geography and geodesy.

From ancient hieroglyphs, hitherto neglected, Stecchini has been able to show that from the earliest dynasties in the third millennium B.C., the Egyptians could measure latitude to within a few hundred feet and do almost as well with longitude—a feat which was not repeated on this planet until the eighteenth century of our era.

The ancient texts and hieroglyphs vindicate Jomard in full, and show that at least as early as the unification of Egypt (ca. 2800 B.C.) the ancient Egyptians knew the length of the circumference of the earth very precisely, the length of their country almost to the cubit, and the geographical coordinates of all the main points in their realm from the equator to the Mediterranean. To do so the Egyptians must have been able to make astronomical observations with almost the exactness afforded by the modern telescope and chronometer.

From a twenty-year study of the mathematical and astronomical data contained in the cuneiform tablets of the ancient Sumerians and Babylonians, Stecchini has derived the evidence that astronomical observations of great

176

accuracy could be, and were, performed in Mesopotamia as well as Egypt in the third millennium B.C.

From his analysis of the pyramids and stepped ziggurats of the Middle East, Stecchini has demonstrated that they not only incorporate the basic techniques for projecting and mapping the hemisphere of the heavens but for mapping the terrestrial hemisphere; they also reveal a high level of mathematics, capable of resolving and simplifying the problems of trigonometry.

Stecchini points out that Herodotus, who has been ridiculed by scholars for his reported dimensions of Egypt, and accused of having lied about his travels there, turns out to have described ancient Egypt with great accuracy in terms of meridians and parallels carefully worked out by ancient Egyptian astronomers.

Stecchini found a glyph carved on the thrones of virtually all the Pharaohs since the Fourth Dynasty which contained geodetic data and hence astronomical data of extraordinary subtlety, enabling him to determine that the Egyptians used three figures for the tropic of Cancer: a simplified one of 24°, a precise one of 23° 51′, and one of 24° 06′ required for observing the sun's shadow at the summer solstice.

The sophistication of the ancients is demonstrated by the fact that they placed their observatory near Seyne on the island of Elephantine, 15′—or half a diameter of the sun—north of the actual tropic because they understood that it was not the center of the sun but its outer rim which had to be observed.

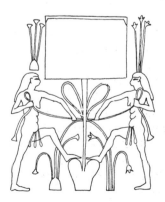

The most important Egyptian text deciphered by Stecchini was a set of three identical hieroglyphs on the back of standard Egyptian measuring rulers found at the temple of Amon at Thebes, the geodetic center of Egypt since the Middle Kingdom. These, says Stecchini, give the clue to the exact dimensions of ancient Egypt.

Ludwig Borchardt, an eminent German Egyptologist, who first published the texts in an article in *Janus* in Vienna in 1921, assumed *a priori* that the figures could not refer to actual latitudes computed astronomically, and did

Knotted ropes beneath Pharaoh's throne are used to symbolize the union of Lower and Upper Egypt at the thirtieth parallel, where the apex of the Delta crosses the prime meridian of Egypt, just north of the Great Pyramid.

Three pairs of short horizontal lines at the bottom of the picture are symbols of three distinct values given by the ancient Egyptians to the tropic of Cancer, basic to the geodetic mensuration of Egypt. The central one of these three lines represented the conventional latitude of the tropic at 24°; the lower line represented the actual latitude at 23° 51'; and the upper line a latitude of 24° 6', which was 15' north of the true tropic, at Syene, where astronomical observations were made.

not even bother to test them: "One must absolutely exclude the possibility that the ancients may have measured by degrees." Succeeding Egyptologists also failed to compare the texts with actual parallels and meridians. Stecchini found them to apply with astonishing precision.

The texts—which for stylistic reasons have been assigned to the Old Kingdom (third millennium B.C.)—state the length of Egypt to be 20 *atur* from Behdet on the Mediterranean to Pi-Hapy (the apex of the Delta just north of the Pyramid of Cheops) and another 86 *atur* south to the First Cataract of the Nile.

This means that 106 *atur* would span an arc of 7° 30' from the Mediterranean to Syene. From a composite of texts and geographic evidence an *atur* is the equivalent of 15,000 royal cubits or 17,000 of Jomard's cubits of .4618 meter. This would make Egypt from Behdet at 31° 30' to Syene at 24° 00' a length of 1,800,000 of Jomard's cubits, or 831,240 meters. The *Smithsonian Geographical Tables* give the distance from 31° 30', to 24° 00' as 831,002 meters. Computing from the third millennium B.C. text, the mean length of a degree of latitude in Egypt would be 110.832 meters. The modern estimate is 110.800 meters.

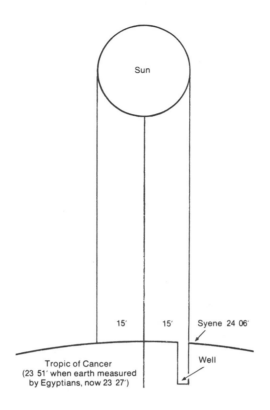

To observe the exact moment the sun fills a well without shadow as it reaches its farthest point north, at the summer solstice, the observation would have to be made under the northern rim of the sun, 15′ further north than the line of the tropic.

When the tropic was at 23° 51′, the ancient Egyptians observed it at Syene at 24° 06′.

Today the tropic is at 23° 27′. By establishing the moment of solstice at the tropic, the ancient astronomers were able correctly to compute the circumference of the earth by the use of deep wells and obelisks.

Sun

15′ | 15′ | Syene 24 06′

Well

Tropic of Cancer
(23 51′ when earth measured by Egyptians, now 23 27′)

The island of Elephantine in the Nile near Syene, where the ancient Egyptians had an astronomical observatory and a nilometer to gauge the flood of the Nile.

Royal Egyptian cubit of Memphis. It was divided into 7 palms of 4 fingers each, for a total of 28. The basic unit from which this cubit is derived is the foot of 300 millimeters. One and a half of these feet made a cubit of 450 millimeters, divided into 6 palms of 4 fingers, for a total of 24 fingers. The royal cubit was obtained by the addition of one extra palm, for a total of 7, or 28 fingers, the equivalent of 525 millimeters.

Stecchini points out that a septenary unit was common to Mesopotamia, Egypt and Greece, because it allowed simple solutions to problems of practical measurement. With a π of 22/7, it was simpler to have a septenary cubit; a square of side 7 was considered to have a diagonal of 10, and a square of 10 as having a semi-diagonal of 7.

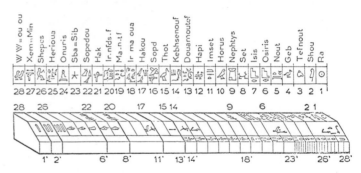

According to Stecchini, once the Egyptians were in possession of the true proportions of their country, they devised a means of simplifying their geodetic data into a geography that was easily committed to memory without recourse to portable maps, using such obvious natural landmarks as the cataracts on the Nile and the extremities of the Nile Delta as geodetic points for rectangles and triangles with easily remembered angles.

The prime meridian of Egypt was made to split the country longitudinally precisely in half, running from Behdet on the Mediterranean, right through an island in the Nile just northeast of the Great Pyramid, all the way to where it crossed the Nile again at the Second Cataract.*

To simplify the dimensions of Northern Egypt, the Egyptian geographers accurately marked it as a triangle exactly 1° deep, with its apex where the Nile splits (just north of the Pyramid of Cheops), fanning out 1° 24′ east and west to where its widest branches flow into the sea. This became an actual Δ-shaped delta, whose angles were designated by the shadows cast by the northeast and northwest corners of the Great Pyramid.

Southern Egypt was made to run precisely 6° to the First Cataract of Aswan on the tropic of Cancer. Two lines drawn parallel to the prime meridian, starting at the side mouths of the Nile in the Delta, running to the tropic, made a simple rectangle of Lower and Upper Egypt.

Stecchini says that when this particular geodetic system of ancient Egypt was established, the tropic of Cancer was at 23° 51′, which corresponds to a place on the Nile just south of the First Cataract called Parembole in Hellenistic times. On the island of Elephantine—15′ farther north—was the famous "well," whose bottom was said to be completely

* Close to the Mediterranean the meridian may have been marked by a northern pyramid. In 1800 the French Expedition saw the remains of a pyramid near Benha in the Delta, but its superstructure has since disappeared.

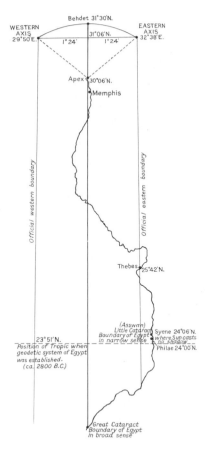

WESTERN
AXIS
29°50'E.
Behdet 31°30'N.
EASTERN
AXIS
32°38'E.
31°06'N.
1°24'   1°24'
Apex 30°06'N.
Memphis

Official western boundary   *Official eastern boundary*

Thebes 25°42'N.

(Asswan)
Little Cataract Syene 24°06'N.
Boundary of Egypt where Sun casts
in narrow sense no shadow
Philae 24°00'N.

23°51'N.
*Position of Tropic when
geodetic system of Egypt
was established.
(ca. 2800 B.C.)*

Great Cataract
Boundary of Egypt
in broad sense

The first cataract, near Syene on the Upper Nile, was fabled to have been a land of the deaf because of the constant roaring of the waters over the outcroppings of granite.

This ancient boundary of Southern Egypt was the source of the hard pink granite from which the monolith beams of the King's Chamber were chiseled, as well as the many great obelisks, weighing as much as a thousand tons, which were set up in Egypt as sundials and geodetic markers.

illumined once a year when the sun stood directly overhead at the solstice.

Were it possible to reconstruct exactly when the tropic was at 23° 51' it would give a firm date for the establishment of the ancient system of geography; unfortunately no astronomer has yet been able to calculate mathematically the exact rate at which the tropic has moved since ancient times to its present 23° 27'. Schwaller de Lubicz figures it was at Elephantine between 2500 and 3000 B.C.

Cities and temples, says Stecchini, were deliberately built at distances in round figures and simple fractions from the tropic or the prime meridian. The predynastic capital of Egypt was set near the mouth of the Nile at Behdet, right on the prime meridian, at 31° 30'. This gave a length to Egypt of 1,800,000 geographic cubits. Memphis, the first capital of united Egypt, was again laid out on the prime meridian and at 29° 51', precisely 6° north of the tropic. The northern limit of the Two Kingdoms was set at 31° 6', and the country was measured by a newer unit, the royal cubit, of which there were 1,500,000 in the length of Egypt.

The geodetic point determining the location of Memphis was called Sokar after the god of orientation (whose name and location are preserved in the present village of Saqqara),

Omphaloi, or "navels," used as geodetic markers.

Geodetic omphalos found by Reisner in the great temple of Amon.

which is exactly on the main axis of the meridian of Egypt, in the necropolis of Memphis.

As each of these geodetic centers was a political as well as a geographical "navel" of the world, an omphalos, or stone navel, was placed there to represent the northern hemisphere from equator to pole, marked out with meridians and parallels, showing the direction and distance of other such navels. In Thebes the stone omphalos was placed in the main room of the temple of Amon, where the meridian and parallel actually cross.

To obtain such precision in their geodesy, says Stecchini, the ancients must have made remarkable astronomical observations.

For the ancient Egyptians to have laid out an absolutely straight meridian of 30° of latitude from the Mediterranean to the equator, over 2000 miles, and drawn two more, equidistant, east and west, as boundaries of the country, must have required an enormous amount of personnel and careful astronomical sightings. Even more sophisticated was their method of establishing longitude, as reconstructed by Stecchini.

With the aid of an elementary system of telegraphy, consisting of a series of beacons, the Egyptians, says Stecchini, were able to note what star was at its zenith at a certain moment, and flash the data, via a string of flares, to other observers so many degrees to east and west.*

H. G. Wood, author of *Ideal Metrology,* assumes that if the Great Pyramid was originally an observatory, signal stations east and west of it once existed which are now in ruins or altogether lost. Wood quotes a Dr. Lieder's description of a little pyramid far to the west in the Libyan desert which could once be seen from the top of the Great Pyramid as the sun went down, but is now lost.

Traveling farther afield, the ancient geographer could establish his longitude with great precision on the basis of accurate tables of the nightly transit of celestial bodies as observed at the Pyramid.†

Fragmented data obtained from such accurate tables, says Stecchini, percolated to the Alexandrine Greeks such as Eratosthenes and Ptolemy, who mixed the accurate data with the inaccurately estimated coordinates of their own period, creating a hodgepodge of good and bad geography. It was not possible to disentangle and correct their work until the development of the chronometer in the eighteenth century of our era.

Because of the advanced geodetic and geographic science of the Egyptians, Egypt became the geodetic center of the known world. Other countries located their shrines and capital cities in terms of the Egyptian meridian "zero," including such capitals as Nimrod, Sardis, Susa, Persepolis, and, apparently, even the ancient Chinese capital of An-Yang.

All of these localities, says Stecchini, were set and oriented on the basis of the most exact sightings. The same applies to the centers of worship of the Jews, the Greeks, and the Arabs.

According to Hebrew historians the original Jewish center of worship was not Jerusalem, but Mount Gerizim, a strictly geodetic point 4° east of the main axis of Egypt. It was only moved to Jerusalem after 980 B.C.

The two great oracular centers of Greece—Delphi and Dodona—were also geodetic markers according to Stecchini.

---

* Fires such as were lighted by the Druids at the moment of the midsummer solstice may have been the origin of the "midsummer fires" and the Beltane fires of May Day, described in *The Golden Bough.*

† Because every observable star comes to the meridian of every place on the globe once in 24 hours, the interval which elapses between the same star coming upon the meridian of two different places is the difference in longitude of the two places.

Delphi is 7° and Dodona 8° north of Behdet, the northernmost part of Egypt, on the prime meridian of Egypt.

The Moselm shrine of Mecca is 10° east of the western meridian of Egypt and 10° south of Behdet. According to Stecchini the sacred black stone of the Kaaba was originally part of a set of four, placed in what he calls a pyramidical triangle from which the trigonometric functions of the shrine could be derived.

Islamic tradition stresses the point that the Kaaba was originally a geodetic center. The essential element of the Kaaba consisted of four stones marking a square with diagonals running north-south and east-west. The diagonal north-south with the northeast and southeast sides formed what the Egyptians called a pyramid. The angle formed by the diagonal with the southeast side was 36°, from which Stecchini concludes that the trigonometric functions of the shrine were measured along the northeast side.

The northwest side of the building of the Kaaba is completed by a semicircular wall: according to tradition this semicircular wall existed since the very beginning. Most likely, this was used, says Stecchini, as a sighting device.

To make a map projection of the northern hemisphere, the ancient Egyptians found a simple mathematical and geometrical means of reducing the curved surface of the globe to a flat surface suitable for mapping, and with a minimum of distortion: they used the stepped pyramid, or ziggurat, each face of which could represent a 90° quadrant of the hemisphere, and each level of which could represent a mappable zone between two parallels of latitude.

Professor Maspero describes the ziggurats of Mesopotamia as "miniature reproductions of the arrangement of the universe." Professor C. P. S. Menon in his *Early Astronomy and Cosmology* says of the ziggurats: "We can deduce that the shape of the Earth, which appears to have served as a model for the temples, was a terraced pyramid with corners pointing to the South, West, North and East."

Ziggurats at Ur, Uruk, and Babylon reached a height of three hundred feet. The ziggurat of Nabu at Barsipki was called the "House of the Seven Bonds of Heaven and Earth" and was in seven stages said to have been painted in seven "Planetary colors."

The sophistication of the ancients, says Stecchini, is illustrated by the ziggurats of Babylon. These stepped "Towers of Babel," long a mystery to mankind, turn out to incorporate a series of Mercator projections, several thousand years before the advent of the Flemish cartographer.

For the purpose of mapping, the northern hemisphere was reduced to a series of flat surfaces represented by the

Reconstruction of Babylonian stepped pyramid or ziggurat. According to H. G. Wood, the ziggurat of Jupiter Belus at Babylon had an ideal basis in the number 360. In his *Ideal Metrology* it is described as a seven-staged pyramid in which each of the six upper stages is 360 inches shorter than the one next below it; the base side was 3,600 inches, and the total height of the structure was 3,600 inches. According to Wood, the entire system of ancient Babylonian metrology appears to have been derived from $360 \times 360 \times 100$, or 12,960,000.

faces of the stepped ziggurat. The area between the equator and the pole was divided into seven bands or "zones" as the Greeks called them, each diminishing in width to correspond to the shrinking degree of longitude. The base line represented the equator, the first step the thirtieth parallel. Thus, each façade represented a 90° quadrant of hemisphere.

Stecchini says the limits of these four quadrants were established with great precision. Egyptian texts, Greek mythology (including the *Argonautica* and the *Odyssey*), and Greek and Roman writers from Herodotus onward unanimously agree in setting this western limit of the Mediterranean quadrant at 9° 54′ East. Another limit, says Stecchini, was known as the Golden Chersonnesos, that is to say, the peninsula of Malaya at meridian 99° 54′ East at a point where the equator cuts the western coast of the island of Sumatra.

Cuneiform tablets indicate that each level of the ziggurats had a specific area corresponding to standard units of land measure.

Nineteenth-century authors illustrated the ziggurats as astronomical observatories, with bearded Babylonians gazing from the battlements; but John Taylor maintained that such high terraces afforded no better vantage than the ground.

On the other hand, a square or tubular shaft of several hundred cubits, built into their interiors, would have made first-rate telescopes for observing the skies. In Mexico the Pyramid of Xochicalco near Cuernavaca contains a tubular well down which the sun shines perpendicularly without a shadow on a specific day of the year.

185

Nineteenth-century idea of Babylonian astronomers atop a ziggurat, published by the French astronomer Camille Flammarion.

Sir John Herschel pointed out that "from the bottom of deep narrow pits, such as a well, or the shaft of a mine, such bright stars as pass the zenith may even be discerned by the naked eye."

John Taylor indicated the reference in Ezekiel (XXIX: 10 and XXX: 6) to a "Tower of Syene," suggesting that perhaps the famous well at Syene was inside a sighting tower.

Reconstructing the ziggurat of Babylon on the basis of the cuneiform text known as the Smith tablet, Stecchini established that it rose in seven diminishing steps, each face of which was smaller than the one below it. For mapping, this allows meridians to cross the parallels at right angles, as in Mercator's projection, but avoids his distortion by shrinking each rectangular face in proportion to the shrinking degree of longitude as it approached the pole.

186

The ziggurat of Babylon, says Stecchini, would have been perfect trigonometrically if the height of the first three steps had been as originally conceived: 30, 48 and 55 1/2 degrees. But the Babylonians raised the first step to 33°, the approximate parallel of Babylon.

The cuneiform description of the ziggurat, known as the Smith tablet, specifically indicates that *each* level of the ziggurat has an area corresponding to standard units of land surface. Particularly important in Mesopotamian land surveying was the square with a side of 60 double cubits—the surface of the third step.

The slope angles at various heights also give important angles, such as $\sqrt{5} - 1$, which is also incorporated into the Great Pyramid. Such triangles, and the number $\sqrt{5} - 1$ (in common practice taken as the magic series 1–2–3) were fundamental in the operations of land surveying.

The third, fourth and fifth steps of the ziggurat make triangles with sides related as the Pythagorean 3–4–5 triangle.

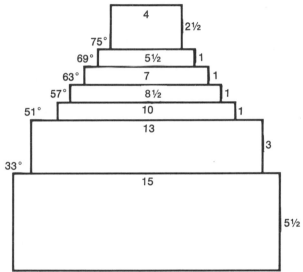

In the original design, says Stecchini, the first step of the ziggurat was intended to represent the thirtieth parallel, but in Mesopotamia it was raised to 33°, the approximate latitude of Babylon. Thereafter the Babylonians made each step rise in units of 6° of latitude. This made it possible for them to obtain an easily remembered cosine value for each step by simply dividing its length by two thirds.

As the Babylonians liked to count by sixes, with a hexagesimal and sexagesimal system, the steps of the ziggurat rose in multiples of 6°. Further to simplify their accounting, the degree of parallel represented by each step could be obtained by multiplying the height of each step by 6; e.g., 6 × 5 1/2 (first step) = 33°.

The system gave the Babylonians an extremely simple way of remembering the trigonometric value of each parallel.

187

All they had to do was divide the length of each step by .666 (or 2/3). Thus, 2/3 of 15 (width of first step) is 10.000, which is the cosine value of the equator. Thereafter the operation produced a simple progression: 8.666, 6.666, 4.666, 3.666, 2.666 for the cosine value of the angles indicated by each step.

The top step, says Stecchini, was rectangular instead of square, because the average of its sides gives 2.5833, which is the cosine of 75° 01′.

XV. THE GOLDEN SECTION

In the Great Pyramid the Egyptians produced a system of map projection even more sophisticated than the one incorporated in the ziggurats.

The apex of the Pyramid corresponds to the pole, the perimeter to the equator, both in proper scale. This fact was inherent in Jomard's conclusions, but got lost in the babble of cubits.

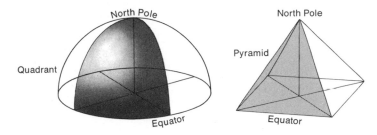

Each flat face of the Pyramid was designed to represent one curved quarter of the northern hemisphere, or spherical quadrant of 90°.

To project a spherical quadrant onto a flat triangle correctly, the arc, or base, of the quadrant must be the same length as the base of the triangle, and both must have the same height. This happens to be the case *only* with a cross section or meridian bisection of the Great Pyramid, whose slope angle gives the π relation between height and base.

John Taylor intuitively suspected something of the sort, but was unable fully to formulate it.

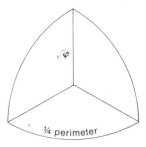

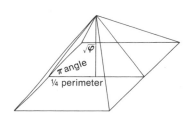

The subtlety of the Pyramid's projection lies in the fact that when viewed from the side, the laws of perspective reduce the actual area of a face (mathematically oversized) to the correct size for the projection, which is the Pyramid's *cross section.*

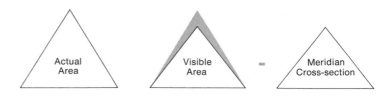

What the viewer saw, and sees, with the aid of perspective is the correct triangle.

The key to the geometrical and mathematical secret of the Pyramid, so long a puzzle to mankind, was actually handed to Herodotus by the temple priests when they informed him that the Pyramid was designed in such a way that the area of each of its faces was equal to the square of its height.

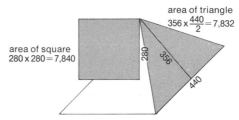

This interesting observation reveals that the Pyramid was designed to incorporate not only the π proportion but another and even more useful constant proportion, known in the Renaissance as the Golden Section, designated in modern times by the Greek letter φ (pronounced *phi*), or 1.618.*

φ, like π, cannot be worked out arithmetically; but it can easily be obtained with nothing more than a compass and a straightedge.

With the incorporation of the Golden Section, the Great Pyramid provides an effective system for translating spherical areas into flat ones.

Anyone who is not anxious to follow the simplified mathematics in this chapter may more simply skip to the following chapter—which contains the answer to the riddle. But he will miss some odd conceits about the relation of

---

* If the 356 cubits of the Pyramid's apothem are divided by half the base, or 220 cubits, the result is 89/55, or 1.618.

190

mathematics to the cosmos and to the creative function of life as embodied in the science of the builders of the Pyramid. The pharaonic Egyptians, says Schwaller de Lubicz, considered φ not as a number, but as a symbol of the creative function, or of reproduction in an endless series: to them it represented "the fire of life, the male action of sperm, the *logos* of the gospel of St. John."

The Golden Section, or φ, is obtained by dividing a line

A _____ B

at a point C

A _____ C _____ B

in such a way that the whole line

A _____ B

is longer than the first part

A _____ C

in the same proportion as the first part

A _____ C

is longer than the remainder.

C _____ B

This will mean that $\frac{AB}{AC} = \frac{AC}{CB} = 1.618$.

This equation, which appears so simple, turns out to be loaded with meaning. Plato in his *Timaeus* went so far as to consider it, and the resulting Golden Section proportion, the most binding of all mathematical relations, and makes it the key to the physics of the cosmos.

In the Great Pyramid the rectangular floor of the King's Chamber (which consists of two equal squares, or a 1 × 2 rectangle) also serves to illustrate and to obtain the Golden Section.

If you split one of two squares in half and swing the diagonal down to the base, the point where the diagonal touches the base will be φ, or 1.618 in relation to the side of the square, which is 1.*

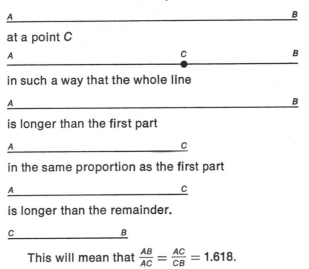

* Pythagoras' theorem will also show that the value of φ will be $1/2 + \sqrt{5/2}$, or 1.618, and that $\varphi - 1$ will be .618.

191

The odd, if not unique, mathematical fact that $\varphi + 1 = \varphi^2$ and that $1 + 1/\varphi = \varphi$ leads to an additive series, known as a Fibonacci series, in which each new number is the sum of the previous two: 1-2-3-5-8-13-21-34-55-89 . . . etc., and their ratio comes closer and closer to φ.*

In Egypt Fibonacci got wind of the additive series and popularized its mystical quality by bringing to Europe the story of the "rabbit problem," or how to find the number of rabbits born in one year, starting with an original pair. Assuming the rabbits to be enclosed by a wall and that every month they produce a pair of rabbits, and that each new pair in turn produce another pair each month, the answer could be obtained by the additive series 1-2-3-5-8-13-21. . . . In this case it is 377 pairs of rabbits.

This mathematical grid, based on the Golden Section, was to become the backbone of the architectural system developed by the great French architect Le Corbusier for his construction of anything from the United Nations building in New York to the closets in a bathroom.

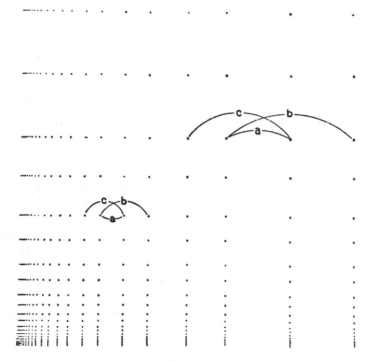

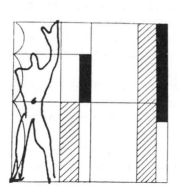

Le Corbusier's "modulor" based on the φ relation in the human body.

The Fibonacci series can be visualized geometrically as a mathematical grid growing larger (or smaller) in which each new unit always bears the relation of φ to its predecessors and successors.

* Leonardo Bigollo Fibonacci, known as Leonardo da Pisa, was perhaps the greatest mathematician of the Middle Ages. Born in 1179, he traveled to Algiers with his father, who acted as consul for the Pisan merchants. From the Arabs Fibonacci learnt the Hindu system of numerals from 1 to 9, which he is credited with having introduced to Europe, where calculations were still being made by the clumsy means of Roman numerals and Greek letters.

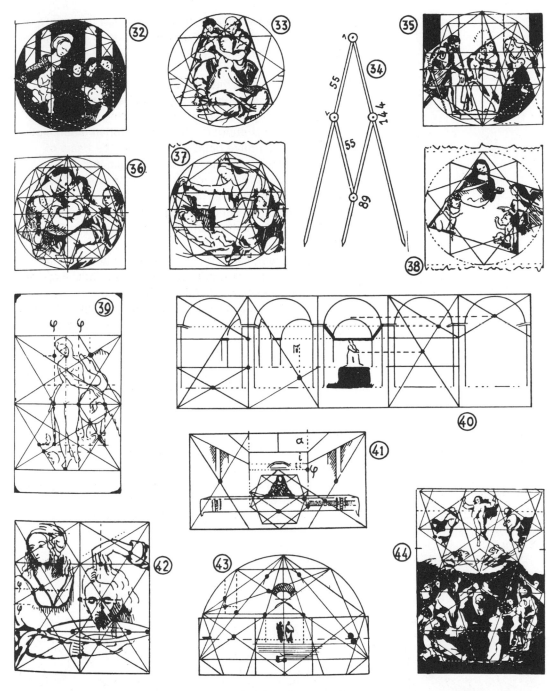

Funk-Hellet's analysis of (32) Mainardi, (33) Michelangelo, (34) Golden Section compass: note 55/89 relation, (35) Veronese, (37), (42), (43) Raphael, (38), (39), (41) Leonardo da Vinci, (40) Fra Lippo Lippi.

In the Renaissance the φ proportion, or Golden Section, as it was called by Leonardo da Vinci, served as the hermetic structure on which some of the great masterpieces were composed. Leonardo illustrated a book on the Golden Section for Luca Pacioli, known as "the monk drunk on beauty," which was published in Venice in 1509.

193

Funk-Hellet has analyzed the φ proportion in a score of masterpieces, including Titian's *Presentation of the Virgin,* Luini's *Sleep of the Infant Jesus,* and Veronese's *The Wedding at Cana.*

The conclusion that the Egyptians of the Old Kingdom were acquainted with both the Fibonacci series and the Golden Section, says Stecchini, is so startling in relation to current assumptions about the level of Egyptian mathematics that it could hardly have been accepted on the basis of Herodotus' statement alone, or on the fact that the φ proportion happens to be incorporated in the Great Pyramid. But the many measurements made by Professor Jean Philippe Lauer, says Stecchini, definitely prove the occurrence of the Golden Section throughout the architecture of the Old Kingdom.

Professor Lauer, for many years the architect for the Egyptian Department of Antiquities, has made thousands of measurements of ancient Egyptian buildings.

Schwaller de Lubicz also found graphic evidence that the pharaonic Egyptians had worked out a direct relation between π and φ in that $\pi = \varphi^2 \times 6/5$.*

In the tomb of Rameses IX there is a strange figure of a royal mummy with one arm raised and an erect phallus. The mummy is lying at the hypotenuse of a sacred 3–4–5 right-angled triangle indicated by a snake.

The length of the body, says Schwaller, is clearly 5 cubits and that of the upright arm is one more cubit, for a total of 6. At the same time the body is divided by the phallus in the proportion of 1 and φ, for a total of φ^2.

This, says Schwaller, makes the outstretched arm give a value for π of 6/5 of the body, or φ^2, which is 3.1416.

On the east side of the temple of Luxor, Schwaller also

Egyptian king as the hypotenuse of a sacred 3–4–5 triangle formed by a snake.
Schwaller de Lubicz shows the king as φ^2, split into a $\varphi + 1$ proportion by the phallus. The king's raised arm gives a 6/5, or $1.2 \times \varphi^2$, proportion, which is exactly 3.1416, or π.

* $2.168 \times 6/5 = 3.1416$.

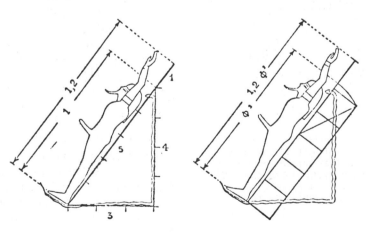

194

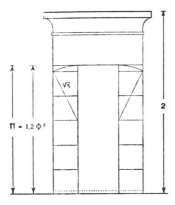

Priests exiting from third pylon of the Great Temple of Karnak bearing the king's barque.

Schwaller de Lubicz shows how the value of π correct to four decimals, or 3.1416, was incorporated into the great gate whose basic measurement was 1 × 2.

Schwaller de Lubicz measured scores of triangular royal napkins and found that lower angles were invariably φ and √φ.

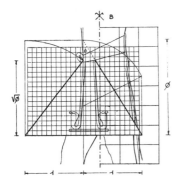

found a relief depicting a cortege of priests exiting from the great temple of Karnak, carrying the king's "solar barque." Schwaller points out that if the width of the gate of the temple, from outside wall to outside wall, is taken as 1, its full height will be 2, and the doorway $\varphi^2 \times 1.2$, or 3.1416; again the value of π, correct to four decimals.

En passant, Schwaller notes the curious coincidence that the Greeks should have adopted for the relation of diameter to circumference the symbol of π, which looks just like the Egyptians' doorway.

Even more extraordinary is Schwaller's resolution of the symbolic meaning of the triangular loincloth worn by the Pharaohs. Schwaller checked several score of these royal napkins for hermetic significance and found that they invariably gave two angles whose values were respectively φ and $\sqrt{\varphi}$.

Because of the location on the body of the royal napkin—similar to the Masonic apron of today—its phallic character, says Schwaller, was unmistakable.

In the Great Pyramid the φ relation is found in the triangle formed by the height, the half base, and the apothem; that is to say, in the basic *cross section* of the structure.

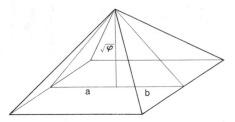

These proportions create a relation between the sides of the triangle such that if the half base is 1, the apothem is φ and the height is $\sqrt{\varphi}$.

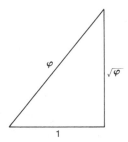

This relation shows Herodotus' report to be indeed correct, in that the square on the height of the Pyramid is $\sqrt{\varphi} \times \sqrt{\varphi} = \varphi$, and the areas of the face $1 \times \varphi = \varphi$.

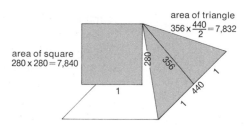

area of triangle
$356 \times \dfrac{440}{2} = 7{,}832$

area of square
$280 \times 280 = 7{,}840$

The simplicity of the system incorporated in the Pyramid makes child's play of the complexities of mathematical map projection. All one need understand is that π is the unchanging value which links a straight diameter to a curved circumference.*

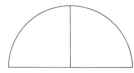

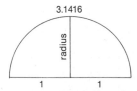

3.1416

* π times the diameter of a circle will equal its circumference. π times one-half the diameter squared will equal the area of the circle.

196

Although the squaring of a circle is an insoluble problem if you use the irrational number of π, it is nevertheless practically resolvable as a function of the Golden Number φ. Because $\pi/2 = 2/\sqrt{\varphi}$ to within a thousandth part, π can usefully be taken as $4/\sqrt{\varphi}$.*

The Pyramid is so designed that for all practical purposes it accomplishes the squaring of the circle. The Pyramid's base is a square whose perimeter is equal to the circumference of a circle whose radius is the Pyramid's height.†

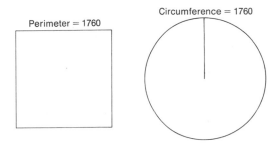

Perimeter = 1760

Circumference = 1760

Superimpose the square on the circle and you get not only an interesting but an extremely useful diagram consisting of the perimeter of the Pyramid and the circumference of the circle it represents.

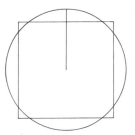

* The following examples are included for the sake of those who might doubt the mathematics; they are not essential to the narrative.

Because π also equals $\varphi^2 \times 6/5$, it is possible to use the Fibonacci series to obtain an accurate relation for the diameter of a circle to its circumference without recourse to π. In the Fibonacci series of 21–34–55, if 21 is taken as the diameter of a circle, its circumference will be 55 × 6/5, or 66, accurate to one-thousandth part, giving the Great Pyramid value for π of 22/7, or 3.14285.

Higher numbers in the Fibonacci series provide increasingly finer values in whole numbers accurate to one ten-thousandth part. Prolonging the series, which goes . . . 89–144–233–377–610 . . . a diameter of 144 gives a circumference of 377 × 6/5, with a value for π of 3.1415; a diameter of 233 gives a circumference of 610 × 6/5, with a value for π of 3.1416; and so on.

† Four times the base of 440 cubits equals 1760 square cubits. The height of 280 cubits × 2π, or twice 22/7, equals 1760 square cubits.

Three more lines will provide the mathematically correct cross section of the Pyramid of Cheops.

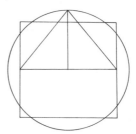

By simply enclosing the diagram in another square, and inserting the φ relationship as it exists in the Pyramid, a key is obtained for readily translating spherical surfaces into flat ones of equal area.

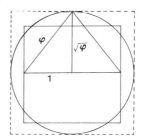

To obtain a rectangle equal in area to the basic circle, two sides of the smaller square need merely be prolonged till they touch the sides of the larger square.

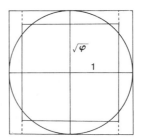

The area of the rectangle is its length times its width, or $2\sqrt{\varphi} \times 2$, which is $4\sqrt{\varphi}$.

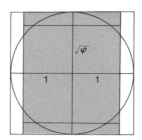

The area of the circle is πr^2, or $\pi\varphi$ in this case, the radius being $\sqrt{\varphi}$. But since $\pi = 4/\sqrt{\varphi}$, the area is also $4\sqrt{\varphi}$, the same as the rectangle.

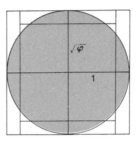

Thanks to the Pyramid's structure it is thus possible, with virtually no mathematics, to draw a rectangle (from the base of the Pyramid and twice its height) which will be equal in area to a circle on its height. This leads directly to being able to draw a rectangle or triangle equal to a spherical quadrant, resolving the main problem of the map maker with the same simplicity.

As the whole circle equals the whole rectangle, half the circle is equal to half the rectangle.

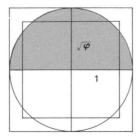
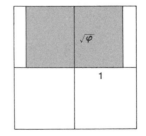

199

But half a flat circle is also mathematically rigorously equal in area to the spherical surface of a quadrant of 90°.

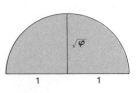

Thus a rectangle of height $\sqrt{\varphi}$ and a base of 2 is equal to a quadrant of height $\sqrt{\varphi}$ and an arc of 2.

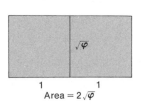

It is thus possible to translate a spherical quadrant of 90° of longitude onto a flat Mercator surface of equal area or onto an undistorted triangle of exactly half that area.

With the Pyramid, the ancient Egyptians had not only squared the circle but effectively cubed the sphere.

XVI. SCIENTIFIC SURVEY GIVES GEOGRAPHICAL PROOF

That the Pyramid of Cheops was intended to represent a geographical rendition of the northern hemisphere was indicated repeatedly in the ancient texts, as Jomard had noted. From a careful analysis of classic Greek authors, Stecchini narrowed the sources of information on the Pyramid —other than Herodotus—down to a single Greek writer, Agatharchides of Cnidus, a peripatetic philosopher who was guardian to the king of Egypt at the end of the second century B.C.

Agatharchides reported that the length of one side of the base of the Pyramid corresponded to 1/8 minute of degree, and the apothem to 1/10 of a minute.

Jomard had hit upon this information and used it to find an almost exact solution: his apothem of 184.722 meters multiplied by 10 gave a minute of 1847.22 meters, which is almost precisely the length of a minute of latitude at the twenty-ninth parallel. This led Jomard to assume that the builders of the Pyramid had chosen to use the mean latitude value for all Egypt, which he figured to be 27° 40′.

What Jomard could not know was that the most ancient geodetic center of Egypt had been placed at 27°45′, precisely halfway between Syene on the Tropic, and Behdet on the coast of the Delta. He could not have known this because the site of the new capital of the young pharaoh Akhnaten called Akhtaten or "Resting point of Aten" had not yet been discovered near the modern Tell el-Amarna, nor had the young Champollion yet deciphered the hieroglyphs.

A stone text found in the ruins of Tell el-Amarna relates to the foundation of the capital. One of the surviving copies is about twenty-five feet high. It gives the length of the new capital as being limited by two boundary stones meticulously set "for eternity" at the extraordinary distance of 6 *atur,* 3/4 of a stadium and four geographic cubits. This indicates an intended accuracy of one in ten thousand. As Stecchini interprets the text, it not only specifically indicates 27° 45′ as the ancient geodetic center of Egypt, but gives the length of the *average* degree of latitude between the equator and the pole to be 240,715 cubits of 111,136.7 meters. The modern estimate is 111,134.1 meters.

As Stecchini points out, Akhnaten's geodetic reform was a return to the predynastic system of computing the length of Egypt in geographic cubits rather than royal cubits.

Had Jomard been able to measure all four sides of the base of the Pyramid with the precision of modern surveyors, he would have realized that the ancient Egyptians intended— quite logically—for the *base* of the Pyramid to indicate the value of a degree at the equator (where they apparently considered the earth to be a true circle and a degree of latitude to be equal to a degree of longitude).

Up until the time of World War I there still remained considerable doubt as to the actual lengths of the four sides of the base of the Pyramid. Petrie had encountered great difficulty in delimiting the exact position of the corners, from which several blocks had been removed. But in 1925, Ludwig Borchardt, then director of the German Institute of Archeology in Cairo, asked to borrow the instruments of the Government of Egypt in order to make a new survey of the Great Pyramid. Borchardt hoped that a really accurate set of measurements might at last separate the strands of fact from fiction in the matter of the geometry of the Great Pyramid.

The Egyptian government agreed to make the survey on condition that Borchardt first clear all the remaining debris from around the base. When this was accomplished, an engineer named J. H. Cole was employed to make a thoroughly scientific survey. Cole used an extensive sounding of the foundations, and was finally able to ascertain to within millimeters the original position of each of the four corners.*

* These were published in *Determination of the Exact Size and Orientation of the Great Pyramid of Giza* (Survey of Egypt, paper 58). Cole gives 230.215 meters (± 6 millimeters) for the south side; 230.454 meters (± 10 millimeters at the west end and ± 30 millimeters at the east end) for the north side; 230.391 for the east side; and 230.253 for the west side.

Stecchini surmises that the apparent discrepancies of a few inches in the lengths of the four base lines might not have been errors on the part of builders who could set casing stones with the precision of a modern optician and dig a descending passage of over 350 feet with a mere 1/4 inch error in azimuth, but *intentional variants* for a definite purpose.

Were the difference in length of the sides to be explained not as the result of imprecision, but as intended skill, it would be possible to explain the lack of squareness in the angles of the base of the Pyramid. In Stecchini's opinion, the Pyramid's sides may have been deliberately planned with angles differing from a right angle in multiples of 15″ in order to correspond to a second time in the apparent motion of the stars.

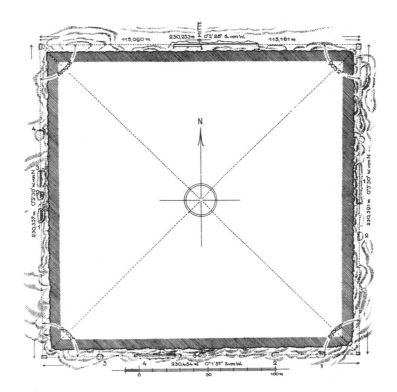

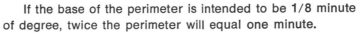

Ludwig Borchardt's measurements of the angles of the base of the Great Pyramid.

Pyramidion, or capstone, from the pyramid of Amenemhet III (1849–1801 B.C.) at Dashur. It is of polished black granite with winged sun disk of gold and carved hieroglyphs.

If the base of the perimeter is intended to be 1/8 minute of degree, twice the perimeter will equal one minute.

Cole's mean figure for twice the perimeter is 1,842.91 meters. The modern figure for a minute of latitude at the equator is 1,842.9 meters.

From the figures it is evident that the ancient Egyptians knew that a degree of latitude is shortest at the equator and lengthens as it approaches the pole.

Schwaller de Lubicz arrived at the same conclusion by noting that the Egyptians counted a minute of arc as being 1000 brasses, or 1000 fathoms of 6 feet. According to Schwaller the brasse was a strictly geodetic measure that varied between 1.843 meters and 1.862 meters, depending upon the degree of latitude at which it was figured. The concordance is remarkable in that a minute of latitude is 1,842.9 meters at the equator, and 1,861.65 at the pole.

Stecchini's analysis of the ancient texts also helps resolve the problem of the apothem of the Pyramid which was said to be 1/10 of a minute, or 600 feet.

Agatharchides of Cnidus reported that the Pyramid of Cheops was topped by a pyramidion, or capstone, of four cubits which could be included in a calculation or excluded depending on the problem to be resolved. Like the obelisks, most pyramids were capped by a pyramidion of precious metal that would sparkle in the first rays of sunlight.

203

Discounting 4 royal cubits for the pyramidion leaves an apothem of 352 cubits of .525 meter each, and solves the whole riddle of the cubits in the Pyramid.

It gives an apothem of 600 geographic feet of .308 meter, or 400 cubits of .462 meter. It also gives an apothem of 500 remen, 220 megalithic yards, 320 *pyk belady* cubits, 100 brasses, 60 decapodes, 40 cannes, 10 short schoenia, 6 plethra, or 1 stadium. It is one tenth of a minute of latitude measured at the parallel of the Great Pyramid.

Jomard had been lucky when he found 600 feet to the apothem of the Pyramid. He had measured short, not knowing about the pyramidion, and come up with a very close 184.72 —which was derided by his colleagues.

Six hundred feet of .308 meter is 184.8 meters. The modern estimate of 1/10 minute of latitude at the parallel of the Great Pyramid is 184.75.

But Jomard had been absolutely right when he said he found 500 old Egyptian cubits of .4618 meter in the base of the Pyramid, and 400 larger *pyk belady* cubits of .5773 meter. These cubits are based on what Stecchini found to be the oldest foot in antiquity, the geographic foot which was still used in classical Greece and which survived in Europe down to our Middle Ages: in Egypt it was still common when Jomard arrived. Stecchini found evidence of this foot in temples in Mesopotamia in the preliterate era as early as 3500 B.C. The same geographic foot forms the edge of a cube or *artaba* which was the standard unit of grain measure in the Near East down to the Persian Empire.

It is now clear that the minute differences that appear in this foot in Persia, Greece, Mesopotamia and Egypt are due to the fact it was computed astronomically, varying a mere fraction of a millimeter depending on the latitude at which it was measured.

The façade of the Parthenon is 100 geographic feet of .3082765 meter, or 1 second of arc at the latitude of Athens, which is 37° 58′. At the equator a foot is a millimeter less, or only .30715 meter; at the mean latitude of Egypt, at 27° 45′, it is .307795. At the latitude of the Great Pyramid it is what Jomard found it to be: .3079. One and one-half of these feet made a geographic cubit of .4618, the same cubit Jomard found in current use when he arrived in Egypt, and which had been current since the time of Al Mamun (by means of which the Arabs could have correctly computed the circumference of the earth).

If you divide the earth into 360 degrees, and again into 60 minutes of 60 seconds, the result is one second of arc, or 100 geographical feet. Translated into meters by multiplying by .308 the result is 39,916.8 kilometers, which is within one quarter of one percent of our modern earth circumference of 40,000 km. By Akhnaten's average degree it was an even closer 40,009.32 kilometers.

Taylor had come within a hair of resolving the problem when he correctly postulated that the builders of the Pyramid had taken a great circle of 360 degrees and divided it first into 60 minutes and then into 60 seconds for a total of 1,296,000 seconds of arc.

Searching for a unit among the ancient measures that would fit this total, Taylor came up with what he called the short Greek foot, or Ptolemaic foot, which was 1.0101 of an English foot. One hundred of the Ptolemaic feet to a second of arc gave an earth circumference of 129,600,000 Ptolemaic feet, or 130,908,960 English feet, which was a bare one thousandth short of the estimate of the earth's circumference in Taylor's day.

Taylor's Ptolemaic foot was, of course, none other than Jomard's foot of .3079, from which was derived the cubit of .4618 meter, 500 of which fit the base of the Pyramid.

But Taylor couldn't make the sums come out because he was using the base computed by Le Père and Coutelle, which was about six feet too long, and into which neither the Ptolemaic foot nor the cubit would fit.

For lack of Cole's precise survey, poor Taylor, who was hot on the scent, was obliged to discard Jomard's thesis that 500 cubits of .4618 fit the base of the Pyramid along with the idea that it was intended to represent 1/8 minute, or 1/480 of a geographical degree. That Taylor was loath to do so is clear from his comment that he was sure that "it is in this direction, if any, that we may hope to find a satisfactory answer to the question: why was the Great Pyramid built?"

Instead, Taylor pursued the confusing idea that the Pyramid had been intended to indicate a polar axis for the earth of 500,000,000 Pyramid inches, and that the Egyptians had measured the base of the Pyramid in units to fit a solar year of 365.2322 days.

Piazzi Smyth, who also sensed there was truth in Taylor's probings, followed him into this apparent cul-de-sac.*

* Even so Taylor and Smyth may have been on the track of a solution. Taylor suggested that the circumference of the earth had been measured in Ptolemaic feet and common cubits, whereas the *polar* axis had been measured in inches and sacred cubits. In his recent *Historical Metrology,* Algernon Berriman supports Taylor's hypothesis by showing that whereas a "sacred" cubit of 25.064 inches is the ten millionth part of the earth's polar radius, a "royal" cubit of 20.6265 inches is a fraction of the circumference of the earth in that it is 206,265 sexigesimal seconds of arc: in other words the radius laid along a circumference of 1,296,000 seconds becomes a radian of 206,265 seconds.

Why Taylor, Smyth, Petrie and Davidson could not, or would not, avail themselves of Jomard's figures is a mystery. The twenty-one volumes of the *Description de l'Egypte* are bulky, hard to come by, and harder to handle (they are in leatherbound folio and double [Atlantic] folio, weighing as much as fifty pounds), and the information is scattered, without an index, through hundreds of pages of text, mixed with thousands of incongruous or irrelevant facts and figures; but the hard facts and figures are there; and Jomard's handling of them is lucid.

More surprising is the dogged determination of Egyptologists and writers on the Pyramid to continue to overlook or deny these facts. Even so eminent an Egyptologist as Jean Philippe Lauer, architect for the Egyptian Department of Antiquities, who certainly had ready access to *Description de l'Egypte* (his father was a curator of the Biblioteque Nationale) continued to dispute Jomard's conclusions even as late as after World War II.

In his book *Le Problème des pyramides,* Lauer writes: "We must recognize that all this pretty hypothesis rests on inexact data. The cubit of .462 meters derived by Jomard from the base and the apothem of the Pyramid appears to be as hypothetical as that of Piazzi Smyth."

Ironically, the Director of the Department of Egyptian Antiquities, M. Etienne Drioton, who wrote the preface to Lauer's book, complained that it is because of their opposition to such theories as Jomard's that Egyptologists are being treated like "naif, blind, refractory dabblers in science whose quiet routines have been disturbed!"

That Jomard's cubit of .4618 or .462 meter is incorporated 500 times in the base of the Great Pyramid and 400 times in the apothem is no longer a matter of debate. Thanks to Cole it is a simple matter of multiplication. Even the confusing report of the Roman historian Pliny that the base of the Pyramid measured 833 1/3 feet and its apothem 666 2/3 feet becomes easily resolvable. The incongruity is rational when it is realized that Pliny's foot was simply 9/10 of a geographic foot. In other words, 833 1/3 of Pliny's feet turn out to be 750 geographic feet, or 500 geographic cubits.

The 500 cubits base is equal to 230.3625 meters (almost exactly Cole's figure) if measured by a geographic cubit computed at the equator, and 230.925 (almost exactly Jomard's figure) if measured by a cubit computed at the parallel of the Great Pyramid. The difference in cubits— which amounts to a fraction of a millimeter—makes no difference whatsoever to the relative values of the other units. For the sake of clarity the accompanying chart uses a cubit of .462 and a foot of .308.

Ancient Units of Measure Contained in the Great Pyramid in Round Numbers or Exact Fractions

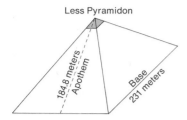

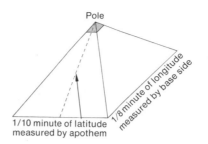

The units of measure, from the short foot of .300 meter, through the various cubits, brasses, megalithic yards, parasangs, and miles, all fit perfectly in either round numbers or exact fractions into the base and apothem of the Great Pyramid because they are *all* fractions of a correct geographical degree of latitude or longitude at the equator. The Great Pyramid is thus a true standard of measure and a scale model of the northern hemisphere.

Apothem	Base
616 Egyptian feet of .300 meter	770 Egyptian feet
600 Greek or geographic feet of .308 meter	750 Greek feet
500 remen of .3696 meter	625 remen
400 geographic cubits of .462 meter	500 geographic cubits
352 royal cubits of .525 meter	440 royal cubits
320 *pyk belady* of .5775 meter	400 *pyk belady*
275 megalithic yards of .84 meter	220 megalithic yards
100 brasses or fathoms of 1.848 meters	125 brasses or fathoms
60 decapodes or rods of 10 feet	75 decapodes
40 rods of 15 feet	50 rods of 15 feet
6 plethra	7.5 plethra
1 stadium of 600 feet (.308)	1 1/4 stadium
1/10 of a mile, or angular minute	1/8 mile or minute
1/600 of a geographic degree	1/480 of a degree

Agatharchides was quite right when he quoted ancient Egyptian sources as saying that the base of the Pyramid was intended to be 1/8 minute of degree at the equator. 500 of Jomard's cubits multiplied by 8 for a minute, by 60 for a degree and 360 for a circumference, equal 86,400,000 cubits.

Relation of the Ancient Egyptian Foot (of .308 meter) and Multiples Thereof to the Circumference of the Earth

In the circumference there are		129,600,000 feet
There are 360 degrees	of	360,000 ft.
3,600 great Egyptian schoene	of	36,000 ft.
21,600 miles	of	6,000 ft.
216,000 stadia	of	600 ft.
1,296,000 plethra	of	100 ft.
2,160,000 schoenia	of	60 ft.
8,640,000 cannes	of	15 ft. (1) cubit
12,960,000 decapodes	of	10 ft.
21,600,000 brasses or ogyie	of	6 ft.
86,400,000 cubits	of	1 1/2 ft.
129,600,000 feet	of	1 ft.
518,400,000 palms	of	1/4 ft.
2,073,600,000 fingers	of	1/16 ft.

Obelisks outside the temple of Amon-Ra at Karnak which was oriented to the solstice. By measuring their shadow at the solstice it was possible to extrapolate the meridian circumference of the planet.

This reveals the source of the Egyptian cubit and foot. There are 86,400 seconds in a day of twenty-four hours, or the time it takes the earth to revolve on its axis. So the distance traveled by the earth at the equator in one second is exacly 1000 of Jomard's cubits.

The builders of the Great Pyramid gave its base a length corresponding to the distance the earth rotates in 1/2 a second. This makes the cubit and the foot doubly earth commensurate: the cubit was equal to 1/1000 of a second of time, the foot to 1/100 second of arc.

How could the ancient observers have established this fact? To compute the polar circumference of the earth the ancients used the sun and the shadows cast by obelisks. To compute the equatorial circumference they observed the passage of stars across fixed points such as obelisks. For the polar circumference they needed merely to measure the distance between two obelisks a few miles apart and the difference in the length of the shadows of the obelisks.

There was no need to measure such a vast distance as separated Alexandria from Syene. The difference in latitude, and hence the fraction of arc separating any two meridian obelisks, can be obtained by the relation of the obelisk's shadow to its height *when measured at the moment of the solstice or equinox.*

To obtain the equatorial circumference, an observer at the base of an obelisk at the thirtieth parallel could signal the appearance on the eastern horizon of a zenith star to an observer at a measured distance in the western desert where the tip of the obelisk would be on the horizon. Noting the interval of time between the signal from the first observer and the moment the star appeared on *his* horizon (and knowing the earth moves through 1,296,000 seconds of arc in 86,400 seconds of time), the observer could figure the equatorial circumference of the earth. At the thirtieth parallel it would vary from the equator by the cosine value of 30° or $\sqrt{3}/2$.

It was thus simply a matter of deciding what *unit of measure* to use in computing these lengths. An observer looking up at the Grand Gallery from a point far enough back to subtend an angle of 2° at the opening, could then note the time it took a star on the celestial equator to cross the opening. He would then possess the necessary data to relate the width of the Grand Gallery to the circumference of the earth.

From the figures it is evident that the ancient astronomers took the earth's daily rotation on its axis as a unit of time and made 1000 cubits the distance traveled by the earth in a second of time.

With a series of obelisks they could physically measure minutes and seconds of meridian arc, along a meridian and extrapolate the distorted distance to the pole.

From many scattered texts Stecchini has deduced that the Egyptians had worked out a simplified method of computing the change in each degree from equator to pole by means of an additive and subtractive series. The geographic cubit was also ideal in that it gave an admirable length for Egypt of 1,800,000 cubits. From Behdet to Syene is 7 1/2 degrees, or 1/48th of the earth's circumference of 86,400,000 cubits.

These cold facts should settle one whole facet of the mystery of the Great Pyramid. Clearly the ancient Egyptians knew the shape of the earth to a degree not confirmed till the eighteenth century when it was established that Newton was correct in his theory that the planet was somewhat flattened at the poles, and they knew the size of the earth to a degree not matched till the middle of the nineteenth

211

century when it was first remeasured with comparable accuracy by the German geodesist Friedrich Wilhelm Bessel. It is equally evident that they could divide a day into 24 hours of 60 minutes and 60 seconds, and produce a unit of measure that was earth commensurate—just as Taylor, Smyth and Jomard had surmised.

So now that Cinderella's foot has been found to fit her lost slipper without pinching or effort, to go on lengthening and shortening the carbuncled feet of her ugly sisters would indeed be like M. Drioton's naif, blind and refractory dabblers in science. On the other hand, a little cooperative effort by experts on ancient Egypt and Sumeria might help bring to light many more fascinating details of the early history of science.

Sexagesimal, Decimal and Quaternary Relations of Ancient Egyptian Units of Measure

60 palms	= 1 canne
60 feet	= 1 short schoenion
60 decapodes	= 1 stadium
60 short schoenia	= 1 Hebraic mile
60 plethra	= 1 Egyptian mile or minute of degree
60 stadia	= 1 grand schoenion
60 Egyptian miles	= 1 degree or moira
60 grand schoenia	= 1 sexagesime
60 sexagesimes	= 1 circumference of the globe
10 Egyptian feet	= 1 decapode
10 Egyptian cubits	= 1 canne or Egyptian pole
10 orgyie or brasses	= 1 short schoenion
10 decapodes	= 1 plethron
10 cannes	= 1 side of land unit of 100 cubits (aroura?)
10 short schoenia	= 1 stadium
10 stadia	= 1 Egyptian mile
10 grand schoenia	= 1 degree of longitude
4 fingers	= 1 palm
4 palms	= 1 foot
4 cubits	= 1 orgyie or brasse
4 cannes	= 1 short schoenion
4 sides of 100 cubits (aroura?)	= 1 stadium

212

Number of Greek or geographic feet of .308 meters.

In circumference of world	360,000 × 360
In a geographical degree	360,000
In a long schoene	36,000
In a geographical minute (or mile)	6,000
In a stadium	600
In a brasse	6
In a cubit (geographical)	1 1/2

Geodetic Values Incorporated in the Dimensions of the Great Pyramid

	Base	Perimeter	Apothem
Egyptian foot of .300 meter	770	3080	616
Greek or geographic foot of .308 meter	750	3000	600
Greek or geographic cubit of .462 meter	500	2000	400
Royal Egyptian cubit of .525 meter	440	1760	352
Pyk belady cubit of .5775 meter	400	1600	320
Megalithic yards of .84 meter	275	1100	220
Brasse of 6 geographic feet (1.848 meters)	125	500	100
Decapodes of 10 geographic feet	75	300	60
Plethra	7.5	30	6
Stadium of 600 geographic feet	1 1/4	5	1
Miles or minute of degree	1/8	1/2	1/10
Parasangs	1/24	1/6	1/30
Long schoene	1/48	1/12	1/60
Geographical degree	1/480	1/120	1/600

XVII. DECLINE OF ANCIENT KNOWLEDGE

What remains a mystery is how all the advanced science of the ancient Egyptians could have been lost for so many centuries.

In his reconstruction of preclassic geographical data, Stecchini has traced an advanced science of geography based on accurate astronomical tables which were kept up to date all the way down to the beginning of the first millennium B.C. He has established that the later Babylonians still had excellent maps for their area of the world between the thirtieth and thirty-sixth parallels, made in segments of 6° of latitude by 7° 12′ of longitude, which gave them perfect squares because of the diminished length of a degree of longitude between those parallels.

This same system, says Stecchini, was in use as late as the reign of Darius the Great of Persia, whose empire, centered on the arbitrary geodetic point of Persepolis, ran precisely 3 units of 7° 12′ east of the Egyptian meridian and three units of 7° 12′ west of the Indian border.

But errors were already creeping into the geography because of a lack of direct observation of celestial phenomena and because of the reliance by geographers on ancient astronomical data that were no longer up to date.

As an explanation for this regression of geographic science, especially during the Hellenistic period, and thereafter almost to modern times, Stecchini suggests that when Alexander the Great destroyed Persepolis in the fourth century B.C. he may have exterminated the Egyptian geographers imported by the Persians to do their figuring, and that when he dismantled the center of Egyptian science at Heliopolis in order to build his own capital at Alexandria, he may have compounded the damage.* The destructions of Persepolis and Heliopolis were considered by Alexander

* Heliopolis, the On of the Bible, was considered the greatest university in the world. It had existed since much earlier times under the domination of the priests, of whom there were said to be 13,000 in the time of Rameses III, 1225 B.C. More than 200 years earlier, Moses was instructed at Heliopolis "in all the wisdom of the Egyptians," which included physics, arithmetic, geometry, astronomy, medicine, chemistry, geology, meteorology and music.

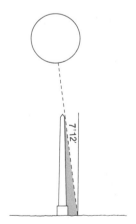

Romantic nineteenth-century depiction of Moses being found in the bullrushes.

Gnomon at Alexandria at summer solstice.

essential in order to destroy the geographic, and therefore the political, basis of the older empires.

Stecchini's evidence shows that far from being the great innovators of geographical knowledge, the Alexandrine geographers of the next half millennium, such as Eratosthenes, Hipparchus and Ptolemy were mainly handling and mishandling traditional data of an advanced science that preceded them, and which they only understood in part.

Current scholarship keeps repeating that the circumference of the earth was first measured by Eratosthenes, the Greek who was put in charge of the library of Alexandria, but it is clear that Eratosthenes merely cited old Egyptian information about the circumference of the earth without really understanding it.

Eratosthenes claimed to have found that a degree of latitude was 700 stadia. This, says Stecchini, was nothing but the traditional Egyptian datum of 14 *atur* to 50 stadia.

Eratosthenes also claimed to have found by observation that when the sun does not cast a shadow at the southern limit of Egypt, it casts a shadow of 7° 12′ at Alexandria.

215

Eratosthenes is said to have measured the circumference of the earth by noting the angle of the sun's rays at Alexandria at the summer solstice, the day he knew the sun would be directly overhead at Syene on the tropic of Cancer.

Finding a shadow angle of 7° 12' at Alexandria, he deduced the distance from Alexandria to Syene to be 7° 12' of the 360° circumference of the globe. As 360/7° 12' = 50, Eratosthenes multiplied the 5000 stadia he believed to separate Alexandria from Syene by 50 and got a figure of 250,000 stadia for the circumference of the earth. Because his various errors canceled out, he was credited with a scientific answer.

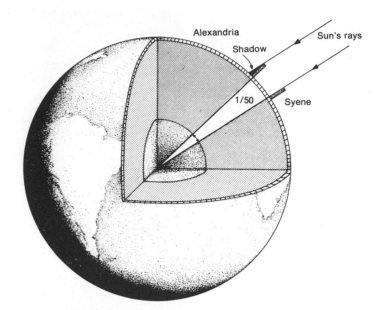

In reality Eratosthenes had read the old Egyptian data (then more than 2000 years old) to the effect that the tropic was at latitude 23° 51' and that the sun did not cast any shadow at Elephantine. What he did not know, and could not measure, was that by his time the tropic had shifted to 23° 45'. Nor did Eratosthenes understand the necessity of adjusting his figures according to the apparent semi diameter of the sun; he believed Alexandria to be 7° 12' north of 23° 51'; he even claimed that Alexandria was on the same meridian as Elephantine, whereas they are apart by about 3°, or 200 miles of longitude.

Furthermore, Eratosthenes used the "great cubit" of Babylon (532.702 millimeters) to obtain his stadium, instead of the more ancient royal cubit of the Egyptians of 525 millimeters, unaware that the first step taken by the Assyrians when they conquered Egypt in the seventh century B.C. was to substitute their own Mesopotamian cubit for the Egyptian one in order to manifest their own dominion.

On the basis of his research into ancient geography, Stecchini is now convinced that there existed on this planet a people with an advanced mathematical and astronomical science several millennia before classic Greece.

216

XVIII. WHO BUILT THE PYRAMID? WHEN? AND HOW?

It would be satisfactory to be able to describe the method by which the Great Pyramid was put together, by whom, and when.

But the builders, whoever they may have been, left no description of their method. No one has even found a *later* Egyptian report of how the first pyramids were built. It is only on the basis of shrewd guessing that Egyptologists estimate the stepped pyramid of Saqqara to be the oldest of the Egyptian pyramids and attribute its construction to the legendary architect Imhotep in the reign of King Zoser of the Third Dynasty.

The stepped pyramid of Medûm, which was the first stepped structure to be converted to a true pyramid, is attributed to Cheops' father Sneferu on similarly sketchy evidence; the same goes for the bent pyramid of Dashur.

Lacking solid history, the Arabs (and the Jews) of the Middle East proliferated legend. The most ancient tradition about the Great Pyramid is that it was erected to memorialize a tremendous cataclysm in the planetary system which affected the globe with fire and flooding.

Arab authors recount that the pyramids were built before the deluge by a king who had a vision that the world would be turned upside down, and that the stars would fall from the sky. According to these Arab sources, the king placed in the pyramids accounts of all he had learnt from the wisest men of the times, including the secrets of astronomy, complete with tables of the stars, geometry, and physics, treatises on precious stones, and certain machines, including celestial spheres and terrestrial globes. They also speak of "malleable glass."

The earliest Jewish reports—other than the vague reference in the Bible to "pillars of stone"—is in Josephus, who says the Sethites were inventors of a wisdom which dealt with celestial bodies and their order in the heavens, and that to preserve their wisdom for all mankind they built two monuments—one brick, the other stone—the stone one being still extant in Egypt in Josephus' time, during the first century after Christ.

The Arab legends maintain that the Great Pyramid not

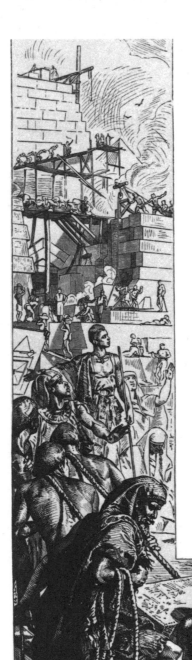

only contained representations of the position of the stars and their cycles, but also a history and chronicle of the times past and future.

As to *who* built the Great Pyramid, Arab historians such as Ibrahim ben Ebn Wasuff Shah say that the Giza pyramids were built by an antediluvian king called Surid or Saurid, who saw in a dream a huge planet falling to earth at the time when "the Heart of the Lion would reach the first minute of the head of Cancer."

Abu Zeyd el Balkhy quotes an ancient inscription to the effect that the Great Pyramid was built at a time when the Lyre was in the Constellation of Cancer, which has been interpreted as meaning "twice 36 thousand solar years before the Hegira," or about 73,000 years ago.

The famous traveler ibn-Batuta, writing 730 years after the Hegira, says that Hermes Trismegistos (the Hebrew Enoch), "having ascertained from the appearance of the stars that the deluge would take place, built the pyramids to contain books of science and knowledge and other matters worth preserving from oblivion and ruin."

According to Basil Steward, a theosophist, author of *The Mystery of the Great Pyramid,* there is no more reason to believe that because the Pyramid stands in Egypt it was built by Egyptians than that the modern Egyptians built the Aswan Dam. Steward says that when all the evidence—archeological and traditional—is coordinated and examined collectively, it leads to but one conclusion: ". . . The seeds of Egypt's greatness were sown by a few colonists who entered the country peaceably and organized the carrying out of great constructional works."

218

Sir George Cornewall Lewis, in *An Historical Survey of the Astronomy of the Ancients,* complained of the arbitrary dating used by Egyptologists which he compared to "the manipulation of the balance-sheet of an insolvent company by a dexterous accountant (who, by transfers of capital to income, by suppression or transposition of items, and by the alteration of bad into good debts, can convert a deficiecy into a surplus)." Lewis pointed out that Baron Bunsen and Dr. Lepsius, both eminent Egyptologists, separated the dates of the figure Sesostris by no less than 3793 years, and asked: "What would we think if a new school of writers on the history of France, entitling themselves Francologists, were to arise in which one of the leading critics were to deny that Louis XIV lived in the seventeenth century, and were to identify him with Hercules, or Romulus . . . or Charlemagne."

The only major historian of ancient Egypt was Manetho, a priest, who wrote a history of Egypt for Ptolemy II, but it was lost. Only scraps of it, translated by authors who lived about six hundred years after his death, have survived. His list of dynasties, checked and modified, forms the framework on which the history of Egypt has been reconstructed. But very little detail is known concerning the political history of the first two dynasties, other than the nearly twenty names of Pharaohs listed by Manetho.

Most Egyptologists consider the First Dynasty to have started with Menes about 2900 B.C., and the Fourth, consisting of Sneferu, Cheops, Didoufri, Kephren, and Mykerinos, to have lasted about 120 years from 2680 to 2560 B.C., as the Old Kingdom.

There followed a first intermediate period, a Middle Kingdom from 2052 to 1785 B.C., a second intermediate period, and a New Kingdom from 1580 to 1085 B.C. Post Empire Dynasties XXI to XXVI follow down to 525 B.C.

According to Steward the colonists were probably a band of Asiatic or Euphratean travelers with a very advanced scientific and mathematical knowledge, who entered Egypt and organized the erection of the Great Pyramid, on completion of which they left the country, taking their knowledge with them.

As Steward puts it, the plans for the Great Pyramid were in existence a long time before the actual construction commenced, and were the design of a single individual "who belonged to the Adamic White civilization endowed with moral, scientific and cultural attainments far in advance of all other contemporary civilizations."

Petrie substantiates this theory to the extent that he believes: "the exquisite workmanship often found in the early period (of Egyptian architecture) did not so much depend upon a large school of widespread ability, as on a few men far above their fellows." Referring to the phenomenal accuracy of the work embodied in the Great Pyramid, Petrie says, "It was limited to the skill of one man."

Recent Soviet authors postulate that the Egyptians may have come from Indonesia when their civilization was devastated some ten to twelve thousand years ago as a result of some cosmic catastrophe such as the falling of an asteroid.

According to Peter Kolosimo in *Terra Senza Tempo,* published in Milan in 1969, the Russians have recently brought to light some fascinating secrets of Egyptian archeology.

The Russians are said to have found astronomical maps of surprising correctness, with the position of the stars as they were many thousands of years ago. The Russians are also reported to have dug up several objects, many not yet identified, including crystal lenses, perfectly spherical, of great precision, possibly used as telescopes. Kolosimo says similar lenses have been found in Iraq and central Australia, but that they can only be ground today with a special abrasive made of oxide of cerium which can only be produced electrically.*

As to the actual dates of construction of the Great Pyramid, apart from the statement that it was built 300 years before the Flood, the legends add little. Egyptologists who worked out that the Fourth Dynasty must have reigned between 2720 and 2560 B.C. believe the Great Pyramid was commenced in 2644; others believe that its construction was begun in 2200 and that 30 to 56 years were required to

* Several attempts to check these data with Soviet academicians have so far been without result.

To Egyptologists Imhotep (above) was a national hero in the reign of King Zoser (below). Imhotep as designer of the stepped pyramid of Saqqara was considered not ony the world's greatest architect but a sage, magician, high priest, medical doctor, diplomat, economist, and poet.

complete it. Still others place the building of the Pyramid a thousand years earlier.

As for the method employed by the builders, the record is equally bleak. I. E. S. Edwards of the Egyptian Department of the British Museum, who spent a lifetime going over the available evidence, points out in his scholarly treatise on the pyramids written in the 1930s that little or no light is thrown on the subject by extant Egyptian records, either written or pictorial.

The result is a congeries of conflicting theories not only about when but about how the Great Pyramid was built.

Nevertheless Egyptologists are in general agreement that the first step required on the Giza plateau was to clear the sand and gravel down to bedrock, then produce a leveled base by removing protuberances and filling in depressions.

R. L. Engelbach, a pupil of Petrie, and for many years Keeper of the Cairo Museum, believes that to obtain a true level the Egyptians surrounded the four sides of the area with low banks of mud from the Nile which they filled with water and through which they cut a network of trenches. The degree of their success is attested by Cole's survey, which found the base rock of the thirteen acre perimeter to be less than 1 inch out of level.

Into the base rock a row of fine rectangular, white limestone slabs were carefully fitted as a pavement on which to lay the first row of casing stones.

When it came to drawing the first straight side, Borchardt and Lauer agree, the correct orientation must have been obtained by means of repeated observations of the rising and setting of circumpolar stars, of which the most likely was alpha Draconis.

The next step would have been to fix the large limestone corner blocks into the rock base so as to form the square corners for the laying of the first rows of casing stones.

Archeologists have had little trouble establishing that most of the limestone blocks for the construction of the Pyramid must have been obtained from the deep Mokattam quarries a few miles across the Nile on the Arabian side of the river, though many of the blocks may have been obtained directly from the Giza hills.

On some of the blocks the names of the quarry gangs were daubed in red ochre, such as "Boat Gang" or "Vigorous Gang."

The nearest source for the 70-ton granite monoliths used to protect the King's Chamber is the Aswan quarry, near Syene about 500 miles up the Nile; from there they were presumably floated downstream on a series of reed barges.

W. Emery has shown that as early as the First Dynasty

The limestone blocks with which the Pyramid is built appear to have been mostly quarried on the spot, or across the Nile in the Mokattam hills about 20 miles away, or from the Turah and Maura quarries opposite Memphis. The 22 acres of casing stones are from the same quarries.

The granite blocks for the Pyramid are believed to have come from Aswan, near the First Cataract, where they were quarried from the face of the rock about a mile from the right bank of the Nile.

Hillsides were hollowed out to provide uniform limestone blocks for the outer casing of the Pyramid.

Limestone was quarried in layers from the top down.

221

The Aswan granite quarries were 500 miles south of the Great Pyramid.

Egyptologists conjecture that in order to cut the stone blocks, the ancient Egyptians must have had some method of tempering bronze unknown in modern times. To cut and finish hieroglyphs and other ornaments would require a tool with an extremely hard-tempered edge.

Few iron tools have been found, probably because of the rapid oxidation of iron in Egypt, where the soil is especially nitrous.

the Egyptians possessed excellent copper tools, including saws and chisels, with which to cut any kind of limestone, and that their technique of working and polishing granite was developed to a truly remarkable art. As an abrasive material in their sawing operations they are believed to have used moistened quartz sand.

To quarry the rock from the hillside, the Egyptians developed a variety of systems, traces of which can still be found on the Mokattam range. Tunnels were dug several hundred feet into the rock, shelves were cut out between the roof and the block to be detached, then a line was chipped away vertically with a wooden mallet and a copper chisel, which must have been highly tempered by some method unknown today. Wedges were inserted which were moistened till they expanded to crack the rock. Sometimes fires were built along the grooved lines, and water poured on the heated stone to obtain a clear fracture.

The only historical description of the manner in which the limestone blocks were taken to the Pyramid is by Herodotus, who claims that he was informed in Egypt that it took twenty years to build the Pyramid and that levies numbering a hundred thousand men were employed for periods of three months to transport stone from the quarries. Herodotus says that to transport the rough blocks from the edge of the Nile up to the top of the Giza plateau, a great causeway was built, which required ten years to complete. The causeway was said to be 3000 feet long and 60 feet wide, of polished stone, over which sleds could pull the heavy stones.

222

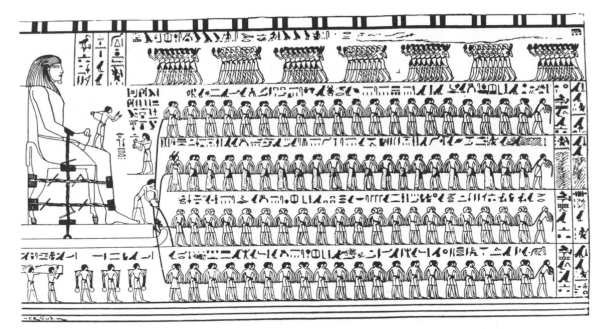

Several score Egyptians transporting a colossal statue with men harnessed in double rank. Note the timekeeper standing on the statue's knee, and a man pouring liquid on runners to decrease friction.

Commander F. M. Barber, an American naval attaché who was stationed in Egypt at the end of the last century and wrote an informed booklet entitled *Mechanical Triumphs of the Ancient Egyptians,* figured that if the causeway had to rise to a height of 120 feet above the Nile, it would have had an incline of 1 foot in 25, which he considered a very easy grade for a greased stoneway.

Barber estimated that it would take a force of 900 men harnessed in double rank on four draft ropes to drag a 60-ton monolith up such an incline. On the causeway the men would cover a space 225 feet long by 16 feet wide, which Barber considered a sufficiently compact and manageable force.

Barber says that such a force would have no trouble dragging the stone, especially if they were drilled to pull together; he concludes that for this reason men and not animals are pictured hauling wrought stones: men could be drilled to march in absolute cadence to a song or time-keeping instrument. A "one-two-three, surge," says Barber, produces a momentary force represented by nearly the weight of the whole mass of men, or several times their ordinary pulling force. Also, vacancies in the ranks caused by sickness could be filled without materially affecting the drill of the remainder. Cattle could never be so well organized.

Pictures show Egyptians hauling stone in the manner described by Barber and include a special artisan pouring some sort of grease on the sled runners to reduce friction.

223

Other Egyptologists have suggested that owing to the great quantity of supplies necessary for building Cheops' pyramid, it was likely that several ramps led from the valley up to the Giza plateau, but very few remains of such possible causeways can now be observed because of modern excavations and the widespread tourist layout.

According to the French scholar E. Amélineau, considerable remains of an inclined plane leading to the pyramid of Kephren still existed at the end of the eighteenth century; and remains of a causeway leading to the pyramid of Mykerinos are still visible today.

The Egyptian archeologist Selim Hassan says that at the edge of the Giza plateau there is a considerable surface composed of large limestone blocks which run in a northeasterly direction and descend to a little less than half the height of the plateau. He believes they may have been part of a construction ramp which was demolished when the Great Pyramid was completed.

Causeway to the pyramid of Kephren.

W. W. Lucker's reconstruction of a pyramid and its causeway to the Nile.

Ahmed Fakhry, another Egyptian archeologist, says that remains of a southern supply ramp composed of rubble mixed with mud still exists a short distance from the south side of the main causeway.

As to how the Great Pyramid was actually constructed, there are differing opinions among Egyptologists. Herodotus reported that the upper portion of the Pyramid was finished first, then the middle, and finally the part nearest the ground. This has been interpreted as meaning that the finished outer casing stones were placed in position against the nucleus starting from the top, presumably by means of a ramp that was removed as the builders worked downward; this would have required four ramps, one against each face.

Herodotus maintains the casing blocks were lifted from the ground, step by step, on pieces of wood, with a machine

225

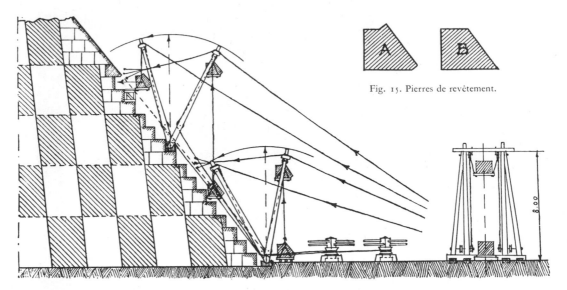

Fig. 15. Pierres de revêtement.

Machine for raising casing stones, as described by Herodotus and reconstructed by H. Straub-Roessler.

A and B are Lauer's indication of how casing stones may have been fitted.

which he does not adequately describe. Cotsworth figures that if the stones had had to be rocked to the top as reported by Herodotus, it would have taken about a month to get each of the final ones up to the summit.

Barber maintains that steel cranes or derricks would have been required to swing such great stones as are found in the Pyramid, and that for lack of such equipment the Egyptians would have had to construct a ramp in order to raise the heavy stones to the required level. Remains of such ramps have been found at the pyramid of Amenemhet at Lisht and also at Medûm. Aerial photographs indicate substantial remains of ramps under the sand at Dashur.

Petrie thinks the casing stones were placed in position at the same time as the core, starting from the bottom and going up course by course. He estimates that about 500 blocks were brought over from the quarries each day and laid in place. As the lower courses contain as many as 50,000 blocks, it would have taken over three months to lay each of these courses.

Petrie says the transporting was done during the three months of inundation, when a vast labor force was available and when advantage could be taken of the flood waters to float the blocks from the quarries downstream and across five miles of swollen Nile. Petrie suggests that even if no more than eight men could work together on an average block of 40 cubic feet weighing about 2 1/2 tons, they could have transported ten such blocks to the Pyramid in three months, taking two weeks to bring the blocks down the causeway from the quarry, a day or two with good wind to ferry the blocks down the Nile, and six weeks to raise them

226

to the required position on the Pyramid. By November the men would be at liberty to return to their usual occupations when the land was again accessible.

Petrie estimated the Great Pyramid to contain about 2,300,000 stones weighing 2 1/2 tons apiece and averaging 50 × 50 × 28 inches. If eight men could bring ten stones in three months, 100,000 men could bring 125,000 stones each season, or the required total in the twenty years reported by Herodotus.

Edwards says there can be little doubt that in addition to the 100,000 men levied for the purpose of transporting the blocks to the Pyramid, many others were engaged in building the Pyramid. These men, says Edwards, consisted of skilled masons and an attendant body of laborers, continually employed throughout the year preparing and laying the blocks and erecting or dismantling the ramps. Presumably these workers could have been housed in the buildings found

Aerial photograph showing ramp under the sand leading to the pyramid of Dashur.

227

Romanticized modern drawing of barges being rowed down the Nile toward the Giza pyramids.

by Petrie west of Kephren's pyramid, where about 4000 at a time could have lived in barracks.

Petrie figures that 40,000 skilled workers living permanently on the spot could easily cut and finish the 120,000 blocks needed each year; a party of four men would have a whole month to handle each block.

Petrie believes the masons finished and laid the casing and some of the core masonry, course by course, on the ground, before raising them. He found horizontal lines carved on the casing stones and on the core stones showing just how they were to be fitted. He believes that skilled masons planned all the work throughout the year and that at flood time gangs of unskilled workmen raised the finished stones to their indicated positions.

Petrie says the casing stones were dressed by very fine picking or adzing and were moved into position from the *inside,* whereas the core was filled in afterward.

Maragioglio and Rinaldi, two Italian scholars who recently made extensive measurements of the pyramids of Giza

228

which they incorporated into four carefully illustrated quarto volumes entitled *L'Architettura delle Piramidi Menefite,* agree that the casing and the nucleus were built up at the same time; they think the casing blocks were slid into place by means of a thin layer of very liquid mortar that served as a lubricant as well as a filler and binder; they also think the casing blocks were levered into position from the back and sides so as not to show marks or chips on the front.

Ballard believes it would have been impossible to place the finished blocks without damaging their fine edges; he thinks the roughly scabbed blocks were put in place and finished off with the aid of templates.

In support of Petrie, I. E. S. Edwards points out that because the lowest course of casing stones lies on the smooth pavement of Turah limestone which projects a couple of feet beyond the Pyramid base, it would have been impossible to lay the casing stones from the *outer* side without damaging the fringe of the pavement which was to remain exposed; nor could they have been dressed *after* being put in position without damaging the pavement.

The fact that some of the limestone slabs of the foundation pavement are seen to be laid *beneath* the nucleus blocks also indicates the nucleus was filled in after the casing blocks had been placed in position.

Petrie believes the casing blocks were placed side by side on the ground and worked so that the back, sides and bottom would fit perfectly when put in place. The only thing left to do on the spot would have been the leveling of the upper faces.

According to the architect Rex Engelbach and the engineer Somers Clarke, authors of *Ancient Egyptian Masonry,* in order to render the sides of the casing blocks perfectly equal they were placed side by side in the yard and a saw was passed between them. However, Maragioglio and Rinaldi could find no trace of saw marks on the vertical sides of any of the remaining blocks.

Petrie claimed to have found traces of red ochre on some of the stone faces which had not been perfectly dressed. From this he deduced that the dressing was done by degrees —as a dentist shapes a tooth—the control being made with facing plates covered with ochre.

In any case, the arrangement of casing blocks must have been worked out in detail well in advance of placement so as to assure a variance in the width and height of the backing stones from level to level, so as to prevent the vertical joints from coinciding.

All the stones presently visible in the Pyramid are backing stones specially cut to dovetail and fit behind the outer casing. They are well dressed and squared, but made with fossilized limestone instead of the pure white.

Behind them the nucleus consists of less well-dressed and roughly faced blocks of greatly varying sizes, for easier construction, and to insure that break joints did not coincide in either sense. They are held together by a mortar composed of sand, lime and crushed red pottery, which gives it a slightly pinkish color.

Maragioglio and Rinaldi attribute the concavity of the sides of the visible backing blocks to a means of preventing the facing courses from sliding, especially in the middle, by wedging the backing stones together at the center. On the north side the concavity has been measured as .94 meter. Maragioglio and Rinaldi believe the casing faces may also have been slightly concave, if only for esthetic reasons, as the optic aberration would thus be corrected, the Pyramid edges would appear sharper, the faces flatter; also,

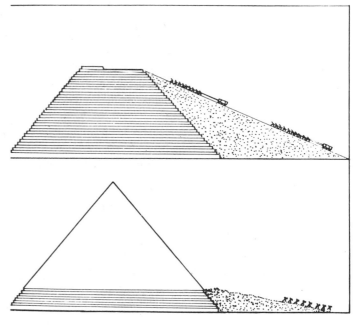

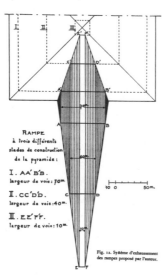

Lauer's idea of how the ramp would grow wider and narrower.

Various methods of building ramps.

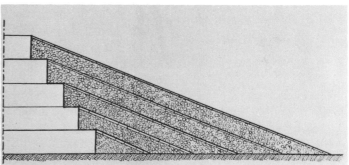

any errors in dressing the faces could be more easily distinguished.

Slight variations in the angle of the outer faces of casing fragments found in the rubble at the Pyramid's base may be explained by such a surface concavity.

To raise each course of casing stones and nucleus all the way up the Pyramid, Petrie believes a ramp was constructed against one face, and he estimates that its volume would have had to be at least equivalent to that of the Pyramid itself.

Barber points out that to carry an inclined plane to the top of the Pyramid at a grade of one in ten, it would have been necessary to start the ramp 6000 feet away in the Nile valley at a point over 1600 feet before the commencement of Herodotus' causeway. Furthermore, says Barber, there would always have been four times as much work to do on the inclined plane as on the Pyramid.

In order to carry the ramp to the top of the Pyramid, Barber estimates that some 75,000,000 cubic feet of Nile bricks would have been necessary, or four times the number of cubic feet of stone still required to finish the Pyramid. With each additional course of masonry the ramp would grow higher and longer, but it would also grow narrower as the Pyramid narrowed at the top. According to Pliny such ramps were composed of niter and salt which could later be dissolved with water, but the idea seems fanciful as it would have required an ocean.

In *Natural History* of November, 1970, Olaf Tellefsen, an engineer, suggests that the Great Pyramid could have been erected with only a few thousand men using a simple piece of machinery consisting of a sturdy wooden arm balanced with counterweights on a fulcrum fixed to wooden skids— much like the machine drawn by the German engineer L. Croon.

This, says Tellefsen, would have done away with the need

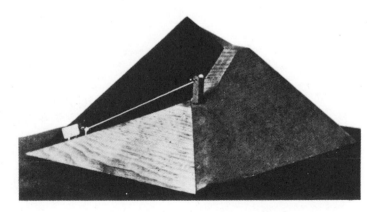

for huge ramps postulated by Egyptologists on the basis of archaeological remains. According to Tellefsen, there was not enough manpower in ancient Egypt to build such ramps beyond the halfway mark of the Pyramid. Egyptologists countered, a little acidly, that from that point on the ramps narrowed rapidly, and that there appeared to be little evidence for Tellefsen's contention.

Cotsworth believes the Egyptians used a more ingenious system for raising the stones by taking advantage of the building itself as a ramp, dragging the stones up the Pyramid's own spiraling outer wall. This would enable the builders to fill in the core as they went up and finish the casing as they came down. Cotsworth says he watched a modern Egyptian peasant build a pigeon house by just this method.

The system has the added advantage that if the south wall of the Pyramid were completed first, the rest of the work could have been carried out in its shade rather than in the broiling sun.

But with or without the broiling sun, if one takes into account the problems of quarrying, roughing out, transporting over two million core stones, and finishing some 115,000 enormous casing stones to a precision of 1/100 inch, then raising, manipulating and mortaring them into their correct

place in a unified polished structure, one must agree with Antoniadi that the mind boggles at the enormity of the effort.

According to Barber's well-trained naval mind, it must have required the organizing capacity of a genius to plan all the work, to lay it out, to provide for emergencies and accidents, to see that the men in the quarries, on the boats and sleds, and in the masons' and smithies' shops were all continuously and usefully employed, that the means of transportation was ample, that the commissariat did not fail, that the water supply was ample and conveniently disposed, and that the sick reliefs were on hand.

Barber points out that public works were essential to keep this population employed and fed during the floods. August Mencken presumes that no less than 150,000 women and children also had to be housed, fed, and policed in nearby settlements. Judging from the texts and the paintings dealing with the subject of forced labor, Barber figures a large portion of the duty of the standing army of 400,000 men must have been that of guards.

Cotsworth says that in the rainless climate of Egypt no housing was needed for the natives who were accustomed to surviving on grain and water, and that the desert provides better sanitation than was available in Victorian England.

The waste chips of the masons were thrown over the

In 1950 the Museum of Science in Boston built a model to the scale of 1:120 showing how they believed the pyramids of Giza to have been constructed with slanting side ramps, three up and one down.

Dows Durham, curator of Egyptian art at the Museum of Fine Arts in Boston, responsible for the technical details, disagreed with the theory of long ramps because every time the building rose a few feet the ramp would become unusable until it was raised and extended.

Durham conceived the side ramps as being about 10 feet wide, or sufficient to handle a sledge with a double row of men to drag the stones over wet timbers for reducing friction. However, turning the corners would not have been easy.

233

cliffs of the Giza hill on both the north and the south sides, where they formed banks stretching out a hundred yards, occupying a space almost half the bulk of the Pyramid. The slopes formed an angle of rest of about 40°, showing the different qualities of refuse thrown away on different days, varying from large chips to mere sweepings.

In pits which had recently been made in part of the heap close to the edge of the cliff, Petrie noted layers of desert flint and sand showing when a piece of desert ground had been cleared to get more space for working. Among the rubbish he found pieces of workmen's water jars and food vessels, chips of wood and charcoal, and even a piece of ancient string.*

The only report on the daily cost of building the Pyramid is given by Herodotus, who says that an interpreter told him the daily sum spent on radishes, onions and garlic for the workmen was inscribed in Egyptian characters on the base of the Pyramid. But the report sounds apocryphal, as does the one passed on by Herodotus to the effect that Cheops became so broke during the operation that he prostituted his daughter by placing her in a chamber and charging each visitor the equivalent of a finished limestone block for her favors.

Kingsland figured that to position an estimated 2,300,000 blocks in a period of 20 years, or 7300 workdays, would have meant placing 315 stones each day, or 26 stones an hour working 12 hours a day.

Mencken, who has such disdain for the mathematical and astronomical knowledge of the ancient Egyptians, considers it remarkable that they were able to solve some of their problems of construction unless they had "more knowledge, better instruments, and far more ingenuity than is generally believed."

Kingsland wonders what means of illumination the Egyptians used while digging down to the subterranean pit and what method they used for getting air to the diggers. He finds it difficult to resist the conclusion that the Egyptians must have had tools and appliances of which we are totally ignorant, and must have employed methods which today would be termed occult.

Some of their solutions may have been no more arcane than Lockyer's suggestion that with one movable mirror and several fixed ones, sunlight could have been reflected to any part of the interior of the Pyramid.

Though legend attributes to the priests of Heliopolis the

* It would be helpful if more fragments could be excavated and carbon-tested.

234

knack of being able to cause tempests and levitate rocks that a thousand men could not move, most Egyptologists argue strenuously against the possibility of sophisticated instruments such as laser beams for cutting surfaces, or ground-effect or antigravity machines for raising weights, insisting that the job was accomplished with nothing but primitive appliances and unlimited manpower. Nevertheless the conscientiously academic Edwards fudges the issue by saying: "Cheops, who may have been a megalomaniac, could never, during a reign of about twenty-three years, have erected a building of the size and durability of the Great Pyramid if technical advances had not enabled his masons to handle stones of very considerable weight and dimensions."

Petrie is more specific and gives substance to the hypothesis of unknown methods, pointing out that in the pyramid of Kephren there is a granite portcullis weighing about 2 tons which is in such a position in a narrow passage that only 6 or 8 men could work on it at once. As it would take a force of 40 to 60 men to manipulate such as a mass, Petrie concludes that the Egyptians must have had some more efficient means which remains unknown to us.

Although the Danish engineer Tons Brunés has demonstrated how a block as large as the beams of the King's Chamber could be comfortably raised by a single man with the dexterous use of balancing and wedges, Petrie is convinced that ancient builders possessed some more efficient means of raising and setting stones than mere rollers, levers, ramps and manual hauling.

But perhaps the most puzzling riddle of the Pyramid, requiring an intellectual game of detection, is the one constituted by the three granite plugs wedged into the end of the Ascending Passage.

XIX. WHY WERE THE PYRAMID PASSAGES PLUGGED? WHEN? AND HOW?

Most Egyptologists conclude that the Pyramid was built as a tomb for some Pharaoh, presumably Cheops. Any mathematical, religious or prophetic theories about the structure they consider to be fanciful, or, at best, coincidental. To Egyptologists the corridors of the Great Pyramid were designed solely as a means of transporting the coffin of the dead Pharaoh to his sarcophagus in the burial chamber, as a means of exiting after the entombment, or as blinds to lead grave robbers away from a hidden chamber.

No other reason is offered for piling up so massive a mound of masonry than to protect the dead Pharaoh from the attention of grave robbers. Oddly, this is the single function which neither the Great Pyramid, nor any of the others, managed to fulfill, there being no reliable report of any body having been found in any of the pyramids, only some fragments of bones whose dates are uncertain.

Even the "unplundered" tomb of Cheops' mother, Hetepheres, found in 1925 by the Harvard-Boston Expedition at the bottom of an 85-foot-deep shaft filled with rubble, appeared untouched in 5000 years: yet the sarcophagus was empty and is presumed to have been so placed within the "burial" chamber.

According to the Egyptologists, who include such eminent figures as Petrie and Borchardt, once the body of a Pharaoh had been laid to rest in the Great Pyramid and the burial party had made its exit, the three huge granite blocks, plus several limestone ones, were allowed to slide down the incline between the ramps of the Grand Gallery till they had completely plugged the Ascending Passage.

Whether the tripping mechanism could have been operated by remote control from a safe distance below the plugged entrance, or whether the technicians responsible for the tripping device were immured for life, or whether they managed to make their escape down what is known as the "well" are theories supported in different degrees by different Egyptologists.

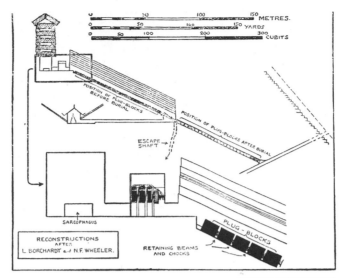

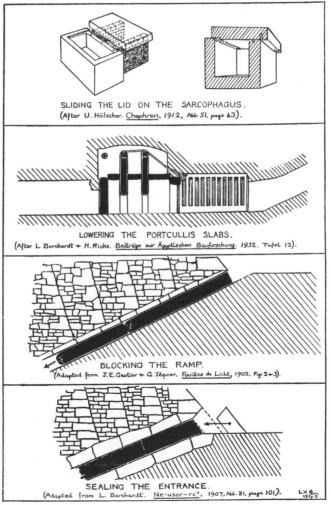

Method of plugging the Ascending Passage as visualized by Cottrell from the ideas of Borchardt and Wheeler.

Ideas of various Egyptologists of the methods of plugging passages, lowering portcullises and sealing sarcophagi.

RECONSTRUCTIONS AFTER L. BORCHARDT and N.F. WHEELER.

SLIDING THE LID ON THE SARCOPHAGUS.
(After U. Hölscher. *Chephren*, 1912, Abb. 51, page 63).

LOWERING THE PORTCULLIS SLABS.
(After L. Borchardt + H. Ricke. *Beiträge zur Ägyptischen Bauforschung*. 1932. Tafel 12).

BLOCKING THE RAMP.
(Adapted from J.E. Gautier + G. Jéquier. *Fouilles de Licht*, 1902. Figs 2+3).

SEALING THE ENTRANCE.
(Adapted from L. Borchardt. *Ne-user-re'*, 1907, Abb. 81, page 101).

237

Modern illustration of the granite plugs in the Grand Gallery.

To account for the three granite plugs and the peculiar arrangement of the Pyramid's passages and chambers, Borchardt put forward the theory that the builders started with one plan, but kept changing it as they went along.

Borchardt believes the "original" intention was to bury the dead Pharaoh in the pit carved out of natural rock at the bottom of the Descending Passage, but that this plan was changed. For some unspecified reason, says Borchardt, it was decided to bury the king higher in the body of the Pyramid, which was already several courses high. The pit was therefore left unfinished. An Ascending Passage was carved up through the already laid courses of masonry, and continued as a new passage up to the level of the Queen's Chamber.

While making a careful study of the walls of the Ascending Passage, Borchardt observed that the stones at the lower end were laid approximately parallel with the ground, whereas nearly all those at the upper end were parallel to the gradient of the corridor. From this he deduced that the Pyramid must have already reached a level corresponding to halfway up the as yet nonexistent Ascending Passage before it was decided to use an upper chamber; at that point the Ascending Passage was dug up through the existing level courses; thereafter it was built with blocks parallel to its slope.

Arrangement of girdle stones 10 cubits apart, to tie the Ascending Passage to body of Pyramid, as drawn by Adam Rutherford, director of the Institute of Pyramidology in Great Britain.

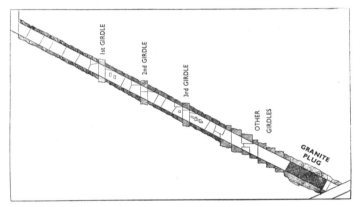

Borchardt's theory is supported by Leonard Cottrell, author of a popular book on the pyramids, *Mountains of Pharaoh,* who suggests that when the builders switched plan they got as far as the Queen's Chamber complete with its air channels before they again changed their minds.

Cottrell says a third scheme brought with it the decision to heighten the Ascending Passage into "the magnificently corbeled Grand Gallery," extending it another 160 feet so as to build yet a third chamber, the King's, as the final resting place for the Pharaoh's body.

According to Cottrell, the change came about as a sort of afterthought, while the great mass of builders was already in the midst of constructing a building whose base and slopes appeared to have been worked out with such extraordinary precision.

Why the Grand Gallery should have been raised to 28 feet, when less than half that height would have been ample for the bearers and for the storage of the plugs, was not explained by Cottrell.

239

Borchardt and Cottrell's theory was disputed by Maragioglio and Rinaldi, who point out that the bottom of the Ascending Passage was *intentionally* cut through the lower courses simply as a means of anchoring it to the body of the Pyramid. The Italians say the lower part of the Passage was not dug out of normal masonry or with normal methods, but in masonry especially erected to anchor the end of the Passage, many of the blocks being exceptionally large, laid flat, vertical and edgewise, and of a different quality from the rest of the nucleus, with joints very thin and finely finished; whereas in other areas where the regular nucleus masonry is visible, the joints are wide and coarse.

The object, say Maragioglio and Rinaldi, was to create a bulwark at the juncture of the Ascending and Descending Passages so that the ceiling and floor of the Ascending Passage would not thrust down on the empty space of the Descending Passage. The Italians point out that several monolithic girdle stones are employed at 10-cubit intervals all the way up the Ascending Passage to reinforce its bond with the nucleus of the Pyramid, and prevent its slipping, but that no such girdle stones appear in the Descending Passage, where they are not needed because the whole passage rests against the solid rock of the Giza hill.

Borchardt produced a further refinement to his theory, which not only found few supporters, even among his fellow Egyptologists, but tended to discredit his whole approach to the problem: namely, that the granite and limestone plugs which filled the Ascending Passage could not have been stored on the Grand Gallery floor between the ramps, because they would have provided an "undignified obstacle" for the funeral train to clamber over. As the plugs were too large to be brought in or out of either the Queen's Chamber or the King's, Borchardt theorized that the blocks were raised onto a wooden platform which was fitted into the grooves which appear halfway up the walls of the Gallery.

This would have allowed the funeral cortege to move beneath them; though how this would have been any less undignified than having to crawl up the low and narrow Ascending Passage is not explained, nor is it explained how the heavy blocks were brought down from the level of the wooden planking to the level of the pavement on which they were to slide.

That Borchardt's hypothesis is unreasonable, say Maragioglio and Rinaldi, is evident from the fact that few archeologists have paid much attention to it.

As for the method of triggering the plugs down the Ascending Passage, Cottrell believes the notches in the

Borchardt's fanciful idea of pallbearers reaching the Great Step at the top of the Grand Gallery, with plug stones supported on a platform above them.

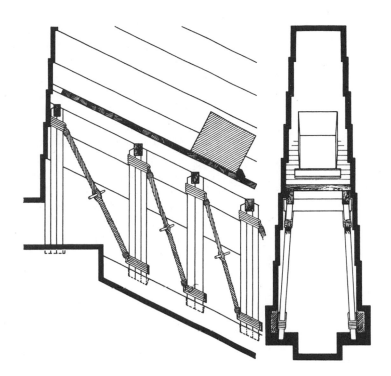

Trestle believed by Borchardt to have raised plug stones to a level half the height of the Grand Gallery.

Goyon's idea of how granite and limestone plugs were held in place by crossbeams fitted into the ramps.

ramp of the Grand Gallery were cut to hold cross beams of wood or limestone to keep each of the massive plugs from prematurely sliding. According to Cottrell, once the funeral cortege had passed, operators standing on the ramps could have released each plug, starting with the bottom one, and allowed them to slide into the Ascending Passage, on the theory that had they all been released simultaneously the momentum and the total weight might have caused damage at the lower end.

The theory raises the question as to what became of the wooden or limestone crosspieces. Had they been made of wood they might conceivably have pulverized and completely disintegrated in the thousands of intervening years. They might also have been carried down the well by the escaping operators, though this would have been something of an ordeal, if indeed possible. The material might also have long since been disposed of by grave robbers. Still, the question is puzzling. Also, why go to all the trouble of plugging the Ascending Passage, only to leave the well shaft as a perfectly simple way for thieves to climb back up to the Grand Gallery? The lower end of the well shaft could have been cleverly concealed; but its whole length could hardly have been plugged or made impassable with fill *after* it had been used as a means of escape.

Part or all of the *Descending* Passage could have been

241

plugged and the Pyramid sealed. This would have been the simplest way conclusively to close up *all* the chambers in the Pyramid, making it an almost superhuman job to chisel out 350 feet of solid limestone.

Petrie disputes the notion that the long Descending Passage could have been filled with blocks; and Maragioglio and Rinaldi suggest that traces of the dismantling of such plugs would have been left on the walls of the Descending Passage, which is not the case, with the exception of a few feet beyond the entrance.

The most sophisticated refutation of the theory holds that the Descending Passage may have been purposely left empty and the pit unfinished as a blind to lead any robber who entered by the trap door to believe that no king had been buried in the Pyramid!

As for the well shaft, Maragioglio and Rinaldi have a completely different theory about its function. They do not think it was ever designed as an escape route; they think it was built in from the early stages as a service shaft and to bring air to the lower end of the Descending Passage.

The Italians say the need which led to the building of such a shaft may have arisen shortly after the beginning of the Ascending Passage, most likely as a means of ventilating the lower shaft. They believe the diggers at the bottom of the Descending Passage had difficulty breathing. Plausible at first sight, the theory is open to two objections: as the building went up course by course, above the level of the rock base, there would have been all the air in the world; whereas digging the well shaft *below* rock level, the diggers would have been as cramped and airless digging the well shaft as digging the Descending Passage, at least until the two met at the bottom—by which time the well would no longer have served its ventilating purpose, the digging having been completed.

Such an air vent might conceivably have been useful to bring air to the pit, had the pit been used for any continuing purpose, such as observing the stars.

The Italians also believe that long before any funeral party entered the Grand Gallery, the entire well shaft was filled from the top with debris and loose material. The bottom entrance was then carefully camouflaged, and a stone was mortared into the upper end in the west ramp of the Grand Gallery to seal and hide the shaft from the top. They cite the fact that from classic times till the nineteenth century no one appears to have spotted the bottom entrance to the well shaft.

Maragioglio and Rinaldi agree with Petrie that the Pyramid was violated by thieves or grave robbers soon after it was finished, during the civil wars, which they date between 2270 and 2100 B.C. At this point the theory of the Italians becomes radical. They maintain it was these early despoilers of the Pyramid and not Al Mamun who cut a hole around the granite plugs at the end of the Ascending Passage. These thieves then worked their way up the Ascending Passage, broke through the lowered portcullis, and entered the "crypt." According to the Italians it was these or successive thieves who found the well shaft by noting a difference in the stones at the bottom of the ramp in the Grand Gallery, which they forced in order to clear out the well shaft in search of treasure. The Italians maintain that the marks in the west ramp around the missing stone appear to have been made with a chisel struck from above. They say it would also have been extremely difficult to remove the stone from below in the very restricted passage which leads to the head of the well shaft.

To explain the way the Ascending Passage was plugged, the Italians maintain the tripping mechanism could have been operated by remote control. They point out that it has recently been discovered that in the bent pyramid of Sneferu, the blocks of granite which plug the Descending Passage could *only* have been moved by gravity and not directly levered by workmen, because there *is* no escape route.

The Italians believe the plugs in the Great Pyramid were slid on liquid mortar and that its forced accumulation accounts for the 10 centimeters of empty space between the first and the second granite plug; though they offer no explanation as to what may have become of the mortar, which could hardly have volatilized in the meantime, unless it was some sort of oil and not mortar.

It is also hard to imagine how the antique grave robbers could have immediately found the exact spot halfway down the Descending Passage from which to dig up past the granite plugs if there is any truth in the story of the plug being covered by a prismatic block.

Maragioglio and Rinaldi suggest there was no such block; paradoxically they give credence to the story that Al Mamun's workers heard a heavy block fall—simply because Al Mamun's passage takes a sudden turn to the east in order to break into the Descending Passage.

Another theory which attempts to account for what could have taken place in the plugging of the Pyramid was produced in 1963 by August Mencken, the engineer from Baltimore who has so little regard for the scientific knowledge of the ancient Egyptians. According to Mencken's somewhat farfetched reconstruction of events, when the Great Pyramid had been built up above the ridge of the roof of the King's Chamber, and work was still going on in the Grand Gallery and in the Antechamber, the structure was suddenly shaken by a severe earthquake. It was then, says Mencken, that the ceiling beams of the King's Chamber were cracked, the fissures opened, and, "to the terror of the builders, the triggering device which held the plugs on the floor of the Grand Gallery was sprung and the blocks slid down the Ascending Passage, blocking all exit from the Pyramid."

According to Mencken, the men inside were trapped, but their plight was not desperate. "As soon as the fright and confusion caused by the earthquake had subsided, the men on the outside discovered what had happened to the men on the inside and opened communication with them through the air ducts leading out from the King's Chamber. By the same ducts the trapped men were supplied with food and water."

Mencken figures that to have chipped out the three granite plugs in the restricted space of the Ascending Passage was out of the question, and that to have tunneled around them would have caused irreparable damage to the passageways. Rather than chip out the granite blocks, the Egyptians, says Mencken, decided to dig the well up from the bottom of the Descending Passage all the way to the end of the Grand Gallery.

The trapped men, says Mencken, were informed of what was being done, "and by the time the tunnel reached the opening in the Gallery they had removed the ramp stone." According to this theory an inspection crew was sent to ascertain the damage and examine the King's Chamber ceiling; for this purpose the small tunnel, later known as Davison's, was dug straight through the lowest of the cushioning chambers.

The plugging of the Ascending Passage, says Mencken, put an abrupt stop to all other interior work and made it impossible for the King's Chamber to be used for a burial, either real or token. "So everything above the plug blocks was abandoned and thus ended the first and only attempt of the ancient Egyptians to build elevated chambers."

In criticism of Mencken's theory it may be asked why, if the building had been constructed to just beyond the peak of the King's Chamber, would it not have been easier to remove several blocks from the upper tiers in order to reach the trapped men rather than go through the trouble of boring hundreds of feet up the whole length of the well? Also, if the builders had no further use for the interior of the building, why go to the effort of finishing off the Pyramid and casing it with 22 acres of finely polished limestone?

An entirely different solution to the problem is provided by David Davidson, the structural engineer from Leeds. According to Davidson, the depth and width of the granite plugs which seal the lower end of the Ascending Passage clearly indicate that the plugs must have been built into the passage *at the time the Pyramid masonry had reached the height of the plugs, or 17 courses.*

Davidson, who spent several months in Egypt studying the Pyramid closely, says the half-inch clearance at the sides of the top of the Ascending Passage would *not* be sufficient to insure the granite plugs being slid from the Grand Gallery without jamming.

This raises the question as to why the builders would have bothered to even build the Ascending Passage if they intended to plug it up immediately with three large granite plugs.

Davidson answers that the inside of the Pyramid was not designed for contemporary use, but was intended to be discovered by people of a much later civilization, rather like our modern time capsules, and that the discoverers would have to break their way in through the series of limestone plugs, much as Al Mamun is reputed to have done.

This raises the question of the presence of the well shaft, which could have led any intrepid explorer straight to the Grand Gallery, bypassing the Ascending Passage. Davidson answers that the well was an afterthought, not planned in the beginning as an escape route after a burial, if for no other reason than because the Pyramid was never intended as a tomb.

Davidson has an ingenious reconstruction of what may have occurred. He maintains that some time not long after the completion of the Pyramid, an earthquake or several disasters severely shook the building. After the disaster the priests or guardians of the Pyramid noted certain subsidence effects on the external surface of the structure, and they decided they must investigate the interior to see if the King's Chamber had collapsed or been badly damaged.

Davidson says this must have happened within a few generations of the completion of the construction, and before precise details and measurements of the internal construction had been lost.

The keepers, says Davidson, entered the Descending Passage and instead of trying to carve their way up through a score or more of limestone plugs in the Ascending Passage, as was later to be done by Al Mamun, they went nearly to the bottom of the Descending Passage and then began to bore a hole upward toward the beginning of the Grand Gallery.

245

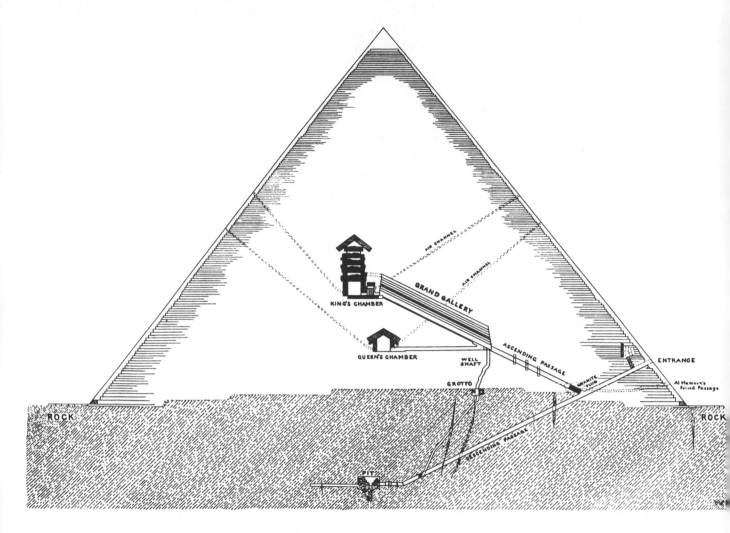

Labels in image: AIR CHANNEL, AIR CHANNEL, GRAND GALLERY, KING'S CHAMBER, QUEEN'S CHAMBER, WELL SHAFT, ENTRANCE, ASCENDING PASSAGE, GRANITE PLUG, Al Mamoun's Forced Passage, GROTTO, DESCENDING PASSAGE, PIT, ROCK, ROCK

Davidson's rendition of the Great Pyramid passages, showing three large fissures in the natural rock.

Their reason for starting so far down, says Davidson, instead of taking a shorter route past the plugged Ascending Passage, was to cut their way through, and carefully observe, two large fissures that had appeared in the bedrock. A third fissure, present at the time of construction, had already been shored up by the builders.

The problem of the priests, says Davidson, was to determine if the fissuring was severe enough to cause further subsidence.

Digging in a gradual upward slope, says Davidson, the keepers worked their way through both fissures, finding them in not as bad condition as they had expected. At the level of the Grotto the keepers made a staging area for tools, for rest, and for the bypassing of workers and material.

From the Grotto they continued their shaft up toward the commencement of the Grand Gallery. Having somehow made an accurate survey of exactly where they were, they

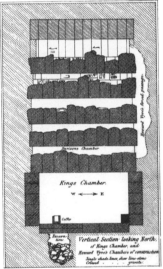

Davidson's rendering of the way the chambers in the Pyramid are aligned just east of the main east-west axis.

then bored straight up and came out beneath the lowest ramp stone on the west side of the Gallery. To Davidson it is clear from the fractured appearance of the ramp around the well entrance that the stone was forced upward and outward.

To accomplish such a feat of accurate digging would have meant knowing the precise internal arrangement and measurements of the Pyramid. Anyone boring blindly could have missed the few feet of Grand Gallery and been obliged to bore several hundred more feet through the limestone courses before coming out into daylight. This goes a long way toward discounting the possibility of the well shaft having been dug by either thieves or explorers.

Once they had reached the Grand Gallery, says Davidson, the keepers dismantled the lower section of the Gallery floor for a dozen or so feet and uncovered the passage to the Queen's Chamber. This they inspected carefully, but found little or no sign of failure.

Proceeding to the King's Chamber, the keepers found indications of possible instability due to the movement. Inside the chamber they found the ceiling beams uniformly cracked along the south ends.

According to Davidson, it was then that the keepers smeared the fractures and open joints with cement and plaster. Petrie was later to report that he had found cement daubed on with fingers for about 5 feet on each side of the joints.

When Petrie carefully examined the King's Chamber he discovered that it had been badly shaken, probably by an earthquake, which caused the whole room to expand

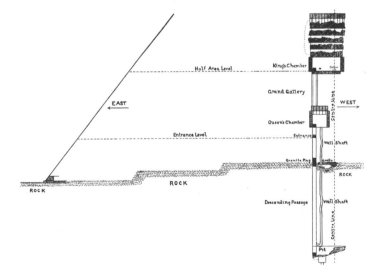

247

Cracks in granite beams at the south end of the King's Chamber.

an inch or so. Every single beam had been wrenched more or less loose from the south end, and cracked through; the whole ceiling, weighing some 4000 tons, was held up solely by "sticking and thrusting." As Petrie summed up the situation, the downfall of the King's Chamber "is a mere question of time and earthquakes." What has saved it so far was not being bonded to the main structure.

Davidson says the five construction chambers were especially designed to take a considerable impact. Instead of resting the uppermost beams on a hard granite wall, the builders rested them on limestone, which could more easily crush and flow in case of subsidence, taking the strain off the lower rows of rafters and keeping the walls of the King's Chamber intact. Davidson says that a more rigid design, uniform from the lowest to the highest chamber, would have been disastrous.

248

To permit this buffer effect being fully developed, the rafters of the chambers were not tied into the east and west walls. Instead, two immense limestone walls, wholly outside of, and independent of all the granite floors and supporting blocks, were built on the east and west sides. As Petrie put it: "Between these great walls all the chambers stand, unbonded and capable of yielding freely to settlement."

To gain access to these important construction chambers above the King's Chamber, the keepers, says Davidson, next drove an opening into the east wall of the Gallery, starting at its upper, or south, end.

In support of the theory that this hole was bored by keepers who were precisely acquainted with the layout of the Pyramid (rather than by later explorers or thieves), Davidson points out that the hole is bored in exactly the right place, and takes off at the precise angle and direction to reach the lowest of the upper chambers.

Once inside the first chamber (later to become known as Davidson's), the Pyramid keepers, says Davidson, found that the indications of instability were not so serious as they had feared. The great granite beams were indeed cracked, but the damage did not seem to be enough to cause any further crumbling or subsidence, nor warrant their boring any higher into the overlaying chambers. Instead, the keepers again daubed the cracks with plaster so as to be able to return at a later date and observe if any further movement had taken place.

According to Davidson, the keepers then climbed back down the well, the bottom end of which they camouflaged, and left by the swivel-stone entrance on the north face.

There is nothing inherently illogical about this version of events. It would have been no easy job to tunnel upward through the solid rock and the various courses of masonry—altogether hundreds of tons of material would have had to be chipped away and taken out of the Pyramid up the Descending Passage—but it would not have been impossible.

It would also have been a problem to get light and air to the men doing the chiseling, and it would have been tricky to raise a platform or system of suspension while chiseling upward; also it would have been a nuisance to have the fragments fall constantly in the face of the chiselers and those below them; but all of this would not have been impossible.

What militates against this theory is the observation of Maragioglio and Rinaldi that the walls of the well shaft upward from the Grotto are built and lined with regular blocks of limestone, apparently as a feature of the original structure.

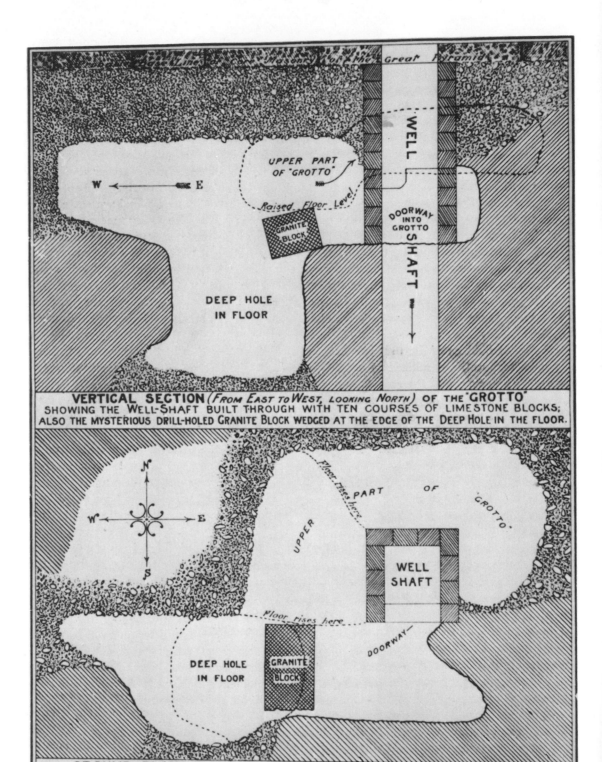

VERTICAL SECTION *(From East to West, Looking North)* OF THE "GROTTO"
SHOWING THE WELL-SHAFT BUILT THROUGH WITH TEN COURSES OF LIMESTONE BLOCKS;
ALSO THE MYSTERIOUS DRILL-HOLED GRANITE BLOCK WEDGED AT THE EDGE OF THE DEEP HOLE IN THE FLOOR.

GROUND PLAN OF THE "GROTTO" IN THE GREAT PYRAMID OF GIZEH
SHOWING THE POSITION OF THE WELL SHAFT, THE GRANITE BLOCK, AND THE DEEP HOLE IN THE FLOOR.
SINGLE SHADED LINES INDICATE NATURAL ROCK.

Grotto showing walls of the well shaft built out of masonry from the level of the Grotto to the first course of masonry of the Pyramid.

Conceivably these walls could have been lined by the keepers, operating from the Grotto, perhaps to insure a stable surface in this final section of the shaft.

Clear indications that it was *not* designed from the beginning were found by Petrie in the fact that the shaft is irregular and tortuous through the rest of the masonry, and that blocks with sharp corners were left in an irregularly curved shaft.

A French professor of architecture, J. Bruchet, who went to the spot to verify and measure, and who published an illustrated book on the subject in Aix-en-Provence in 1966, agrees with Davidson that the granite plugs could not have been slid down the Ascending Passage; he believes they were put in place at the moment of construction, when the Pyramid was still a truncated body. To have slid them down, with so little clearance, says Bruchet, would have required walls as smooth as glass, whereas he found the walls of the corridor roughly finished.

But Bruchet disagrees with Davidson that the well shaft could have been dug from the bottom up, giving as his reason the fact that the bottom of the well shaft goes slightly below the level of the Descending Passage. Bruchet believes that this would not be so if the shaft had been started from below.

For the well shaft to have been dug from above, the operation could only have been completed *before* the Ascending Passage was plugged, or *after* the opening of "Al

Mamun's hole.'' In a closed upper Pyramid there would have been no place to store the carloads of rubble from the digging of the well shaft: the King's and Queen's chambers would not have been sufficient, and storage in the sloping Grand Gallery would have required crosspieces and sacks.

Bruchet points out that the well shaft could not have been dug *after* Al Mamun, because the lower end of the Descending Passage was filled by him with the refuse of broken limestone plugs, which were not cleared out till 1817 by Caviglia. Also, says Bruchet, there are no graffiti to indicate the presence of visitors in the lower passage after the date of the Hegira.

Another Frenchman, Georges Goyon, who collected reproductions of all the graffiti on the Pyramid, which he put into a book dedicated to King Farouk, also does not accept the idea that the service shaft was used as an escape way. He too believes the Pyramid was violated a short time after it was built, and that "Al Mamun's hole" was made at this early period. He even goes so far as to suggest that the first violators entered by the tunnel now attributed to Al Mamun, and that Al Mamun's violation was made *after* the ablation of the Pyramid casing, which is in strict contradiction with the historical record.

Maragioglio and Rinaldi find some of Goyon's theories tenable, but are awaiting the publication of a booklet by Goyon in which he promises to add further material on the subject.

In a recent article in *Revue Archéologique,* entirely devoted to the mechanism of the closing of the Great Pyramid, Goyon suggests that one or two men alone could have manipulated the whole train of blocks down the Ascending

Goyon's view of how a single man could have eased a train of granite plugs down the Ascending Passage with the help of unguents and wooden wedges.

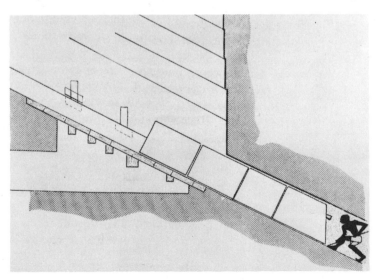

Passage by simply sliding them on clay mixed with cows' milk for greater viscosity, controlling the downward motion by means of wooden wedges on either side of the first block.

Goyon says there are indications on the lowest granite block of two slots 7 centimeters wide intended for wedges.

Goyon's arrows indicate slots in the granite plug for the insertion of wedges to control its downward movement.

Goyon disputes the point made much of by Davidson that the purely stylized portcullis outside the King's Chamber indicates it was never used to seal an actual tomb.

Goyon believes that the granite slabs—long since removed by grave robbers—could have been lowered in the appropriate side slots by ropes run on wooden rollers, and that the four vertical slots carved in the face of the portcullis were intended to allow free play for the ropes.

In the final analysis, the theory which stands up best, and is not in conflict with Davidson's findings, is that of the astronomers Proctor and Antoniadi, which is supported by Kingsland and John and Morton Edgar, that the truncated Pyramid served as a stellar observatory by means of which the ancient Egyptian priests were able to make accurate maps and tables of the visible stars from which to create their entire science of astronomy, geography and geodesy. Once they had obtained what they needed for their astronomical and astrological predictions (and for the secrets of surveying and map making), they may have decided to wall up their instrument so that no one else could know how their lore was obtained.

253

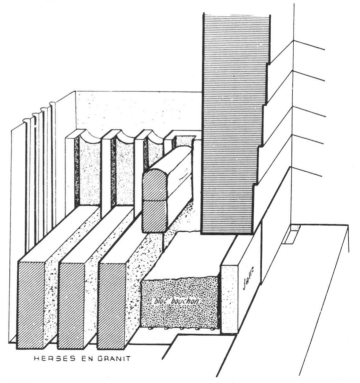

Borchardt's idea of how ropes around wooden rollers could have been used to lower the granite slabs of the portcullis.

Goyon's rendition of granite blocks plugging passage to the King's Chamber.

HERSES EN GRANIT

bloc bouchon

Jalie

It would then have made sense to place the granite and limestone plugs in the Ascending Passage while the top of the Grand Gallery was still open to the level of the King's Chamber. To satisfy this theory, the well shaft could have been carved upward, as suggested by Davidson, or it could have been built in earlier to serve the builders for a variety of reasons, including to serve as a means of coming and going to the pit while the Descending Passage was blocked by a reflecting pool. In any case, the shaft could have been comfortably filled from the top before the builders finished off the building to its apex to serve as a sundial and almanac.

Donald Kingsbury, a professor of mathematics at McGill University, suggests that the well could have been used for observing the passage of stars at the zenith above the Pyramid. There are two vertical sections of the well which could have served this purpose admirably and at different moments in the construction. There is a short vertical passage dug into the plateau which is served by the Grotto and linked to the Descending Passage so that signals could have been freely passed between polar and zenith observers. Another vertical section leads from the bottom of the Grand Gallery and could have been used for zenith observation in conjunction with the Ascending Passage looking south and reflecting north. Kingsbury points out that with two such wells a short distance apart the circumference of the earth could have been computed by observing the passage of a zenith star.

Duncan Macnaughton in *A Scheme of Egyptian Chronology* subscribes to the slightly different theory that ancient scientists used the truncated Pyramid as an observatory, but that a later generation finished it off as a tomb for some Pharaoh.

The custom of burying distinguished citizens in national monuments that were not originally designed for that purpose is common to the world, as in Westminster Abbey, the Invalides, the Pantheon, and Maes-Howe.

Then there is the idea that the sarcophagus was never an actual tomb, but "an open tomb" symbolic of the resurrection, and of a reawakening of the dormant spirit of the great initiates.

XX. TEMPLE OF SECRET INITIATION

Several authors have expressed the opinion that there is a close connection between the Great Pyramid and what are known as the Egyptian mysteries, that is to say, the secret knowledge possessed by a hierarchy of initiates which was communicated to those who could prove their worthiness by passing a long period of probationary training and severe trials, the sort of system that was perpetuated or debased by such societies as the Templars, the Rosicrucians, and the Masons.

In due course the initiates are said to have been shown the great laws and principles of the cosmos and of man's relation thereto, which could not be explained to the more or less ignorant, "who could not rise above the level of a crude realism which takes things to be what they *seem.*"

The Egyptian temple order is described by modern Free Masons as a gradual process of initiation and admission, in which the Great Pyramid was probably used for the initiation of the highest degree, or the three highest degrees in the order.

Throughout the graduated admission, which is said by Masonic writers to have lasted twenty-two years, the prospective initiate was taught the various sciences, of which geometry and numbers were among the most important. "In this context," says Tons Brunés, author of *The Secrets of Ancient Geometry,* "it is not surprising that they should have worked this knowledge into the structure of the initiation temple."

Knowledge of the astronomical cycles and their application also formed part of the ancient initiatory teaching. In those days, says William Kingsland, astronomy was not the mere science of the mechanism of the heavens, but was intimately connected with astrology, "a profoundly esoteric science connected with the great cycles of man's evolution, understood only by the Adepts."

Kingsland adds that if the Great Pyramid was built by initiates for initiates, "What could be more likely than that some of the deeper forces of nature were used in its construction, and that these would—did we but know of them—solve the problems of construction which still remain an enigma to us."

The theosophist H. P. Blavatsky in *The Secret Doctrine* says the Pyramid not only indicated the courses of the

According to Manly P. Hall, the illumined of antiquity passed through the mystic passageways and chambers of the Great Pyramid, entering its portal as men and coming forth as gods.

"The candidate," says Hall, "was laid in the great stone coffin, and for three days his spirit—freed from its mortal coil—wandered at the gateways of eternity. His *Ka,* as a bird, flew through the spiritual spheres of space. He discovered that all the universe was life, all the universe was progress, all the universe was eternal growth. Realizing that his body was a house which he could slip out of and return to without death, he achieved actual immortality. At the end of three days he returned to himself again, and having thus personally and actually experienced the great mystery, he was indeed an Initiate—one who beheld and one to whom religion had fulfilled her duty bringing him to the light of God."

stars in heaven but was "the everlasting record and the indestructible symbol of the Mysteries and Initiations on Earth." In *Isis Unveiled* Madame Blavatsky elaborated, saying that whereas externally the Pyramid "symbolized the creative principle of Nature, and illustrated also the principles of geometry, mathematics, astronomy and astrology," within the building itself was the site of the mysteries of initiation—"a temple of initiation where men rose towards the Gods and the Gods descended towards men." To Blavatsky the coffer was "a baptismal font upon emerging from which the neophyte was born again and became an adept."

Brunés says that during the ceremony of initiation, the candidate was placed by the temple leader in a deathlike trance symbolizing death itself. On awakening from this condition, "having wandered in the world of the gods," he was regarded as having been reborn.

257

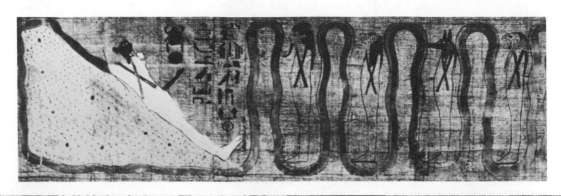

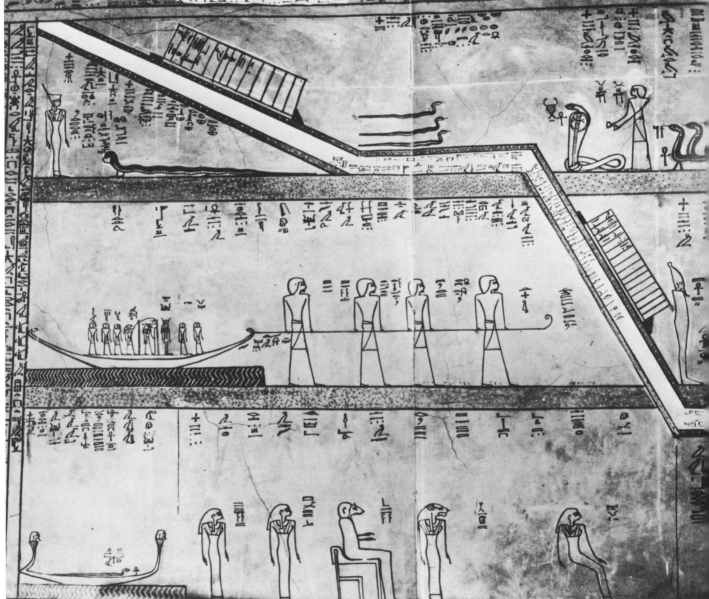

Blavatsky describes the ancient rite: "The initiated adept, who had successfully passed through all the trials, was attached, not nailed, but simply tied on a couch in the form of Tau . . . and plunged into a deep sleep (the 'Sleep of Siloam'). He was allowed to remain in this state for three days and three nights, during which time his Spiritual Ego was said to confabulate with the 'gods,' descend into Hades, Amenti, or Patala (according to the country) and do works of charity to the invisible beings, whether souls of men or Elemental Spirits; his body remaining all the time in a temple crypt or subterranean cave. In Egypt it was placed in the Sarcophagus in the King's Chamber of the Pyramid of Cheops, and carried during the night of the approaching third day to the entrance of a gallery where at a certain hour the beams of the rising Sun struck full on the face of the entranced candidate, who awoke to be initiated by Osiris, the Thoth and God of Wisdom."

For such a rite to have been possible, either the Pyramid must still have been truncated, or it contains secret passages at present undiscovered.

Most of the ancient philosophers and great religious teachers, including Moses and St. Paul, acknowledged or are acknowledged to have derived their wisdom from the Egyptian initiates. Individuals who admitted or hinted they were initiates include Sophocles, Solon, Plato, Cicero, Heraclitus, Pindar and Pythagoras.

Some of the ceremonies of what are sometimes referred to as the lesser mysteries have survived in a more or less degraded and merely formal manner in the ritual of Masonry and of the Christian churches. Kingsland believes the secret of the Pyramid is even known to present-day initiates, but is probably "one of those matters which they do not see fit to disclose to the world at large."

According to Norman Frederick de Clifford, author of *Egypt, the Cradle of Ancient Masonry,* ancient Masonry had its origin long centuries before the dawn of authentic history; he claims the ancient brotherhood "possessed a far greater knowledge of mechanical arts and sciences than is known to architects of the present day."

Several authors, including W. Marshal Adams, believe the Pyramid represented in monumental form the doctrine which *The Book of the Dead* sets forth in script, containing in an allegorical and symbolic manner the secret wisdom of the initiates, or the laws which govern and direct the universe, enabling the initiate to know "how he came into being in the beginning."

The Book of the Dead is the title generally given to a collection of Egyptian inscriptions and papyri found in tombs

These illustrations from Albert Champdor's *The Book of the Dead* show a mummy with phallus erect sliding into the Seventh Region of the Lower World, described as being "filled with serpent's coils and the four sons of Horus who protect the viscera of the dead." This Twenty-first Dynasty drawing has lost the precise φ proportions of the earlier renditions of the same subject shown in earlier illustrations.

259

or in mummy wrappings. Sir E. A. Wallis Budge translated it as *The Book of the Mistress of the Hidden Temple.* One late text found with a mummy was on a papyrus roll 20 meters long divided into 165 chapters. It is now in the Turin Museum.

The ancient Egyptians attributed *The Book of the Dead* to Thoth, Lord of Wisdom, and recorder of the deeds of men, which were produced when the soul came to judgment.

Egyptologists in general label it a collection of funerary and ritual texts of different periods in different forms, used by ancient Egyptian priests in their burial ceremonies. But Henri Furville in his *La Science Secrète* claims that the texts of *The Book of the Dead* are incomprehensible to those who never made a careful study of them from the point of view of psychic science. The obscure texts, says Furville, "shine in the light of initiation, and the practices which seem extraordinary and even absurd to the profane, are, on the contrary, the result of the most profound science."

The problem of translating hermetic language from hieroglyphs is highlighted by Giorgio de Santillana when he points out that in the Erman-Grapow Egyptian dictionaries there are thirty-seven terms for "heaven." As a result, says Santillana, the elaborate instructions in *The Book of the Dead* referring to the soul's celestial voyage translate into "mystical" talk, and must be treated as holy mumbo-jumbo. Modern translators, says Santillana, believe so firmly in their own invention, according to which the underworld has to be looked for in the interior of our globe—instead of in the sky—that even 370 specific astronomical terms would not cause them to stumble. He gives as an example the goddess Hathor being described as "lady of every joy," when the literal translation is "the lady of every heart circuit." The determinative sign for "heart," explains Santillana, often figures as the plumb line coming from the astronomical or surveying device, the *merkhet.* "Evidently," says Santillana, "the heart is something very specific, as it were, the center of gravity."

J. Ralston Skinner in *The Source of Measure* was convinced that the Pyramid was not a tomb, but a temple of initiation. He went further and linked the Pyramid to the Jewish cabala, a system of allegorical symbolism among the initiated which sets forth the secret teachings of the Bible, concealing the great cosmic principles of man's origin.

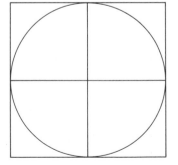

According to Skinner the key to the cabala was said to be the geometrical relation of the area of the circle inscribed in the square, or the sphere in the cube. This gave rise to the relation of the diameter to the circumference of a circle, with the numerical value of the relation expressed in integrals, such as 22/7.

The relation of diameter to circumference, says Skinner, was considered a supreme one, connected with the god names Elohim and Jehovah, the first being the circumference, the second the diameter, which were numerical expressions of these relations.

Tons Brunés, who dedicated his *The Secrets of Ancient Geometry* to the Fraternity of Free Masons, shows that the Great Pyramid, like most of the great temples of antiquity, was designed on the basis of an advanced but hermetic geometry known only to initiates, only fragments of which percolated to the classic and Alexandrine Greeks. According to Brunés, the secret of this ancient geometry was so well guarded that the whole of it was not revealed until the publication of his book in 1969.

Brunés shows how the ancient Egyptians used the basic design of a circle inscribed in a square to divide both circle and square geometrically into equal parts from 2 to 10, and all their possible multiples, without recourse to measuring or arithmetical calculations, with the aid of nothing but a straightedge and a compass—common emblems, along with the Pyramid, of the Masonic orders of yesterday and today.

In Brunés' reconstruction of the secret geometry, the cross emerges as the first geometric addition to the circle and square, and is the key not only to the solution of geometric problems but to the development of numerals and the alphabet.

By including the diagonals, every number both Latin and Arabic and all the letters of several alphabets may be obtained.

According to Brunés, both mathematics and the alphabet sprang from geometry, not the reverse. He says that nowadays we use numbers as the primary factor in our calculations, and geometry only as a subsidiary, whereas he believes the Egyptians reversed the order. He uses a detailed analysis of the Rhind Mathematical Papyrus to demonstrate that the ancient Egyptian system of counting was directly governed by geometric factors and that their ideas and theories were bound in geometric rules.

Brunés found that the circle was indeed considered sacred by the Egyptians, as were the square and the cross and the triangle, all of which are intimately incorporated into the Great Pyramid with its square base and triangular faces designed to represent the "sacred" circle.

Brunés demonstrates how the circle inscribed in a square and quartered by a cross enabled the ancient Egyptian geometer to inscribe in a circle the basic figures of pentagon, hexagon, octagon and decagon.

Of these the pentagon with its five-pointed star is perhaps

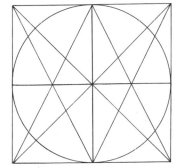

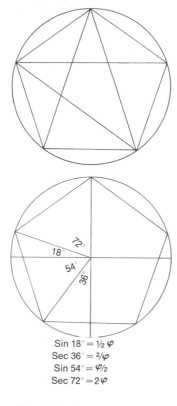

Sin 18° = ½ φ
Sec 36° = ²/φ
Sin 54° = φ/2
Sec 72° = 2φ

The circle in a square with a cross and diagonals, plus a pentagon or decagon, enabled ancient mathematicians to measure lengths of $\sqrt{2}$, $\sqrt{3}$, $\sqrt{5}$, as well as multiples and fractions thereof without arithmetical computation.

the most important: it automatically produces the Golden Section and the φ proportion in the simplest geometric manner.

Each line of the five-pointed star—the symbolic sign of recognition of the initiated Pythagorean, whose hermetic meaning it meant death to reveal—cuts the other in the proportion of major to minor: the Golden Section.

Furthermore, the side of a pentagon inscribed in a circle whose circumference is equal to the perimeter of the Pyramid will be equal to the apothem, or slant height, of the Pyramid, which will be the value of φ.

A pentagon divides a circle in 72° segments. With the main cross, the pentagon radii form angles of 18°, 36°, 54° and 72°.

Though Greece has been looked upon as the birthplace of mathematics—largely because of surviving written material on the subject of mathematics and geometry—Brunés points out that Pythagoras, the founder of Greek mathematics, spent 22 years in Egypt as a priest of the temple, and only returned to Greece after Cyrus the Great, king of Persia, burnt the temples at Memphis and Thebes in 527 B.C. and dragged him off as a prisoner to Babylon.

Back in Greece, Pythagoras taught mathematics on the basis of what he had learnt in Egypt; but after his death his followers were persecuted and had to take refuge abroad. Some eighty years later, Plato left Athens after the execution of Socrates and joined the Pythagorean societies. He traveled to Egypt, where he too was initiated into the lower degrees of learning in the temple, which were slowly recovering from being disbanded by the Babylonian-Persian conquerors.

Plato collected documents and writings connected with Pythagoras. In the end he produced the concept that the cosmos was represented by the five regular solids that can be inscribed in a sphere.

Brunés maintains that Plato incorporated into the body of his writings, and especially in the *Timaeus,* the secret teachings of the Egyptians, which he had sworn not to divulge directly, but which he handled in a hermetic language for which Brunés provides a solution.

Brunés says that Moses, who was also an Egyptian priest, had knowledge of the ancient geometry, which he passed hermetically in his instructions for building the Tabernacle, data which eventually reached Jerusalem and were incorporated into holy teaching.

The French archeologist and mathematician Charles Funk-Hellet, in his *La Bible et la Grande Pyramide d'Egypte,* agrees that the cubit of the Bible can only be the Egyptian

262

royal cubit, which he makes a hair, or 1/2 millimeter, shorter than Stecchini's. According to Funk-Hellet the cubit was incorporated into the Temple at Jerusalem as $\pi/6$, or 523.6 millimeters, instead of Stecchini's 524.1.

Funk-Hellet points out that Solomon had Hiram Abiff build a temple whose columns were 18 cubits high and 12 cubits around. In other words, one cubit equaled the twelfth part of the circumference of the arc of 30°, or $\pi/6$.

By subtracting the circumference from the height, they obtained 6 cubits in a straight line, which was equal to half the circumference, or the exact value of π; so that a thousand years before Christ the Hebrews knew that a cubit was a mathematical entity dependent on the circumference, and were able to resolve π to four points of decimal.

Using *one unit* of measure as the radius of a circle, the ancients found the trigonometric value of 30° to be $\pi/6$, which was the value of the royal cubit, or .5236 of the unit used.

$$\frac{3.1416}{6} = .5236$$

SERIES P

I	II	III	IV	V	VI	VII	VIII	IX	X	XI	XII	XIII	XIV	XV	XVI	XVII	XVIII
1	5	6	11	17	28	45	73	118	191	309	500	809	1309	2118	3427	5545	8972
2	10	12	22	34	56	90	146	236	382	618	1000	1618	2618	4236	6854	11090	17944
3	15	18	33	51	84	135	219	354	573	927	1500	2427	3927	6354	10281	16635	26916
4	20	24	44	68	112	180	292	472	764	1236	2000	3236	5236	8472	13708	22180	35888
5	25	30	55	85	140	225	365	590	955	1545	2500	4045	6545	10590	17135	27725	44860
6	30	36	66	102	168	270	438	708	1146	1854	3000	4854	7854	12708	20562	33270	53832
7	35	42	77	119	196	315	511	826	1337	2163	3500	5663	9163	14826	23989	38815	62804
8	40	48	88	136	224	360	584	944	1528	2472	4000	6472	10472	16944	27416	44360	71776
9	45	54	99	153	252	405	657	1062	1719	2781	4500	7281	11781	19062	30843	49905	80748
10	50	60	110	170	280	450	730	1180	1910	3090	5000	8090	13090	21180	34270	55450	89720
11	55	66	121	187	308	495	803	1298	2101	3399	5500	8899	14399	23298	37697	60995	98692
12	60	72	132	204	336	540	876	1416	2292	3708	6000	9708	15708	25416	41124	66540	107664
. . . . . .																	
24	120	144	264	408	672	1080	1752	2832	4584	7416	12000	19416	31416	50832	82248	133080	215328

Funk-Hellet found another additive series made by adding 5 to 1, and so on; 1, 5, 6, 11, 17, 28. . . . He developed the series in 18 columns and 36 lines horizontally, with some extraordinary results, including values for π, φ, and the royal cubit; this led him to conjecture that the royal cubit might have had a theoretical value before it had a practical one.

The first line gives the numbers 11, 17 and 28, which are divisions of both the royal cubit and the Chaldean cubit; furthermore, $11 \times 17 \times 28$ equals 5236, which is Funk-Hellet's figure for the royal cubit in millimeters, or $\pi/6$.

The fourteenth column of the series gives the φ^2 value of 2.618, the royal cubit value of 5236, and the π value of 3.1416.

The second row produces the φ, or Fibonacci-type, series of $1/\varphi$, 1, φ, φ^2 with 618, 1000, 1618 and 2618.

The seventh column gives the divisions of a 360-degree circle in halves, quarters, eighths, etc.

Funk-Hellet maintains that as early as the fourth millennium B.C. the Chaldeans had a mathematical series which gave the exact values of the cubit, the meter and π. What's more, he insists that the present *meter,* as developed by the French in the nineteenth century, was already a hermetic measure known in antiquity, and was linked trigonometrically with the cubit.

To Funk-Hellet the Great Pyramid is a geodetic gnomon, or pillar, incorporating values for both the meter and the cubit. He says the finger, palm and cubit are built into the apothem. In the King's Chamber, he says, the double square of the floor is 5.236 meters by 10.472 meters—which varies from Petrie's and Davidson's measurements by a few millimeters.

Funk-Hellet says the basic meter unit from which the cubit was derived had to be kept a deep secret, presumably so that all the calculations, including the means for obtaining the exact length of the year, would remain the sole property of the officiating priests.

Schwaller de Lubicz in *Le Temple de l'Homme* corroborated the evidence that the Egyptians knew the meter, pointing out that on the whole length of a surrounding wall of the Third Dynasty (3000 to 2000 B.C.), "one finds three lines painted at the time, of which the distance between two lines is exactly one meter," adding that this is not an isolated case, "but one of thousands." In ancient constructions of Troy, Heinrich Schliemann found a unit of measure which was exactly half a meter, or 50 centimeters.

Funk-Hellet says the meter and the cubit depended from each other and were both defined by geodetic measurements. He suggests the way the meter was derived by the ancients was by watching from a measured height the moment a light disappeared on the horizon.

At the beginning of the nineteenth century, Sir John Herschel tried to calculate the radius of the earth with two observers placed 10 feet above the sea who ceased to see each other at 12,873 meters. This gave Herschel an earth radius of 6797 kilometers instead of the correct 6378, or an error of 419 kilometers.

Funk-Hellet believes the ancient Egyptians did better. He points out that the full apothem of the Pyramid including the pyramidion is 10,000 fingers long, or 187 meters. He then computes that if 1870 meters is taken as an arc of 30°, the resulting radius will be 3570 meters. Modern experiments indicate that a light disappears on the horizon at 3570 meters when the eye of the observer is exactly 1 meter above the ground.

José Alvarez Lopez of Argentina, in his work *Fisica y*

Creacionismo, says that a cubit of 523 millimeters—about half a millimeter shorter than Funk-Hellet's and 1 millimeter shorter than Stecchini's—is exactly half of what he calls an *absolute meter,* which he says occurs as a natural unit in the solar system.

According to Alvarez Lopez the planets of our system orbit in harmonic distances from the sun which are multiples of a single unit of length—his *absolute meter*—in an arrangement which is naturally decimal.

Alvarez Lopez says that beginning with Mars, the planets are disposed in the order of the colors in the solar spectrum —with Mars as red, Jupiter yellow, Saturn yellowish-green, Uranus green, Neptune blue, and Pluto violet. According to Alvarez Lopez the Pyramid may once have been painted with the colors of the spectrum starting with red for Mars, just below the gilded pyramidion representative of the sun, and diminishing through yellow and blue to violet at the base, symbolizing the construction of the solar system both geometrically and with color.

The only evidence that the Pyramid may have once been painted, apart from the legends of the Arab storytellers, are some fragments of casing stone found in the early nineteenth century which were covered with what appeared to be red paint. Subjected to careful chemical and spectrographic

Alvarez Lopez's rendition of the dimensions of the coffer used by the Egyptians for basic astronomical ratios.

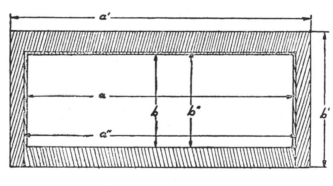

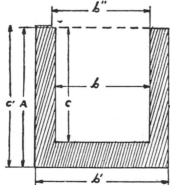

analysis at the Sorbonne, it was determined that the casing stones had once been covered with a layer of paint with a red ochre base, and that the paint could not have been caused by any chemical recomposition of the stone itself.

The Great Pyramid, says Alvarez Lopez, represents a decimal schema of the solar system. He figures the height of the Pyramid to be a millionth part of the distance to the sun, measured from the limit of the earth's atmosphere, and its base to be the ten-thousandth part of the surface of the earth.

The dimensions of the granite coffer in the King's Chamber, as worked out by the Argentine professor, are arranged to form a perfect "astronomical atlas": he says the inner measure gives an *absolute cubic meter,* but that the coffer was not designed as a cube so that its various inner and outer measures could also represent the various astronomical constants of the solar system.

He says there was just one way to build a coffer so that it would include not only the distance from the earth to the sun (a basic astronomical unit), but the weight of the earth, the weight of the earth and the moon, the weight of the sun in relation to the earth, the weight of the sun in relation to the earth and the moon, the weight of the earth in relation to the moon, the value of the absolute cubic meter, and the polar radius (one-half the diameter from pole to pole) of the earth in terms of an absolute meter.

Alvarez Lopez considers the original discovery of these figures to have been perhaps the hardest job yet mastered by man, and says this explains the care and trouble taken by the builders of the Pyramid to secrete the information in the heart of the building. Were the coffer not so badly chipped and worn, says Alvarez Lopez, it might give us more exact astronomical figures than we now possess.

All these astronomical constants, says the professor, depend on a precise knowledge of the solar parallax; he is amazed that the builders of the Pyramid could have known the parallax and the earth's polar radius so exactly without the help of telescopes and cameras. It will be interesting, he says, to compare our new figure for the sun's parallax with that of the granite coffer, as determined by the near passage of the small planet Eros, which occurs every 37 years and is due in 1975.

Stecchini is more *terre-a-terre.* He can show that the half meter found by Schliemann is really a Babylonian cubit of .49907 meter and that the meter of Funk-Hellet and de Lubicz is in fact three feet of .3329 meter, both derived from the geographic foot and cubit.

When I reminded Stecchini that Petrie had found the

coffer in the King's Chamber to be designed in even numbers of fifths of a cubic cubit, Stecchini resolved the millennial riddle of the coffer by showing that it contains exactly 40 *artaba,* or 40 cubes whose sides are one geographic foot, and that its outside volume is twice this amount, or 80 cubes of one geographic foot.

Would it not be worthwhile, nonetheless, for academic institutions, so admirably equipped with computers and talent, carefully to analyze such conceits as those of Alvarez Lopez and Funk-Hellet and either refute them or support them with reliable data? Some of their ideas may turn out to be no wilder than those for which Jomard, Taylor, Smyth and maybe even Davidson were unjustly lampooned.

Napoleon's French Institute in Cairo.

XXI. MORE SECRET PASSAGES AND CHAMBERS

Many Egyptologists and explorers were convinced—and many still are—that the Pyramid conceals one or more secret and yet undiscovered chambers. It is also believed that the Pyramid is connected by subterranean passageways to other pyramids, to the Sphinx, and to long-demolished reception halls, small temples and other enclosures.

The engineer of the Australian railways, Robert Ballard, believed the Giza pyramids may also have been built above a vast series of catacombs, with chambers and galleries, like the pyramids of Lake Moeris, which are said to have vast subterranean residences for its priests and keepers.

Ballard suggests that much of the limestone for the structure of the pyramids of Giza may have been quarried from such catacombs. He suggests that a good diamond drill with two or three hundred feet of rods be used to make tests on the Giza plateau. Ballard believes that when this subterranean city is discovered, it will be found that it had access passages for the priests and the surveyors linking it to every pyramid.

While the pyramids appeared to the outside world to have been sealed up as mausoleums for the dead, says Ballard, the sealing may simply have rendered more mysterious and private the recesses and abodes of the priests who entered from below, and who were possibly enabled to ascend by private passages to their very summits.

When Perring and Howard-Vyse were exploring the bent pyramid at Dashur in 1839, they noticed an extraordinary phenomenon. The workmen clearing the passages were suffering from intense heat and lack of oxygen when suddenly a strong cold wind began to whistle through the passages. It blew so fiercely for two days that the men had trouble keeping their lamps lit. Mysteriously it stopped and no one has yet figured out the mystery.

Ahmed Fakhry, working in the same pyramid in the 1950s, heard weird noises which led him to conclude that there must be undiscovered passages within or under the bent pyramid.

Edgerton Sykes, an archeologist and author, who is perhaps the best living authority on ancient Atlantis, also

Herodotus speaks of a palace complex of 3500 chambers half above and half below ground at Moeris. The Egyptians called it "the temple at the entrance to the lake." Herodotus called it a "labyrinth," and considered that it outranked the pyramids as a wonder.

believes there is a whole maze of corridors and passages dug into the Giza hill. Sykes quotes an ancient Arab source to the effect that the designers of the Pyramid made "several doors, built over underground vaults of stone, each with a secret stone door revolving upon a hinge."

Peter Kolosimo believes there are more tombs and caves beneath Saqqara, Abydos, and Heluan, of very ancient dynasties, and reports the legends of hidden doors "that could be opened by a mysterious force" such as a supersonic wave length, or specially resonant voice.

According to the Baron de Cologne, as quoted by Robert Charroux in *Le Livre des Secrets Trahis* (Paris, Laffont, 1965), there is an underground kingdom under the Egyptian desert similar to the "Agartha" of Tibet.

Commander Barber, the American attaché who gave such attention to the construction of the Pyramid, wrote that "when one considers the inexplicable and yet exact arrangement of the various chambers and galleries, and that there is room for 3700 more such chambers, provided we could find them, we can almost be tempted to believe that we have not yet discovered all the chambers or even the true chamber of Cheops."

Piazzi Smyth was equally convinced that there was an undiscovered chamber in the Great Pyramid "which will prove to be the very muniment room of the whole monument."

269

Bent pyramid at Dashur. Arrow points to a secondary entrance to pyramid high on the north side.

When a multitude of chips of black diorite rock were discovered on the Pyramid hill, Smyth surmised that the undiscovered chamber might be lined with black diorite.

Thomas Holland, a Thirty-third Degree Free Mason, believed that if the granite leaf were removed from the portcullis it would disclose the way to "magnificent passages and chambers hitherto undiscovered."

Louis P. McCarty, in a privately printed booklet, *The Great Pyramid of Jeezeh,* published in San Francisco in 1907, says he believes the Pyramid contains at least three more chambers located between the King's Chamber and the apex, and at least one with double the capacity of the King's Chamber. McCarty believes the next largest chamber will be found at the 75th course, and the largest at the 100th course, and that the largest should be of an equal capacity to the three below it. He believes there is a fifth and final chamber on the 120th course of masonry, and that this one should be just half the capacity of the King's Chamber. McCarty also subscribes to the theory that there is a passage somewhere beneath the northeast corner of the Pyramid which leads to the Sphinx.

Funk-Hellet suspects there might have been a room on top of the present platform, now destroyed.

William Kingsland, in his two-volume work on the Pyramid, suggested generating radio waves of 5 meters length in the King's Chamber, and by noting the strength of reception at measured intervals all round the outside of the Pyramid, determine if some hidden chamber might exist.

In the late 1960s Dr. Luis Alvarez, the 1968 Nobel Prize winner for physics, developed a machine for recording the passage of cosmic rays through the pyramid of Kephren, by means of which he hoped to discover any secret chambers or passages within its body.

The operation, which required a team of scientists, turned into an expensive venture in which twelve United States and United Arab Republic agencies became involved, including the U.S. Atomic Energy Commission, the U.A.R. Department of Antiquities, the Smithsonian Institution and the Faculty of Science of the Ein Shams University in Cairo.

Alvarez's project was based on the fact that cosmic rays, which bombard the planet day and night, lose part of their energy as they pass through an object, in proportion to the density and thickness of the object.

By placing a "spark chamber" in the subterranean vault of the pyramid the scientists planned to monitor the number of cosmic rays which made their way through the pyramid walls. Those rays which passed through a void in the body of the pyramid would reach the chamber more frequently than those traversing solid rock, and the variance would indicate the presence of a secret chamber or passage in the pyramid.

The path of each ray is recorded electronically and stored on a magnetic tape. The tapes are then fed into a computer to calculate and memorize the point at which each recorded ray penetrated the surface of the pyramid.

To pinpoint the location of any cavities which showed up, the scientists planned to shift the "spark chamber" and obtain a sort of stereo picture.

Were any hidden chamber located, it would then be possible to dig directly to it without risking great damage to the rest of the pyramid. The operation would consist of drilling a small hole upward in the indicated direction of any cavity that appeared on their "X-ray plate." Modern optical tools would allow archeologists to look into the chamber through a long hole, perhaps 100 feet long and only 3/4 inch in diameter.

Dr. Alvarez chose the pyramid of Kephren because he considered it unlikely that Kephren, as the son of Cheops, would have had such an imposing pyramid erected without incorporating some secret system of passages and chambers such as have been discovered in the Great Pyramid.

Alvarez assumed that Cheops' architects must have had a choice of clever ideas for secreting chambers, some of which had to be left out of his pyramid, but could have been applied to Kephren's. "My hunch," says Alvarez, "was that younger architects working on Cheops' pyramid would have had their ideas rejected. Later, in Chephren's time, they could have persuaded Chephren to use them, or some other improved plans."

271

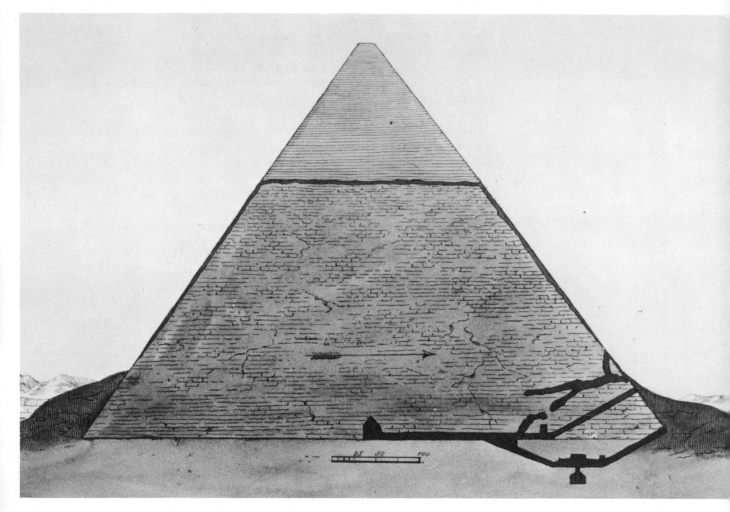

On this tenuous assumption Alvarez hoped to find a secret chamber in Kephren, and perhaps even the sarcophagus of the dead Pharaoh: an Egyptologist's dream.

Alvarez also chose Kephren's pyramid because its central chamber was more convenient for setting up his complex electronic equipment. The subterranean vault discovered in 1818 by the Italian explorer Giovanni Belzoni had recently been cleared of rubble, and other chambers and passages in the pyramid had been lit with electricity by cable from the nearby Mena House.

By September of 1968 two million cosmic-ray trajectories had been measured: these were considered ample for finding any hidden vault within the field of view of the upward-looking equipment. When the tapes were run through the local computer in Cairo for the first analysis, the results looked wonderful. They clearly

272

In 1818 the Italian adventurer Giovanni Belzoni tried to find an entrance to the second pyramid of Kephren.

He found what appeared to be the original entrance close to the ground plugged by three granite blocks. The passage was cleared all the way down to a funerary chamber containing only a granite sarcophagus. On the west wall of the chamber an inscription in Arabic indicated the chamber had been penetrated some time after the Hegira.

Portrait of Giovanni Belzoni used as a frontispiece for a book edited by his wife commenting on his exploits in Egypt.

showed up the corners and the faces of the pyramid as outlined by the passing cosmic rays, recorded in the central chamber. The equipment appeared to be functioning excellently. But there were some mysterious developments.

As Dr. Lauren Yazolino, Alvarez's assistant, returned to the United States to analyze the tapes on the most up-to-date computer at Berkeley, a correspondent from the London *Times* visited Cairo to check on the results locally. At Ein Shams University, John Tunstall found an up-to-date 1130 IBM computer surrounded by hundreds of tins of recordings.

"It defies all known laws of physics," Tunstall quoted Dr. Amr Goneid, who had been left in charge of the pyramid project since the return to America of Dr. Yazolino.

According to Tunstall's report, each time Dr. Goneid ran the tapes through the computer a different pattern would appear, and the salient points which should have

273

been repeated on each tape were absent. "This is scientifically impossible," Tunstall quoted Goneid, explaining that earlier recordings which had raised the hopes of a great discovery were now found to be a jumbled mass of meaningless symbols with no guiding pattern whatever.

Tunstall asked Goneid: "Has all this scientific know-how been rendered useless by some force beyond man's comprehension?" To which Goneid is reported to have answered: "Either the geometry of the pyramid is in substantial error, which would affect our readings, or there is a mystery which is beyond explanation—call it what you will, occultism, the curse of the pharaohs, sorcery, or magic; there is some force that defies the laws of science at work in the pyramid."

At Berkeley, Alvarez refuted Tunstall's account, insisting that the equipment was functioning admirably. In the 35° cone scanned by the spark chamber there was no sign of any hidden passageway or chamber. This was the area believed by the scientists to be the most likely to contain them, though there was still hope of finding something in the remaining sections.

As soon as further funds were available the team of scientists planned to resume their scanning of Kephren. Dr. Yazolino added that if sufficient funds were available they might even move their equipment to the Queen's Chamber in Cheops to see if they could find any unknown passages or chambers in the Great Pyramid.

Yazolino explained that the only trouble they had encountered had been poor readings when the spark chamber ran out of neon and produced some mysterious dark spots which looked like a possible chamber till they were carefully analyzed and found to be caused by the gap between two spark chambers.

Alvarez stressed his confidence in Dr. Goneid as a very able physicist, saying that he thought so much of him he had invited him to spend a year at his lab at Berkeley. "If I thought for a moment that he had said any of the nonsense attributed to him, you can be sure I wouldn't want him as a member of my research group."

Yet there remains something mysterious about the pyramid which needs to be explained.

When a Frenchman, M. Bovis, visited the Great Pyramid he noticed that some garbage cans in the King's Chamber contained dead cats and other small animals that had apparently wandered into the Pyramid and died.

There was something odd about these corpses: there was no smell or decay to them. Curious as to the cause

Diorite statue of Kephren dating from the Sixth Dynasty found by Marietta Bey in the so-called Temple of the Sphinx, now in the Cairo Museum.

275

of this phenomenon, Bovis examined the animals and found them dehydrated and mummified, despite the humidity in the chamber.

Bovis wondered if the mere shape of the Pyramid could have been responsible for this natural process of embalming: so he made a wooden model of Cheops with a base three feet long, and oriented it due north. Inside the model, a third of the way up, he placed a freshly dead cat. After a few days it mummified. Bovis then placed other organic materials in the model, especially matter that normally decays very quickly, such as calf's brains, and when these failed to putrefy, he concluded there must be something about the shape of the Pyramid which prevents decay and causes dehydration.

A Czechoslovakian radio engineer named Karel Drbal read Bovis's reports and made some further experiments with pyramid models, concluding that there is "a definite relation between the shape of the space inside the pyramid, and the physical, chemical and biological processes going on inside that space."

The same phenomenon has been noted in Italy and Yugoslavia where milk packaged in pyramidal cartons keeps fresh indefinitely without refrigeration. A French firm has also patented a pyramidal container for yogurt.

Drbal wondered if the shape might be responsible for an accumulation of electromagnetic waves or cosmic rays,

277

or of some unknown energy. Placing a used razor blade within a six-inch-high cardboard model of Cheops' pyramid, oriented to true north, Drbal found that the edges of the blade automatically recovered their sharpness after use, that he could shave with one Gilette blue blade as many as 200 times. He concluded that the environment inside the pyramid somehow made the crystals in the blade return to their original form. Drbal was issued patent no. 91304 by the Czechoslovak patent office and began manufacturing "Cheops Pyramid Razorblade Sharpeners" out of cardboard. Today they are being made of styrofoam.

An engineer and former professor of radio, L. Turenne, maintains that all sorts of different forms—being combinations of different frequencies—act as different types of resonators for energy in the cosmos. This has led to speculation that the Pyramid might be some sort of gigantic lens which is able to focus an unknown energy simply by means of its shape.

Even the coffer in the King's Chamber has been considered such a device by Worth Smith, who points out that the cubic capacity of the coffer is *exactly* the same as that of the biblical Arc of the Covenant.

According to Maurice Denis-Papin, descendant of the famous inventor, the Arc of the Covenant was a sort of electric capacitor capable of producing an electrical charge of 500 to 700 volts. The Arc is said to have been made of acacia wood, lined inside and out with gold: that is to say, two conductors separated by an insulator. On either side were garlands which may have served as condensors. Denis-Papin says the Arc was placed in a dry spot where the magnetic field reached a normal 500 to 600 volts per vertical meter.

Insulated from the ground, the Arc is said to have given off fiery rays, acting like a Leyden jar. According to Denis-Papin the capacitor was discharged to earth by means of the garlands. To move the Arc, two golden rods were slid through rings attached to the exterior.

The similarity of such an "energy accumulator" to the orgone box developed by Wilhelm Reich, which was such a puzzle to Albert Einstein, is also striking.

Sir W. Siemens, the British inventor, related that one day while he was standing on the summit of Cheops' pyramid an Arab guide called his attention to the fact that whenever he raised his hand with his fingers outspread an acute ringing noise was heard.

Raising just his index, Siemens felt a distinct prickling in it. When he tried to drink from a wine bottle he had brought along he noted a slight electric shock. So

Siemens moistened a newspaper and wrapped it around the bottle to convert it into a Leyden jar. It became increasingly charged with electricity simply by being held above his head.

When sparks began to issue from the wine bottle, Siemens's Arab guides became distrustful and accused him of practicing witchcraft. One of the guides tried to seize Siemens's companion, but Siemens lowered the bottle towards him and gave the Arab such a jolt that he was knocked senseless to the ground. Recovering, the guide scrambled to his feet and took off down the Pyramid, crying loudly.

Such weird but soberly recounted tales about the Pyramid are tame compared to the wilder conceits that have been propounded by pseudoscientific, science-fiction and sensational authors. According to one science-fiction theory, the Pyramid was used as a huge protecting baffle for ancient scientists who had found a way to tap the energy of the Van Allen belts by letting it flow on an ionized path through the atmosphere to the peak of the Pyramid, possibly on a laser beam. The authors of this science fiction recount how an error was committed in the length of time the energy was allowed to flow, causing an avalanche of power which knocked the planet off its axis.

Another popular idea is that the truncated Pyramid served not merely as an observatory but as a landing pad for extraterrestrial space ships. The polished sides of the Pyramid would have made such a platform inaccessible to the hoi polloi, so that godlike visiting astronauts could have confabulated in security with the high priests who had access to the platform from interior passages. Herodotus lends romance to the idea that ziggurats and pyramids were steppingstones for the gods from heaven and that the King's Chamber—which Petrie found to be built quite separately from the surrounding Pyramid— could have served as a reception room on the truncated platform.

Herodotus describes a reconstructed ziggurat which he visited in Babylon. "On the topmost tower there is a spacious temple, and inside the temple stands a great bed covered with fine bed-clothes, with a golden table by its side. There is no statue of any kind set up in the place, nor is the chamber occupied at night by any but a single native woman who—say the Chaldean priests—is chosen by the deity out of all the women of the land. The priests also declare—but I for one do not credit it—that the god comes down in person into this chamber, and sleeps upon the couch."

In the light of recent scientific discoveries, one more theory must be added to this world of fable: that the Great Pyramid was built not only as an astronomical observatory but as an astrological one in order to make accurate large-scale horoscopes for the reigning monarch.

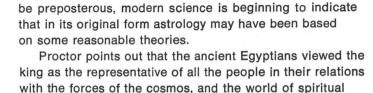

XXII. ASTROLOGICAL OBSERVATORY

Though many of the doctrines of astrology appear to be preposterous, modern science is beginning to indicate that in its original form astrology may have been based on some reasonable theories.

Proctor points out that the ancient Egyptians viewed the king as the representative of all the people in their relations with the forces of the cosmos, and the world of spiritual powers.

On the theory that what was good for the king was good for the country, Proctor suggested that the Egyptians made no move in either domestic or foreign policy without the recommendation of their astrologer priests, whose opinions were based on the movement of heavenly bodies as scanned from a pyramidal observatory.

Once the king was dead, Proctor believes, his body may have been buried within the pyramid and the platform finished off to a point.

The idea that the shifting of heavenly bodies bears some relation to man's fate is so ingrained that people are still called martial, jovial, saturnine or lunatic; the days of the week are still named for sun, moon and planets; and our religious festivals are still based on the astrological system of ancient Egypt, with Christmas tied to the winter solstice and Easter to the spring equinox.

In his *The Scientific Basis of Astrology,* published in 1969, Michel Gauquelin describes some of the effects of the motions of the sun and moon upon terrestrial phenomena. Apart from such obvious effects as the seasons, the growth of vegetation and the tides, he deals with the less apparent but equally powerful effects of the eleven-year cycle of sunspots on our flora, fauna and inhabitants.

Sunspots, which appear like dark flowers on the surface of the sun, spring up, develop and disappear. As they do so, the sun spews up fantastic incandescent clouds of gas, and whips up huge magnetic whirlwinds.

Rotating on its axis in a twenty-seven-day cycle, the sun periodically aims these spots and eruptions directly at the earth. The result is an increased projection of waves and particles towards the earth. In the words of Gauguelin, "we terrestrians can regard ourselves as living in the interior of the sun."

The position of the earth in its orbit also affects the sunspots: when Venus and Earth are on the same side of the sun, their effect on the sunspots is combined. The sun's vagaries induce earthquakes and even alter the duration of the day; the earth's magnetic fields are disturbed; there are radio interferences and other such mysterious phenomena. At the same time the earth is subject to bombardment by galactic particles such as Alvarez's cosmic rays, which also have their effect.

Sunspot activity has been related to such different phenomena as the number of icebergs in the North Atlantic, the level of water in lakes, the concentric rings in the growth of trees and the number of rabbit skins taken by the Hudson's Bay Company. Even the quality of wines in Burgundy is affected, excellent vintages corresponding to periods of maximum solar activity.

Sunspots have been proved to affect the smallest cells, and the world of microbes is disturbed to the point that waves of epidemics can be generated. Gauguelin quotes a Doctor Fauré to the effect that the frequency of diphtheria cases in Central Europe and of smallpox victims in Chicago follow the eleven-year cycle of sunspots, as did the recurrent great plagues of typhus and cholera in Europe.

Indirectly, most of the phenomena of weather, such as barometric pressure and the rate of winds, depend on the eruptions of sunspots. Gauguelin wonders if there may not be more subtle effects on the air we breathe, on our physical and mental states, and even on the way we think.

Recent experiments indicate that subjects breathing air charged with positive ions are likely to feel discomfort, headaches and giddiness; whereas when the atmosphere is full of negative ions the same subjects feel cheerful, relaxed and in top form.

The concentration of positive and negative ions in the air we breathe depends in the final analysis on solar activity. The ionosphere is filled with positive and negative ions. Particles which induce a very high ionization in the upper atmosphere are directed toward the earth by the sun. Unfortunately, negative ions have a tendency to attach themselves to clouds, whereas positive ions tend to accumulate on the ground.

Such data tie in with the theories of Wilhelm Reich about the healthful effects of what he calls "orgone energy" and the toxic effects of its counterpart "deadly orgone," which was reputed to turn rocks brown, make strong men giddy and bring on women's menses out of season.

Current research and experiments behind the Iron Curtain as reported by Ostrander and Schroeder in their *Psychic Discoveries Behind the Iron Curtain** have added even more fantastic details to the use of astrology as a science.

These authors describe a Czechoslovak Ministry of Health center, complete with modern computers, run by gynecologists and psychiatrists. It is called Astra Research Center for Planned Parenthood and uses astrological data, or the position of sun, moon and planets in relation to the birth of an individual, in order to assure a safe and reliable means of birth control without pills, contraception or operations. The same system is being used to help seemingly sterile women become fertile, help women who have had nothing but miscarriages deliver full-term babies, and even allow them to choose whether they will have a boy or a girl child.

In a book called *Predetermining the Sex of a Child,* Eugen Jonas, a Czech medical doctor who developed the Astra clinic, maintains that women's cycles are affected not only by the phases of the moon, but that each individual at birth is affected by the basic pattern of sun, moon and planets. From this basic pattern Dr. Jonas claims to be able to figure out the exact days in a woman's entire lifetime when she can conceive, as well as the ones which are the best or worst for a forthcoming child. The woman may then take advantage of such days, or avoid them.

Jonas found that dead, deformed and retarded children were produced when women conceived during certain oppositions of the sun, moon and major planets.

The system is now being tested in Hungary as well as Czechoslovakia, where Dr. Kurt Rechnitz, former director of the Budapest Obstetric Clinic prescribed astrological birth control for one hundred twenty women. None was reported pregnant.

It has been too short a period to establish the validity of such data, but the endeavor could prove more rewarding than voyaging to the moon. It would certainly be simpler for a lady in New York to step into the booth of an astrological computer in Grand Central Station in order to arrange her calendar of engagements for the year. And it might do wonders for an overpopulated planet.

Jonas' good-humored complaint is that most gynecologists know as little about astronomy as astronomers know about obstetrics, and that both believe

* Prentice-Hall, Englewood Cliffs, New Jersey, 1970.

astrology to be superstitious nonsense. If the disciplines were combined, the results, says Jonas, might be great for mankind. Had the designers of the Great Pyramid been able to monitor the sunspots with a screen across the Grand Gallery, as suggested by Proctor, and had they been aware of such phenomena as has been described by Dr. Jonas, they may well have been able to use the Great Pyramid as a means of providing accurate astrological data on which to formulate the charts for individual behavior, if not for the thronging masses, at least for the pharaohs, priests or nobles.

In his book on the Great Pyramid William Kingsland declares flatly that the ancient Egyptians used "their profound knowledge of what we call the outer facts of astronomy" to connect them astrologically with the principles of man's relation to the cosmos, and that this formed part of the concealed knowledge contained in the mysteries.

Kingsland notes that from the very remotest antiquity the Egyptians believed firmly in an afterlife and were not afraid to think cosmically in terms of millions of years. He quotes an introductory hymn to *Ra* in *The Book of the Dead* as saying: "millions of years have gone over the world; I cannot tell the number of those through which thou hast passed. . . ."

To Kingsland *The Book of the Dead,* though it appears to be a ritual for funerary rites of a deceased king or high official, was actually a description of the trials, temptations and difficulties which the adept had to meet and overcome as he progressed from knowledge to knowledge and from power to power, as he penetrated the superphysical regions from plane to plane. The ultimate goal of initiation, says Kingsland, was "the full realization of the essential *divine nature of man,* the recovery by the individual of the full knowledge and powers of his divine spiritual nature, of that which was his source and origin, but to the *consciousness* of which he is *now* dead through the 'Fall of Man' into matter and physical life."

The old Greeks, says Kingsland, learning from the Egyptians, embodied these trials and difficulties of the great initiates into the legends of their heroes and demigods.

Manly P. Hall, a lifelong researcher into the mysteries of ancient initiation, says the Great Pyramid was dedicated to the god Hermes, the personification of Universal Wisdom; it was not only a temple of initiation but a repository for the secret truths which he calls the foundation of all the arts and sciences. The time will come, says Hall, when the secret wisdom shall again be the dominating religious and philosophical urge of the world: "Out of the cold ashes of lifeless creeds, shall rise phoenix-like the ancient Mysteries . . . . The unfolding of man's spiritual nature is as much an exact science as astronomy, medicine and jurisprudence."

Whatever mystical, occult or science-fiction tales may be associated with the Great Pyramid, it is still an extraordinary piece of masonry, and its designers must have been extraordinary beings. Who they were and when they built their Pyramid remains a mystery. So the quest continues.

But certain facts must be confronted, and the textbooks amended to conform with them. Eratosthenes was obviously not the first to measure the circumference of the earth. Hipparchus was not the inventor of trigonometry. Pythagoras did not originate his famous theorem. Mercator did not invent his projection—though he did visit the Great Pyramid and leave his graffito to prove it.

Whoever built the Great Pyramid knew the dimensions of this planet as they were not to be known again till the seventeenth century of our era. They could measure the day, the year and the Great Year of the Precession. They knew how to compute latitude and longitude very accurately by means of obelisks and the transit of stars. They knew the varying lengths of a degree of latitude and longitude at different locations on the planet and could make excellent maps, projecting them with a minimum of distortion. They worked out a sophisticated system of measures based on the earth's rotation on its axis which produced the admirably earth-commensurate foot and cubit which they incorporated in the Pyramid.

In mathematics they were advanced enough to have discovered the Fibonacci series, and the function of π and φ. What more they knew remains to be seen. But as more is discovered it may open the door to a whole new civilization of the past, and a much longer history of man than has heretofore been credited.

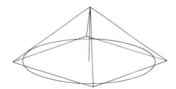

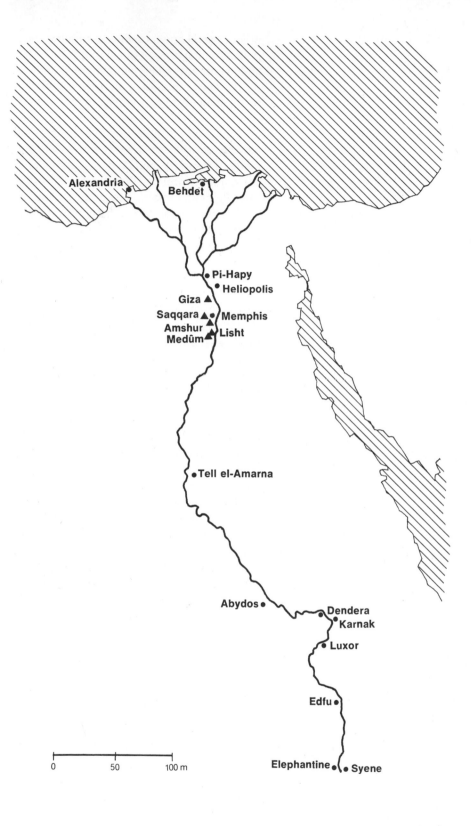

Alexandria

Behdet

Pi-Hapy
Heliopolis
Giza ▲
Saqqara ▲ ● Memphis
Amshur ▲ ● Lisht
Medûm ▲

Tell el-Amarna

Abydos ●
Dendera ●
Karnak
Luxor ●

Edfu ●

Elephantine ● ● Syene

0   50   100 m

NOTES ON THE RELATION OF ANCIENT MEASURES TO THE GREAT PYRAMID

by LIVIO CATULLO STECCHINI

The following pages constitute an abstract from a lifelong research into the history of measures. I became interested in this subject toward the end of my secondary education, when I was trying to put to some use my eight years of Latin and Greek grammar. It was then that I became an acolyte of Angelo Segré, whom I knew as a fellow law professor with my father at the University of Catania. Segré was a scholar of Roman law, but, coming from a family of distinguished scientists and mathematicians, had specialized in the study of ancient measures.

Upon completing my secondary education, I ended my study with Segré to register as a student at the University of Freiburg, Germany. Since at that age one believes that a thinking person must have a philosophical foundation, I chose Freiburg because it was the university where Husserl taught, whose philosophy appealed to me because of its mathematical rigor. But at Freiburg at the moment the focus of attention was the philosopher Heidegger, who had just announced to the world the discovery of something called existentialism. I did not share the excitement of my fellow students for the new dispensation (although I liked the lectures on existentialist mathematics by Oskar Becker), but there were a couple of things that I learned from Heidegger. One was that the idea of the progress of human civilization, on which practically all historians operate, is a theological doctrine developed by the Church Fathers. The other, more specific, was that scholars of Greek culture have murdered the texts of early Greek philosophers, on the assumption that since they were early philosophers they must have had infantile conceptions. In the area of my vocational studies, I identified myself with a group of professors, led by Fritz Pringsheim, who had dedicated themselves to one topic, the contract of sale in ancient times. Since seminar work consisted in interpreting contracts from several areas of the eastern Mediterranean, I focused my attention on the clauses relating to measures, which these contracts contain in abundance. My teachers were tolerant of my passion; for instance, Otto Lenel in his *privatissimum,* dedicated to the development of postclassical Roman law, allowed me to read a paper on the length of the miles in the Syro-Roman Law Book.

After the Freiburg group was disbanded by Hitler, I returned to Italy, where I received a doctorate in the field of Roman law. On that basis I became assistant to the chair of history of Roman law at the University of Rome and a member of the Institute of Roman and Oriental Law of that University. During my Roman years, I learned the most from Edoardo Volterra, later holder of the chair of Oriental law at the University of Rome; he was sympathetic to my interests, since he was the son of the famous mathematician Vito Volterra.

When World War II brought me to the United States, since my interests were historical rather than legal, I registered as a candidate for a doctorate in ancient history at Harvard University. There I discovered that those who come to ancient history from literature have a completely different view of the ancient world from the practical, realistic, and utilitarian view which prevails in legal studies: in substance they see the ancient world as the realm of poetic fantasy. My Harvard teachers used to admonish me to understand "the spirit of the ancients," but the only image that their perorations could stir in my mind was the image of the ancients in a constant state of alcoholic stupor. As to my special field of research, my teachers thought that my notion that the Greeks were concerned with precision in measurement was intellectually preposterous and historically impossible.

The terms of the controversy were clarified for me by Werner Jaeger, who tried to support me by suggesting that I write under him a thesis on the concept of *akribeia,* "precision," in Greek thought. In outlining the proposed thesis, Jaeger explained that with Isocrates there was developed in Greece a new conception of humanism opposed to *akribeia.* Jaeger was impliying that my critics were followers of Isocratean humanism. Because of youthful stubbornness, I declined the flattering offer of Jaeger, being convinced that what counts is to put precision into practice, rather than to talk about it. I tried to prove my point by submitting a thesis on "The Origin of Money in Greece." It was accepted as containing much that was valuable, but I received the advice that before publishing it I should cut down on "all those numbers."

After this, I thought that I could still achieve a result by expanding my documentation. From the study of Greek monetary weights and the operation of Greek mints, I passed to the topic of the dimensions of Greek temples. The study of Greek temples much later led me to the study of ancient geography and geodesy. But I was gradually forced to accept the fact that scholars of ancient history do not read numbers, neither in ancient texts nor in research papers. I noticed a number of times, when I submitted a paper for judgment to a specialist of a particular area, that he would quickly turn a page if he saw numbers on it. In many different guises I was told that "numbers do not constitute evidence in ancient studies." Finally, I learned that I had no choice but to pursue my interests in splendid isolation.

About ten years ago I exchanged manuscripts with Hertha von Dechend, who was then beginning to write her book *Hamlet's Mill.* As an expert of ancient cosmology, she raised a strong objection to the fact that I would discuss length, volume, and weight for hundreds of typewritten pages, without ever mentioning time, whereas the ancients were dominated by the preoccupation with cosmic time, with the movement of the vault of heaven. I answered that she was right, but that I had not yet found in the texts anything that would establish a connection between time and other measures. Giorgio de Santillana, who was writing *Hamlet's Mill* together with Dechend, teased me in a friendly way by saying that I had become so stuck in the mire of economic documents that I could not lift myself out of it; I replied in the same half-serious tone that I was willing to lift my eyes to heaven only on condition of being sure that my feet remained firmly planted on the ground.

Although I recognize that astronomical measurements are extremely important, I have always been wary of dealing with them, because studies of ancient astronomy have become cluttered with metaphysical and theological doctrines. My opposition to the view that the ancients lived in a world of fantasies or even of outright hallucinations (as it is specifically claimed by scholars of ancient astronomy) is such that, after years of dealing with all sorts of measurements, I still feel most at ease with agrarian measures in cuneiform tablets, rates of money exchange in Greek inscriptions, or the volume of jars in papyri from Egypt. Yet the techniques of land surveying used in Meso-

potamia are a key to the understanding of how the ancients mapped the sky.

Because of my horror of metaphysical or pseudo-metaphysical intrusions, I had several times picked up and then dropped the problem of the dimensions of the Great Pyramid of Giza. It was only after Peter Tompkins took upon himself the task of organizing the literature in the field, separating sense from nonsense, that I gained the courage to deal with the problem to the point of some conclusion. In the course of discussing with me the geometry of the Great Pyramid, Tompkins explained how the Great Pyramid with its galleries could have been used to measure the movements of the vault of heaven. In describing the possible procedures, he pointed out how a second of time in the motion of the vault of heaven corresponds to a definite length on earth. For me this was a Galilean revolution in that it permitted me to see ancient astronomy in terms of observational techniques based on measurements, rather than systems based on the theological persuasions or the psychological projections of the modern investigators. Once I was able to link time together with length, volume, and weight, a number of scattered researches suddenly became related to each other. Up to that moment I had had the uncanny feeling that somewhere there was a piece missing, and I knew that a missing piece, even a little one, is vital when one deals with measurements.

Since Tompkins has asked me to write a summary of my findings that relate to the problem of the Great Pyramid, I have tried to comply with his request.

I. EGYPTIAN GEODETIC SYSTEM

1. The present Arabic name of Egypt is *al Miṣri,* which is the equivalent of the biblical *Miṣraîm.* This name is derived from the Semitic root which in Akkadian gives the verb *aṣaru,* "to cut, to delimit, to delineate," and hence "to draw a picture, a plan," and the noun *eṣertu,* "drawing plan, representation," applied in particular to the specifications for the construction of a building. In Semitic language an "m" before the root of a verb forms what we would call a past participle: Egypt is the country built according to a geometric plan.

The Egyptians expressed this idea by calling their land *To-Mera,* "the land of the *mr.*" The word *mr* is used to refer to the pyramids, but more specifically it refers to the meridian triangle of a pyramid, whose hypotenuse is the apothem. The *mr* essentially is a right triangle with an angle of 36° and another angle which of necessity is 54°.

Since the Egyptians did not have trigonometric tables, they used this triangle to obtain the value of trigonometric functions. They conceived of this triangle as the basic building block of the cosmos. They used this triangle or modifications of it by a few degrees in geometric constructions, in the planning of buildings, in surveying, and in geography.

In the last century the Egyptologist Karl H. Brugsch noticed that the hieroglyphic sign for *mr* when used in the name *To-Mera* is accompanied by a determinative in the form of a fret or Greek key. In hieroglyphic writing a determinative is an extra sign which helps in understanding the meaning of a word by indicating the class of concepts to which the word belongs. Brugsch observed that this fret is "a peculiarly shaped geometric figure which in principle could represent the entire land *Mera* and must have a meaning pertaining to a specific peculiarity of Egypt." But, although he was much more sympathetic to science than Egyptologists usually are, he did not pursue this line of reasoning. He resisted accepting the notion that the Egyptians conceived of their country as having an exact geometric shape.

The Egyptians were proud that their country had some unique geographic features which could be expressed in rigorous geometric terms and had a shape which related to the order of the cosmos as they saw it. They believed that when the gods created the cosmos they began by building Egypt and, having created it perfect, modeled the rest around it.

2.   Everybody knows that Egypt is a most peculiar, almost unique, country. Since it seldom rains there, the entire life of humans, animals, and plants depends on the water of the Nile. It is also known that the Egyptians linked the regular flood of the Nile with the movement of the sun and other heavenly bodies, such as the star Sirius. But the Egyptians put great stress also on the geographic peculiarities of the course of the Nile.

The Nile originates at the equator from lakes so immense that their water could be identified with the primeval water of the ocean. From the equator it moves north following substantially the meridian of its source at Lake Albert. It follows this line up to latitude 30°, one-third of the distance from the equator to the pole.

The key geographic position in Egyptian geography was the southern tip of the island today called al-Warraq, at the northern limit of the city of Cairo, where the Nile begins to divide into branches to form the estuary which the Greeks called Delta, after the triangular shape of the fourth letter of their alphabet. The apex of the Delta, the tip of the island al-Warraq, is cut by meridian 31° 14′ east. This meridian indicates the main line of the course of the Nile from the equator to the apex of the Delta and divides the Delta into two equal parts. It was considered the main axis of Egypt.

But in terms of latitude the apex appeared at first not as perfect as it should have been, since it was at latitude 30° 06′ north and not at the perfect latitude 30° 00′ north, which is the latitude of the Great Pyramid of Giza. But the Egyptians reassured themselves by observing that the southern limit of Egypt is indicated by the First Cataract. The upper edge of this cataract is at the perfect latitude 24° 00′ north, whereas its lower edge is at 24° 06′ north. Hence, they could say that Southern Egypt has an extension of 6° 00′, which may be counted either from 24° 00′ to 30° 00′ north or from 24° 06′ to 30° 06′ north. They adopted as a principle that geographic distances are measured by units of 6 minutes (1/10 degree). They assumed that the interval between the equator and the pole was divided into belts (in pictures they portrayed actual belts with clasps) of 6′; on the basis of this the Greeks introduced into our geography the term zone, which in Greek means "belt."

For the benefit of those who understand mathematics, I may add that the Egyptians analyzed curves by dividing the area under a curve into a series of rectangles, which is the basic principle of integral calculus. It seems that in analyzing the curvature of the earth, they used rectangles 6′ wide.

Geographically Egypt is divided into two different parts. Southern (or Upper) Egypt is essentially a canyon cut into the desert plateau by the Nile; it is long and narrow. Northern (or Lower) Egypt is a typical estuary, swampy and wide. In spite of the efforts of the rulers to stress the unity of the country, the two parts continued to be conceived as different even in political and administrative terms. This is the reason why the Hebrew word for Egypt, Miṣraîm, has the grammatical form of the dual. The Pharaoh wore two crowns on his head: a red straw hat for Northern Egypt and a white wool cap for Southern Egypt.

Although not much is known about the history of pre-dynastic Egypt, it seems rather well established that in this period the two Egypts were unified for a time, with a capital at Behdet at the extreme north of the curved coastline of the estuary, as far north as one could go in Egypt. Although archeologists have not yet identified the location of Behdet, the data of geography indicate that Behdet, either as a geodetic point or as an actual city, was at 31° 30′ north 31° 14′ east. It was on the main axis of Egypt and of the

Nile, on the meridian of the apex of the Delta, at a distance of 7° 30' (1/12 of arc of meridian) from the southern boundary of 24° 00' north and at a distance of 1° 24' = 1.4° from the apex. The distance from latitude 30° 00' north is 1° 30', so that it could be assumed that Southern Egypt relates to Northern Egypt as 4:1. Southern Egypt is 1/15 of arc of meridian and Northern Egypt is 1/60. We shall see that the total length of Egypt from 24° 00' north to Behdet was calculated as 1,800,000 geographic cubits. Since 400 cubits is a stadium and 600 stadia is a degree, it is a length of 4500 stadia (3600 stadia for Southern Egypt and 900 stadia for Northern Egypt).

This is the way in which the dimensions of Egypt were rationalized in the predynastic period.

3. The dynastic period begins with the final unification of the two Egypts. At this moment Egypt emerged from prehistory, because writing was invented in the form of hieroglyphs. At the same time the geodetic system of Egypt was revised, stressing the importance of the number 7 and linking the geography of Egypt with the geography of the heavens.

The main feature of the map of the sky is that the sun follows a course which is at an angle with the equator. The circle marked by the sun is called the ecliptic and the angle of this circle with the circle of the equator is the angle of the ecliptic (roughly 24°). The ecliptic cuts the plane of the equator at two points and reaches its highest and lowest points in relation to the equator at celestial latitudes which are marked on the surface of the earth by the tropics.

The moon and the planets in their movements around the earth follow substantially the line of the ecliptic, being at times north and at times south of the course of the sun. (The body which deviates most sharply from the ecliptic is Mercury. Mercury can be as much as 7° 00' north or south of the ecliptic.) For this reason it was conceived that there was marked in the heavens a great "highway" (*hodos* in Greek) in which there moved the sun, the moon, and the planets. This path is 14° wide and is the origin of the concept of the zodiacal band. Since Mercury determines its dimensions and determines them by a perfect figure, in ancient religions this planet was associated with the god of measurement. It was conceived that the sun, the moon, and the planets were engaged in competing with each other running in the racing course of the zodiacal band. Another conception was that there were two walls, running parallel 14° apart, within which there was going on a ball game. The notion of a wall accounted for the fact that the heavenly bodies could not go beyond a given distance from the ecliptic; they appeared to run away from the ecliptic, hit a wall, and bounce back past the ecliptic to hit the wall on the other side. This is the ritual origin of racing competitions (such as the Olympic races, on foot or in chariots) and of ball games. The most vivid expression of the second conception is the famous ball court in the Mayan city of Chichen Itzá; the structure of this ball court can be understood when one realizes that its two parallel side walls are unfolded cylindrical projections of the sky.

The zodiacal band was conceived to be the inhabited part of the sky; the rest of the sky was still and lifeless (*erēmos,* "desert, desolate," in Greek), because nothing moved in it, except for the rotation of the vault of heaven in a solid block. Hence, in order to make a map of the sky for the study of the moving heavenly bodies, it was enough to draw a map that reaches latitude 31° (24° + 7°). Such a map could be drawn in the form of a cylindrical projection without substantial deformation; this cylindrical projection was unfolded to form a rectangle.

On the basis of this conception, stress was put on the fact that Egypt begins at the line of the tropic of Cancer (the upper edge of the First Cataract is at 24° 00′ north) and extends north for 7°, so that Egypt could be considered as the equivalent on earth of the northern half of the zodiacal band. For the sake of mapping the earth from the equator to the northern limit of Egypt, one could use a cylindrical projection. The maximum deformation in such a type of projection could be determined; it was established that a degree of longitude at parallel 31° 06′ north is exactly 6/7 of a degree of longitude at the equator. According to the Clarke Spheroid a degree of equator is 111,321 meters, of which 6/7 is 95,418 meters; according to the same Spheroid a degree of longitude at 31° 06′ is 95,407 meters. To the north of latitude 31° 06′ north there was the expanse of the Mediterranean, the "Great Green" for the Egyptians, which could be compared with the expanse of the empty sky, north of the same celestial latitude.

The angle of the ecliptic has decreased slowly (today it is 23° 27′; it was about at 23° 45′ in the age of Ptolemy), and accordingly the tropic of Cancer has moved south. This movement is due to the gravitational pull of the planets, particularly Jupiter and Venus. Nobody as yet has succeeded in constructing a valid formula for calculating the angle of the ecliptic in ancient times. But, it is a fact that when the second geodetic system of Egypt was established it was assumed that the tropic of Cancer was at 23° 51′ north. Greek scholars living under the rule of the last Egyptian dynasty, the Ptolemies, continued to quote this figure, although it was not correct at their time.

If the tropic is at 23° 51′ north, it would follow that the southern border of Egypt is out of place. But the discrepancy was rationalized by considering the fact that when one follows the movement of the sun along the ecliptic by observing the shadow cast by a pointer, there must be introduced a correction of about 15′. The position of the shadow is not determined by the center of the sun, but by the upper limb of the disk. The apparent diameter of the sun is about half a degree; calculating exactly, it varies between 32′ 30″ and 31′ 28″, according to the seasons, but, considering the corrections that have to be made for the phenomenon of irradiation, the figure of 15′ for the half diameter of the disk of the sun is satisfactory.

If the tropic of Cancer is at 23° 51′ north, the point at which the sun is at the zenith at noon of the day of the summer solstice is at 24° 06′ north, that is, at the latitude of the lower edge of the First Cataract. Hence, the Egyptians conceived that the line of the tropic of Cancer was marked by three parallels: 23° 51′, 24° 00′, and 24° 06′ north.

For this reason the hieroglyphic symbol for Southern Egypt consists essentially of three parallel lines with a vertical line rising at the middle. Since hieroglyphic writing aims at being colorful and pictorially decorative, this symbol was stylized in the shape of a trunk of a tree from which there sprout three parallel tiers of branches. Egyptologists who do not want to recognize the existence of scientific thought in Egypt have stressed the incidental vegetal appearance of this symbol. They have understood that the name for Southern Egypt, which is *To-Shemau,* "the land of the heat, of the sun, of the summer solstice," means "the land of the plant *sh-m-a.*" But if there was such a plant associated with Southern Egypt (which as yet has not been identified), it is possibly the same plant which is called *šamšu,* "sunflower" in Akkadian; the word *šamšu* means "sun" in Akkadian (Hebrew: *šemeš*). In a text of the Old Kingdom in which the hieroglyphs are drawn with particular care, in the symbol for *shemau* there is only one tier of branches, but the trunk starts from a little arc, a semicircle, which obviously symbolizes a parallel. But what probably is most revealing is that in most hieroglyphic texts the tiers of branches sprout from the bottom of the trunk and not from its top.

4. Once the latitudes of the southern limit of Egypt were rationalized by identifying the line of the tropic with three parallels (the first of which cuts the lower edge of the First Cataract at 24° 06′, the second cuts the upper

edge of it at the perfect latitude 24° 00′, and the other cuts the Nile at 23° 51′ north, at a place which the Greeks called Parembole, "supplement, addition"), it became possible to rationalize the boundary between Southern Egypt and Northern Egypt. This boundary was understood as marked by three parallels, the first at 30° 06′, the latitude of the apex of the Delta, the second at the perfect latitude 30° 00′, and the third at latitude 29° 51′.

In the administration of Egypt, the area between 29° 51′ and 30° 06′ north was organized as a special district which did not belong either to the list of nomes (provinces) of Southern Egypt nor to that of nomes of Northern Egypt. The hieroglyph for this district is a rectangle which is either empty or filled with water or fish. A distinguished Egyptologist, being at a loss for a better explanation, has read this hieroglyph as "fishpond." He did not realize that a rectangle, either empty or filled with water or fish, is the symbol of the Square of Pegasus. In *Hamlet's Mill,* de Santillana and Dechend have presented illustrations of this symbolism occurring all over the globe (between pages 434 and 435). There are in the sky four stars which are at a distance of about 15° from each other and mark a square with sides that run according to the celestial meridians or parallels; these four stars form the Square of Pegasus. In iconography this square was at times portrayed as filled with water or fish, because it was in the constellation of Pisces. The Square of Pegasus was considered the starting point in the mapping of the sky. The ancients, from the Sumerians to the Romans, in surveying land began by marking a square of a standard dimension and then proceeded to measure out of it in a checkerboard pattern. In cuneiform texts the name *ikū* is given to the basic surveying square, to a unit of land surface, and to the Square of Pegasus. The hieroglyph used to refer to the district extending for 15′ from Memphis-Sokar to the apex of the Delta indicates that this district was considered the basic reference unit from which there started the mapping of Northern and Southern Egypt.

The capital of united Egypt was established at Memphis, at latitude 29° 51′ north. But, since the capital city of necessity had to be on the bank of the Nile, which here runs slightly east of the apex, the geodetic point was set to the west of the city in the funerary area (the city of the dead is always to the west of the city of the living), on the basic meridian 31° 14′ east. This was the point called Sokar, the name of which is preserved by the present village of Saqqara (29° 51′ north, 31° 14′ east). In the religion of the Old Kingdom, Sokar is an important god of orientation

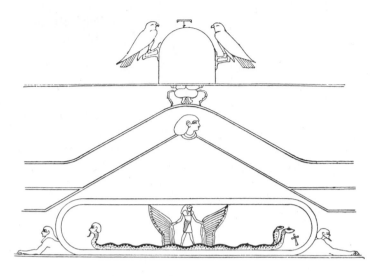

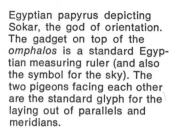

Egyptian papyrus depicting Sokar, the god of orientation. The gadget on top of the *omphalos* is a standard Egyptian measuring ruler (and also the symbol for the sky). The two pigeons facing each other are the standard glyph for the laying out of parallels and meridians.

and of cemeteries. The god and the geodetic point were represented by the stone object which the Greeks called *omphalos,* "navel"; it is a hemisphere (the northern hemisphere) resting on a cylinder (the foundations of the cosmos). Usually on top of Sokar, as on top of any *omphalos,* there are portrayed two birds facing each other; in ancient iconography these two birds, usually doves, are a standard symbol for the stretching of meridians and parallels.

The practice of placing the geodetic center in the city of the dead was followed by King Darius the Great, when he established a new capital for the Persian Empire, Persepolis. Historians have wondered why Darius should have chosen for Persepolis a most inconvenient location; actually the capital of Persepolis was seldom used except for ritualistic purposes. Persepolis is at latitude 30° 00′ north and three units of 7° 12′ east of the main axis of Egypt (31° 14′ east). The reason for choosing units of 7° 12′ is that the Persian Empire was mapped by drawing a series of geodetic squares, east and west of Persepolis, which extend 6° in latitude from 30° 00′ to 36° 00′ north and have a width of 7° 12′ of longitude, since 7° 12′ of longitude is equivalent in actual length to 6° of latitude at the middle point between 30° 00′ and 36° 00′ north. Hence, these geodetic squares are true squares. The geodetic point of Persepolis, 30° 00′ north, 52° 50′ east, is north and west of the wide expanse of the royal buildings and is identified by the tomb of King Darius, around which there were built the tombs of his successors. At the geodetic point 30° 00′ north, 52° 50′ east, there could be erected tombs, but there was not the kind of ground on which there could be stretched a capital city.

The location of Memphis-Sokar had the advantage of being exactly 8° north of the point where meridian 31° 14′ east cuts again the course of the Nile at the Second Cataract. In a new imperialistic spirit, Egypt in a wide sense was understood to end at the Second Cataract.

5. According to the new conception which links Egypt with the sky, if Southern Egypt extends 6° from the tropic, Northern Egypt must extend only 1° to the north of the apex, in order to be in agreement with the order of the cosmos. Hence, the northern limit of Egypt was set at parallel 31° 06′ north.

This was achieved by identifying the northern limit of Egypt with the line that joins the two outer ends of the estuary of the Nile. This line extended 1° 24′ = 1.4° east and west of the axis 31° 14′ east. Hence, there was marked a triangle, which the Greeks called the Delta, with a base line extending from 31° 38′ to 29° 50′ east along parallel 31° 06′ north and a vertex at the long-established point of the apex of the Delta. This isosceles triangle is divided by meridian 31° 14′ into two right triangles of the type *mr*. In calculating the proportions of this triangle, one must keep in mind that at latitude 31° 06′ north, 1.4° of longitude corresponds to 1.2° in actual length, since the degree of longitude is shrunk by 1/7 at this latitude.

The base line of the mathematical triangle of the Delta fell perfectly at the eastern end. Here the corner of the Delta coincides with the well-defined natural boundary point Pelusium, along the shore. On the western side the corner of the Delta did not fall right on the shore, but at the middle of a coastal lagoon; even today the eastern boundary of the Western Desert province of Egypt passes through it.

The old geodetic center of Behdet was not completely ignored, since it could be fitted into the system by considering that it is 1.4° north of the apex of the Delta.

I have stated earlier that it was assumed that at latitude 31° 06′, the degree of longitude is 6/7 of the degree of equator. This calculation permitted the rationalization of the shift of the key positions of Egypt by 6′ to the north of the perfect latitudes 24° 00′ and 30° 00′ north. The shift was related to the polar flattening of the earth, which, according to the septenary order of the cosmos, was assumed to be 1/280. If the earth were a perfect sphere, the degree of longitude which is 6/7 of degree of equator would be at latitude 31° 00′ (cosine 31° 00′ = 0.85717; 6/7 = 0.85714).

Anticipating what I will explain in greater detail later, I must mention here that the dimensions of Egypt were recalculated in terms of a new unit of length, the royal cubit, which is obtained by adding a seventh hand to the usual six which compose a cubit. In terms of this longer cubit, the length of Egypt from 31° 06′ to 24° 00′ north was set at 1,500,000 cubits. The royal cubit summed the septenary spirit of the new geodetic system.

In hieroglyphic writing the name for Northern Egypt is *To-Meḥu*. Most Egyptologists, following the line of reasoning which I have mentioned in relation to Southern Egypt, have understood that *To-Meḥu* means "the land of the papyrus," but the name of the papyrus is *ḥly,* and the symbol for Northern Egypt cannot be compared with a papyrus plant by any stretch of the imagination. The name of Northern Egypt can be explained when we consider that it is similar to the name of the cubit (*maḥe* in Coptic), which comes from a root which means "to fill up." Hence, *To-Meḥu* may mean "the land which fills up the dimensions of Egypt." Northern Egypt corresponds to the seventh hand added to the cubit.

From what we have of early writing attempts from predynastic Egypt, it is absolutely clear that the symbol for Northern Egypt used to be the red straw hat. With the beginning of the dynastic period, the creation of hieroglyphic writing, and the new geodetic system, the symbol of Northern Egypt becomes a plant with three stems springing from one root. In some cases the reference to the triangularity of the Delta is emphasized by putting at the end of each stem a flower with a triangular calyx. In carefully drawn representations the plant springs from a rectangle either empty or filled with the wavy line for water, which is the symbol for the intermediary district, extending from 29° 51′ to 30° 06′ north.

At times the stems in the symbol for Northern Egypt are broken and bent at the top. This may be a reference to the fact that in the new geodetic system the northern limit was lowered from 31° 30′ to 31° 06′ north.

On the two sides of the throne of the Pharaoh there was a design which Egyptologists call "Unity of Egypt." We know it well because it appears in all statues of Pharaohs sitting on the throne; the series of such statues starts with the Fourth Dynasty, but occasional drawings indicate that the design "Unity of Egypt" is older. In the course of centuries the design varied somewhat and the artists who carved the throne stylized it according to different tastes; but on the basis of what I have explained above, one can always recognize that it represents the geodetic system of Egypt.

The center of the design is the hieroglyphic sign for the verb "to unite," which is a windpipe with two lungs.

However, in the design "Unity of Egypt" the windpipe is stretched, so that it looks like a long trunk of a tree, in order to indicate the main axis of Egypt; the lungs are reduced to a diminutive size. On one side of the windpipe there is the symbol for Northern Egypt and on the other side the symbol for Southern Egypt. But what is most significant is that the entire drawing is tied together by a system of ropes and knots, which indicate the geodetic lines and points of Egypt.

The design called "Unity of Egypt" is the standard decoration of the royal throne, because it symbolizes all that the Egyptians held fundamental in their political, ethical, religious, and cosmological conceptions, a cluster of ideas which they summarized by the word *maet,* a word with which I will deal in a following chapter. Nevertheless, this design has received only casual attention. The best way in which I can convey in brief how this design is pregnant with meaning is by referring to Hebrew Cabalistic literature. The Cabala is a Hebrew underground religion or philosophy. The starting point of Cabalistic doctrine is that God in creating the world began by creating the ten numbers and arranged them according to a diagram of points and connecting lines, which proves to be modeled on the design "Unity of Egypt." Actually, what gave me the first insights into the Egyptian geodetic system was the reading of the Italian Renaissance scientists who were influenced by Hebrew Cabalists.

The state of Israel has adopted as its national emblem the Cabalistic symbol of two overlapping triangles. These two triangles should be seen as inscribed in a circle: they represent the poles, the tropics, and the ecliptic, besides having the added meaning of the male and female elements coming together to generate the cosmos. The Founding Fathers adopted as the seal of the United States a pyramid; they wanted to convey the notion that a perfect society had been organized, and in order to convey it they adopted a symbol which, through the tradition transmitted by masonic societies, goes back to the Egyptian idea of *maet.*

6. The geodetic system established at the beginning of the Old Kingdom was modified in part with the advent of the Twelfth Dynasty, the most dynamic of the Egyptian dynasties as far as we know. The advent of this dynasty marks the beginning of what scholars call the Middle Kingdom period. But probably more significant in Egyptian terms was that the advent of this dynasty coincided with the beginning of the age of Aries. It became necessary to revise the system of cosmology, since the sun had moved out of the constellation of Taurus to enter into that of

301

Aries. The kings of this dynasty identified themselves with the god Amon, symbolized by the ram. The first king of the dynasty called himself Amenemhet, introducing the custom of theophoric names, that is, of personal names composed with the name of a god. The god Amon was made to spring from relative obscurity into the position of the main official divinity of Egypt. It seems that up to that time Amon was a local god of the desert area west of Thebes or that Amon was identified with a local god of that area.

The Twelfth Dynasty moved the capital and the geodetic center of Egypt to a more central position, Thebes. The longitude of the new capital was determined by the point where the eastern axis of Egypt (32° 38′ east) cuts the course of the Nile. The latitude was 2/7 of the distance from the equator to the pole (25° 42′ 51″ north). This latitude was marked by the central room of the temple of Amon, in which the god and the geodetic point most probably was indicated by the same object, the *omphalos,* "navel," which used to represent the god Sokar. What is certain is that when centuries later in the capital of Nubia, Napata, there was built a second temple of Amon in order to link Nubia with Egypt politically, in the center of this temple there was placed such an object.

Egyptologists have tried to torture Egyptian linguistics in order to explain why the Greeks should have given the name Thebes to a city which the Egyptians called Wast. The likely explanation is that the Greeks learned the name of the city from the Phoenicians, who in their own language called it *thibbûn,* "navel." There is textual evidence that in Hebrew, which is practically the same language as Phoenician, the word *thibbûn* is used to refer to a geodetic navel.

The choice of the latitude emphasized the septenary system of Egyptian geography. The ancients divided the space between the pole and the equator into seven zones. This is indicated not only by Greek writers of geography, but also by the ziggurats of Mesopotamia and the earliest pyramids of Egypt, which are step pyramids.

7.   It was possibly on the occasion of the transfer of the capital and geodetic center to Thebes, which stresses the importance of the eastern meridian of Egypt (32° 38′ east), that something was done to rationalize the longitude of the First Cataract. The First Cataract happened not to be included in the rectangle of Egypt, being somewhat to the east of meridian 32° 38′, at 32° 53′ east. The lower edge of the cataract, at 24° 06′ north, 32° 53′ east, is 15′ north of the right position and 15′ west of it. It must have been

disturbing that the southern boundary of Egypt should not fit with the system of three meridians passing through the three angles of the Delta triangle. Hence, the area of the First Cataract was extended southward along the course of the Nile up to the point where meridian 32° 38′ east cuts the course of the Nile. This point happens to be at 23° 00′ north. The new point 23° 00′ north, 32° 38′ east was called Sacred Sycamore and was set as the legal boundary of Egypt. The stretch of the Nile from the Sacred Sycamore to the First Cataract was attached to the district of the First Cataract. In Hellenistic times this attached district was called Dodekaschoinos, which in Egyptian would be "twelve *atur*." The *atur,* as I will explain later, was a unit of length such that slightly more than 14 (14 in practical computations) went into a degree. If the distance of 51′ between 23° 00′ and 23° 51′ north, the correct line of the tropic, is calculated as 12 *atur,* it means that counting exactly a degree would be 14.11765 *atur.* The Egyptians used two types of *atur:* an *atur* of 17,000 geographic cubits (7848.8 meters) and an *atur* of 15,000 royal cubits (7862.2 meters). Now, 51′ at latitude 23° to 24° is about 94,135 meters, whereas 12 *atur* of the first kind is 94,186 meters and 12 *atur* of the second kind is 94,346 meters.

Even though the district Dodekaschoinos was attached to Egypt purely for mathematical reasons, it continued to be included in Egypt into the Roman period.

I suggest that the establishment of the supplementary district Dodekaschoinos with a new southern boundary of Egypt at 23° 00′ north was linked with the transfer of the capital to Thebes, because there is a text which gives the dimensions of Egypt from the sea at Pelusium (eastern corner of the triangle of the Delta) to the end of the district Dodekaschoinos, that is, all along meridian 32° 38′ east. The distance is divided into two-thirds from Pelusium to Thebes and one-third from Thebes to the Sacred Sycamore. If we round the latitude of Thebes from 25° 42′ 51″ north to 25° 42′ north, the calculation is perfect:

$$31° \ 06′ \text{ to } 25° \ 42′ \text{ north} = 5° \ 24′$$
$$25° \ 42′ \text{ to } 23° \ 00′ \text{ north} = 2° \ 42′$$

When the southern boundary of Egypt is moved to the Sacred Sycamore by adding the district Dodekaschoinos, the Temple of Amon in Thebes is in a rational position not only in relation to arc of meridian, but also in relation to the extension of Egypt.

The text that gives the information just mentioned indicates also that the latitude of Thebes has a further peculiarity: at this latitude the degree of longitude is 9/10 of degree of equator.

303

II. EGYPTIAN UNITS OF LENGTH

1. All the measures of length, volume, and weight of the ancient world, including those of China and India, constituted a rational and organic system, which can be reconstructed starting from a fundamental unit of length. I have not yet completed the gathering of data concerning the units of pre-Columbian America, because these are difficult to obtain, since the metrology of the American continent has received meager attention; but the figures that I have succeeded in establishing so far suggest that the American units agree with those of the Old World. The units used in Europe up to the adoption of the French metric system were the ancient ones or modifications of them introduced for specific reasons. The ancient system of measures continues to be used today in the form of English measures; we find the basic units of the English system, such as the pound of 453.8 grams, used in Mesopotamia in the third millennium B.C.

The effort to reconstruct the original and unitary system of measures was started by scholars of the Renaissance as a result of the beginning of the age of geographical discoveries. Their investigations, although they took the form of antiquarian research, had two practical purposes: to interpret correctly the data provided by ancient geographers and to establish an absolutely reliable and fixed standard of length. Although the major concern of Renaissance investigators of measures was to establish the exact value of the ancient Roman foot, they were also concerned with a tradition to the effect that all measures were derived from the Egyptian ones. This is the reason why John Greaves went to measure the Great Pyramid of Giza, in order to complete his researches on the length of the ancient Roman foot. In Egypt Greaves met with Burattini, who had gone to measure the monuments of Egypt, in order to establish the linear starting point (for which he coined the name *meter*) in his proposal for a new metric system which would be strictly decimal, like the one later adopted as the French metric system. Greaves had the advantage of having spent a long time in Rome measuring buildings, vessels, and weights and of being provided with accurate measuring tools, based on English units; Burattini had the advantage of having already measured a number of Egyptian buildings. Greaves and Burattini joined forces in measuring the Great Pyramid of Giza, which they hoped would provide a solution to their problems. After this survey Greaves returned to England, leaving his measuring tools with Burattini, who continued the study of Egyptian monuments. On his return Greaves published the results obtained at Giza, results which were later interpreted by Newton. But Burattini had the ill luck to be robbed of his notes by Hungarian brigands while on his way to Poland. As a result, when he published his proposal for a decimal metric system, for lack of a better alternative, he advocated that one should start with the English foot and divide the cube of this foot decimally in order to obtain the units of volume and weight.

The study of Egyptian measures received a new impulsion with the Napoleonic expedition to Egypt and the consequent decipherment of Egyptian hieroglyphs by Champollion. This decipherment had been unsuccessfully attempted by Father Athanasius Kircher, who had sponsored Burattini's expedition to Egypt. In the first half of the nineteenth century, it was established that the Egyptians had a septenary system of linear units.

In the ancient world one measured by feet and cubits. The cubit is equal to 1 1/2 feet. The cubit is divided into 6 hands of 4 fingers each (24 fingers) and the foot is divided into 4 hands (16 fingers). The division of the foot into 12 inches, with which we are familiar, became common only with the Romans. According to the Roman reckoning the cubit is 16 inches. The inch was considered to be the thickness of the thumb; generally in the ancient world one preferred to reckon by fingers, assumed to be the thickness of the other four fingers. It must be kept in mind, however, that terms like foot, cubit, finger, and inch were introduced in order to give a name to units obtained scientifically, units which correspond only vaguely to the natural units of the same name.

Scholars of Egyptology concluded that the Egyptians had started with a foot of 300 millimeters and a corresponding cubit of 450 millimeters, divided into 16 and 24 fingers as in the rest of the ancient world, but then had adopted as their linear basic unit a cubit, called a royal cubit, of 525 millimeters. The royal cubit is composed of 7 hands, or 28 fingers: it is an ordinary cubit with a seventh hand added.

2. One can find examples of septenary units also outside Egypt. The use of measuring rods of seven feet is common in medieval and early modern Europe. A typical example of septenary units is the Russian *sajen'*, which is composed of 7 English feet and is divided into 3 *arshin* of 28 inches. The *sajen'* was the basis of the Russian system of measures until the Soviet government adopted the French metric system in 1918.

The reason for the occurrence of septenary units is that they were convenient in practical reckonings. Agrarian units of surface were arranged in a series in which each was double of the preceding one. It was assumed in practical

Egyptian measuring rule carved out of wood showing various fingers, palms, and cubits (at present in the Turin Musem).

305

reckonings that a square with a side of 100 was the double of a square with a side of 70 and the half of a square with a side of 140. This implies that $\sqrt{2} = 1.414214$, taken as equal to 1.4. A typical example of this reckoning is the area of 5000 square cubits, within which a Jew can move on the Sabbath, which is described by the Talmud as "the square of seventy cubits." When greater precision was desired in practical reckonings, one averaged the results of considering the diagonal of a square as 10/7 of the side and as 14/10 of the side ($1.42857 + 1.4/2 = 1.41428$).

Septenary units were used also in order to facilitate other practical reckonings. The height of an equilateral triangle being equal to $\sqrt{3}/2$ of the side, the relation can be taken as 7:6, since $12/7 = 1.71428$ and $\sqrt{3} = 1.73205$.

According to the septenary system of reckoning, the circumference was considered 22/7 of the diameter; the approximation $\pi = 3 \ 1/7 = 3.142857$ is still used today as an adequate approximation in many problems of engineering.

The figure 22/7 used to obtain the value of π in practical reckonings is related to the fact that the ancients used both septenary and undecimal (i.e., eleven-based) units in order to achieve easy computations in practical reckonings. Undecimal linear units were common in the ancient and early modern world; an example of them is the English chain of 66 feet. An acre, originally a square with sides of 70 yards, is now 10 square chains (4840 sq. yards).

An important practical problem involving the number π was solved by the use of undecimal units. Units of volume were legally defined as cubes, but measuring vessels were built as cylinders. All that an ordinary potter, who could be an illiterate person, had to know was that, in order to construct a cylinder equal in volume to a given cube, he had to take the height and width of the cube and use them as the height and diameter of the cylinder, provided he measured the cylinder by a ruler based on a unit of length increased by 1/10. The procedure results in a cylinder of slightly excessive volume. If we assume a cube with a side of 10 fingers, its volume is 1000 cubic fingers. A cylinder with a diameter of 11 fingers and height of 11 has a volume of 1045.4 cubic fingers. But this small excess was automatically corrected in practice, since a measuring vase must have a rim and cannot be filled to the brim. A filling line marked on the measuring vase slightly below the brim took care of the difference. I first became aware of this procedure in interpreting cuneiform mathematical texts, but later I found it referred to in Athenian inscriptions and applied concretely in Athenian measuring vessels.

By combining calculations by the factor 7 and calculations

by the factor 11, one could solve practically a number of geometric problems involving irrational numbers. This practice is one of the reasons why the builders of the Great Pyramid began their plan with a height of 280 royal cubits and a side of 440.

A simple example of the combination of reckoning by septenary and undecimal units is the following. As I have said, in agrarian units it was assumed that a square with the side of 100 is the double of a square with a side of 70 and half of a square with a side of 140. This procedure would result in units of the following surface:

$$49,000$$
$$100,000$$
$$196,000$$

In order to make the series more regular, the middle unit was often taken as a square with a side of 99, so that the series became:

$$49,000$$
$$98,010$$
$$196,000$$

When Herodotus reports the surface of the sides of the Great Pyramid, he reckons by units of surface calculating by the second pattern.

Although the use of septenary units had been common in ancient times and later, in Egypt the septenary cubit became a national symbol related to the essential structure of Egypt and of the cosmic order.

3. In the second half of the nineteenth century, some scholars of ancient measures tried to derive them from the Egyptian units of length. Although in the last fifty years it has become fashionable among scholars of ancient cultures to deny that they had any knowledge of a scientific system of measures, all serious scholars of ancient and medieval measures have always known that all measures of volume and weight are derived from the units of length. Units of volume were obtained by cubing the units of length. Units of weight were obtained by filling the units of volume with rain water at ordinary temperature; this water has the same density as distilled water at 4° Centigrade adopted by the French metric system, since in the earlier procedure the impurities of the rain water compensated for the higher temperature.

Friedrich Hultsch, who was the most authoritative investigator of ancient measures in the later part of the last century, concluded his lifelong research by announcing just before his death that all ancient measures could be derived from the Egyptian foot of 300 millimeters and from the corresponding ordinary (not septenary) cubit of 450 millimeters. He also supported the view expressed by others that the Egyptian unit of weight called *qedet,* of 9 grams, is the basic unit of weight of the ancient world.

But Hultsch left a difficulty unsolved. If we cube an Egyptian foot of 300 millimeters, we obtain a cube of 27,000 cubic centimeters or grams, which is divided into 3000 *qedet* of 9 grams. If we cube an Egyptian ordinary cubit of 450 millimeters, we obtain a cube of 91,125 cubic centimeters or grams, which is divided into 10,000 *qedet* of 9.1125 grams. Sample weights indicate that both *qedet* were used in Egypt. A *qedet* of 9 grams relates to a *qedet* of 9.1125 grams as 80:81.

The same discrepancy occurs all over the ancient world. Prince Mihail Sutzu, Director of the National Bank of Rumania, having dedicated his life to the study of ancient weights, in 1930 concluded that the *qedet* of 9 grams is the *bazele fundamentale ale metrologiei ponderale din antichitate,* but, in order to explain the mentioned discrepancy in weights, supposed that there had been a gradual decrease from a unit of 9.20 grams established in the neolithic period.

But in presenting this explanation Sutzu contradicted one of his basic assumptions, which is the amazing stability of measures throughout history. From the very beginning of literate cultures, documents indicate an extreme concern with the preservation of exact metric standards. The concern with precision seems to have lessened in the course of history. Early modern Europe was less careful than medieval Europe. The Greeks of the Hellenistic age were less careful than those of the classical age. Even though the Greeks of the classical age seem to have been obsessed with the problem of correct standards, they did not reach the subtlety of Egypt and Mesopotamia. One of the reasons why the study of the history of measures was actively pursued in the late Renaissance was that by that time standards had started to waver.

There were two factors which determined extreme concern with absolutely exact standards: units of length were used to measure geographic distances, and units of weight were used to measure gold and silver used as means of exchange.

The amazing stability of measures is indicated by the circumstance that the kilogram was established by relating it to the Paris livre which was directly related to the Roman *libra.* The official definition of the kilogram is such that the livre equals 489.5058466 grams. Since the livre was divided into 9216 grains (16 ounces of 24 scruples of 24 grains), the Paris grain according to this definition is 0.05311478 gram. Historically the Paris livre was established by fixing the Paris grains as 1/6100 of the ancient Roman *libra,* the Roman *libra* being 324 grams (5000 English grains) or 36 Egyptian *qedet.* If the original standard had been preserved, the grain of Paris would have been found at the moment of adoption of the French metric system to be 0.05311475 gram and the livre to be 489.5055737 grams. In substance the standard of the Paris livre and hence of the Roman *libra* appear to have been well preserved, even though those who established the French metric system did not consider the theoretical foundations of the livre, but simply averaged several sample weights which were available. However, scholars of the seventeenth century complained that Paris measures were not very clearly defined and had concluded that English units of weight were more exactly defined.

The English grain has remained stable as 1/5000 of a Roman *libra.* English weight units have not changed at all since Sumerian times. The oldest weights of which I have found mention in an archeological report are those excavated at Tepe Gawra in Iraq, near the present oil center of Mosul. The lowest strata of Tepe Gawra embody the very first steps of the transition from village life to urban life. The earliest weights of Tepe Gawra precede by about a millennium the invention of writing. According to my interpretation these weights are fractions of the present English ounce avoirdupois of 28.350 grams (1/16 pound, which is 7/5 of a Roman *libra*).

4. Before explaining why there was a *qedet* of 9 grams and a *qedet* of 9.1125 grams, I must deal with a much more serious difficulty met by Hultsch.

He assumed that all measures of the ancient world can be derived from the Egyptian foot, but could not solve the absolutely essential problem of explaining how the Roman foot of roughly 296 millimeters could be derived from the Egyptian foot of 300 millimeters.

The key to the solution of this problem was provided to me when in 1942 the archeologist August Oxé, at the end of lifelong research, published a monograph explaining that almost all units of volume and weight of the ancient world exist in two varieties, related as:

12.5	25	50	62.5	75	100	125	150
12	24	48	60	72	96	120	144

He called the first series units *brutto,* and the second series units *netto.* The reason for the existence of the second series is that it is impossible from the practical point of view to divide decimally a cube into smaller cubes.

Developing the discovery of Oxé, I arrived at the logical consequence that units of length must usually occur in two varieties, one which is the edge of a cube containing a unit *brutto* and one which is the edge of a cube containing a unit *netto.* The two varieties of units of length are related as $\sqrt[3]{25}:\sqrt[3]{24}$. I call the first group of units of length by the name of *natural* units and the second group by the name of *trimmed* units.

From an Egyptian cubit of 300 millimeters we derive:

> Basic talent *brutto* of 27,000 cubic centimeters or grams
> 1000 Roman ounces of 27 cubic centimeters or grams
> 3000 Egyptian *qedet* of 9 grams

It follows that the cube of the Roman foot (which the Romans called *quadrantal,* or *pes quadratus*) must be 24/25 of the preceding unit:

> Basic talent *netto* of 25,920 cubic centimeters or grams
> 960 Roman ounces of 27 cubic centimeters or grams
> 2880 Egyptian *qedet* of 9 grams

The Roman quadrantal or basic talent *netto* is divided into 80 librae of 324 grams (12 ounces or 36 *qedet*). The libra is equal to 5000 English grains.

Accordingly I could establish that the Roman foot relates as $\sqrt[3]{24}:\sqrt[3]{25}$ to the Egyptian foot of 300 millimeters, and hence is a unit of 295.9454 millimeters, which is a figure in agreement with the empirical evidence.

Having established the theoretical basis of the Roman foot and of the Roman quadrantal, I could dispose of a difficulty which had bedeviled scholars since the Renaissance. By examining the empirical evidence it had been established that the Roman foot existed in two varieties, one shorter (called *pes Statilianus* by Renaissance scholars) and one longer (called *pes Aebutianus*). Correspondingly, there were two varieties of Roman libra.

The explanation for this difference is that units of volume and weight may occur in two varieties related as 80:81, with a difference which I call discrepancy komma. In 1909 Jean Adolphe Decourdemanche, at the end of his book on Arabic measures, added a proviso explaining that all Arabic units of weight and volume occur in two varieties related as 80:81. My teacher Angelo Segré, in studying the measures of Hellenistic Egypt, found that, although the cube of the cubit is 3 3/8 of the cube of the foot, given that $(1\ 1/2)^3:1^3 = 3\ 3/8:1$, often this relation between the cube of the cubit and the cube of the foot is taken as a relation 3 1/3:1 for the sake of easy reckoning, with the result that there is a discrepancy of 1/80, since 3 1/3:3 3/8 = 80:81.

The most striking example of the discrepancy komma (1/80) is that next to the quadrantal (cubed Roman foot) of 80 librae there is a quadrantal of 81 librae. This larger quadrantal has an edge which constitutes a special Roman foot of 297.1734 millimeters (instead of 295.9454 millimeters), which was called geometric foot in the Middle Ages. The Roman foot of the geometric variety was the scientific foot of early modern science. Scientists began to calculate by the French *pied de roi* (which originally was the undecimal version, 11/10, of the Roman foot) after Picard used it in his famous calculation of the circumference of the earth, and Newton quoted Picard's figures in presenting the empirical proofs for the theory of gravitation. The *pied de roi* was used in calculating the length of the Paris meter, theoretically defined as 1/10,000,000 of the arc of meridian: the meter is 1/10,000,000 of 30,784,440 *pieds de roi,* which was then the assumed length of the arc of meridian from the equator to the pole.

By dividing the quadrantal of 81 librae into 80 librae, the Romans obtained a libra of 328.050 grams, which was called the *geometric libra* in the Middle Ages. The edge of the larger quadrantal, the Roman *geometric foot,* was the standard unit in the planning of most monuments of classical Athens.

The larger Roman quadrantal (81 regular librae = 80 librae of the geometric variety), cube of a Roman geometric foot 297.1734 millimeters, contains 26,244 cubic centimeters or grams. It survived up to recently as the Russian *chetverik* (this Russian term has the same meaning as the Latin *quadrantal*). The law of 1918 that introduced the French metric system in the Soviet Union fixed the *chetverik* at 26,239 cubic centimeters.

The reason for the small difference is that Czar Peter the Great, according to his westernizing policy, had the length of the Russian *sajen'* readjusted to make it equal to 7 of the feet used in England. But the exact standard of the English foot had been lost in the Elizabethan age, and the length of the English foot has wavered until in England there was established the Imperial Yard of 1824, which makes the foot equal to 304.79974 millimeters, and in the United States the foot was defined by the Paris meter as 304.8 millimeters (act of Congress of 1928). The reform of Peter the Great caused uncertainties in the definition of Russian measures. The action of one autocrat extended the damage caused by another. As far as I can understand the record, the problem of the length of the English foot arose when Queen Elizabeth, following her policy which aimed at reducing the power of the municipal body of London, downgraded the authority of the standard of Guild Hall (*pes Curiae Londinensis*), which was considered by scholars the best standard of English foot. Incidentally, Piazzi Smyth suggested that a way to reconstruct the authentic value of the English foot is to compare the actual dimensions of the King's Chamber of the Great Pyramid with the report of the survey conducted by Greaves.

On the other side, I have examined the reports about the dimensions of the Church of St. Sophia in Novgorod, the oldest stone monument of Russia, in order to establish what was the original value of the Russian counterpart of the English foot. From the point of view of my investigations, it is lucky that an effort has been made to restore this church exactly as it was before it was destroyed by the German army in World War II.

5.   Once I was able to establish the relationship between the Roman foot and the Egyptian foot (the former being the trimmed version of the latter) and succeeded in clarifying the history of the units called Roman by distinguishing two varieties of libra related as 80:81, I came to the conclusion that the root of the ancient system of measures is not the Egyptian foot of 300 millimeters, but another unit which is the geographic foot of 307.7957 millimeters.

If we take 9/8 of a Roman quadrantal of 80 regular librae or 10/9 of a Roman quadrantal of 81 such librae, we have a unit of 90 librae, which metrologists call the *artaba*. Artaba is the Persian name of this unit. Metrologists employ it because after this unit was adopted as the official standard by the Persian Empire, the use of its Persian name became general in the ancient world: we find it in Greek, Latin, Hebrew, Syriac, and Arabic texts. But the unit itself is as old as any other known unit of the ancient world.

The artaba has the following contents:

          29,160 cubic centimeters or grams
              90 Roman librae
            1080 Roman ounces of 27 cubic centimeters or grams
            3200 Egyptian *qedet* of 9.1125 grams
            3240 Egyptian *qedet* of 9 grams
         450,000 English grains

The artaba was a unit of paramount importance in Egypt and several other areas of the ancient world, because it was the standard ration of wheat for a month. This was the ration for an adult free male; women, slaves, and children were assigned fractions of it. The artaba was also the standard monthly ration of rice in China.

In cuneiform mathematical and economic texts the most common unit of volume is a pint (*sila* in Sumerian, *gā* in Akkadian) of 486 cubic centimeters, which is 1/60 artaba. The pint of cuneiform texts is divided into 60 sheqels of 8.10 grams (9/10 of an Egyptian *qedet*).

The paramount importance of the artaba continued up to

312

modern times. I have established that the key to the metric systems of medieval Europe is an ounce of 29.160 grams, which is 1/1000 of an artaba of water. This ounce was made important in Europe by the monetary reforms enacted by the Frankish Kings Pepin and Charlemagne. The artabic ounce was known in Europe as the Cologne ounce, because Cologne was the seat of one of the important mints of the Carolingian Empire. In England the artabic ounce was called ounce Tower, after the mint of the Tower of London.

In England the ounce Tower remained stable at 450 English grains (29.160 grams) or 16/15 of ounce Troy. The ounce Tower is no longer used today because it was used only to weigh coins. On the European continent the Cologne ounce remained less stable, because often it was computed as 451 grains (to my knowledge this figure is first mentioned in a document A.D. 1275). The reason for this shift was an effort to adjust the Cologne ounce to a shift in the Paris livre. The Paris livre was divided into 9216 grains (16 ounces of 24 scruples of 24 grains). For technical reasons of monetary economics, the Paris ounce had to be 22/21 of an artabic ounce. Hence, in the early Middle Ages the Paris ounce was 30.54857 grams and the Paris livre 488.77714 grams, with a grain of 0.0530357 gram. Since there were 6109.1 of these grains in the Roman libra of 324 grams, in the later part of the Middle Ages, in order to relate easily the Paris units to a well-established standard, the Paris grain was recalculated as 1/6100 of a Roman libra and the Paris ounce and livre were increased accordingly (livre of 489.50557 grams). The Paris grain (0.05311475 gram) came to be 50/61 of the English grain. This small and apparently reasonable readjustment of the Paris units was enough to create a spreading wave of uncertainty in the value of European weight units which did not come to rest for centuries. For instance, one can trace its consequences in metric and economic documents of the Low Countries, Scandinavia, and Russia.

Because of the increase in the Paris units, the Cologne ounce came to be often calculated as 451 English grains instead of 450. At the beginning of the nineteenth century, when the German states were taking steps toward national unity, it was thought expedient to try to unify the German coinage in terms of the Cologne ounce. A survey conducted in 1829 established that in Cologne itself the Cologne mark (8 ounces) was 233.8123 grams; 8 artabic ounces would be 233.280 grams and 8 ounces of 451 English grains would be 233.79840 grams. The standards of other German cities were found to be slightly different from that of Cologne, reaching a minimum with the mark of the mint of Bonn, which was

313

233.612 grams. On July 30, 1838, the German states signed a convention to establish a uniform monetary mark defined in terms of the French metric units as 233.855 grams; but the mine administration of Saxony continued to consider as correct the mark of Dresden, which had been set at 233.5804 grams in an assembly for the testing of monetary weights (*Münzprobationstag*) held at Regensburg in 1737. Apparently the assembly of Regensburg had followed the pattern of the medieval Assizes of Weights and Measures, who when called to resolve discrepancies between different standards of the same measure usually settled the matter by selecting an intermediary value. I may finally mention that when the French metric system was adopted in Spain, it was decreed that the pound of Aragon, composed of 12 ounces, would be thereforth considered equal to 350 grams; 12 artabic ounces is 348.720 grams.

6. The edge of the cube containing an artaba is a foot of 307.7957 millimeters (cubit of 461.6935 millimeters), which I call geographic foot, because it was the unit most commonly used in geographic measurements in all areas of the ancient world, Egypt being excepted for reasons that I will explain.

The multiple of the geographic foot is the stadium of 600 feet (400 cubits). The stadium is 1/600 degree, so that there are 360,000 geographic feet in a degree. It was assumed that a stadium (184.677 meters) corresponds to a double minute of march, implying that a man makes a step of 5 feet in a second. It was assumed that a man marching or a ship under oars covers 30 stadia (5540.3 meters) in an hour. Since it was assumed that a man can march or row for 10 hours a day, 300 stadia was considered the distance normally covered in a day. There are a great number of texts from Egypt and other areas of the ancient world which have not been understood, because they speak of 1,2,3,4, . . . days of march, when they mean a geographic distance of 30′, 1°, 1° 30′, 2°. . . . It was assumed that the speed of a ship under sail is 5/4 of that of a ship propelled by oars, so that a ship under sail covers 37.5 stadia in an hour and 900 stadia (1 1/2 degrees) in 24 hours.

In the ancient world the degree of latitude was usually reckoned as 360,000 feet (600 stadia). Sailors and travelers of the eastern Mediterranean and of the Middle East reckoned the degree of longitude as roughly 500 stadia, or 300,000 geographic feet (92,339 meters); this calculation is correct between parallels 34° and 35°.

The calculations of the degree of latitude as 360,000 geographic feet (240,000 geographic cubits) proves to be of Egyptian origin, since a degree of 110,806.5 meters proves to be correct at parallel 27° 45′ north, which is the middle latitude of Egypt according to the predynastic geodetic system, which counted 7° 30′ from Behdet to the southern limit of Egypt, latitude 24° 00′ north. According to the *Smithsonian Geographical Tables,* a degree at parallel 27° 45′ is 110,803.0 meters.

The Egyptians preferred to reckon by cubits (stadium of 400 cubits and degree of 240,000 cubits), because it is expedient to divide the circumference of the earth not only into 360 degrees but also into 24 hours. According to the second system a degree is equal to 4 minutes of time and a minute of degree is equal to 4 seconds of time. I shall deal with this matter more extensively later.

Two great scholars of this century who have dedicated their lives to the study of ancient measures concluded that these are so strictly defined and so rigorously organized that they must have a basis on some absolute natural standard. Since it is obvious from the reading of ancient texts that the ancients had a deep concern with cosmic time, with the movement of the vault of heaven, these two scholars concluded that the system of measures must have coordinated not only length, volume, and weight, but also time.

The first of these two scholars, Sir Flinders Petrie, whose major concern was Egyptian measures, thought that the starting point of ancient measures was the length of the pendulum. He advanced the theory that the Egyptians began with a pendulum that swings 100,000 times a day at the latitude of Memphis (29° 51′ north). Having established that this pendulum has a length of 740.57 millimeters, they would have taken as standard of length the side of a square the diagonal of which is the length of the pendulum. This would be the origin of the Egyptian royal cubit. Calculating by this procedure, the royal cubit would be 523.66 millimeters, but Petrie estimates it as about 524 millimeters.

Carl Friedrich Lehmann-Haupt, a scholar of ancient history who, after the death of Hultsch, took over the role of the great German specialist of ancient measures, making them his major concern up to his death in 1936, followed the same line of reasoning. Since he started his activities as one of the decipherers of the Sumerian language and was particularly competent in the reading of cuneiform mathematical texts, he argued that the ancient system of measures was organized in Mesopotamia from the pendulum that beats the second at latitude 30°. The early inhabitants of Mesopotamia would have taken the half of this length as their cubit (cubit of 491.16 millimeters according to Lehmann-Haupt).

315

The idea was not completely new: in the period of the adoption of the French metric system, there occurred to a scholar of ancient measures that the Roman foot might have been calculated as the length of the pendulum that beats the half-second.

Unfortunately, Petrie and Lehmann-Haupt were not so well informed about the history of measures as they should have been. Soon after Galileo discovered the law of isochronism of the pendulum, since scholars were debating among themselves the project for a new decimal system of measures, it was suggested by several of them that the new system should be based on the length of the pendulum, in order to link together time, length, volume, and weight. But in the course of the eighteenth century it was realized that the pendulum does not provide a reliable standard of length. First of all, it was established that the period of oscillation of the pendulum changes according to the latitude; this led to the discovery of the polar flattening of the earth. It was also successively established that the period of oscillation is influenced by the density of the earth and by any presence of large masses of matter, since the period depends on the gravitational pull. Hence, by the time of the adoption of the French metric system, it had been decided that the new decimal system should limit itself to coordinating length, volume, and weight.

When the Constitution of the United States was drafted, there was included a special clause to prepare the ground for the adoption of a new decimal system of measures, which was advocated by all enlightened people. When the French Revolution in one of its first steps put into law the decimal metric system, the Congress of the United States considered adopting the French system. But Thomas Jefferson, whom Congress respected as the authority on such matters, opposed the plan on the ground that the French system was inadequate, since it did not coordinate time with length, volume, and weight. This opposition from inside the camp of the progressive forces doomed the adoption of the decimal system in the United States.

Jefferson was correct in principle, and so were Petrie and Lehmann-Haupt. A truly desirable system of measures should coordinate time, length, volume, and weight, but what these people did not know is that the ancients had found an easy and reliable method to coordinate length with time. All that is needed is to relate the unit of length to the speed of the rotation of the vault of heaven, since this is the basis of our calculations of time. As I will explain later, today we calculate time by the length of the mean solar day, but since this is a highly artificial concept, astronomers set the

316

length of the solar day by the apparent motion of the vault of heaven (sidereal time), which flows evenly.

The problem of coordinating time with the other measures is so important that after decades of research on ancient measures I was still fumbling for one element which would allow me to fit all my findings together, until Peter Tompkins ripped the veil from my eyes by pointing out to me that speed of rotation of the vault of heaven is 1000 geographic cubits a second.

The Egyptians set their standards of length in a manner that permits an easy correlation with time, but still the standard which was scientifically defined had to be the standard of length.

7.   The tradition of what was the ancient procedure has been preserved by the scientist and mathematician Girolamo Cardano (1501–1576). Like other Renaissance scholars he was concerned with the establishment of an absolutely inalterable standard of length. In his book *De Subtilitate* (Chapter XVII, edition of Basel, 1553, p. 475) he discusses the length of the ancient Roman foot and passes from it to the problem of how to base length and weight on a *mensura perpetua*. He observes that such an absolute standard should be searched for in the heavens, but, since this is impossible for practical reasons, he declares that the standard is provided by the pyramids of Egypt, the Labyrinth of Thebes, cities like Cairo, and the river Nile. The meaning of this statement is perfectly clear, when we consider the geodetic system of Egypt, as I have reconstructed it; but its form is cryptic. This should not be surprising, since it is known that Cardano has been cryptic in announcing some of his major mathematical discoveries. It had been the practice of scientists and mathematicians up to the age of Newton to put into print the data which they considered of essential importance in a form such that the meaning would become obvious only after an explanation had been communicated orally, because this was the only method they had of protecting their copyright.

The Egyptians decided that the distance of 7° 30′ from Behdet to the southern boundary of Egypt should be reckoned as 1,800,000 geographic cubits. According to the *Smithsonian Geographical Tables* the interval from 31° 30′ to 24° 00′ is 831,091 meters. According to my findings 1,800,000 geographic cubits are 831,048 meters. The figures of the *Smithsonian Geographical Tables* are an estimate of the average length of the degree of latitude, based on the assumption that the earth is a regular geometric body. It would be necessary to consider what is the actual length of the degree in Egypt. Up to now I have deliberately avoided obtaining this information, because I did not want my interpretation of the texts to be influenced by the knowledge of the possible results.

In order to appreciate the nicety of the Egyptian figure, we must keep in mind that in the first French legislation the length of the meter was established by assuming that the arc of meridian is 30,794,580 *pieds de roi,* on the basis of the survey conducted in 1740. Later the length of the meter was revised to the present one, because according to the survey conducted in 1792–98 the arc of meridian is 30,784,440 *pieds de roi.* After this survey the meter was no longer revised, although it has been ascertained that the arc of meridian is about 2000 meters more than 10,000,000 meters.

8. From the geographic cubit, defined as 1/1,800,000 of the length of Egypt, there was derived the geographic foot of 307.7957 millimeters. By cubing this there was fixed the volume of the artaba as 29,160 cubic centimeters.

The artaba was divided into 64 pints of 455.6250 cubic centimeters, that is, into 64 cubes with a side of a hand (4 fingers = 1/4 foot). This unit is the standard pint of Egypt. The pint was divided into 50 *qedet* of 9.1125 grams, employed to weigh gold and silver used as a means of exchange. Sutzu is correct in concluding that, although the *qedet* of 9 grams is the more current unit of weight in advanced civilizations, the heavier *qedet* appears common in prehistoric or early times.

From the artaba there was derived a unit of 3 artabas, which is the cube of the Roman cubit. This is the origin of the Roman foot. There was also derived a unit which is the *brutto* version of the preceding one; since in the cube of the Roman cubit there are 9600 *qedet,* this second unit contains 10,000 *qedet* of 9.1125 grams. The edge of the cube which corresponds to this second unit is the ordinary Egyptian cubit of 450 millimeters. This cubit implies a foot of 300 millimeters. The cube of this foot is the talent of 27,000 cubic centimeters or grams, which was divided into 3000 *qedet* of 9 grams or 1000 Roman ounces of 27 cubic centimeters or grams. The *netto* version of this unit is the cube of the Roman foot (25,920 cubic centimeters or grams). Since the cube of the Roman foot is 8/9 artaba, this cube was divided into 80 librae of 36 *qedet* of 9 grams, whereas the artaba is composed of 90 librae. Three *qedet* of 9 grams makes the Roman ounce of which 1000 makes the cube of the Egyptian foot of 300 millimeters (27,000 cubic centimeters or grams). However, following the reckoning of a *qedet* of 9.1125 grams there continued to be in common use a larger quadrantal (Russian *chetverik*), the edge of which is the Roman geometric foot, and which contains 80 geometric librae

(81/80 of regular libra of 324 grams). This larger quadrantal is 9/10 of artaba.

The organization of the units according to this pattern had a practical purpose. The unit of 3 artabas was the cube of the cubit (443.9181 millimeter) called Roman, a unit of 87,470 cubic centimeters or grams. This was considered a unit *netto,* to which there corresponded a unit *brutto* (25/24) of 91,125 cubic centimeters or grams, which is the cube of the common Egyptian cubit of 450 millimeters. The units of 87,470 grams and of 91,125 grams, that is, the weight of the cubes of the Roman and of the common Egyptian cubits filled with water, are called by me basic load *netto* and basic load *brutto.* I have given them these names because they were considered the standard amount that could be carried by a pack ass. In Akkadian these units are called *imēru,* which means "ass." The Masoretic text of the Old Testament uses a different punctuation of vowels under the consonants to distinguish between the term *ḥmr* as referring to an ass and the same term as referring to the unit of measure, but there are puns in the Old Testament which indicate that one could confuse one meaning with the other. Since the language of measures is very international, there is a transfer of terms among Semitic, Indo-European, and Fenno-Ugrian languages, in which the same terms are applied at times to the measure and at times to the animal. Some easy examples are the following. In Hellenistic Egypt the ass was called *gomarion,* from *gomos,* "load"; the ass is called *gomari* in modern Greek. In Italian the ass is called *somaro,* from the Greek *sagma,* "pack saddle." The corresponding English word is *sumpter,* which corresponds to a German *Saumtier,* a term in turn corresponding to the Italian *bestia da soma,* "pack animal." In German *Saum* means "burden" and also refers to a large unit of measure. In Italian *salma* is both a large unit of weight or volume and a corpse carried on a stretcher, which has on the average the weight of what I call a basic load.

The cube of the foot was called talent in Greek or by equivalent terms in other languages of the ancient world. There was a basic talent *netto* of 25,920 grams and basic talent *brutto* of 27,000 grams, which were respectively the cube of the Roman foot of 295.9454 millimeters and the cube of the Egyptian foot of 300 millimeters. Names such as talent refer to the fact that these weights were considered half of the amount that could be transported by a man. It was assumed that a man transports burdens by suspending them at the two ends of a carrying yoke. At each end of the yoke there were weights, which ideally had to be identical; each of these weights was called a talent. It is evident that

319

this is the origin of the idea of equilibrium and of the measuring scale. Incidentally, I may also mention that it was assumed that the carrying yoke has a length of 2 cubits or three feet.

9.   Since the development of units from the artaba had started with the cube of the Roman cubit, which is equal to 3 artabas, there was developed a unit equal to 5 artabas. The edge of the cube containing 5 artabas is the origin of the Egyptian royal cubit. Five artabas were the volume of a basic load of barley (barley was assumed to have a specific gravity between 0.6 and 0.666).

The edge of the cube which contains 5 artabas was interpreted as the septenary version of the Egyptian cubit of 450 millimeters, that is, as a cubit of 7 hands (28 fingers) instead of the normal 6 hands (24 fingers). But, if we reckon exactly, the cube of the cubit of 525 millimeters contains 144,703.125 cubic centimeters, which is something less than 5 artabas = 145,800 cubic centimeters. A unit of 5 artabas should contain 16,000 *qedet*. By dividing the cube with an edge of 525 millimeters by 16,000 there is obtained a *qedet* of 9.043945 grams, which is intermediary between the *qedet* of 9 grams and the *qedet* of 9.1125 grams. The analysis of the distribution of the weights of Egyptian sample weights indicates that there were in use three standards of *qedet:*

9.000000 grams
9.043945 grams
9.112500 grams

Correspondingly, the study of the monuments and of the measuring rods indicates that there were three values of the royal cubit:

524.1483 millimeters
525.0000 millimeters
526.3231 millimeters

The first royal cubit is the edge of the cube containing 16,000 *qedet* of 9 grams. It is the standard of the Great Pyramid and of the immense complex of buildings erected by the architect Imhotep around the pyramid of King Zoser of the Third Dynasty. This royal cubit was the scientific unit of Egypt, employed in the calculation of geographic distances.

The second royal cubit was exactly 7/6 of the Egyptian cubit of 450 millimeters. It was the one most commonly used in ordinary life. It is the standard of the Second Pyramid of Giza.

The third royal cubit had the virtue of being the edge of the cube containing exactly 5 artabas (16,000 *qedet* of 9.1125 grams). It is the standard of the coffers of the mentioned two pyramids of Giza.

The royal cubit had the advantage of being a septenary unit, a type of unit which had been found convenient in the practical solution of problems involving irrational roots such as $\sqrt{2}$, $\sqrt{3}$, and π. But, when the reorganization of the Egyptian geodetic system with the unification of Egypt stressed the number 7 as the link between the dimensions of Egypt and the order of the heavens, the septenary royal cubit was raised to the status of a national symbol and became the official standard of the Egyptian monarchy.

It may be worth pointing out, in order to indicate how the great majority of scholars deal with these problems, that Eduard Meyer, whose ideas and method dominate contemporary history of antiquity and of Egypt in particular, explained the origin of the royal cubit by asserting that the Pharaohs demanded contractors to build by the cubit of 7 hands, but exercised their royal prerogatives by paying them as if they had employed the regular cubit of 6 hands (a discount of 37 percent). Let us not forget that the current opinions about the Egyptian ability to measure time astronomically are based on the calculations of Eduard Meyer.

10.   According to the second geodetic system of Egypt, the length of Egypt, from the base line of the Delta (31° 06′ north) to the usual southern boundary at 24° 00′ north, was recalculated as 1,500,000 royal cubits of 524.1483 millimeters. This is the reason why the cubit of 524.1483 millimeters became the one used in geographic measurements.

This second calculation of the length of Egypt is derivative and, hence, is not as precise as the one that made the geographic cubit equal to 1/1,800,000 of the length of Egypt. The length of Egypt according to the dynastic system is 7° 06′; 1,500,000 royal cubits equals 786,222 meters. According to the *Smithsonian Geographical Tables,* the interval from 31° 06′ to 24° 00′ is 786,741 meters. There is a difference of about 1000 royal cubits.

For the sake of geographical calculations the royal cubit was given as multiple the *atur* of 15,000 royal cubits, so as to make Egypt equal to the perfect figure of 100 *atur*. The term *atur* literally means "river"; it could be translated as "river measure." It was understood that an *atur* (7862.2 meters) corresponds to an hour of navigation along the Nile.

The *atur* fitted the septenary spirit of the system of measures, since it could be assumed that a degree of latitude is 14 *atur*. This was a practical approximation, which was corrected by adding decimal points to the figure of 14 *atur,* reaching a maximum of 14.1 *atur* at the north of Egypt.

A degree of 14.1 *atur* is 110,857.4 meters. According to the *Smithsonian Geographical Tables,* degree 30°–31° is 110,857.0 meters.

The length of Egypt was divided into 14 *atur* for Northern Egypt and 86 *atur* for Southern Egypt. If we divide 100 *atur* by 7° 06′, we have a degree of 14.084507 *atur* = 110,735.6 meters, which is the length of the degree at parallel 23° 00′ (110,736 meters according to Helmert). A reason why the length of Egypt was extended south to the Sacred Sycamore, at 23° 00′ north, appears to have been that of giving a more exact scientific basis to the calculation of the royal cubit as being such that 211,267.605 royal cubits (14.0845 *atur*) makes a degree.

We shall see that the Pharaoh Akhenaten attacked the authority of the Temple of Amon at Thebes by questioning the scientific exactitude of the second geodetic system of Egypt and of the calculations by royal cubits. There is a possibility that the extension of the boundaries of Egypt from latitude 24° 00′ to latitude 23° 00′ north was part of the counterattack against the reforms of Akhenaten. The purpose may have been that of calculating the value of the royal cubit independently of the value of the geographic cubit.

III. COFFER OF THE GREAT PYRAMID

1. On the basis of my reconstruction of the Egyptian system of measures, it is possible to solve the riddle of the coffer placed inside the King's Chamber of the Great Pyramid.

Many investigators have tried to explain the dimensions of this coffer, but none has reached a positive conclusion. However, the majority of the investigators agree on two basic assumptions: the coffer embodies some numerical conundrum and the contents of the coffer corresponds to some standard of volume. According to my interpretation both of these assumptions are correct: the contents of the coffer is 8 cubic royal cubits = 40 artabas (1166.40 liters), and the walls were given a thickness such that the outside volume of the coffer is twice that of the contents, that is, 16 cubic royal cubits = 80 artabas (2332.800 liters).

The investigators who have preceded me have been hampered by not knowing that there were three possible values of the royal cubit. For this reason they could not realize that the standard of measure of the coffer is a royal cubit different from that employed in planning the King's chamber and the rest of the Pyramid. The King's Chamber was planned by the royal cubit of 524.1483 millimeters, because this is the standard of the Pyramid, chosen because this was the royal cubit usually employed by the Egyptians in calculating geographic distances. The coffer, on the other hand, was planned by the royal cubit of 526.3231 millimeters, because this was the unit employed in calculating the fundamental units of volume and weight.

Before the Cole survey of the dimensions of the Great Pyramid, the only datum available to scholars to determine the exact value of the cubit of the Pyramid was the dimensions of the King's Chamber. It was Newton who, on the basis of the survey conducted by Greaves, realized that the King's Chamber measures 10 by 20 cubits. Having established this fact, he calculated that the cubit of the Pyramid is 1732.5/1000 of an English foot and rounded the figure to 1732/1000. Calculating by the British Imperial standard foot established in 1824, the figures of Newton indicate a cubit of 528.0655 or 527.9131 millimeters. Newton was interested in the length of the Egyptian royal cubit, because he wanted to interpret the statement of Eratosthenes that a degree of latitude is 210,000 cubits.

Petrie proceeded to an extremely accurate survey of the dimensions of the King's Chamber, taking into account the fact that the blocks have been spread apart by the action of earthquakes. By deducting from the length of the sides the spaces which today separate the blocks, he concluded that the cubit of the King's Chamber is 20.632 ± 0.004 English inches = 524.0523 ± 0.1016 millimeters. This empirical datum agrees with the figure of 524.1483 millimeters which I have obtained by considering the mathematical structure of the Egyptian system of measures and all the empirical evidence available.

The coffer is not calculated by the cubit of the King's Chamber, but the cubit of 526.3231 millimeters, because this cubit when cubed contains 145.800 liters = 5 artabas = 16,000 *qedet* of 9.1125 grams.

The reports about the dimensions of the coffer show some discrepancies, because the coffer was cut rather roughly. Petrie relates that an entire side was cut by the strokes of a huge saw, which at times was backed up after it had dented the stone as much as one inch out of plumb. However, by comparing the reports of Greaves, Piazzi Smyth, Petrie, and others, I have identified the intended dimensions of the coffer, since I have the advantage of knowing the exact value of the unit of measurement.

The coffer was computed in hands of 1/7 of the cubit of 526.3231 millimeters. Its inner dimensions are:

Width: 9   hands = 676.70 mm
Length: 26.3 hands = 1977.47 mm
Height: 11.6 hands = 872.19 mm

323

The corresponding figures in the reports of Greaves and Petrie are:

26.616 English inches = 676.15 mm   26.81 inches = 680.97 mm
77.856 English inches = 1,977.54 mm   78.06 inches = 1982.72 mm
34.32 English inches = 871.73 mm   34.42 inches = 874.27 mm

The report of Smyth agrees substantially with that of Greaves. Petrie's figures are slightly excessive, because he computed the inner dimensions by deducting the thickness of the walls from the outer dimensions, and he thought that it would be proper to measure the walls at the point of their minimum thickness.

The lateral walls were intended to be 2 hands thick, so that the outside dimentions are:

Width: 13 hands = 977.46 mm
Length: 30.3 hands = 2278.23 mm

Petrie's figures for these two dimensions are:

38.50 English inches = 977.90 mm
89.62 English inches = 2276.35 mm

The height of the outside was intended to be 2 cubits = 14 hands, but in order to establish a link between the coffer and the rest of the Pyramid these two cubits were calculated by the cubit of the Pyramid and the King's Chamber. Two cubits of 524.1483 millimeters is 1,048.29 millimeters. In terms of the cubit of 526.3231 millimeters, this means 13.9422 hands; possibly the figure was rounded to 13.9333 hands = 1,047.63 millimeters. I assume that the bottom of the coffer was given a thickness of 2.333 hands = 175.44 millimeters (Petrie reports 6.89 inches = 175.01 millimeters). I assume that the height was 13.9333 hands = 1,047.63 millimeters (Petrie reports 41.31 inches = 1049.27 millimeters).

According to Greaves's figures the contents of the coffer is 71,118 cubic inches = 1,165.428 liters. According to Petrie's figures the contents is 72,033 cubic inches = 1,180.405 liters; I have explained why Petrie overestimated the inner dimensions. According to my interpretation the contents is 2745.72 cubic hands. Now, 2744 cubic hands is 1,166.400 liters = 8 cubic cubits = 40 artabas.

If the outside of the coffer is 13 by 30.3 by 13.933 hands, its volume is 5488.3 cubic hands. Now, 5488 cubic hands is 16 cubic cubits = 80 artabas.

Since the two volumes of the coffer are 8 and 16 cubic cubits, it is not possible to be certain that a measurement by artabas was in the mind of the builders, although I cannot think of any other reason why the builders should have chosen the cubit of 526.3231 millimeters, unless they intended to choose the cubit which when cubed has a contents of exactly 5 artabas. A clearer proof that the calculation was intended to be by artabas is provided by the similar coffer of the Second Pyramid of Giza.

2. From the dimension of the sides of the Second Pyramid of Giza, it can be established that it was planned by the royal cubit of 525 millimeters. Nevertheless, as in the case of the Great Pyramid, the coffer was planned by the cubit of 526.3231 millimeters.

Petrie reports the following data about the coffer of the Second Pyramid, expressed in English inches:

	Length	Width	Height
Out-side:	106.68 = 2,709.67 mm	41.97 = 1,066.04 mm	38.12 = 968.25 mm
Walls:	21.95 = 557.53 mm	15.28 = 388.11 mm	8.53 = 216.66 mm
Inside:	84.73 = 2,152.14 mm	26.69 = 677.93 mm	29.59 = 751.59 mm

As in the Great Pyramid, the coffer was planned in hands (1/7) of the cubit of 526.3231 millimeters. The dimensions are the following:

	Length	Width	Height
Outside:	36 = 2,706.80 mm	14.2 = 1,067.68 mm	12.88 = 968.43 mm
Walls:	7.4 = 566.40 mm	5.2 = 390.98 mm	2.88 = 216.54 mm
Inside:	28.6 = 2,150.41 mm	9 = 676.70 mm	10 = 751.89 mm

Petrie's figures imply an inside volume of 1,096.554 liters. According to my interpretation the volume is 2574 cubic hands = 1094.137 liters. If we assume that the volume was intended to be 2572.5 cubic hands = 1093.500 liters, the contents of the coffer corresponds to:

> 7.5 cubic royal cubits
> 37.5 artabas
> 12 basic loads *brutto*
> 120,000 *qedet* of 9.1125 grams
> 121,500 *qedet* of 9 grams

The contents of this coffer is 15/16 of the contents of the coffer of the Great Pyramid.

Because the Second Pyramid had been planned by the royal cubit of 525 millimeters, the coffer, although measured by the cubit of 526.3231 millimeters, indicates a volume expressed best of all in basic loads *brutto;* the basic load *brutto* is the cube of the cubit of 450 millimeters, which is the common cubit coresponding to the royal cubit of 525 millimeters.

Petrie's figures imply an outside volume of 2796.883 liters. According to my interpretation the volume is 6584.25 cubic hands = 2798.786 liters. If we assume that the outside volume was intended to be 6585.4 cubic hands = 2799.360 liters, the volume corresponds to:

> 19.2 cubic royal cubits
> 96 artabas
> 32 basic loads *netto*
> 307,200 *qedet* of 9.1125 grams
> 311,400 *qedet* of 9 grams

The outside volume of this coffer is 6/5 that of the coffer of the Great Pyramid.

The coffer of the Second Pyramid was planned so as to embody the key units of the Egyptian system of volumes:

Artaba of 29,160 cubic centimeters (cube of the geographic foot)
Basic load *netto* of 87,480 cubic centimeters (cube of the Roman cubit)
Basic load *brutto* of 91,125 cubic centimeters (cube of the Egyptian common cubit)

IV. DEGREES OF LATITUDE

1. The calculation of the dimensions of Egypt by royal cubits was less precise than that by geographic cubits, but it had the advantage of stressing the number 7 as the key to the dimensions of Egypt and as the link between the structure of Egypt and the order of the cosmos.

Following the septenary system of measurement, the stadium, a tenth of minute of degree, was reckoned as 350 royal cubits (183.45 meters). This stadium is somewhat shorter than the stadium of 400 geographic cubits (600 geographic feet = 184.68 meters). It implies a degree (600 stadia to the degree) of 210,000 royal cubits = 110,071.1 meters. But the calculation of the stadium as 350 royal cubits was considered a first approximation which could be employed in practical computations. Just as in the calculation by *atur,* a degree of latitude was considered basically equal to 14 *atur,* but in exact calculations a decimal point was added to the figure of 14, so in exact calculations a few cubits were added to the figure of 350 royal cubits to a stadium.

In round figuring the Egyptians calculated the stadium at the equator as 354 stadia; but more accurate figures were known. By this round figure they obtained an equatorial minute of degree (10 stadia) of 1855.485 meters, which is 88 millimeters more than the figure of the International Spheroid (1855.398 meters). A stadium of 354 cubits implies an equatorial circle of 76,464,000 cubits = 40,078,491 meters, whereas according to the International Spheroid the equatorial radius is 6,378,388 meters ± 18 meters, so that the equator would be 40,076,594 meters ± 113 meters. Since the Egyptians preferred to count by 90 degrees of equator, the figure of 354 cubit for a stadium of equator contains a numerical game, such as frequently occurs in ancient computations for mnemonic reasons. Ninety degrees of equator is 54,000 stadia of 354 cubits.

Assuming a stadium of 354 royal cubits, a degree of equator is 212,400 cubits, which is a good round figure. We shall see that the Egyptians estimated the exact figure as between 212,380 and 212,392 cubits.

An absolutely exact calculation of the length of the equator was a matter of scientific interest, whereas the Egyptians put much greater stress on the exact calculation of the length of the degrees of latitude, since the anchor of their geodetic conceptions was the course of the Nile.

For the stadium of latitude of the equator they used the figure of 351.6 cubits = 184.2905 meters, which is as exact as any modern calculation can be. According to the Clarke Spheroid a minute of latitude at the equator is 1842.787 meters; according to the International Spheroid it is 1842.925 meters. We shall see that the base of the Great Pyramid is calculated by a stadium of 351.6 cubits.

To those who may not be conversant with these matters, I must explain that, since the shape of the earth is irregular, modern scholars have tried to construct a regular geometric figure, called the spheroid, the dimensions of which fit as closely as possible the actual dimensions of the earth. Different scholars have constructed different spheroids, in part because they have based their work on surveys conducted in different areas of our planet. For instance, in the United States many agencies and institutions continue to use the spheroid calculated by the English geodesist Clarke in 1866, because its data fit rather well with the shape of the earth in North America. Many scholars prefer the computation published by the German Helmert in 1907. But the calculation most usually considered authoritative by scholars is that completed by the American Hayford in 1910, known as the International Spheroid. This calculation is based on a gigantic survey conducted under the auspices of the British Empire from the tip of South Africa to the Equator and then up to the Mediterranean along the Nile. This survey happens to overlap the Egyptian calculations along the course of the Nile.

The stadium of latitude increases as one moves to the north from the equator, reaching the value of 354 cubits, equal to the length of the stadium of equator, between parallel 55° and parallel 56°. It reaches a maximum estimated as 355 cubits at the pole. This figure of 355 cubits for the stadium of latitude at the pole, which indicates a minute of 1860.726 meters, was a convenient round figure which was refined in exact reckonings. A stadium of 355 cubits implies a polar degree of 213,000 cubits = 111,643.6 meters; if 1/2000 was the amount added to the latter figure we would have 213.106.5 cubits = 111,699.4 meters. According to the *Smithsonian Geographical Tables*, degree 89°–90° is 111,699.3 meters.

For navigation along the Nile, there was used the following formula for the length of the degrees of latitude:

211,500 cubits = 110,857 meters at latitude 31° 06′
211,300 cubits = 110,753 meters at latitude 24° 06′
211,100 cubits = 110,648 meters at latitude 15° 36′

Latitude 15° 36′ north is the latitude of the confluence of the White Nile with the Blue Nile.

2. One of the major difficulties of ancient mathematical science was that it could not rely on printed tables, although some numerical tables, such as exponents, roots, and logarithms, are occasionally found in cuneiform tablets. Even maps were so drawn that the key positions could be memorized. The lack of the printing press is the reason why in ancient mathematics we find a variety of formulas and mnemonic devices for obtaining trigonometric functions. In the same spirit the Egyptians had developed a simple formula for calculating the length of the degree of latitude at all parallels between the equator and the pole.

The scheme was based on the circumstances that the Egyptians used three values for the length of the degree of latitude at the equator—an exact value based on a stadium of 351.6 cubits and two rounded values:

A. Exact value. Stadium of 351.6 cubits, degree of 210,960 cubits = 110,574 meters.
B. Value rounded to degree of 211,000 cubits = 110,595 meters.
C. Value rounded to arc of meridian of 19,000,000 cubits, degree of 211,111 = 110.654 meters.

Value B was considered exact for a degree at 9° and value C for a degree at 16°.

The length of the degree was calculated by taking the second value, 211,000 cubits, and assuming that each degree is longer than the preceding degree by a number of cubits equal to the number of the degree.

Degree	Cubits added to degree	Cubits added to length of degree at 0°
1°	1	1
2°	2	3
3°	3	6
4°	4	10
5°	5	15
6°	6	21

This pattern was followed up to degree 36°, which is 36 cubits longer than the degree at 35° and 666 cubits longer than the degree at 0°. For six degrees, from 37 to 42°, the amount added to each degree is 37 cubits. For the following six degrees, from 43 to 48°, the amount added to each degree is 38 cubits. Then for six degrees, from 49 to 54°, the amount added is again 37 cubits. For the remaining 36 degrees, from 55 to 90°, the amount added is the same as that applied to the first 32 degrees but in the inverse order.

The scheme gives immediately the length of the degrees from 24 to 58°, that is, for 35 degrees. For the first 23 degrees and for the last 32 there are introduced simple corrections:

(1) For the first eight degrees, from 1 to 8°, the amount is added to the exact value of the degree (value A, 210,960 cubits to degree). From a degree at 9° one begins to count by value B (211,000 cubits), but 45 cubits is deducted from the amount added to this degree; this deduction is reduced by 3 cubits for each of the following 13 degrees, until 3 cubits is deducted from 23°.

3. At 90° the amount added according to the scheme is added to a basic degree calculated by value C (211,111 cubits). For the 32 degrees from 59 to 90°, an adjustment is

Degree	Cubits added to each degree	Cubits added to 0° degree	Correction	Egyptian ESTIMATE, meters	Helmert's ESTIMATE, meters
1°	1	1		110,575	110,573
2°	2	3		110,576	110,574
3°	3	6		110,577	110,575
4°	4	10		110,580	110,577
5°	5	15		110,582	110,579
6°	6	21		110,585	110,582
7°	7	28		110,589	110,586
8°	8	36		110,593	110,591
9°	9	45	−45	110,595	110,596
10°	10	55	−42	110,602	110,602
11°	11	66	−39	110,609	110,609
12°	12	78	−36	110,617	110,616
13°	13	91	−33	110,626	110,624
14°	14	105	−30	110,635	110,633
15°	15	120	−27	110,640	110,642
16°	16	136	−24	110,654	110,652
17°	17	153	−21	110,664	110,662
18°	18	171	−18	110,675	110,673
19°	19	190	−15	110,687	110,684
20°	20	210	−12	110,699	110,696
21°	21	231	− 9	110,712	110,709
22°	22	253	− 6	110,725	110,722
23°	23	276	− 3	110,738	110,736
24°	24	300		110,753	110,750
25°	25	325		110,766	110,764
26°	26	351		110,779	110,779
27°	27	378		110,793	110,794
28°	28	406		110,809	110,810
29°	29	435		110,823	110,826
30°	30	465		110,839	110,843
31°	31	496		110,855	110,861
32°	32	528		110,872	110,878
33°	33	561		110,889	110,895
34°	34	595		110,907	110,913
35°	35	630		110,926	110,931
36°	36	666		110,944	110,949

Degree	Cubits added to each degree	Cubits added to 0° degree	Correction	Egyptian ESTIMATE, meters	Helmert's ESTIMATE, meters
37°	37	703		110,964	110,968
38°	37	740		110,983	110,987
39°	37	777		111,003	111,006
40°	37	814		111,022	111,025
41°	37	851		111,041	111,044
42°	37	888		111,061	111,063
43°	38	926		111,081	111,083
44°	38	964		111,101	111,103
45°	38	1002		111,120	111,122
46°	38	1040		111,140	111,142
47°	38	1078		111,160	111,162
48°	38	1116		111,180	111,181
49°	37	1153		111,200	111,201
50°	37	1190		111,219	111,220
51°	37	1227		111,238	111,239
52°	37	1264		111,258	111,258
53°	37	1301		111,277	111,277
54°	37	1338		111,297	111,296
55°	36	1374		111,316	111,315
56°	35	1409		111,334	111,334
57°	34	1443		111,352	111,352
58°	33	1476		111,369	111,370
59°	32	1508	+ 3.5	111,388	111,388
60°	31	1539	+ 7	111,406	111,405
61°	30	1569	+10.5	111,423	111,422
62°	29	1598	+14	111,440	111,439
63°	28	1626	+17.5	111,457	111,455
64°	27	1653	+21	111,473	111,471
65°	26	1679	+24.5	111,488	111,487
66°	25	1704	+28	111,503	111,502
67°	24	1728	+31.5	111,518	111,517
68°	23	1751	+35	111,531	111,531
69°	22	1778	+38.5	111,547	111,544
70°	21	1794	+42	111,558	111,557
71°	20	1814	+45.5	111,570	111,570
72°	19	1833	+49	111,582	111,582
73°	18	1851	+52.5	111,593	111,594
74°	17	1868	+56	111,604	111,605
75°	16	1884	+59.5	111,616	111,616
76°	15	1899	+63	111,624	111,626
77°	14	1913	+66.5	111,633	111,635
78°	13	1926	+70	111,642	111,643
79°	12	1938	+73.5	111,650	111,651
80°	11	1949	+77	111,657	111,659
81°	10	1959	+80.5	111,664	111,666
82°	9	1968	+84	111,671	111,672
83°	8	1976	+87.5	111,677	111,677
84°	7	1983	+91	111,682	111,682
85°	6	1989	+94.5	111,687	111,686
86°	5	1994	+98	111,692	111,690
87°	4	1998	+101.5	111,696	111,693
88°	3	2001	+105	111,699	111,695
89°	2	2003	+108.5	111,702	111,696
90°	1	2004	+111.11	111,704	111,697

made for a transition from value *B* to value *C*. Thus, to a degree at 59° there is added 111.11/32 cubits, or practically 3.5 cubits (32 × 3.5 = 112); to a degree at 60° twice as much is added; to a degree at 61° there is added three times as much.

This scheme gives values of the degree of latitude which differ most from the one we use today in the area near the pole. This could be connected with the fraction that the Egyptians used in calculating the polar flattening of the earth. I shall deal with this fraction in a following chapter. According to the scheme, the degree between parallel 89° and the pole is 213,115.11 cubits = 11,703.9 meters. According to the Clarke Spheroid the minute of degree of latitude at the pole is such that the corresponding degree is 111,699.36 meters; but in 1880 Clarke revised the figure to 111,702,06 meters. According to the International Spheroid the figure is 111,700 meters.

4. The scheme which I have presented provides excellent values for the length of the degree of latitude, but probably was intended to be only a practical device, not the most exact calculation. There is evidence which suggests that efforts were made to calculate the lengths of the degrees with greater mathematical refinement.

The Egyptians invented the column as an architectural element. If one observes the decoration of Egyptian columns with a scientific attitude, he will recognize that the column represents the map of Egypt: the capital is Northern Egypt and the shaft is Southern Egypt. This explains why among the Greeks, who learned the use of the column from the Egyptians, for the Doric order, the most conservative of the Greek orders, there was the rule that the shaft should be six units high and the capital one unit high. In the Greek orders the base of the column preserves the arrangement on three horizontal lines, which are the symbol of the tropic of Cancer (parallels 24° 06′, 24° 00′, and 23° 51′ north). The column basically represents the three meridians of Egypt and through its curvature suggests the extension of the system of meridians to the east and west of Egypt. But, since the column is circular, the structure of the column was related to the problem of presenting the map of Egypt as part of a cylindrical projection of the surface of the earth from the equator to latitude 31° 06′ or latitude 31° 30′ north. The elaborate numerical rules for the proportions of Greek columns, which archeologists treat as numerological superstitions, can be explained when one considers the two interrelated problems of describing mathematically the curvature of the earth and of projecting a curved surface on a flat map. The theory of conic sections, which is considered the highest achievement of Greek mathematics, may have been developed in order to solve these problems. Greek columns taper from the bottom to the top, but to the rectilinear line of the shrinking there is applied a curved line, so that the column seems to swell slightly toward the middle. If we consider the scheme I have presented for the calculation of the lengths of the degrees, a scheme in which a basic simple progression was modified by the addition of another progression, we can understand why Greek columns diminished in diameter from bottom to top according to a combination of two lines. In the case of the columns of the Parthenon, the added curvature, called *entasis* by the Greeks, is a hyperbolic curve, but in other temples we meet with more complex mathematical curves. It may be enough to say this much here: if one assumes that the bottom of the colonnade of the Parthenon represents the equator and its top the latitude of Athens, the proportions of the entire colonnade can be readily explained.

V. TEXTUAL EVIDENCE

For lack of space, it is impossible for me to present here the evidence for what I have stated to be the Egyptian estimates of the length of the degrees of latitude, since this evidence was obtained by gathering scores of scattered pieces of information, the interpretation of which often involves delicate issues of textual interpretation. But the preoccupation with geographical distances was so dominant in Egyptian civilization that one can find many documents the meaning of which is obvious; several of these documents are well-known texts. It has taken me a great deal of painstaking research to fit these documents together, in order to arrive at a unified view of what was the Egyptian system of geography; but the interpretation of single documents *per se* in many cases did not present difficulty. What is difficult to explain is why Egyptologists have stubbornly refused to accept these documents at their face value. In order to illustrate how Egyptologists operate in order to slough off the evidence, I shall present two examples of such nature that the issues involved can be understood by the non-specialist.

Inscribed Cubit Rules

1. In 1921 the famous Egyptologist Ludwig Borchardt wrote a report on three Egyptian measuring rules found at the Temple of Amon in Thebes. These three royal cubit rules

bear an identical inscription. The inscription appears to be a traditional one; for reasons of style the text of the inscription has been ascribed to the Old Kingdom, although the rules themselves belong to a later period. It is known that at times measuring rules were given a sacred meaning, although nobody has ever asked why; it should be evident to the reader of these pages why a measuring rule could be a sacred object for the Egyptians. The cubit rules studied by Borchardt, according to his report, seem to be of the type used as sacred objects rather than as instruments of actual measurement.

Borchardt did not test the length of these rules, but concentrated his attention on the inscription. The essential meaning of the inscription is open and clear, even though a professional Egyptologist may find difficulty with some of the hieroglyphs, as it often happens when archaic hiero-glyphic texts were copied centuries later when the language and the writing style had changed. The inscription states that the distance between Behdet and Syene, the area of the First Cataract, is 106 *atur,* and divides this distance into 20 *atur* from Behdet to a place called Pi-Hapy, and 86 *atur* between Pi-Hapy and Syene.

Borchardt considered the evident possibility that the distances should be understood as differences of latitude, but dismisses it outright: "one must absolutely exclude the possibility that the ancients may have measured by degrees." No further words are added to justify this drastic pronounce-ment. Then he states that it must be a matter of measure-ments taken along the actual course of the Nile, the only measurements of which the Egyptians were capable. By referring to modern data about the length of the line of navigation along the Nile, he concludes that the inscription expresses a rough estimate.

He proceeds by remarking that the inscription provides an excellent opportunity to establish the value of the important Egyptian linear unit *atur.* He observes that by reading documents that contain calculations in *atur* one gathers that the value of the *atur* in royal cubits must be expressed by numbers such as 5000 or 10,000. Finally, he concludes that, given the length of the course of the Nile from one end to the other of the country of Egypt, the *atur* must be 20,000 royal cubits.

I have concluded that the *atur* is 15,000 royal cubits (7862.225 meters), and this inscription bears me out. The difference of latitude between Behdet and the southern limit of the First Cataract is 7° 30′. Now, 106 *atur* is 1,590,000 royal cubits = 833,395.8 meters. The distance between 24° 00′ and 31° 30′ is 831,091.6 meters according to the

333

Smithsonian Geographical Tables. The Egyptian figure is in excess by 2300 meters, or 2/7 *atur.* The excess is not surprising, since the calculation of the length of Egypt as ending at Behdet was originally related to the geographic cubit and not the royal cubit. I have explained that the geographic cubit was defined as 1/1,800,000 of the length of Egypt to Behdet. In *atur* of 17,000 geographic cubits, this length could be expressed as 106 *atur* (1,802,000 geographic cubits) = 831,971.7 meters, with only a small excess over the initial figure of 1,800,000 geographic cubits = 831,048.4 meters.

The calculation of the length of Egypt to Behdet as 106 *atur* of 15,000 royal cubits has the virtue of indicating the length of the arc of meridian from the equator to the pole; since the length of Egypt to Behdet is 7° 30′, it is 1/12 of this arc. Multiplying 106 *atur* by 48, we have a great circle of 5088 *atur* = 40,002,998 meters, which is an excellent figure (212,000 cubits to a degree); Helmert's figure of 40,008,268 meters differs by less than an *atur.*

The purpose of the inscription on the rules which were found at the Temple of Amon in Thebes is to stress the scientific value of the calculations by the septenary royal cubit, which was a matter of essential political interest to this temple, as I will explain in the second part of this chapter.

The calculation of the length of Egypt as 106 *atur* had also the purpose of indicating by one of the usual numerological games that the average degree of latitude is 212,000 royal cubits = 111,119.4 meters; 212,000 was the Egyptian round figure for the average length of the degree of latitude (stadium of 353,333 royal cubits). If the average degree is identified with the middle degree, the degree at parallel 45°, this figure is only 2 cubits short of the Egyptian estimate of 212,002 cubits = 111,120.5 meters for this degree. The estimate of the *Smithsonian Geographical Tables* is 111,121.0 meters.

2. The inscription on the rules divides the interval of 106 *atur* into 86 *atur* from Syene to Pi-Hapy and 20 *atur* from Pi-Hapy to Behdet. It occurs immediately that the two figures must refer to Northern and Southern Egypt. But the figure of 20 *atur* is slightly too much for Northern Egypt and that of 86 *atur* is slightly too little for Southern Egypt.

If the degree is calculated as 212,000 royal cubits, 20 *atur* = 300,000 cubits is too much for the interval between Behdet and the apex of the Delta, since 1.4° × 212,000 = 296,800 cubits. Conversely, 86 *atur* would be 1,290,000 cubits, whereas the distance from 24° 00′ north to the apex is 6.1°, and 6.1° × 212,000 = 1,293,200 cubits. In either case there is a difference of 3200 cubits. Hence, the breaking point in the calculations must be somewhat south of the apex of the Delta.

Even though Egyptologists ignore scientific geography, there are specialists of Egyptian toponymy, that is, the study of local names. These have wondered about the identification of the locality of Pi-Hapy, "House of the Nile," mentioned in the inscription we are discussing. They have observed that in Egyptian texts Pi-Hapy is usually mentioned together with Kher-aha, although Pi-Hapy is a different place. They have concluded that Pi-Hapy was on the right bank of the Nile about 2 kilometers south of Kher-aha. But specialists of Egyptian toponymy have failed to identify Kher-aha, which was a fundamental point of Egyptian geography; Kher-aha, called Kerkasoros by the Greeks, was the apex of the Delta, the point 30° 06′ north, 31° 14′ east, at the southern tip of the island al-Warraq. Pi-Hapy, called Nilopolis by the Greeks, was on the right bank of the Nile, facing the southern tip of the island al-Warraq. Since the Nile in its course comes to the island al-Warraq from the west, the point Pi-Hapy was on meridian 31° 14′ east and could be considered to be on the right bank of the Nile directly opposite the apex of the Delta, or point Kher-aha. The width of the Nile between Kher-aha and Pi-Hapy, measured along meridian 31° 14′ east, fits well with what I have calculated to be the distance between the apex and Pi-Hapy (3200 royal cubits = 1,677 meters).

The breaking of the distance of 106 *atur* into a segment of 20 *atur* by establishing a new reference point called Pi-Hapy may have been influenced by the calculation of the length of Egypt up to the base line of the Delta as 100 *atur* (1,500,000 royal cubits).

In the inscribed royal cubit rules, the original estimate of 106 *atur* of 17,000 geographic cubits was interpreted in terms of 106 *atur* of 15,000 royal cubits, in order to link more closely the dimensions of Egypt (1/12 of arc of meridian counting to Behdet) to the measurements of the arc of meridian. As I have stated, 12×106 *atur* = 1272 *atur* = 19,080,000 royal cubits = 10,000,749.6 meters is an excellent estimate of the length of the arc of meridian, obtained with an extreme economy of reckoning. Let us not forget that the French metric system was established on the assumption that the arc of meridian is 10,000,000 meters. Even today in practical reckoning we take 111,111.1 meters as the round figure for the average degree of latitude, whereas the figure of 106 *atur* for the length of Egypt indicates a round figure of 212,000 cubits = 111,119.4 meters, which is more precise, and is almost perfect if we take 212,000 cubits to mean the length of the degree at the middle parallel.

Akhet-Aten

1. Because Egyptologists have ignored the issue of geodetic points and of the linear units, the figure of the revolutionary Pharaoh Akhenaten has turned out to be the most mysterious and controversial in the long history of the Egyptian monarchy, although this Pharaoh was unusually articulate and self-expressive in his utterances. The archeologist Cyril Aldred, who is the author of the most recent study of the reign of Akhenaten, begins his book (page 11) with this observation.

> With the possible exception of Cleopatra, no ruler of Ancient Egypt has provoked a greater flow of ink from the pens of historians, archaeologists, moralists, novelists and plain cranks than the Pharaoh Akhenaten who governed almost half the civilized world for a brief span during the fourteenth century B.C.

The Pharaoh Akhenaten.

The reason why even "plain cranks" write interpretations of the historical role of Akhenaten is that professional scholars have given the example. Because they have resisted accepting the solidly documented facts, established scholars have devoted their energies to debating theories such as that Akhenaten was impotent, was a practicing homosexual, or a woman masquerading as a man; there are historians who profess to be informed about the intimate relations between him and his wife, the beautiful Nefertiti. Since the picture of Akhenaten has remained indefinite and blurred, scholars have used it to project their own emotions. Those who do not like Akhenaten present him as a psychopath and dispute about the clinical definition of his illness. In the middle are those who describe him as a playboy Pharaoh. Those who admire him have chosen to portray him either as some sort of Christian evangelist, an Anabaptist preacher thrown into the midst of the history of Egypt, or, at the opposite end of the psychological personality scale, as an *artiste* type, bent on freeing Egyptian culture from its formalistic tradition in order to release untrammeled individualistic self-expression. If one were to look for a common denominator among all the conflicting interpretations, one fact could be considered as universally accepted, in spite of the heated controversies, namely, that Akhenaten was as far as possible from being a rational scientific thinker. Nevertheless, the documentary evidence suggests a style of thought that today we would call scientific naturalism.

There is a phrase which occurs again and again in the pronouncements of Akhenaten and represents his effort to summarize his program by a slogan: "Living in *maet.*" This is so obvious that Aldred declares (page 67):

> There is in Akhenaten's teaching a constant emphasis upon *maet,* "truth," as is not found before or afterwards.

It is agreed that *maet* was the central concept of Egyptian civilization and that the role of a Pharaoh was to be the defender and the living embodiment of *maet.* This concept was so basic in Egyptian culture that Aldred has no difficulty in explaining it in a few words (page 25):

The king was the personification of *maet,* a word which we translate as "truth" or "justice," but has the extended meaning of the proper cosmic order at the time of its establishment by the Creator. For it was believed that the gods had first ruled Egypt after creating it perfect.

Akhenaten, his wife Nefertiti, and two daughters (Berlin Museum).

The reader can easily grasp what was meant by *maet* by referring to what I have said about the geodetic system of Egypt. But, having admitted what is indisputable, that Akhenaten saw himself as the Pharaoh who would truly uphold *maet,* Aldred stops cold and does not draw the implications. Like other interpreters, he wanders afar and regales us with a chapter entitled "The Pathology of Akhenaten."

2. If instead of trying to imagine what were the hieroglyphic notes of the psychoanalyst of the royal family, we consider the documented facts, the most important action in the revolutionary reign of Akhenaten proves to be the establishment of a new capital for Egypt, the city of Akhet-Aten, "Resting-point of Aten." The miles-long remains of the buildings of this city have been found and excavated in the locality today known as Tell el-Amarna. During the reign of Akhenaten a substantial percentage of the national resources was dedicated to the construction of this city.

337

Scholars of the last century, who had not yet adopted the psychologizing fashion, at least recognized the political meaning of the shift in the location of the capital of Egypt. Akhenaten intended to cut at the root the power of the priests of the Temple of Amon in Thebes, who through their control of the national oracle, identified with the god of this temple, had usurped the royal functions. But what these scholars did not know is that the Temple of Amon was the geodetic center of Egypt, the "navel" of Egypt, being located where the eastern axis (32° 38′ east) crosses the Nile, at the parallel which is at 2/7 of the distance from the equator to the pole (25° 42′ 51″ north), and that the god Amon was identified with the hemispheric stone which marked this point.

The new city which was intended to replace Thebes as the capital and geodetic center of Egypt was planted in a position which seems most undesirable in terms of what we would consider the function of a capital city. Some scholars have interpreted this fact as further evidence of the mental derangement of its founder. It was in an area of difficult access, where there had never been any known significant center; some scholars have doubted whether even villages had existed there. It did not provide large flat areas for a major urban development. When maintenance was suspended after the fall of Akhenaten, large sections of the new buildings were washed away by the rainwater rushing down torrentially from the surrounding cliffs. Even the climate was inferior to that of many other areas along the course of the Nile. Unless one assumes that there was a compelling mathematical reason for choosing this location, one must agree that there is justification in claiming that what is often called the "Tell el-Amarna Revolution" was the product of a playful young man, or a religious fanatic, or a degenerate obsessed with his sex problems. Akhenaten himself relates that his courtiers raised objections to the selection of the new site, although he states that it was pointed out to him directly by his father, the god Aten.

The new capital for the god Aten, who was raised to the status of the one true god, was set at latitude 27° 45′ north, at the middle point between the northernmost point Behdet and the southern limit of Egypt at latitude 24° 00′ north. The longitude could not be equally as significant, since the capital had to be on the banks of the Nile. It was one degree east of the western axis of Egypt, that is, 30° 50′ east.

The longitude, although it was not as crucial as the latitude, was significant according to the system that the Egyptians used to describe the east coast of Africa. In order to describe this coast, down to the equator, the

338

Aerial view of the Tell el-
Amarna (RAF photo).

Egyptians used a system of right triangles, in which one side
was one of the three axes of Egypt and the other a
perpendicular to it; the hypotenuse usually indicated the
course of a segment of the east coast of Africa. The most
important of these triangles was one obtained counting from
Behdet 19° 30' south along the central axis of Egypt and
then 19° 30' to the east, to reach a point 12° 00' north,
50° 44' east, near Ras Alula (11° 59' north, 50° 46' east), a
point which was considered the extreme limit of the Arabian
Gulf. The ancients took the Gulf of Suez, the Red Sea, and
the Gulf of Aden as a single entity, the Arabian Gulf, which
at times they described as a river similar to the Nile. The
geographical point in question is called Notou Keras, "horn
of the East," by Strabo; it had a counterpart in the "horn of
the West," the innermost point of the Gulf of Guinea on the
west coast of Africa. The segment of parallel reaching the
"horn of the East" from the meridian of Behdet marks the
basic latitude 12° 00' north, halfway between the equator
and the basic latitude 24° 00' north, and bisects Lake Tana,
the source of the Blue Nile. The Nile was considered to have
two sources, one at the equator (White Nile) and one at
latitude 12° 00' north (Blue Nile). This system of calculations
for the geography of the area east of the course of the Nile
has an importance which carries beyond ancient history,

339

since the establishment of a geodetic point 10° south of Behdet and 10° east of the western axis of Egypt explains the origin of the religious importance of Mecca. The essence of this system of calculations was that points to the east of Egypt were identified by drawing perpendiculars to the course of the Nile. Considering this system in relation to the position of Akhet-Aten, if one counts east from it as much as it was south of Behdet, that is 3° 45', one reaches the sea at a point presently called island Ghānim (off Cape Az Zaytīyah, called Drepanon Promontory by Ptolemy, which is at 27° 47' north, 33° 35' east); Cape Az Zaytīyah together with the island south of it was considered the southernmost limit of the Gulf of Suez on the Egyptian side; it was assumed that the line drawn from Behdet to this point gave the course of the coast of Egypt on the Gulf of Suez.

3. The most revealing pieces of evidence uncovered in the area of the new capital established by Akhenaten are the so-called "Boundary Stelae." Along the outskirts of the new city there have been found huge inscriptions, either cut on pillars or cut on the cliffs, which contain a text substantially identical in the fourteen samples which have been uncovered so far. These inscriptions proclaim what was for Akhenaten the leading idea behind the establishment of the new capital.

The inscribed text relates in detail the rituals performed in the establishment of Akhet-Aten, "Resting-point of Aten"; but the greatest emphasis is placed on the setting of two boundary pillars, one at the extreme north and one at the extreme south of the sacred territory of the city, at a distance of 6 *atur,* 3/4 *khe,* and 4 cubits from each other. After setting these pillars the King took a solemn oath, to be repeated at regular intervals, never to remove or displace them and to restore them in the same identical place in case they were moved or damaged.

It should be obvious that the figure of 6 *atur,* 3/4 *khe,* and 4 cubits, given with numerical precision, is the key to the reason for the establishment of the new capital. Nevertheless, only one Egyptologist has made an effort to interpret these figures. This effort was a half-hearted one; it ignored Egyptian geographical texts and parallel occurrences of the terms *atur* and *khe* in Egyptian writings. Nevertheless, ever since, scholars quote this interpretation if they bother to mention the dimensions of Akhet-Aten in dealing with its establishment. The interpretation took as a starting point the distance between the relatively northernmost and the relatively southernmost of the fourteen inscriptions which have been found, and divided this distance by 6 to conclude that an *atur* must be 4000 royal cubits. It can be objected

Boundary stelae at Tell el-Amarna.

that the pillars which in some cases were erected to carry the text of the inscription cannot be the boundary pillars of which the inscription is speaking, since the latter must be of such a nature and form that their position could be established to the inch. It stands to reason that when, after the collapse of the revolution, masons were sent to demolish or deface the monuments of the accursed Akhenaten, not sparing even the tombs of the members of his family, the work of destruction must have started with the boundary pillars; we are not likely to find them, unless broken pieces were scattered around. In any case, the Egyptian texts which mention distances measured in *atur* positively exclude that an *atur* can be as short as 4000 royal cubits (2097 meters).

341

As to the *khe,* the interpretation stated in a hit-or-miss manner that it is equal to 100 royal cubits. Nobody asked why Akhenaten should have selected a figure refined not only to 3/4 of *khe,* but also to 4 cubits. It was a matter of such precision that the inscribed text indicates that even knocking the limit markers or hitting them with stones would interfere with their function.

According to Egyptian practice, geographic distances could be measured either in geographic cubits or in royal cubits. The natural multiple of the geographic cubit was the stadium, called *khe* in Egyptian, of 400 geographic cubits (600 geographic feet), whereas the natural multiple of the royal cubit was the *atur* of 15,000 royal cubits. But the two systems were merged by using an *atur* of 15,000 royal cubits (7862.2 meters) and an *atur* of 17,000 geographic cubits (7848.8 meters), and a *khe* of 350 royal cubits (183.45 meters) and a *khe* of 400 geographic cubits (184.68 meters). In the case of the inscriptions of Akhet-Aten, the occurrence of the figure of 3/4 of *khe* suggests that a calculation by geographic cubits is involved, since 3/4 of a stadium of 350 royal cubits would be an odd figure. It is my understanding that the dimensions of the district of Akhet-Aten were:

> 6 *atur* of 17,000 geographic cubits
> 3/4 of a stadium of 400 geographic cubits
> 4 geographic cubits
> Total: 102,304 geographic cubits = 47,233.1 meters

4. Even without considering the exact value of the units mentioned by Akhenaten, the figure of 6 *atur* should have rung a bell in the mind of Egyptologists, calling to their attention the traditional figure of 106 *atur* for the length of Egypt. Akhenaten wanted to emphasize that the "Resting-point of Aten" was at the middle point of Egypt. By giving to the new geodetic center a dimension of 6 *atur,* he left 50 *atur* from it to Behdet and 50 *atur* from it to parallel 24° 00′ north. This was particularly significant since there was another basic estimate of the length of Egypt as 100 *atur,* from the base line of the Delta (31° 06′ north) to parallel 24° 00′ north.

Before proceeding any further I must remind the reader that the traditional figure setting the length of Egypt at 106 *atur* did not intend to convey information only about Egypt itself, but also to indicate the length of the arc of meridian, 12 × 106 *atur.*

Since the length of the geographic cubit was defined by considering the distance from Behdet to parallel 24° 00′ north equal to 1,800,000 cubits, if the district of Akhet-Aten had had an extension of 0° 25′ 30″, it would have had a length of 6 *atur* = 102,000 cubits. This length was increased to 6 *atur,* 3/4 stadium, 4 cubits = 102,304 cubits, in order to indicate that the average degree of latitude on earth is 240,715 cubits.

The figure of Akhenaten indicates that the average degree of latitude was estimated as 240,715 cubits, since 0° 25' 30" of a degree of 240,715 is 102,303.875 cubits. A degree of 240,715 cubits is 111,136.6 meters; the corresponding arc of meridian is 21,664,375 geographic cubits = 10,002,301 meters. Hayford's figure is 10,002,286 meters.

Akhenaten wanted to prove that Thebes could not properly claim to be the geodetic center of Egypt and that he had chosen the geodetic center conforming to an absolutely rigorous interpretation of *maet,* the cosmic order of which the dimensions of Egypt were an embodiment. In order to follow absolutely exact standards of measurement, he reverted to the predynastic geodetic system which counted in geographic cubits starting from Behdet. This system was more precise than the system which counted in royal cubits (septenary units) starting from the base line of the Delta, making Egypt equal to 100 *atur* of 15,000 royal cubits. Thebes could claim to be a geodetic center only in terms of the second system, which is septenary and makes the meridian of Thebes coincide with the eastern corner of the Delta. In terms of the system based on the predynastic capital of Behdet, there could be no question that Akhet-Aten is the "true and just" navel of Egypt.

This conclusion implies that one should reevaluate the entire historical role of Akhenaten, taking as the starting point what he himself considered the initial step in his program to establish true and just conformity with *maet.* There is a possibility that his revolutionary reforms, which extended from religion to art and family relations, were understood as a general return to predynastic ideas and practices.

5. Since the Egyptian monarchy set the style for the trappings of royal power thorughout the world, the prescriptions of Akhenaten about the dimensions of the territory of his capital did not remain without parallel in history. A striking parallel can be found in what may appear a most unlikely time and place, Saxon England.

Scholars are so bent on principle to interpret the history of measures and measurement in terms of the most crude primitivism, that in most works of history that deal with English measures one reads that the English foot was originally set by the length of the foot of an English king. The name of the king whose lower extremities were so decisive varies from scholar to scholar, although, when one thinks about it (which is not done in matters of measurement) kings of average human size should be excluded. There is agreement among scholars that the king in question reigned in the centuries following the Norman conquest, since it is assumed and often stated that before this time England did not have set units of measure. A variant of the fairy tale about the English foot is provided by the historians who tell us that it was not a matter of the foot but of the arm of a king which decided the length of the yard (three feet). Usually the length of the arm of King Henry I (1068–1135) is mentioned in this connection.

Such statements are made in spite of the fact that it is not necessary to be a specialist in the history of measures to find out that a foot equal to the English foot was the basic standard of Russia, from the time of the first available historical records to the Soviet revolution. I grant that it takes a specialized historical training to trace the linear standard of England and Russia to the ancient Orient, but I may also observe that there are well known Greek temples which have been planned in English feet, and that archeologists of English and American nationality have studied them without realizing what they had before their eyes.

Historians could have developed less benighted notions about the origin of English measures, even without extending their horizon beyond the British isles, because there is a law of King Athelstan (924–940) which defines the length of the English foot. The text of this law is included in the standard collections of medieval English laws. The words of law of Athelstan were repeated exactly in the legislation about measures issued by King Henry I. The law of Athelstan provides the most fundamental text for the study of English measures, but it has been ignored.

Athelstan prescribed that the king's girth shall extend from the royal residence for a distance of 3 miles, 3 furlongs, 9 acres, 9 feet, 9 palms, and 9 barleycorns. The King's girth was the area considered a direct extension of the King's place of residence and as such the area in which the King's peace was in force. This was the area in which attacks on private persons were crimes against the Crown.

The picturesque language of the law means that the King's girth extends for a radius of 18,250 feet, since it is a matter of the following units:

mile	5280 feet
furlong	600 feet
acre	66 feet
palm	3/4 foot
barleycorn	1/3 inch

344

The law employed a form of expression which had a particular numerological rhythm and at the same time defined the value of the multiples and submultiples of the foot.

My understanding of the law of King Athelstan is that the radius of the King's girth was defined as 3 minutes of latitude. The King's girth extended 6 minutes or 1/10 of degree from north to south. This implies that a degree was understood to be 365,000 English feet, which is the length of the degree at the latitude of towns like Winchester.

A more detailed analysis of the law of Athelstan belongs to a study of English measures. What is important to stress here is that the English foot was defined by length of a stretch of 1/10 latitude around the king's place of residence. The political conditions of the feudal society of Saxon England were very different from those of Pharaonic Egypt, but the method used by King Athelstan in order to relate his power to the system of measures and to the cosmic order bears a remarkable similarity to that adopted by the Pharaoh Akhenaten.

VI. DEGREES OF LONGITUDE

1. When the Egyptians fixed the value of their fundamental unit of length, the geographic cubit, they chose as standard degree the degree of latitude at 27° 45′ north, taken as the middle latitude of Egypt. When they recalculated the dimensions of Egypt in terms of royal cubits, they chose as the middle latitude 27° 33′ north. These latitudes were chosen taking into account the length of a degree of longitude at the equator. Latitude 27° 45′ is the half of latitude 55° 30′ and latitude 27° 33′ is the half of latitude 55° 06′. The Egyptians assumed that at the two higher latitudes a degree of latitude is equal in length to a degree of equator.

According to the *Smithsonian Geographical Tables,* a degree of latitude at parallel 55° 30′ is 111,324.7 meters, but probably the Egyptians calculated it as 361,680 geographic feet = 111,323.5 meters: this degree is equal to the fundamental degree of 360,000 geographic feet (600 stadia) plus 2.8 stadia or plus 1/214.28. According to the *Smithsonian Geographical Tables* a degree at parallel 55° 06′ is 111,317.3 meters. According to the Egyptian table of the lengths of the degrees of latitude which I have reconstructed, it is 212,378.5 royal cubits = 111,317.3 meters. This length could be expressed also as 361,660 geographic feet = 111,317.4 meters, that is, as 600 stadia plus 2.7666 stadia. This implies that the Egyptians estimated the equatorial circle either as 130,204,800 geographic feet = 40,076,478 meters or as

130,197,600 geographic feet = 40,074,261 meters. I suspect that they began with an estimate of 130,200,000 geographic feet (degree of 361,666 feet = 360,000 feet plus 1/216) = 40,075,000 meters, and then modified the figure in order to establish a relationship between the equatorial degree and the degree of the middle latitude of Egypt. The Egyptian estimate agrees with our current ones: the equator is 40,075,452 meters, according to the Clarke Spheroid and 40,076,596 meters according to the International Spheroid.

Very revealing is that a base line was marked along parallel 45° 12′ north on the north side of the Black Sea. This base line started from the mouth of the Danube, cut across the Crimea, and ended at the foot of the Caucasus. Beginning from this base, Russia was surveyed for a length of 10 degrees, along the three meridians which formed the three axes of Egypt, up to latitude 55° 12′ north. The river Dnieper was understood to be a symmetric counterpart of the Nile, running between the same meridians. Key positions along the course of the Dnieper were identified with corresponding key positions along the course of the Nile, up to the point of transferring Egyptian place names to Russia. The information about the existence of this geodetic system is provided by the description of a map of Russia which is based on it. The description of the map indicates that it was used at the end of the sixth century B.C., but the map may be older; in any case there are other sources of information about the base line which indicate that it was marked in very early times.

The figures of the geodetic system on which the map of Russia was based are most intriguing. The base line at parallel 45° 12′ north suggests that it was decided that it is at this latitude that the degree of latitude has a length equal to the average length of the degree of latitude. The fact that the meridians of Egypt were followed for 10° up to parallel 55° 12′ north suggests that it was decided that a degree of latitude at this parallel is equal to the length of a degree of equator.

The designation of 45° 12′ north for the location of the average degree indicates what the Egyptians assumed to be the degree of ellipticity of the earth. According to the *Smithsonian Geographical Tables,* the length of the degree of latitude at the point 45° 12′ north is 111,134.9 meters; from this figure we would get an arc of meridian of 10,002,141 meters. According to the Egyptian table of the length of the degrees of latitude that I have reconstructed, the degree at the point 45° 12′ north is 212,028.6 royal cubits = 111,134.4 meters; this length implies an arc of meridian of 10,002,099 meters. According to the *Smithsonian Geographical Tables* the degree ending at parallel 55° 12′ is 111,319.3 meters; if this is taken as the length of the degree of equator, the equatorial circle is 40,074,948 meters. According to the Egyptian table of the length of the degrees of latitude, the degree at 55° 12′ north is 212,381 royal cubits = 111,319.1 meters; this would indicate an equatorial circle of 76,457,160 royal cubits = 40,074,890 meters (stadium of equator = 353.96833 cubits).

2. In performing astronomical observations it is necessary to express differences of longitude in terms of units of time. The equator and all parallels are divided into 360 degrees, but considering the rotation of the earth it is expedient to divide the equator and all parallels into 24 hours. Given 360/24 = 15, a minute or a second of time is equal to 15 minutes or 15 seconds of degree.

In astronomical calculations, there are employed two different kinds of time, solar time and sidereal time. Solar time is our ordinary time. Solar time assumes that the day is the interval between two successive passages of the sun at the meridian. The length of the day so defined varies greatly according to the seasons of the year; it varies by more than 1/90. The reason for this variation is that the speed of the earth along its orbit around the sun is not constant and that the apparent motion of the sun around the earth does not follow the line of the equator, but of that of the ecliptic. Hence, in ordinary life we reckon by mean solar time, which is obtained by assuming that a fictitious sun moves along the celestial equator at a speed equal to the average speed of the sun along the ecliptic.

Mean solar time is a highly artificial concept and we can use it because we have mechanical clocks. The ancients calculated by sidereal time, which they could measure by observing the apparent movement of the vault of heaven. Sidereal time has the advantage of flowing evenly. There are small variations due to the nutation of the earth under the influence of the gravitational pull of the moon and the planets; but these variations are too small to be relevant to the calculations we are considering.

A sidereal day is the interval between two passages of a star at the meridian. A sidereal day is shorter than a solar day. If one observes a star at the meridian today, that star will be again at the meridian in less than a solar day. In other words, if one counts by solar time, the vault of heaven rotates about one degree more than a full circle in a day. The difference between mean solar time and sidereal time can be easily computed, because in a year the vault of heaven makes exactly one more circle around the earth than the number of circles made by the sun.

347

Hence the ancients could reckon:

$$\frac{\text{Solar time}}{\text{Sidereal time}} = \frac{366}{365} = 1.00273972$$

or more precisely:

$$\frac{\text{Solar time}}{\text{Sidereal time}} = \frac{366.25}{365.25} = 1.00273785$$

They did not need a formula more precise than the second one; today we reckon by the ratio 1.00273791.

The ancients simplified this complex matter by counting by the speed of movement of a point at the equator. That speed was taken by them as constant; the infinitesimal variations in speed of the rotation of the earth on its axis are relevant only to some calculations of modern astronomy.

The speed of a point at the equator in terms of mean solar time was obtained by dividing the length of the equator into 24 hours = 1440 minutes = 86,400 seconds. But the ancients were concerned particularly with the speed of a point at the equator in terms of sidereal time. A minute of time (solar time) corresponds to the length of 15 minutes of degree of equator. A minute of time (sidereal time) is equal to the same length multiplied by 365.25/366.25, that is, it is shorter.

3. When the Egyptians standardized their system of measures by establishing that the degree at the middle latitude of Egypt is 240,000 geographic cubits (360,000 geographic feet = 600 stadia) or that 1/48 of great circle measured from 24° 00′ north to 31° 30′ north is 1,800,000 geographic cubits, they must have had in mind the following equivalence:

1 second (sidereal time) = 1000 cubits
1 minute (sidereal time) = 60,000 cubits =
1/4 length of degree of latitude in Egypt

This calculation was convenient, but implied an equatorial degree (degree of latitude in Egypt × 1.00273785) of 111,109.8 meters, which is slightly too short; it is the length of a degree of longitude at about 3° 30′ from the equator.

In order to obtain the right length of the second and minute of sidereal time, one must take as reference a degree of latitude further north than Egypt. The degrees at the latitudes of Dodona and Delphi provided the correct values.

Classical Greece was not a unified country, being divided into cities proudly clinging to their absolute political independence; but, most incongruously, it had a national oracular center, just as Egypt, a strongly unified country, had a national oracular center at the Temple of Amon in Thebes. In Greece there were two centers which competed

Another Greek conception of an *omphalos* as derived from the Egyptians.

Omphalos of Delphi depicted with two pigeons (usually facing each other), evidently carrier pigeons used for establishing geographic distances. According to Greek legends, a central geodetic point was obtained by loosing two birds of equal strength and using the mean of the time employed in flight. This would allow for differences in wind current and other variables. By repeated flights even more accurate measurements could be obtained.

for the role of national oracle, Dodona and Delphi. The oracle of Dodona was considered more ancient and many Greeks considered it more authoritative, but it was at a practical disadvantage because it was located beyond the limits of solidly Greek territory in an area of most difficult access. In modern Greece, which extends more widely than ancient Greece, Dodona is near the Albanian frontier. The position of the oracle of Delphi, even though not as surprising as that of the oracle of Dodona, was peculiar; it was located in the mountains, north of all major centers of Greece.

The Greeks narrated that two doves flew from the temple of Amon in Egypt in order to establish the oracles of Dodona and Delphi. In ancient literature and iconography the flight of two doves is the standard symbol for the stretching of meridians and parallels.

Because the oracle of Delphi was less isolated, it received more attention and consequently we are better informed about it. Delphi was considered the geodetic center of Greece. The god of Delphi, Apollo, whose name means "the stone," was identified with an object, the *omphalos,* "navel," which has been found. It consisted of an ovoidal stone (the ovoidal shape indicated the lengthening of the degrees of latitude as one moves north) covered by a net. The net was the symbol of what even today we call the net of meridians and parallels. The *omphalos* of Delphi was similar to the object which represented the god Amon in Thebes, the "navel" of Egypt. In 1966 I presented to the annual meeting of the Archeological Institute of America a paper in which I maintained that historical accounts, myths, and legends, and some monuments of Delphi, indicate that the oracle was established there by the Pharaohs of the Ethiopian Dynasty. This is the reason why the Greek portrayed Delphos, the eponymous hero of Delphi, as a Negro.

The relevance of the latitude in the location of Delphi is indicated by a number of Greek accounts which associate Delphi with Sardis, the capital of the kingdom of Lydia in Asia Minor, which is on the same parallel (38° 28′ north).

The role of geography in the oracular importance of Delphi is indicated also by the method employed in obtaining oracular responses. Modern scholars who have been impervious to the rational elements of ancient thought and prefer to ignore that Apollo, the god of Delphi, was a god of reason and scientific thought, are generally inclined to think that the oracular responses were given by a priestess who, put in a trance by drug fumes, uttered gibberish. But there is abundant pictorial evidence which shows vividly how the oracle was consulted. An object which resembles a roulette

Egyptian *omphali* with twin birds. Carrier pigeons are depicted in Egypt as early as the Fourth Dynasty, and were evidently used to establish parallels and meridians from prehistoric times. Homing pigeons, which fly in a straight line (as the crow flies!), could cover the more than five hundred miles from one end of Egypt to the other in a single day.

wheel, and actually is its historical antecedent, was centered on top of the *omphalos*. The spinning of a ball gave the answers; each of the 36 spokes of the wheel corresponded to a letter symbol.

In studying ancient computing devices, I have discovered that they were used also to obtain oracular answers. This is the origin of many of the oracular instruments we still use today, such as cards and ouija boards. The psychological foundation of this phenomenon is simple. If I have a problem in interpreting an ancient text or an archeological report, I "consult" my calculating machine which "gives me the answer." By stretching this imagery further, one could assume that the calculating machine is an oracle. The roulette wheel of Delphi originally was a special kind of abacus for calculating in terms of angles.

The latitudes of Dodona and Delphi are significant. The length of the degree of latitude at the parallels of these two oracular centers gave the length of the minute or second of sidereal time, that is, the distance covered by a point at the equator in a sidereal minute or second of rotation of the earth.

Dodona is at 39° 32′ north. According to the *Smithsonian Geographical Tables* a degree at this parallel is 111,014.0 meters. This means that the degree must have been calculated as 360,673 geographic feet (360,000 plus 1/535) = 111,013.6 meters. If we multiply this length by 1.00273785, we obtain 361,660 geographic feet, the length of the degree of latitude at parallel 55° 06′, which is equal to the length of a degree of longitude at the equator.

If the figures employed in the reckoning of Dodona are rounded to a degree of 360,600 geographic feet and to a second of sidereal time of 1001.666 geographic cubits (that is, 1000 plus 1/600), we obtain the length of the degree of latitude at the parallel of Delphi, which is 38° 28′ north. A degree of 360,600 geographic feet is 110,991.1 meters; a degree at parallel 38° 28′ is 110,993.5 meters according to the *Smithsonian Geographical Tables* and 110,992.1 meters according to the Egyptian table of the length of degrees of latitude. Latitude 38° 28′ north may also have been chosen because it is at the standard distance of 6′ from latitude 38° 34′ north, which is at 3/7 of the distance from the equator to the pole, whereas the Temple of Amon in Thebes was set at 2/7 of this distance.

4. Metrologists of the past have wavered in establishing the value of the geographic foot (and hence of the artaba), because they confused this unit with a similar one, the Greek foot, which is about half a millimeter longer.

Roman writers mention a Greek foot which is 25/24 of

the Roman foot and a Greek stadium which is equal to 600 Greek feet or 625 Roman feet. The Romans used the two units in conjunction. Roman roads were divided into miles of 5000 Roman feet, but at times between the milestones there were smaller markers which divided the road into 8 Greek stadia ($8 \times 625 = 5000$). In giving itinerary distances, writers of the Roman period usually reckon by Roman miles on land and by Greek stadia at sea.

Because Roman authors indicate that the degree is 75 Roman miles or 600 Greek stadia, since the Renaissance metrologists have been concerned with establishing the exact value of the Greek foot; but in examining the empirical evidence they met with data that appear conflicting, for the reason that they did not separate sources of information which apply to the geographic foot. Travelers and sailors of the eastern Mediterranean and the Middle East used to assume that a degree of latitude is 600 geographic stadia (110,806 meters) and a degree of longitude is 500 geographic stadia (92,339 meters); Greek and Roman travelers and sailors used to assume that a degree of latitude is 600 Greek stadia = 75 Roman miles (110,980 meters) and a degree of longitude is 500 Greek stadia = 60 Roman miles (92,483 meters). As a result scholars have confused information concerning two different types of units. The confusion occurs easily, unless one assumes high standards of precision and accuracy in ancient measurements, since we have:

Geographic foot	= 307.7957 millimeters
Geographic cubit	= 461.6935 millimeters
Greek foot	= 308.2764 millimeters
Greek cubit	= 462.4147 millimeters

A degree of latitude of 600 Greek stadia = 75 Roman miles is correct at parallel 37° 42′, which is the latitude of Mycenae. The system of calculation used by the Greeks and Romans goes back to the Mycenean ancestors of the Greeks.

Archeologists assume that, if the Greeks of the classical period measured badly, the Greeks of the Mycenean age did not measure at all. It is assumed that when the Myceneans erected their buildings they placed one stone on top of another without much of a plan. However, we know that the Myceneans were engaged in extensive long-distance trade and through it they accumulated huge quantities of gold of African origin; long-distance navigation and exchange of precious metals were the two activities which created for the ancients the most compelling need for exact standards.

By examining the dimensions of Mycenean citadels, I

351

have established that they were planned by a foot which is 15/16 of the Roman foot, a foot of 277.4488 millimeters. This foot has been called Oscan or Italic by metrologists of the last century, who noticed its occurrence in pre-Roman Italy and in the earliest remains of Rome. I call this foot Mycenean.

The Mycenean foot not only is 15/16 of the Roman foot of 295.9454 millimeters, but also is 9/10 of the Greek foot of 308.2764 millimeters. The Greek foot is 25/24 of the Roman foot and $25/24 \times 16/15 = 400/360 = 10/9$.

A degree of 360,000 Greek feet (75 Roman miles), a degree of latitude at the parallel of Mycenae, is equal to 400,000 Mycenean feet. The occurrence of the factor 4 indicates that a calculation by time units is involved, since there are 4 minutes of time in a degree. A minute of time is equal to 100,000 Mycenean feet. Hence, by using the Greek cubit and the Mycenean foot, one could obtain the following easy formula:

Second of time = 1000 Greek cubits
Minute of time = 100,000 Mycenean feet

These units are slightly too short for a second and a minute of sidereal time. If we take the degree of 360,000 Greek feet = 400,000 Mycenean feet = 110,979.5 meters and multiply it by 1.00273785, we obtain a degree of 360,986 Greek feet = 110,283.4 meters, which is the length of a parallel circle at about 1° 30′ from the equator.

But the numerical structure of the units indicates how the exact length of the degree of equator was obtained by introducing an easy correction. One starts with these data:

1000 Greek cubits = 1 second of time
Day of 86,400 seconds = 86,400,000 Greek cubits
100,000 Mycenean feet = 1 minute of time
Day of 1440 minutes = 144,000,000 Mycenean feet

These figures can be modified as follows:

Equator = 86,666,666 Greek cubits = 40,075,939 meters
Equator = 144,444,444 Mycenean feet = 40,075,939 meters

Similarily, one may start with the Greek foot and obtain

100 Greek feet = 1 second of degree
Circle of 1,296,000 seconds = 129,600,000 Greek feet

The last figure can be modified to

Equator = 130,000,000 Greek feet = 40,075,939 meters

All that was needed in order to obtain the exact length of the equator was to assume that a circle is equal to 1,300,000 seconds of degree, instead of 1,296,000.

It is possible that this formula was used to calculate the actual length of the solar day in the different seasons of the year. Today almanacs assign the value of 1200 to the length of the mean solar day and list a figure greater or smaller than 1200 in order to indicate the actual length of the solar day for each day of the year. Possibly the ancients proceeded in a similar way, assigning the value of 1300 to the mean solar day.

Archeologists and historians assume that the Myceneans had no concern with science, but the most famous remains of Mycenean civilization proclaim otherwise.

Lion Gate at Mycenae.

The best known monument of Mycenae is the entrance gate which today is called the Lion Gate, because he who approaches the city is overpowered by a huge relief sculpture on the triangular capstone of the entrance; the relief consists of a column between two facing lions. The column is sandwiched between two sets of parallel horizontal lines. At the bottom the column rests on a support on which three parallel lines are strongly marked. These three lines are the same three lines which occur in the hieroglyphic symbol for Southern Egypt; they represent the tropic of Cancer, which was identified with parallels 24° 06′, 24° 00′, and 23° 51′ north. The column represents the three basic meridians of Egypt; the curvature of the column suggests the development of the system of meridians to the east and the west of Egypt. On top of the capital of the column (symbol for Northern Egypt) there rests what appears to be a segment of a floor. This segment of floor is on three levels. The bottom and the top levels are two horizontal lines, whereas the middle level consists of four circles. I have explained the significance of the factor 4 in the Mycenean system of linear units. The top part of the relief represents the parallel of Mycenae.

The grave circle at Mycenae excavated by Schliemann. A geodetic point for astronomical observation similar to the circular henges and mounds of the second millennium B.C. elsewhere in Europe.

The two lions which face each other on the sides of the column represent a circle closing on itself. The easiest way to convey the meaning of this symbol is to refer to pieces of ancient jewelry which consist of a bracelet open at one side with a head of a lion on each open end. The lions represent the summer solstice. The stance of the lions, with the front paws on the line of the tropic and their hind paws extending below it (this stance will later become the heraldic symbol of the lion rampant), indicates the spread of the zodiacal band north and south of the ecliptic. The ancients established their astronomical system when the spring equinox was in Taurus, which ceased to be true at the beginning of the second millennium B.C.; for them the point zero of the sky was between the two horns of Taurus. Today we count from the constellation of Aries, although the spring equinox has not been in Aries since the time when the Roman Emperor Antoninus Pius (A.D. 138–161) celebrated the end of the age of Aries and introduced new cults and religious beliefs in accordance with the beginning of a new cosmic age. When the spring equinox was in Taurus, the summer solstice was in Leo.

The cosmological meaning of the Lion Gate of Mycenae should not have been lost to archeologists, since next to

354

this gate there is the second most impressive relic of ancient Mycenae, the so-called Grave Circle. It consists of a circular arrangement of stone blocks. If excavators had not been completely blinded by their belief in the primitiveness of the Myceneans, they would have immediately assumed that this circle must have some cosmological meaning. Instead the Smithsonian Institution spent time and energy to proceed to measurements of the skeletons found buried within the circle, arriving at the conclusion that they were bones of ordinary size men and not of giants. But the dimensions of the stone circle have not received attention; it may be enough to report here that the inner diameter of the circle is 100 Mycenean feet.

When the first circuit of walls of Mycenae was erected, the Circle was outside the walls directly in front of the Gate; the middle of the Gate is on the line of the north-south diameter of the Circle. Later the circuit of the walls was extended so as to include the Circle within the citadel.

5. A splendid illustration of the Mycenean system of linear units is provided by the Parthenon of Athens.

The Parthenon of Athens is the only Greek temple which has been surveyed with an adequate level of accuracy. But unfortunately for my investigation of the dimensions of Greek temples, the system of proportions of the Parthenon is an aberrant one. I have established the mathematical formula that determined the dimensions of Greek temples and the mathematical formula that determined the dimensions of Mycenean throne rooms; the Parthenon conforms to the latter and not to the former. The reason is that the Parthenon was built as a replacement on a larger scale of the Temple of Athena destroyed by the Persians, when they sacked Athens in 480 B.C. The old Temple of Athena in turn was built on top of a Mycenean throne room, some remains of which have been found by deep excavations. For this reason the Parthenon was planned in Mycenean feet, whereas most of the other monuments of the Acropolis of Athens were planned in Roman feet. However, the major dimensions of the outer colonnade of the Parthenon were so chosen that they could be expressed also in Greek feet, which was easy since Mycenean foot and Greek foot relate as 9:10.

For the study of the Parthenon we can rely on data that are satisfactory for some of the major dimensions, because at the middle of the last century an English architect and scholar of the history of architecture, Francis Cranmer Penrose, who was also an outstanding dilettante astronomer, on the basis of reports on the mathematical curvatures of the lines of the temple became convinced that the Parthenon

The so-called Treasury of Atreus at Mycenae built into a mound with corbeled roofing similar to the Maes-Howe mound.

had been planned and executed with high standards of mathematical skill. In order to prove his point he measured it accurately with the precision of one-thousandth of an English foot.

Penrose, however, was ridiculed by archeologists, and no other Greek temple has been surveyed with comparable care ever since. The Archeological Institute of America does not support any survey or publication which does not assume that the maximum precision achieved in construction of reference foot rules by the ancient Greeks was a fifth or at the very best a tenth of centimeter. Naturally, the precision achieved in the construction of buildings was much less than the precision of the official reference rules.

Penrose was not able to convince scholars of his major contention, because he was obsessed as an architect with the notion that buildings should have perfectly square corners. He put this notion into practice when he planned the building of the British School of Archeology in Athens, of which he was director for two short periods, after its foundation in 1882. Because of this obsession, when Penrose found that the western front of the Parthenon is longer than the eastern front and that the south flank is longer than the north flank, he concluded that this was the result of mistakes in construction. His opponents were quick to point out that, if it is so, his major contention is disproved.

Penrose believed that the difference in the lengths of the sides of the Parthenon results from mistakes in the marking of the four corners which were intended to be perfectly square. In reality, the four corners of the Parthenon

356

Nineteenth-century view of the Parthenon.

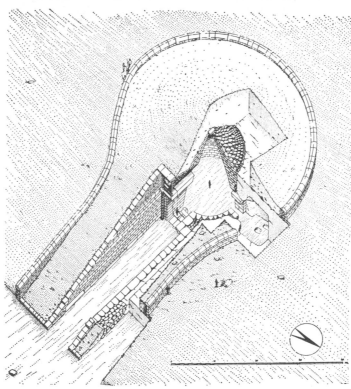

The Treasury of Atreus at Mycenae (isometric view, after Hood), which has a striking resemblance to the Maes-Howe burrow and appears to have been designed for azimuth and zenith observation, like the subterranean chambers of the pyramids.

were not intended to be exactly square, but to deviate by set small amounts from a right angle, as is the case with the four corners of the Great Pyramid. I have established that the west front of the Parthenon was intended to be 1/48 of a Mycenean foot longer than the east front, and that the south flank was intended to be longer than the north

357

flank by the same amount. The two longer sides join at the southwest corner, which is also higher in level over the other three corners. Taking these intended deviations into account, the actual findings of Penrose about the length of the sides agree almost perfectly with the theoretical dimensions obtained by mathematical principles.

Even with the intended lengthening of the west and south sides, the northeast corner, which joins the two most important sides, could have been a right angle, but instead it was acute by a figure close to a minute of degree. Unfortunately, Penrose measured the angle of this corner rather casually, because he thought that the lack of exact squareness was the result of a mistake in construction, and nobody else has tested the angle of this corner again in more than 120 years.

East end of the Parthenon.

There are many problems in the architecture of the Parthenon that cannot be solved, because archeologists prefer to go on building fanciful theories rather than establish the facts by an accurate survey. It is a basic principle of epistemology that our ability to reject erroneous theories increases in proportion with the precision and accuracy of the measurements; the converse is true, and this is what archeologists like, because, as they put it, it permits the spirit to soar. For instance, if one were to accept the loose standards of measurement dogmatically adopted by the Archaeological Institute of America, it would not be too difficult to present an argument to the effect the the surface of the earth is concave.

In the specific case of the Parthenon, I can point out that Penrose tested the orientation of the north flank, and that on the basis of his finding I could establish that the Parthenon is correctly oriented according to the latitude and longitude of Athens. But details of construction have led me to realize that the orientation of the inner part of the temple, the cella, was a trifle different. Since the difference of azimuth between the two longitudinal axes of the Parthenon has never been tested, I am left in the dark about the fine points in the orientation of the Parthenon.

An essential datum is that there are similarities between the mathematical structure of the Parthenon and that of the Great Pyramid. In both constructions the corners deviate deliberately from a right angle. I have established that the elevation of the fronts of the Parthenon was calculated by the factor φ and that the elevation of the flanks was calculated by the factor π. According to the data available, I have interpreted the elevation of the Great Pyramid to be such that the north side was calculated by the factor φ and that the west side was calculated by the factor π.

Here, I will deal only with the horizontal dimension, width, of the two fronts of the Parthenon, because it is directly connected with the Mycenean system of measures.

Before Penrose proceeded to a careful measurement of the sides of the Parthenon in the winter 1846–47 (the season of winter was deliberately chosen in order to reduce the effects of changes in temperature which may be macroscopic under the sun of Greece), an attempt at careful measurement was conducted in 1753, under unfavorable political and physical circumstances, by the painter James Stuart and the architect Nicholas Revett, who had become interested in the measurements of ancient buildings while studying in Rome. The expedition of these two English antiquarians had been carefully planned and created great stir in Europe at the time. One of their specific aims, indicated in the campaign for the raising of the necessary funds, was to ascertain the exact length of the Greek foot and by inference of the Roman foot, which is 24/25 of Greek foot. The Parthenon is called *Hekatompedon,* "one hundred foot temple," in Greek texts and these texts indicate also that its width was 100 feet. Earlier visitors to the Parthenon had concluded that the two fronts of the temple measured 100 Greek feet. For this reason Stuart and Revett provided themselves with highly reliable instruments of measurement and paid the greatest attention to the measurement of the two fronts.

They were so concerned with the length of the Greek foot that they reported the dimensions of the temple in such a way as to arrive at the results that were expected. Their figures for the length of the fronts are scanty. But they

359

arrived at the conclusion that the value of the Greek foot is 12.137 English inches = 308.2795 millimeters, which agreed well with what scholars had estimated to be the length of the Roman foot (24/25 of Greek foot). According to my reckonings the Greek foot is 308.2765 millimeters.

Stuart and Revett used a yard rule prepared by the famous instrument-maker John Bird of London. A few years later (1762) Bird prepared a yard rule on behalf of the Parliamentary Committee appointed in 1758 "to inquire into the original standards of weight and measure of this kingdom." Although Bird had to follow the instructions of the committee, it can be presumed that the rule he built in 1762 did not differ in a manner significant for the present research from those he had built earlier. The Bird rule of 1762 was the main basis in the calculation of the Imperial Standard Yard made legal by Parliament in 1824.

What Stuart and Revett did not know is that the fronts of the Parthenon were intended to be slightly more than 100 Greek feet.

If the fronts had had a length of 100 Greek feet = 111.111 Mycenean feet = 111 1/9 Mycenean feet, they would have had a length equal to a second of degree of latitude at the parallel of Mycenae (37° 42′ north), whereas the latitude of Athens is 37° 58′ north.

The fronts of the Parthenon were planned to have a length of 100 1/5 Greek feet = 111 1/3 Mycenean feet. This length was increased by 1/48 of a Mycenean foot on the west front. Hence, the lengths of the fronts, according to my interpretation, was:

Eastern front = 30,889.3 millimeters
Western front = 30,895.1 millimeters

Penrose reported the following findings:

Eastern front = 101.341 English feet = 30,888.7 millimeters
Western front = 101.361 English feet = 30,894.8 millimeters

The western front is better preserved.

These figures prove how accurate was the planning of the Parthenon and how justified was Penrose in testing the dimensions of this temple with the greatest care of which he was capable.

But all the horizontal lines of the Parthenon have a parabolic curvature. The sides of the temple have a double parabolic curvature: they are curved upward and inward. The spacing of the columns proves that dimensions that were relevant were those measured along the parabolic line.

The two parabolic curvatures increased the length of the sides. What I have been able to establish with certainty is the effect of the combined double parabolic curvature on

the edge of the sides, because of necessity the spacing of
the columns which were placed all along the sides had to
be based on the actual length of the edge of the sides.
The two curvatures added 8/48 = 1/6 of foot to the length
of the fronts, so that the eastern front measured 111 1/2
Mycenean feet = 100.35 Greek feet = 30,935.5 millimeters,
when measured along the edge of the blocks. But in
calculating the width of the temple one should consider
only one parabolic curvature, the curvature upward, that
is, in substance, the curvature of the floor. Before expressing
exact conclusions I would like to see the results of a new
survey of the curvatures of the Parthenon, but I can definitely
state that the width of the temple measured along the
curvature of the floor was halfway between 111 1/3 and
111 1/2 Mycenean feet, that is, close to 111 5/12 feet =
30,912.4 millimeters.

If we add to this amount the 1/48 foot added to the
western front, we have a length of 111 7/16 feet =
30,918.2 millimeters. This length would indicate an equatorial degree of 111,305.5 meters and an equatorial circle
of 40,069,988 meters.

It can be concluded that the width of the fronts of
the Parthenon was intended to indicate the length of a
second of degree of longitude at the equator. But further
testing of the dimensions of the Parthenon is necessary in
order to establish what was exactly the length of the second
of degree that the builders had in mind.

As I have indicated, the Mycenean system of measures,
which was followed by the Greeks of the classical age,
assumed an equatorial circle of 144,444,444 Mycenean
feet and hence a second of degree of equator of 111.45404
feet. This would imply a width of the Parthenon of 30,922.8
millimeters.

VII. DIMENSIONS OF THE GREAT PYRAMID

1.   Since the dimensions of the Great Pyramid have
been endlessly debated, and studies of them have often
degenerated into mysticism, it is proper that in approaching
the subject I clarify my method. The essence of my method
is to be absolutely pedestrian. I have spent years of my
life in trying to ascertain the exact length of the Roman foot,
eliciting from the academy the reaction that it is a disgrace
for a classical scholar to waste energy on such mechanical
trivialities. Similarly, after reading scores of studies on the
architecture of the Parthenon, I set myself two tasks: to
determine the length of the foot employed in the construction, and to compare item by item all available modern

361

reports on the actual dimensions of this temple. I followed this line of research although I was warned by the learned that a person guilty of such *banausia,* which in Greek means behavior worthy of a manual wageearner, would always remain blind to the lofty mind of the ancient Greeks. In dealing with the geometry of the Pyramid, I have taken as starting points my conclusions about the length of the Egyptian royal cubit and the survey of the dimensions of the Pyramid conducted by Cole, who was not an Egyptologist but a professional surveyor.

Up to now the Cole survey has been neglected. Trust has been put on the survey conducted by Petrie, but, although Petrie considered himself an expert of measurements (he started his career as an Egyptologist under the guidance of his father, who was an engineer) and used all the diligence of which he was capable, his survey proves to have arrived at misleading results when compared to that of Cole.

In order to justify my method, I shall refer to another great scientific issue which, as we shall see, happens to be related to the problem of the dimensions of the Pyramid. In the *Principia* Newton argued that because of the centrifugal force generated by its rotation, the earth must be flattened at the poles. Reasoning purely on mechanical grounds, he concluded that the polar flattening is 1/230, which means that the polar radius is shorter than the equatorial radius by 1/230 of the latter. The calculation was based on the assumption, which is not true, that the earth is a homogeneous fluid body. Following the survey of Picard, for which Newton waited before publishing his *Principia* in 1686, other scholars of the French Académie des Sciences applied themselves assiduously to the problem of determining by geodetic surveys what was the actual shape of the earth. Their results were contradictory, but they were such that for seventy years after the publication of the *Principia* the empirical evidence could be understood to indicate that the earth, far from being flattened at the poles, was elongated. This caused most serious controversies in the field of physical theory. I have reexamined the records of this gerat debate to find that the French scholars were successful in advancing mathematical theory, in developing correct methods of triangulation, and in refining the techniques of astronomical observation, but had neglected the need of setting a reliable unit of linear measurement. The several surveys of the length of the degree of latitude, up to and including the famous survey conducted by Father Ruggiero Boscovich in Italy in 1751–53 (a survey which took as a starting point the Roman milestones of the Appian Way), kept using standards of the *pied de roi* which were different from each other.

The history of these surveys is a comedy of errors. This was sensed by the keen mind of Voltaire who, when Maupertuis announced triumphantly that his survey of the degree conducted in Lapland had proved that the earth is flattened at the poles, called him *le grand aplatisseur,* "the great flattener," building a pun on the extracurricular activities of Maupertuis with a Lappish maid.

The difficulties of scientists arose from the circumstance that the original standard of the *pied de roi* had been lost. The *pied de roi* used to be a fraction of the ancient Roman foot, and good reference standards of the Roman foot and of the *pied de roi* were kept by French trade guilds. But, the French absolute monarchy followed a policy of eliminating the public functions of the guilds. Finally the minister Colbert issued an ordinance prescribing that the only reference rule that could be used should be that kept at the Châtelet, the seat of royal administration and justice in Paris. But the standard of the Châtelet was poorly defined and badly protected from accidental damage. This is the reason why many scholars could arrive at the startling scientific conclusion that the earth is elongated at the poles. The intellectual confusion came to a rest because the engraver Langlois built his own private standard of the *pied de roi,* by assuming that the *pied de roi* is the edge of a cube that contains 70 Paris livres of water. Langlois's standard was used in establishing the Paris meter of the French metric system.

2. Although Petrie's survey of the length and orientation of the sides of the Great Pyramid proves to be unreliable, his survey of the dimensions of the King's Chamber proves to be superior to the several ones conducted since the seventeenth century. Since Petrie's survey of the King's Chamber has established that the royal cubit of the Pyramid measured 524.05235 ± 0.1016 millimeters, it permits the conclusion that the royal cubit employed in the construction was 524.1483 millimeters.

Cole began his survey of the length and orientation of the sides of the Pyramid by trying to establish the exact location of the corner points. By an extensive sounding of the foundations, he located the corner points with a possible margin of error which he estimated as follows:

> West side: 30 millimeters at either end
> North side: 6 millimeters at either end
> East side: 6 millimeters at either end
> South side: 10 millimeters at the west end
>   30 millimeters at the east end

363

Next, Cole examined the alignment of the four sides and concluded that they meet to form angles which deviate as follows from a right angle:

Northwest corner: —0° 00' 02"
Northeast corner: +0° 03' 02"
Southeast corner: —0° 03' 33"
Southwest corner: +0° 00' 33"

I interpret these data to mean that the west side was drawn first and that the north side was intended to be perfectly perpendicular to it. The east side was intended to be at an angle of 3' with the perpendicular to the north side, and the south side was intended to be at angle of 30" with the perpendicular to the west side. In other words, the four corners were intended to deviate from a right angle according to the following pattern:

Northwest corner: 0
Northeast corner: +3 minutes
Southeast corner: —3 1/2 minutes
Southwest corner: + 1/2 minute

Having established the alignment of the sides according to the figures mentioned above, Cole calculated the length of the sides to be the following:

West : 230,357 millimeters
North: 230,253 millimeters
East : 230,391 millimeters
South: 230,454 millimeters

There is a contradiction in Cole's report about the length of the north side. In the summary of the lengths of the sides, Cole states that this side is 230,253 millimeters; but in an earlier part of his report he states that the north side is divided into a segment of 115,090 millimeters and a segment of 115,161 millimeters (total of 230,251 millimeters) and confirms these figures by explaining that the difference between the two segments is 71 millimeters. This contradiction is most unfortunate, because it is a conclusion of mine that the lengths of the two segments of the north side provide a key to the determination of the vertical dimensions of the Pyramid. I am inclined to infer that Cole found the north side to have a length of 230,251 millimeters.

I interpret Cole's figures to mean that the basic length of the side was 439 1/2 cubits = 230,363.18 millimeters. According to Cole the average length of the sides is 230,363.25 millimeters. Each side was intended to have a length of 1 1/4 stadia according to the stadium of 351.6 cubits; for the Egyptian this was the stadium (1/10 minute) of the degree of latitude at the equator. The perimeter of the Pyramid was intended to be 1758 cubits = 921,452.71 millimeters; Cole reports a perimeter of 921,453 millimeters. The perimeter was intended to be equal to 1/2 minute of latitude at the equator. The length of the minute of degree of latitude at the equator was calculated 3516 cubits = 1842.905 meters; it is 1842.925 meters according to the International Spheroid.

In the calculation of the Pyramid the royal cubit was divided into 24 fingers, each finger being 21.8395 millimeters. Egyptian measuring rods indicate that the royal cubit, which in principle is composed of 28 fingers (fingers such that 24 make an Egyptian common cubit), at times was divided into 24 fingers according to the ordinary division of the cubit. There are Egyptian measuring rods in which the royal cubit is divided into 28 fingers on one face and 24 fingers on the other face.

The west side was drawn first and then the north side was drawn perpendicular to it. The south and the east sides were at an angle different from a right angle with the two neighboring sides. This caused variations in the length of the sides, but steps were taken in order to assure that the average length of the sides remained 439 1/2 cubits.

The south side was intended to be at an angle 90° 00′ 30″ with the west side. Reckoning by tangent 0° 00′ 30″, this would cause a lengthening of the east side of 33.494 millimeters. Apparently this lengthening of the east side was computed as 1 1/2 fingers = 32.758 millimeters. The lengthening of the east side was compensated in part by shortening the west side by 1/4 of finger. In other words, the south side was moved backward by 1/4 of finger. The west side came to be 439 1/2 − 1/96 cubits = 230,363.1778 − 5.4597 millimeters = 230,357.72 millimeters. The east side was lengthened by 1 1/4 fingers, so that it came to be 439 1/2 + 5/96 = 230,363.1778 + 27.2994 = 230,390.48 millimeters.

The western side was rotated at the middle point by 3 minutes, so as to shorten the north side and to lengthen the south side. Multiplying the length of half of a side by tangent 0° 03′ 00″, there would be a shortening and a lengthening of 100.519 millimeters, which could be understood as 4 5/8 fingers = 101.008 millimeters. Since the east side had been lengthened by 1 1/4 fingers and the west side had been shortened by 1/4 finger, there remained an increase of a finger to be compensated. Hence, the north and south sides were shortened by 1/2 finger each. In other words, the east side was moved backward by 1/2 finger.

The length of the north side came to be 439 1/2 cubits − 4 5/8 fingers − 1/2 finger = 439 55/192 cubits = 230,251.250

365

millimeters. The length of the south side came to be 439 1/2 cubits + 4 5/8 fingers − 1/2 finger = 439 129/192 cubits = 230,453.266 millimeters. The difference between the two sides is 74/192 cubits = 202.016 millimeters.

This analysis of the method followed in planning the base of the Pyramid arrives at the striking conclusion that my estimates of the lengths of the sides, based on theoretical principles, do not differ by a millimeter from those obtained empirically by Cole (length of sides expressed in millimeters).

	My estimate	Cole's report
West side:	230,357.72	230,357
North side:	230,251.25	230,251
East side:	230,390.48	230,391
South side:	230,453.27	230,454
	921,452.72	921,453

3. In his survey Cole paid attention to a detail which in my opinion provides the key to the entire geometrical structure of the Pyramid. The Egyptologist Borchardt had noticed that, at about the middle of the north side, a small line is marked on the pavement which extends outward from the bottom of the Pyramid. Cole measured the position of this line and found It to be at a distance of 115,090 millimeters from the northwest corner and 115,161 millimeters from the northeast corner, with a difference of 71 millimeters between the two distances. He stated that this line is "probably the original line of the axis." Cole apparently did not pay much attention to this detail, since he reported also that the north side has a length of 230,253 millimeters. Reginald Engelbach, in presenting Cole's findings to the academic world, failed to notice the discrepancy in Cole's figures. I suspect that the figure of 230,253 millimeters for the length of the north side crept into the Cole report as a result of a mistake of 2 millimeters in placing the end of the tape against the pin that marked the position of the line of the axis.

If the north-south axis of the Pyramid is off center, it follows that the apex was off center. Petrie, when he surveyed the slope of the Pyramid, on the basis of preliminary tests suspected that each face of the Pyramid had a different slope, but did not try to establish whether this suspicion was justified. Instead he concentrated his efforts on establishing the slope of the north face, which is the best preserved one. As far as I know, none of those who tried to interpret the geometry of the Pyramid on the basis of Petrie's report considered the possibility that the four faces of the Pyramid had different slopes. Nobody has ever utilized Cole's survey in order to interpret the geometry of the Pyramid. If the four faces have different slopes, it follows that the apex is off center.

I have concluded that the north side had a length of 439 55/192 cubits = 230,251.250 millimeters. Hence, I understand Cole's figure to mean that the line which divided the north side into two parts is at a distance of 219 137/192 cubits = 115,162.479 millimeters from the northeast corner, and a distance of 219 55/96 cubits = 115,088.771 millimeters from the northwest corner. The difference between the two segments is 27/192 cubits = 73.708 millimeters. I suspect that there was a mistake of 2 millimeters in setting the end of the tape against a pin at the middle of the north face; this is the reason why Cole reports that the north side has a length of 230,253 millimeters with an excess of 2 millimeters. This type of mistake is common in surveying.

A great number of those who have tried to explain the geometry of the Pyramid can be placed into one of these two categories: those who conclude that the Pyramid was calculated by the factor π, and those who believe that the Pyramid was calculated by the factor φ. In my opinion both explanations are correct, in the sense that the slope of the west face was calculated by the factor π and the slope of the north face was calculated by the factor φ. The inclination of the other two faces was affected by the fact that the angles at the northeast and the southwest were more than right angles.

For reasons that I shall explain below, I have concluded that the height of the Pyramid was either 279.53 cubits = 146,515.174 millimeters or a figure very close to 279.53 cubits.

According to what I have said above, the distance of the apex from the west side was 115,088.771 millimeters. If the west face was calculated by the factor π, the height of the Pyramid had to be $\pi/4$ of the base of the meridian triangle of the west side. Now, 146,515.174 millimeters relates to 115,088.771 millimeters as 0.78550752, which would imply $\pi = 3.142030$. If π was reckoned as 3.1420, the height would have been 146,516.522 millimeters. By the exact value of π, the height would have been 146,535.569 millimeters.

Because of Cole's report we know the distance of the apex from the west side, but we do not have direct information on the distance of the apex from the north side. However, it can be presumed that the west-east axis was not displaced from the middle position. It can also be presumed that the line of the west-east axis was set according to the basic length of sides, before the length of the sides was altered by the widening of the southwest and northeast corners. Since the basic length of the sides is 439 1/2 cubits = 230,363.178 millimeters, it can be presumed that the apex was at a distance of 219 3/4 cubits = 115,181.589 millimeters from the north side. If this is the length of the base of the meridian triangle of the north face, and the height of the Pyramid is 279.53 cubits = 146,515.174 millimeters, the base of the meridian triangle of the north face is 0.78614103 of the height. If the north face was calculated by the factor φ, the height should have been equal to $\sqrt{1/\varphi}$ of the base of the meridian triangle. If one had recokoned by the exact value of φ, the height would have been 146,513.250 millimeters. If the height was 146,515.174 millimeters, as I tentatively assume, and the northern half of the north-south axis was 115,181.589 millimeters, $\sqrt{1/\varphi}$ was reckoned as 0.786141 (the exact value is 0.7861514) and hence $1/\varphi$ was reckoned as 0.61801767.

If $1/\varphi$ was reckoned as 0.6180, the height would be 146,517.274 millimeters, which would imply $\pi = 3.141985$. Therefore, I would conclude that the height possibly was reckoned as 279 15/28 cubits = 279.53714 cubits = 146,518.169 millimeters. According to Petrie the slope of the north face is 51° 50′ 40″ ± 1′ 05″. If the north face had been calculated by the exact value of φ, the slope would have been 51° 49′ 38″. This angle can be easily calculated, because if the meridian triangle of the north side is calculated by φ, the secant and the tangent of the angle of the slope must be equal to each other, that is, must be equal to $\sqrt{\varphi}$. If the west side had been calculated by the exact value of π, it would have had a slope 51° 51′ 14″.

4. Most interpreters agree that the Pyramid had a height of 280 cubits. Even Borchardt, who is so opposed to the idea that Egyptians had any knowledge of mathematics that he calls Herodotus an "idiot" for having said that the Pyramid was calculated by φ, agrees that the Pyramid had a height of 280 cubits.

In general one could establish a consensus of the responsible interpreters to the effect that the meridian triangle of the Pyramid was the following:

Height: 280 cubits
Base: 220 cubits
Apothem: 356 cubits

In my opinion, this triangle was purely the starting point of the calculations. It was chosen in order to indicate the relation π and the relation φ, since 22/28 is the value of $\pi/4$ used in practical reckonings ($\pi = 3\ 1/7$), and

356/220 = 89/55 = 1.6181818 is an approximation to the value of φ according to the initial terms of the Fibonacci series. But the initial meridian triangle was modified for several reasons, the first one being that it is impossible to construct a right triangle with sides 280, 220, and 356, since we have:

$$280^2 = 78,400$$
$$220^2 = 48,400$$
$$356^2 = 126,736$$

We have seen that the basic length of the sides was reduced to 439 1/2 cubits (semiside of 219 3/4).

In my opinion, the height of 280 cubits was chosen in order to indicate the polar flattening of the earth. The Egyptians calculated the polar flattening as 1/280, but this was a round figure adopted on the assumption that the order of the cosmos must be septenary.

Information about the Egyptian estimate of the size and shape of the earth is provided by Chapter LXIV of the *Book of the Dead.* This chapter was the most important one: reciting it was considered almost as effective as reciting the entire book. In one of the papyri of the *Book of the Dead* there is an annotation to the effect that this chapter was found in the shrine of the solar boat during the reign of Udimu, the fourth or fifth Pharaoh of the First Dynasty. Chapter LXIV states that the spirits of the Nether World (that is, all that is below the surface of the earth) are 4,601,200 and that each is 12 cubits high. The occurrence of the factor 12 indicates that it is a matter of geographic cubits. Now, $12 \times 4,601,200$ cubits = 55,214,000 cubits = 138,036 geographic stadia, is equal to two diameters of the earth. In order to explain the figure of 138,036 stadia, one must assume that the Egyptians reckoned as if the polar flattening occurs only in the northern hemisphere. On the basis of this assumption the figure of 138,036 stadia can be decomposed into the following four earth radii:

34,538 stadia = 6,378,388 meters = equatorial radius
34,538 stadia
34,538 stadia
34,422 stadia = 6,356,966 meters = polar radius
─────────────
138,036 stadia

These figures imply that the flattening of the North Pole is 116/34,538 = 1/297.74.

With extreme economy of numerical expression the Egyptians had arrived at values which are as good as the best modern ones. The figure for the equatorial radius happens to coincide to the meter with that calculated by Hayford. But Hayford calculated the polar flattening as 1/297. Helmert, however, set the polar flattening at 1/298.3, a figure which has been adopted in several of the recent surveys and calculations of the size of the earth which aim at achieving the maximum possible exactness.

At the beginning of the dynastic period the above mentioned figures were revised in order to make them fit into the septenary system of measures and cosmic order. The polar flattening was set at 1/280. This was achieved by decreasing slightly the polar radius and increasing slightly the equatorial radius. The equator which used to be reckoned as 217,000 geographic stadia = 40,074,999 meters, was calculated by a stadium (1/10 of minute) of 354 royal cubits, which made it 40,078,476 meters. It is conceivable that the data mentioned in the *Book of the Dead* was reinterpreted as follows:

34,540 geographic stadia = 6,378,758 meters = equatorial radius
34,540 geographic stadia
34,540 geographic stadia
 34,416 geographic stadia = 6,355,858 meters = polar radius
138,036 geographic stadia

The figure of 1/280 for the polar flattening was adopted because it fits into septenary reckoning also in a second and more subtle way. If the polar flattening is 1/280, the arc of meridian is 0.7840 of equatorial diameter. Now, $0.784 = 280^2/100,000 = 78,400/100,000$. This is the reason why Herodotus put emphasis on the fact that the surface of each face of the Pyramid is 78,400 square cubits, being equal to the square of the height, which is 280 cubits. However, the figures reported by Herodotus apply only to the initial plan of the Pyramid. When the figures were further refined the height was calculated as 279.53 cubits. If the polar flattening is 1/297.74, the arc of meridian is 0.7408 of equatorial diameter. This means that an arc of meridian is $0.78408/\frac{1}{4}\pi = 279.53/280$ of a fourth of equator. Hence, the height of the Pyramid in the final plan indicated the correct figure for the polar flattening.

VIII. ADDITIONAL REMARKS ON THE DIMENSIONS OF THE GREAT PYRAMID

1. Herodotus provides only two pieces of information about the dimensions of the Great Pyramid. He states that the surface of each face is equal to the square of the height, which means that the Pyramid was calculated by the Golden Section (by the factor φ). He states also that this surface of each face is equal to 8 Egyptian acres. The Egyptian acre is a square with a side of 1000 royal cubits (2747 square meters). The Egyptian acre, the amount plowed in a day, is similar to the Roman acre (*jugerum*), which is 2524 square meters. Herodotus's figure indicates that he had in mind a

height of 280 royal cubits. He reckoned by half acres, which, as I have explained earlier, were taken to have sides of 70 cubits. If the Pyramid has a height of 280 cubits, the square of the height is 16 half acres (78,400 square cubits). If Herodotus assumed a side of 440 cubits, in order to have this surface the faces should have had an apothem of 356.4 cubits; but if he assumed a side of 439 1/2 cubits the apothem should have been 356.8 cubits. But Herodotus's figure for the surface of the faces was not intended to be exact.

The Roman geographer Pomponius Mela (I,9) paraphrases Herodotus in these terms: *quatuor fere soli jugera sua sede occupat, totidem in altitudinem erigitur,* "it occupies almost four acres with its base, and it rises as much in height." Mela expresses himself awkwardly, but the main point is clear. In order to make the reckoning more easily comprehensible he counts by double acres which have sides of 140 cubits. If the Pyramid had a height of 280 cubits, it would be immediately clear that the square of the height is 4 (double) acres. But Mela states that the surface of the faces and the square of the height is *almost* 4 acres. It was a current practice in all ancient cultures to double units of measure, while continuing to refer to them by the name of the simple unit. Mela erroneously speaks of the surface of the base, whereas it is a matter of the surface of the faces. The error probably originated through an inept translation from a Greek author who used the technical term *epipolēs,* which means "in elevation, by the lateral surface," but may also mean "in surface." The same error occurs in Pliny. It is likely that the error in translation originated with Varro, who almost certainly was the common source of Mela and Pliny. The polymath Varro, who lived in the first century B.C., proves inept in mathematical matters, and Mela and Pliny were certainly no more adept in these matters. But, the text of Mela, in spite of its shortcomings, supports my contention that the height of 280 was merely an initial figure in the calculation of the Pyramid, a figure which was reduced in the course of the development of the calculation.

I have analyzed all other ancient authors who provide information about the dimensions of the Pyramid. By a careful collation of their words and phrases, I have established that they all draw, directly or indirectly, on a single source. These authors wrote in Greek or in Latin during the first century of the Roman Empire. They are the historian Diodorus of Sicily (I, 63), the geographer Strabo (XVII, 1, 33), the encyclopedist Pliny the Elder (XXVI, 12, 78–80), and the engineer Philon of Byzantium (*Wonders of the World,* II). Their common source is the Greek grammarian Agatharchides of Cnidus, who toward the end of the second century B.C. was guardian to one of the Ptolemy kings of Egypt. Quotations from Agatharchides' lost works indicate that he wrote extensively on the geography of Egypt, with particular emphasis on natural science.

The interesting feature of Agatharchides' report about the dimensions of the Pyramid is that he excludes the pyramidion from the reckoning. We know from the descriptions of other pyramids that the very top of the structure was a small pyramid of metal, usually a precious metal such as gold or silver, which shined in the sun. From Agatharchides' account one gathers that the Great Pyramid of Giza was topped by such a pyramidion, "small pyramid," as the Greeks called it. In the case of this Pyramid, at least, the pyramidion was used to achieve a mathematical result.

In ancient mathematics extensive recourse was made to a mathematical procedure which we no longer use, but which was extremely convenient. If the square root of a number cannot be expressed by an integer, the number is conceived as the product of two integers of which the second is the same as the first, but increased or decreased by a small quantity, usually the unit. Similarly, if the cubic root of a number cannot be expressed by an integer, the number is conceived as a cube in which one side is longer or shorter than the others. For instance, the number 8400 is conceived as a cube with sides 20, 20, and 21. This procedure is called *basi* in Sumerian. I have established that the calculation by what I call near-squares and near-cubes was common not only in theoretical mathematics but also in architecture, land surveying, and the construction of measuring vessels.

The procedure just described was applied in geometry by removing a small part of a figure. For instance, a problem of geometry could be solved by cutting off a slice from a side of a parallelogram. Most commonly the procedure was applied by cutting off a corner of a triangle; this is the reason why the part cut off is called *gnōmōn* in Greek. Most usually *gnōmōn* means "pointer of a dial" in Greek; hence, the term applies perfectly in our case in which the top of the Pyramid was conceived as cut off in the computation presented by Agatharchides.

An essential point of Agatharchides' account is that he describes the Pyramid as having an apothem which measures a stadium up to the pyramidion and having a side which measures 1 1/4 stadia. The term stadium has a double meaning: it refers to 1/10 minute of degree and it refers to a specific unit of measurement. Agatharchides uses the term in both senses.

I have already indicated that the base of the Pyramid has a length of 1 1/4 times 351.6 royal cubits, which for the Egyptians was the length of the stadium (1/10 minute) of the degree of latitude at the equator. From the authors who drew on Agatharchides we gather that he said that the perimeter is 5 stadia, that is, 1/2 minute of degree.

One would have expected the perimeter of the Pyramid to have been calculated by the length of the degree of longitude at the equator, but the builders instead calculated by the degree of latitude, because their concern was the length of the arc of meridian. From Agatharchides we learn that the apothem up to the pyramidion had a length of a stadium, that is, 1/10 of a minute of degree. This permits us to understand what was the specific function of the pyramidion. Since the degrees of latitude increase in length from the equator to the pole, the apothem of the Pyramid up to the pyramidion gave the length of the shortest degree of latitude, the degree at the equator. The pyramidion may have been graduated, giving the length of all the degrees from the equator to the pole. According to Egyptian reckonings, the stadium of the degree of latitude at the equator is 351.6 royal cubits and increases to a length which at the pole the Egyptians assumed to be 355 cubits in practical reckonings and slightly more than 355 cubits in exact reckoning. The apothem of the full Pyramid came to be something less than 356 cubits.

Agatharchides interprets the dimensions of the Pyramid also by taking the word stadium as referring to the stadium of 600 geographic feet. The geographic stadium was the unit most commonly used by the ancients in calculating geographic distances. A stadium was 600 geographic feet, and 600 stadia made a degree. This calculation was correct for the degree of latitude at the middle latitude of Egypt, for the latitude of the capital built by the Pharaoh Akhenaten. According to Agatharchides the side of the Pyramid is 1 1/4 stadia or 750 feet (230,847 millimeters), and the apothem is a stadium or 600 feet. The side of the base of the pyramidion is 9 feet. The figures indicate that Agatharchides was not concerned with presenting the actual dimensions of the Pyramid, but in illustrating the mathematical principles according to which the Pyramid had been conceived.

The figures quoted from the text of Agatharchides by later authors suggest that he began his analysis of the meridian triangle of the Pyramid by presenting a triangle with the following dimensions:

Height: 480 feet
Base: 377 feet
Apothem: 610 feet

This approach gives excellent values of φ and π.

$$\varphi = 610/377 = 1.6180371 \text{ (exactly } \varphi = 1.6180339887)$$
$$1/\varphi = 377/610 = 0.6180328 \text{ (exactly } 1/\varphi = 0.6180339887)$$
$$\pi/4 = 377/480 = 0.785\,41666$$
$$\pi = 3.14166$$

It is impossible to construct a right triangle with sides 480, 377, and 610, since we have:

$$480^2 = 230,400$$
$$377^2 = 142,129$$
$$610^2 = 372,100$$

But the calculation I mention is less off the mark than the calculation by the triangle 280, 220, and 356, which was the one with which the builders of the Pyramid actually began.

Having started with the mentioned meridian triangle, Agatharchides cut off the side so as to reduce the apothem to 600 feet and the base to 371 feet, excluding the part of the base below the half of the pyramidion.

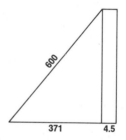

Since Pliny in quoting Agatharchides does not give the length of a side of the pyramidion (which another author describes as being 9 feet), but the combined length of two sides, I have concluded that the pyramidion had an average side of 9 feet, but had different lengths of different faces.

I presume that Agatharchides presented two different meridian sections of the Pyramid, one calculated by the factor φ and one calculated by the factor π.

By φ:

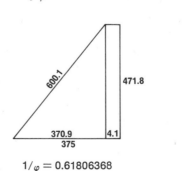

$$1/\varphi = 0.61806368$$

By π:

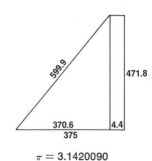

$$\pi = 3.1420090$$

The two possible meridian sections were combined so as to obtain two faces calculated by π and two faces calculated by φ. The Pyramid seen from above would have had the following dimensions:

Like Herodotus, Agatharchides was not concerned with reporting the exact dimensions of the Pyramid, but with presenting the general principles of the mathematics of the Pyramid. This was the point which was of the greatest interest to a Greek audience.

I do not pretend to have reconstructed the authentic reckoning of Agatharchides, but I feel confident that I have understood the general drift of his interpretation. It seems to me that he intended to improve on the presentation of Herodotus, who had only mentioned the factor φ, by stressing the roles both of the factor φ and of the factor π. Agatharchides wanted also to emphasize that the dimensions of the Pyramid were related to the length of the degree of latitude. This was a point of essential importance which had not been mentioned at all by Herodotus.

2. The Egyptians ascribed the invention of the art of building with stone to Imhotep, vizier and architect of King Zoser, who reigned about fifty years before the building of the Great Pyramid. And in fact there has not been found any important building made only of stone blocks which dates before the reign of Zoser. The Egyptians described Imhotep as a sort of Leonardo da Vinci of Egypt, mathematician, scientist, engineer, and architect. Not many years after his death he was made into a demigod, son of Ptah, the god of craftsmen and technicians. Up to recently there were Egyptologists who insisted that Imhotep was a legendary figure. One argument was that there is no other instance in Egyptian history of an ordinary person having bene divinized. But more basic was the argument that a person with all the gifts ascribed to Imhotep could not have existed in the Old Kingdom. It is only in the last few years that it has been definitely accepted that Imhotep was a real person, since it has been possible to gather some specific details of information even about his physical appearance. His genius was recognized even during his life, since King Zoser

375

covered him with all sorts of honors, although he was a man of humble origin.

But, even though it is now granted that the Egyptians were not living in dreams when they idolized the genius of Imhotep, Egyptologists have failed to investigate what were the scientific achievements of Imhotep other than that he was the first one to have designed a pyramid, the step pyramid of Saqqara. This pyramid is just one element in an enormous group of buildings which is known as Zoser's Complex. This group of buildings is not only so extensive but also so elaborate that nothing of the sort was produced again in the long history of Egypt. In spite of this, not one Egyptologist has tried to investigate this monument and other constructions directed by Imhotep in terms of what the Egyptians said were his talents. Scholars are willing to grant that a man with the name of Imhotep walked on the land in Egypt, but they are not yet willing to grant that Egypt could have produced a mind like his.

The French archeologist Jean Philippe Lauer has dedicated many years to the study of Zoser's Complex. He is a highly competent archeologist and essentially factual and realistic. Actually he has been criticized for insisting too much on technical problems of architecture. For instance, the German Egyptologist Herbert Ricke has disputed point by point Lauer's interpretation of the monuments of Zoser's Complex, claiming that the architecture must be understood in terms of the conflict between the psychological attitudes of nomadic hunters and that of sedentary agriculturists. But Lauer has learned how far the academic community is willing to go in tolerating rational thought in the area of ancient studies. In 1944 he published a short paper in which he tried to deal with the geometry of the pyramids and enlisted the cooperation of a professional mathematician, Paul Montel. But, four years later, when he published the book, *Le Problème des pyramides,* he backtracked and dismissed any mathematical interpretations.

In reporting about Zoser's Complex, Lauer keeps stumbling into mathematical problems, but ignores them. For instance, he found that the wall that surrounds the entire Complex forms a rectangle 544.90 by 277.60 meters. He concludes that it is a matter of a dimension of 1040 by 530 cubits. I would understand that the intended dimensions were 545,114 by 277,799 millimeters, according to the cubit of 524.1483 millimeters. Lauer is surprised at meeting with the figure of 1040 cubits, whereas he would expect 1000 cubits, and explains it away by assigning arbitrarily 40 cubits to the thickness of the walls. But in another part of his work he points out that the same proportions occur in some First Dynasty royal tombs which have dimensions of 54 by 27 meters. It may be enough to point out here that the dimensions of the enclosure of Zoser's Complex are based on the near-square with sides 52 and 53, a mathematical entity of which I have spoken earlier. It is a matter of two near-squares with sides of 520 and 530 royal cubits. It is relevant to what follows that such a near-square has a diagonal of 742.49579, which is 6 times 123.749.

Lauer notices in Zoser's Complex four instances of the occurrence in important positions of the anomalous dimensions of 123 cubits, whereas in the Complex dimensions are generally decimal multiples of the cubit. One of the most impressive remains of the Complex, the monumental entrance gallery, has a length of 123 cubits. Lauer suggests that the Egyptians may have been fascinated by a magic number composed by the first three integers. This is a way of shunting off a problem by appealing to that undefinable entity called magic and by implying, at the same time, that the Egyptians, and their hero Imhotep in particular, were frivolous in matters of mathematics.

Lauer did not realize that the number 123 is an expression in terms of integers of the number $2/\varphi = \sqrt{5} - 1 = 1.236068$. In his book on the pyramids Lauer had denied the occurrence of the factor φ in their architecture.

It is a matter of the right triangle with an angle of 36° which the Egyptians called *mr.* I have suggested that the name *To-Mera,* which the Egyptians gave to their country, was a reference to this triangle. If a right triangle has an angle of 36° and the longer side is 100, the hypotenuse is $2/\varphi\ 100 = 123.6068$, the other side being 72.6542.

Since I have argued that the Great Pyramid was calculated both by the factor φ and by the factor π, I might point out here that there is a close relation between these two numbers, which goes beyond the fact that there is a numerical similarity between $\pi/4 = 0.7853981$ and $\sqrt{1/\varphi} = 0.7861514$. The number φ was used to obtain the value of circular functions, since we have

$$\sin\ 18° = \cos\ \ 72° = 1/2\varphi$$
$$\sin\ 54° = \cos\ \ 36° = \varphi/2$$
$$\sec 36° = \operatorname{cosec} 54° = 2/\varphi$$
$$\sec 72° = \operatorname{cosec} 18° = 2\varphi$$

In practical reckonings the right triangle with an angle of 36° was taken as a triangle with a side of 100 and a hypotenuse of 123. The side opposite the angle of 36° was taken as being 72; this permits us to calculate in terms of half degrees all the trigonometric functions of the angles between 0° and 36°. Since the angle of 36° is 2/5 of a right angle and 1/10 of a full circle, one can calculate from the mentioned triangle the trigonometric functions for all angles.

377

This is the reason why the triangle *mr* was considered the basic constituent of the cosmic order.

In order to recognize the importance of the right triangle with an angle of 36°, one may start by considering how much attention it received in Euclid's *Elements*. It plays an even greater role in early Greek mathematics. The symbol of the Pythagorean sect, the five-pointed star, was a combination of such triangles.

I have explained that the right triangle with a hypotenuse of 123 was a practical simplification of the triangle of 36° built according to the Golden Section. A further simplification was the right triangle with sides related as 3:4:5. If this triangle is enlarged to the scale of the one with hypotenuse of 123, it has sides 120, 100, and 75, instead of 123, 100, and 72.

I need to point out that the Great Pyramid incorporates the relation 4:5 in the proportion between the length of the apothem up to the pyramidion and the length of the side. This provides a point of transition to an analysis of the dimensions of the Second Pyramid.

The Great Pyramid tried to compress a great number of mathematical relations, whereas the Second Pyramid limited itself to embodying the triangle *mr.*

The basic idea of the Great Pyramid was that it should be a representation of the northern hemisphere, a hemisphere projected on flat surfaces, as is done in mapmaking. This was the principle according to which was built the ziggurat of Babylon, the biblical Tower of Babel, and according to which were built the earlier pyramids. The Great Pyramid was a projection on four triangular surfaces. The apex represented the pole and the perimeter represented the equator. This is the reason why the perimeter is in relation 2π with the height. The Great Pyramid represents the northern hemisphere in a scale 1:43,200; this scale was chosen because there are 86,400 seconds in 24 hours. But then the builders became concerned with the problem of indicating the ratio of polar flattening of the earth and the length of the degrees of latitude which depends on the ratio of this flattening. Next, they incorporated into the Pyramid the factor φ as the key to the structure of the cosmos. The Second Pyramid, on the contrary, limits itself to embodying the trangle *mr,* which is based on the number φ, at least as far as I have been able to establish up to the present moment.

According to Petrie's survey the sides of the Second Pyramid have the following lengths:

West: 215,278 millimeters
North: 215,186 millimeters
East: 215,269 millimeters
South: 215,313 millimeters

The royal cubit of this pyramid is that of 525 millimeters. The basic length of the sides is 410 cubits = 215,250 millimeters.

The meridian triangle of the pyramid is a triangle with proportions 3:4:5. The base is 205 cubits, the height is $4/3 \times 205 = 273.33$ cubits, and the apothem is $5/3 \times 205$ cubits = 341.66 cubits.

Reckoning by third of cubits, we have:

Base: 123×5
Height: 164×5
Apothem: 205×5

Possibly the pyramid was calculated by a rod of 5/3 of a cubit, which is called *nbyw* (*nebiu* in Coptic).

It is clear that this pyramid was intended to incorporate the number 123 as a round figure for $2/\varphi$.

The slope of the pyramid is the same as the angle of problems 67–69 of the Rhind Papyrus. The tangent $164/123 = 1.3333$ corresponds to a slope 53° 07′ 48″. The angle of the apothem with the height is 36° 52′ 12″. This angle was intended to be an approximation to the perfect angle 36°.

The geometry of the Second Pyramid could be considered crude in relation to the sophisticated one of the Great Pyramid, but it emphasizes the importance that the Egyptians attached to the triangle *mr*.

3. Petrie's survey of the Second Pyramid helps in clarifying the problem of the orientation of the sides of the Great Pyramid.

Petrie reported that the four sides of the Second Pyramid are oriented as follows:

West side: 0° 04′ 21″ west of true north
North side: 0° 05′ 31″ north of true east
East side: 0° 06′ 13″ west of true north
South side: 0° 05′ 40″ north of true east

Petrie warns that the triangulation of Egypt existing at his time did not permit him to establish the direction of north with absolute certainty. Hence, his figures can be taken only as an indication of the angle of the sides in relation to each other.

Petrie's figures prove that the deviation from the right angle in three of the four angles of the Great Pyramid was intentional and not the result of mistakes in construction, as claimed by professional archeologists. The north side of the Second Pyramid is shortened in relation to the south side, as it occurs also in the Great Pyramid. But in the Second Pyramid the shortening of the north side and the lengthening of the south side was achieved by constructing a more regular figure. The base of the Second Pyramid has the shape

379

of a trapeze or a trapezoid. The north and south sides were drawn parallel to each other. Possibly the west side was intended to be at an angle of one minute with the north-south axis, and the west side was intended to be at an angle of half a minute with the north-south axis.

In any case the approximate findings of Petrie indicate that, if one proceeded to a new survey of the Second Pyramid and then surveyed the orientation of the sides of other pyramids and possibly of other major constructions of the Old Kingdom, one could recognize a pattern on the basis of which it could be established what was the purpose in making the angles of pyramids and possibly of other major constructions different from a right angle. It is impossible to formulate a reliable explanation for the differences among the angles of the base of the Great Pyramid without establishing what was the general practice in establishing the angles of the base of pyramids.

I have come across the same difficulty in dealing with the dimensions of Greek temples. I have ascertained that the four angles of the Parthenon were intended to deviate slightly from a right angle. Further, in the case of the Parthenon the north side is shorter than the south side, as in the case of the two major pyramids of Giza. But it is impossible to advance hypotheses in order to explain the differences among the angles of the Parthenon, as long as the angles of other temples are not surveyed so as to make possible the identification of a regular pattern.

There is one further problem to be considered in relation to the orientation of the faces of the Great Pyramid. The west face, which in my opinion was drawn first and is the basic face, is not oriented to the north, but is oriented 2′ 30″ west of true north.

This deviation from orientation to the north is the result of the precession of the equinoxes.

From cuneiform texts one gathers that in Mesopotamia there was a distinction of roles between the mathematician who formulated the general plan of a building and the architect who executed the plan. Whether this distinction existed in Egypt or not, it can be assumed that in the construction of a pyramid the first step was the drawing of a mathematical plan. This plan would include the alignment of the stars to be observed in establishing the direction of the north. If my interpretation of Egyptian sky charts is correct, the line that indicates the north used to be marked so as to pass through the celestial pole and through the pole of the ecliptic.

In any case, it appears that there was drawn a plan of the Great Pyramid which included the calculation of the stars to be observed in order to obtain the direction of the north. After this plan was drawn, the ground of the Pyramid had to be cleared in order to proceed to the ceremony called "stretching of the cord," which for the Egyptians was the equivalent of our laying of the first stone. This ceremony had the purpose of establishing the direction of true north and, as the Egyptians saw it, suspending the building from the sky by tying the building with an imaginary string to the axis of rotation of the vault of heaven.

If there had passed exactly three years from the drawing of the plan to the ceremony of the "stretching of the cord," the clustering of stars, which gave the exact north of the moment of the drawing of the plan, would give an orientation 2′ 30″ west of north, because of the precession of the equinoxes, which displaces the star taken as the polar star in practical calculations to the west at a rate of about 50″ a year.

The Second Pyramid too is oriented west of true north, but unfortunately Petrie's figures for the orientation of this pyramid are not exact, as he himself warns.

The question to be asked is whether the incorporation of the rate of the precession of the equinoxes into the dimensions of the Great Pyramid and of the Second Pyramid was accidental or intended. I am inclined in favor of the second alternative, since in the case of the Great Pyramid the angle corresponds exactly to three years in the precession of the equinoxes. In their book *Hamlet's Mill* de Santillana and Dechend have used mythological and iconographic evidence in order to prove that all ancient cultures of the world were deeply preoccupied with the phenomenon of the precession of the equinoxes. They intended to prove that the movement by which the celestial pole in about 25,920 years (Platonic year) makes a full circle around a point called the pole of the ecliptic was conceived as the basic movement in the life of the universe. This cycle determined all other movements, including biological developments, and determined the length of human life (taken as equal to 72 years, or the time that it takes the celestial pole to move a degree) as well as historical events. The authors of *Hamlet's Mill* have kept their conclusions vague, probably in the hope that thereby their findings would be less readily attacked by the academy. They open their book with the statement: "This is meant to be only an essay. It is a first reconnaissance of a realm well-nigh unexplored and uncharted." This is a most gentle way for a professor of the history of science at the zenith of his career to present a thesis which, if accepted, should have the impact of a Copernican revolution on current conceptions of the development of human culture. Since the essence of my method is quantitative, I cannot indulge in the luxury of such linguistic niceties. I have collected a mass of numerical evidence which shows that the inhabitants of the ancient world were acquainted with the rate of the precession of the equinoxes and attached a major significance to it. But in order to deal with this evidence, I would have to open an entirely new topic. I beg the indulgence of the reader in asking him to remain satisfied for the moment with the mere hint that there is yet another lesson about the level of Egyptian science to be drawn from the stark nakedness of the Great Pyramid.

GLOSSARY OF NAMES AND TERMS

Abd-al-Latif (1179–1231)

Arab historian who taught medicine in Baghdad. Author of one of the early Arab histories of Egypt: *Relation de l'Égypte.* In 1220 he explored the Great Pyramid, reporting that he came out of it "more dead than alive."

Abdullah Al Mamun (d.833)

Caliph of Baghdad, son of Harun al-Rashid. Patronized literature and science; built an astronomical observatory outside Baghdad; ordered a degree of latitude to be measured across the plain of Palmyra. Is reputed to have broken into the Great Pyramid in 820 in search of treasures, but to have come away empty-handed after opening the way to the King's Chamber.

Agatharchides of Cnidus

Greek historian and geographer who lived in the time of Ptolemy Philometor (181–146 B.C.) and dealt with the geography of the Near East.

Akhnaten (1388–1358 B.C.)

Revolutionary pharaoh of the Eighteenth Dynasty who changed his name from Amenophis IV, and broke with the priests of Amon at Thebes. He built a new capital, Akhtaten, between Thebes and Memphis near the site of Tell el-Amarna. Of his religious reform, which was monotheistic and recognized the sun as the symbol of living energy, Petrie remarked: "no such grand theology had ever appeared in the world before."

Akhtaten (Resting point of Aten)

Capital built by the young pharaoh Akhnaten at the predynastic geodetic center of Egypt, halfway between the Tropic and the Mediterranean coast, near the site called Tell el-Amarna. The city, which was decorated with splendid temples and palaces, was destroyed after Akhnaten's death.

Ali Gabri (1830–19?)

Arab guide, sometimes referred to as Alee Dobree, who was an assistant to Howard-Vyse, Piazzi Smyth, Sir Flinders Petrie, and Moses B. Cotsworth over a period of nearly seventy years, helping them explore and measure the Great Pyramid.

Alvarez, Luis Walter (1911–   )

Nuclear physicist. Professor of physics at Lawrence Radiation Laboratory, Berkeley, California. Nobel Prize winner for physics in 1968. Developer of radar. Helped develop A-bomb and flew in B-29 observer following the plane that bombed Hiroshima. One of the youngest members to be elected to the National Academy of Science. Author of several scientific articles. Adapted spark chamber to X-ray the pyramids with cosmic rays.

Amèlineau, Emile (1850–1915)

Studied Egyptian and Coptic under Maspero. Did much excavating but was criticized by Petrie and Maspero for unscientific methods. Professor of history of religions in École des Hautes Études in Paris, where he died in 1915. Author of several volumes on ancient Egyptian history and science.

Amenemhet

Four Pharaohs of the Twelfth Dynasty, the first of which reigned from ca. 1991 to 1962 B.C.

383

Amon	A god who was related to the wind, promoted to an imperial divinity at the beginning of the Twelfth Dynasty as Amon-Ra. Amon was considered the creator of other gods, and to have had no beginning and no end.
Ancient Empire	From the Third to Sixth dynasties, variously estimated, but approximately 2780 to 2280 B.C. There is little historical data on this period, most of the relevant papyri having disappeared. Under the influence of King Zoser and his architect Imhotep, brick structures gave way to stone. The political center was at Memphis.
anomalistic year	365 days, 6 hours, 13 minutes, 48 seconds. The time it takes the earth to return in its elliptical orbit to the point nearest the sun —about 4¾ minutes longer than the sidereal year.
apothem (of a pyramid)	The distance from the apex down one face to the center of a base side.
Arya-Bhata (b. 476–?)	Hindu astronomer and mathematician, author of Aryabhatiya which gave the rules of mathematics as known in his time. Most of his work deals with astronomy and spherical trigonometry. Gave a value for π of 3 177/1250, or 3.1416. Taught that the daily rotation of the heavens was an appearance due to the earth's rotation on its axis.
Aten	God of the solar orb, raised to a prime position by Akhnaten. Represented by a golden disc radiating rays that end in hands. Was considered a universal deity who could have held sway over a universal empire.
azimuth	Angle of arc around the horizon, or angular distance of an observed point from geographic north (or other fixed point).
Ballard, Robert T.	Australian engineer who made a study of the pyramids in 1882 which he wrote up in "The Solution of the Pyramid Problem; or, Pyramid Discoveries with a New Theory as to Their Ancient Use."
Barnard, Professor F. A. P. (1809–1889)	President of Columbia University (1864) and president of the American Association for the Advancement of Science. An authority on weights and measures, he took issue with the conclusions about the Pyramid drawn by Piazzi Smyth and other pyramidologists.
Behdet	Town in lower Egypt which was the capital of Egypt in predynastic times. In Ptolemaic times it was the capital of a nome and was known to the Romans as Hermopolis Parva. In Stecchini's reconstruction of the ancient geography, Behdet was the northern limit of Egypt, 7 1/2° north of the Tropic.
Belzoni, Giovanni Battista (1778–1823)	Italian explorer and adventurer. A large and powerful man, six feet seven inches, who exhibited himself in feats of strength. He came to Egypt to demonstrate a hydraulic machine he had invented, but when the machine proved unsuccessful he turned to archeology and discovered several tombs as well as the entrance to Kephren's pyramid. A narrative of his exploits was published in 1820.
Biot, Jean Baptiste (1774–1862)	French physicist, professor of mathematics at Beauvois and professor of physics at the Collège de France. A prolific writer, he covered a wide field of physical science, becoming a member of the Academy of Sciences and a commander of the *Légion d'Honneur.* He was especially interested in the astronomy of the ancient Egyptians.

384

The Book of the Dead	An Egyptian collection of hermetic inscriptions and papyri purportedly providing funerary and ritual texts.
Borchardt, Ludwig (1863–1938)	German Egyptologist. Studied Egyptology at Berlin University under Professor Johan Erman. Worked at Philae in Egypt in 1895, and conducted many excavations in subsequent years. Inaugurated the great Catalogue of Cairo Museum with Professor Gaston Maspero. Founded German Institute of Archeology in Cairo. A bibliography of his many writings was issued in 1933.
Bouchard, Pierre-François-Xavier, Captain (1772–1832)	Engineer working on Fort Julien near Rosetta, 70 kilometers east of Alexandria, in 1799 found the Rosetta Stone as part of an old wall.
Brugsch, (Pasha) Karl H. (1827–1894)	German Egyptologist sent to Egypt by the Prussian government in 1853. Consul general in Cairo, 1864, then professor of Egyptology at Göttingen, 1868. Director of School of Egyptology in Cairo. Published a demotic grammar, a hieroglyphic dictionary, and a history of Egypt.
Brunés, Tons	Danish consulting engineer and Freemason who devoted a score of years to resolving the problems of ancient geometry. In 1967 he published a six-hundred-page two-volume book, *The Secrets of Ancient Geometry,* in which he attempted to substitute a "Sacred Cut" for the Golden Section or phi relation.
Budge, Sir Ernest Alfred Wallis (1857–1934)	Orientalist. Keeper of Egyptian and Assyrian Antiquities at the British Museum. Large published output including popular and semipopular works. Compiled an Egyptian dictionary, and a full edition of *The Book of the Dead.*
Burattini, Tito Livio (16?–1682)	Italian follower of Father Athanasius Kircher. Made several trips to the Great Pyramid and took measurements with Greaves which were used by Newton in his first calculations for the theory of gravitation. A Venetian by birth, Burattini spent the better part of his maturity in Poland. Author of works on standards of measure and the use of pendulums.
Cabala	A system of mystical interpretation of Scriptures practiced by certain medieval Jewish rabbis and certain Christian sects, on the assumption that Scriptures have an occult meaning.
Campbell, Patrick, Colonel (1779–1857)	Army officer and diplomat. British consul general in Egypt, 1833 to 1840. Associate of Colonel Howard-Vyse in exploration of pyramids, who named for him one of the construction chambers above the King's Chamber in the Great Pyramid.
Cardano, Girolamo (1501–1576)	Milanese doctor, mathematician, and astronomer, author of several books. His works in mathematics include treatises on arithmetic and algebra. He referred to ancient traditions as indicating the Great Pyramid incorporated an earth commensurate unit of measure of great exactness.
cardinal points of the compass	North, east, south, west.
cartouche	An oblong figure containing a Pharaoh's name.
Cayce, Edgar (1877–1945)	American clairvoyant whose thousands of readings while in trance are filed in a foundation created in his memory at Virginia Beach, Virginia. Had many memories as a being at the time of Atlantis and the construction of the Pyramid, but readings lack solid data.
Cassini, Gian Domenico (1625–1712)	French astronomer and geodesist of Italian origin, founder of a family of geodesists. He measured meridian arc through Paris.

385

Was assisted by his son Giacomo (1677–1756), who was assisted by his grandson Cesare Francesco (1714–1784). His great-grandson, Giacomo Domenico, also a geodesist and astronomer, was born in Paris in 1747 and died 1845.

Caviglia, Giovanni Battista (1770–1845)

Genoese mariner, owner and master of a trading vessel in the Mediterranean based on Malta. Regarded himself as a British subject. Explored the pyramids and the Great Sphinx, from whose base he had great quantities of sand removed. An ingenious excavator, he discovered the outlet to the well in the Great Pyramid and was in charge of several hundred men excavating for Colonel Howard-Vyse until they quarreled. Caviglia was given to occultism and mysticism, and spent his final years in Paris as a protégé of Lord Elgin.

celestial equator

A great circle produced by projecting the earth's equator outward to the celestial sphere.

Champollion, Jean-François (1790–1832)

At 16 at the Academy of Grenoble, Champollion presented a thesis in support of Father Athanasius Kircher's idea that Coptic was a degeneration of ancient Egyptian. The discovery of the Rosetta Stone by Napoleon's troops helped Champollion to decipher the system of ancient Egyptian hieroglyphs.

clinkstone

Compact grayish rock which clinks like metal when struck.

clinometer

A device to measure angle of slope.

Cole, J. H.

British surveyor who carried out the official survey of the Great Pyramid for the Egyptian government in 1925. His measurements made it possible to know the dimensions of the base of the Pyramid to within a few millimeters, and put an end to years of controversy.

corbeled masonry

An arrangement of stones in which successive courses project beyond those below.

Cotsworth, Moses B. (1859–1943)

British legislative enthusiast who wrote a series of pamphlets and books advocating a more rational almanac and demonstrating how the pyramids, obelisks, Druid circles, and mounds were erected as yearly almanacs. Expatriated to Canada, where he died during World War II.

Cottrell, Leonard (1913–   )

British author of several books on Egyptian history and the pyramids. Writer and producer for radio and television.

Davison, Nathaniel (?–1783)

Accompanied Edward Wortley Montagu on his travels in the East. Arrived at the Great Pyramid in July of 1765, where he discovered the first construction chamber over the King's Chamber, which has since been named for him. Was later British consul general at Algiers until his death in 1783.

decans

Ten-day periods marked by the passage of constellations by which the Egyptians divided the year into thirty-six units.

declination

Angular distance of a heavenly body north or south of the celestial equator; analogous to latitude on the stellar vault.

Dendera

Ancient site of a Ptolemic temple compound about 60 kilometers north of Luxor on the east bank of the Nile dedicated to Hathor and Isis. Several temples are believed to have been constructed on the site, attributed to Cheops, Pepi I, and earlier monarchs. A zodiac on the ceiling of an upper room was removed and is now on display at the Louvre where it has been the object of heated controversy as to its age and significance.

Denon, Baron Dominique Vivant (1747–1825)	French antiquary and man of letters. Joined Napoleon's expedition and made many remarkable drawings. Published *Voyage dans la basse et la haute Egypte,* 1802, which was an instant success; translated into German and English. Appointed director-general of French Museums.
Didoufri	Fourth Dynasty king who succeeded Cheops and preceded Kephren.
Diodorus Siculus	Greek historian of the first century B.C. Published a history, or *Bibliotheca historica,* the first surviving book of which deals with Egypt, to which he traveled about 60 B.C. In his geography he quotes various lost sources.
diurnal pattern	The apparent movement of the stars in each rotation of the earth.
Dümichen, Johnnes (1833–1894)	German Egyptologist. Professor of Egyptology, Strassbourg, 1872–1894. Several publications. Traveled frequently to Egypt.
dynasties	Thirty dynasties of Egyptian kings were listed by the priest Manetho, from Menes to Ptolemy II Philadelphus. Though erratic, the list has formed the basis of Egyptian history for succeeding Egyptologists.
Edfu	Ancient temple said to have been built during the Third Dynasty. Capital city of second nome of Upper Egypt on the west bank of the Nile, 100 miles downstream from Thebes. Site of huge sandstone temple dedicated to Horus, constructed in Ptolemaic times, and found half buried in the sand by Napoleon's forces during their campaign in Upper Egypt.
Edwards, I. E. S. (1909–)	British author and Egyptologist. Keeper of Egyptian Antiquities British Museum since 1955. Visiting professor at Brown University, 1953–1954.
Egyptian mysteries	Secret knowledge of the cosmos possessed by initiates.
Elephantine	Island in the Nile just north of the first cataract, which was used as a geodetic point. Known as the city of the elephants, capital of the first nome in Upper Egypt on the border of Nubia. Opposite Syene, the modern Aswan.
Engelbach, Reginald (1880–1946)	British engineer and Egyptologist. Assisted Petrie in several digs. Appointed Chief Inspector in Upper Egypt for the Services des Antiquités. Keeper of Cairo Museum 1931. Published work on obelisks and Egyptian masonry.
equinox	Time at which the sun crosses the equator in March and September (vernal and autumnal) when day and night are of equal length all over the earth.
Fibonacci, Leonardo Bigollo (1179–1250)	Italian mathematician, known as Leonardo da Pisa. His *Liber Abaci* (1202) was for years a standard work on algebra and arithmetic. In *Practica Geometriae* (1220) he organized and extended material in geometry and trigonometry. The Fibonacci series, which he popularized in Europe in the thirteenth century, appears in the construction of the Great Pyramid several millennia earlier.
Fibonacci series	A sequence of numbers in which each is the sum of the two previous numbers—1, 2, 3, 5, 8, 13 . . . The limit of this series gives the exact value of φ.
Firth, Cecil Mallaby (1878–1931)	British Egyptologist. Served thirty years in Service des Antiquités.
geodetic gnomon	A vertical pillar whose shadow can be used to determine time, distance, and latitude.

387

Golden Section (φ proportion)	Division of a line (or geometric figure) so that the proportion of the smaller section to the larger is the same as that of the larger to the whole. For example, in the line below, the Golden Section is such that AB:AC = AC:CB.

A ———————————————— C ———— B

Greaves, John (1602–1652)	Mathematician and antiquarian. Son of Rector of Colemore in Hampshire. Educated at Baliol College, Oxford. Professor of geometry at Gresham College, London. Traveled to the East to collect Arabic and Persian manuscripts. Made the first accurate survey of the Great Pyramid during a trip to Egypt in 1639. Author of *Pyramidographia*. Appointed Savilian professor of Astronomy in reign of Charles I; dismissed by Roundheads.
Hapy	The animating spirit of the Nile, self-engendered; lord of the fish represented by an androgynous divinity crowned by a papyrus reed.
Hathor	Egyptian goddess, originally a personification of the sky. In the Dendera cult, Hathor was considered the wife of Horus. The Greeks identified Hathor with Aphrodite.
heliacal rising (or setting)	Observation of a star as close as possible to the rising or setting of the sun.
heliocentric pattern	The arrangement of the planets in orbits around the sun.
Heliopolis (or On or Annu)	Northeast of Cairo on the edge of the desert; believed to be the capital of a prehistoric state. City of the Sun, embellished by a series of kings from the Third Dynasty on, it was the seat of temple of priests who numbered as many as twelve thousand. Ancient center of theological learning. It was reduced by Alexander the Great in the fourth century B.C. One of the earliest obelisks was found still standing at Heliopolis.
Herodotus (484–425 B.C.)	Greek historian born in Asia Minor. Visited Egypt towards the end of the first Persian domination. In his *History* he devoted a book (called Euterpe, after the muse of lyric song) to Egypt, giving many interesting and accurate details of geography.
Herschel, Sir John (1792–1871)	Astronomer, only son of astronomer Sir William Herschel. Made a fellow of the Royal Society at twenty-one for a brilliant mathematical investigation. Author of books on mathematics and astronomy considered among the elevating influences of the century.
Horus	Prehistoric Egyptian sky god in the form of a falcon whose eyes were the sun and moon; also called the "Behdetite" in the form of a winged sun-disk. Later incorporated in the Osiris cycle. Identified by the Greeks with Apollo.
Howard-Vyse, Colonel (later Major General) Richard William (1784–1853)	Son of General Richard Vyse and grandson of Field Marshal Sir George Howard. Retired as Colonel of Second Life Guards, 1826. Equerry to the king of Hanover. Member of Parliament. Traveled to the Middle East in 1835, where he organized excavation of the pyramids in 1837, employing Caviglia and hundreds of other workers. Discovered original casing stones and found chambers above Davison's. Author of *Operations Carried on at the Pyramids of Gizeh in 1837*.
Hyksos	Asiatic kings who invaded Egypt and formed the Fifteenth and Sixteenth dynasties. They were chased out of Egypt by Ahmosis I who founded the Eighteenth Dynasty.

ibn-Batuta (ca. 1352)	Mohammedan traveler. Said the pyramids were built by Hermes, who is the same person as the biblical Enoch, to preserve the arts and sciences, and other scientific acquirements, during the flood. Said dream occurred to King Surid that the Pyramid would be opened on the north side, so he deposited a sum of money equal to the expense of excavation.
Imhotep (ca. 2800 B.C.)	King Zoser's architect, who is accredited with the building of the stepped pyramid of Saqqara, of limestone. He is reputed to have been an author, diplomat, architect, and physician.
Ka	Metaphysical part of human being. Lived only on the essence of foods and was satisfied with facsimiles of food and mock buildings which had only façades.
Lepsius, Karl Richard (1810–1884)	German Egyptologist. Led Prussian expedition to Egypt and Nubia. Published seventeen folio volumes of *Denkmäler,* mostly epigraphic material. Keeper of Egyptian collections of Berlin from 1873.
Lieder, Rudolph Theophilus (1797–1865)	German missionary. Member of the Egyptian Society of Cairo, 1836. Collected antiquities.
Lindsay, (Lord) Alexander William Crawford (afterwards 25th Earl of Crawford and 8th Earl of Balcarres) (1812–1880)	Traveler and writer on art. His *Letters from Egypt,* etc., contain particulars on Caviglia.
Lockyer, Sir Joseph Norman (1836–1920)	English astronomer, educated on the continent of Europe; knighted for his work in spectroscopy and for identifying helium in the sun. The author of several books on the astronomy of ancient peoples, he was the first to demonstrate convincingly how ancient Egyptian temples were used as solar and stellar observatories and almanacs.
Luxor	Part of the ancient site of Thebes. A huge temple dedicated to the god Amon was built in the reign of Amenhotep III, and altered by succeeding Pharaohs, especially by Rameses II, who had many colossal statues of himself erected on the grounds.
Mandeville, Sir John (fl. 1356)	Fabulous writer of traveler's guidebooks. Most of his data were available in contemporary travel books and encyclopedias. His "voyages" are believed to be the work of a notary in Belgium who never traveled abroad.
Manetho	Egyptian priest and annalist in the reign of Ptolemy I who wrote a history of Egypt in Greek, only fragments of which remain. His division of the kings of Egypt into thirty dynasties is still the basic structure underlying Egyptian history.
Mariette, (Pasha) Auguste (1821–1881)	French Egyptologist. Traveled to Egypt to collect Coptic manuscripts and engaged in excavations. Appointed Conservator of Egyptian Monuments by the Khedive and settled in Egypt, where he made numerous finds which became the nucleus of the Cairo Museum.
Maspero, Sir Gaston Camille Charles (1846–1916)	French Egyptologist of Italian origin. Professor of Egyptology at Collège de France. Succeeded Mariette as director of the Services des Antiquités. Wrote many scientific memoirs and a large number of popular books and reviews.
mastaba	An oblong masonry structure with sloping sides and a flat top, usually above a deep pit.

389

Menes (fl. 3400 B.C. [3500?])	First historic ruler of the First Dynasty of ancient Egypt, who is reputed to have united the southern and northern kingdoms and settled on a new capital on the Nile at the point of juncture at Memphis.
mensuration	The science of measurement.
meridian	A great circle passing through the poles of the celestial sphere and the zenith of a fixed point on earth.
Meroe	Village in the Sudan on the Nile north of Khartoum which still has ruins of temples and pyramids.
Middle Kingdom	Twelfth to Fourteenth dynasties, from 2000 to 1600 B.C. Follows first intermediate period of chaotic conditions. The capital was at Thebes.
Minutoli, Johann Heinrich Carl, Freiherr von (1772–1846)	Prussian officer of Italian origin. Collected large quantities of antiquities. Published *Mes souvenirs en Egypte.*
New Kingdom	Covers Eighteenth and Nineteenth dynasties, 1580–1350 and 1350–1200 B.C. The Hyksos invaders were crushed and a military state embarked on wide conquest from as far as Cush to the Euphrates.
nilometer	An instrument for measuring the height of the Nile.
Nubia	Ancient region, originally called Cush, extending from the Nile Valley near Aswan southward to the modern Khartoum, east to the Red Sea and west to the Libyan desert.
obelisk	A tapered four-sided pillar used for measuring shadow length, usually inscribed with hieroglyphs proclaiming the achievements of a Pharaoh.
omphalos	Navel, or a central point on the surface of the earth.
Pepi	Two pharaohs of the Sixth Dynasty.
Perring, John Shae (1813–1869)	British civil engineer. Assistant to manager of public works for Khedive Mohammed Ali. Assisted Colonel Howard-Vyse in survey and exploration of the pyramids. In 1839 wrote and drew pictures for a large folio, *The Pyramids of Gizeh from Actual Survey and Measurement on the Spot.*
Petrie, Sir (William Matthew) Flinders (1853–1942)	Egyptologist, son of William Petrie, a civil engineer, and Anne, daughter of Matthew Flinders, the explorer of Australia. Surveyed ancient British sites such as Stonehenge before making first scientific survey of Giza hill. Founded the British School of Archaeology in Egypt. Responsible for many excavations and numerous books. He is considered the father of modern scientific archeology.
ϕ (phi) proportion	See Golden Section.
π (pi)	The constant by which the diameter of any circle may be multiplied to give its circumference.
Picard, Jean (1620–1682)	French astronomer, noted for having made the first accurate modern measurement of a degree of the earth's meridian. His figures enabled Newton to calculate the force of gravitation. Occupied the chair of astronomy in the Collège de France in 1655. Largely responsible for the establishment of the Paris Observatory and the appearance of *Connaissance des temps,* the first two volumes of which he authored.
Pococke, Richard (1704–1765)	Traveler and divine, bishop of Ossory (1756–1765). Ascended the Nile as far as Philae. The manuscript journal of his travels is in the British Museum.

precession of the equinoxes	Each year at the spring equinox the constellation in the sky where the sun rises due east appears to have fallen back about twenty minutes. This phenomenon, or precession, is caused by a slow toplike wobble of the earth on its axis which takes about 26,000 years to cycle.
Proctor, Richard Anthony (1837–1888)	English astronomer and popular writer on scientific subjects. Founded the popular scientific magazine *Knowledge.* Lectured in the United States and Australia. Author of many books on science and astronomy. Developed the theory that the Great Pyramid had been designed and used as a great astronomical observatory while still a truncated body at the level of the King's Chamber.
Ptah	Called Hephaistos by the Greeks. Egyptian god of the city of Memphis, portrayed as a human figure in a tight mummy wrapping. Considered the creator of the world who produced visible phenomena through thought and the word. The protector of artisans. His high priest was the doyen of master craftsmen.
Pylon	A double tower with rectangular base pierced by central door to a temple. The temple of Karnak had ten pylons.
Pythagoras' theorem	The square of the hypotenuse of a right triangle is equal to the sum of the squares of the other two sides.
Ra	The sun, later deified. Creator of the world, was said to be swallowed at night by Nut and recreated fresh each day.
Reisner, George Andrew (1867–1942)	American Egyptologist (Ph.D., Harvard University, 1893). Director of the Hearst expedition to Egypt 1905–1907. Excavated for Harvard University for many years in Egypt, particularly at Giza. Professor of Egyptology at Harvard (1914–1942). Curator of Egyptian Department, Boston Museum of Fine Arts (1910–1942). Author of several books on archeological excavations.
Rhind, Henry Alexander (1833–1863)	Scottish lawyer and traveler. Owing to ill health was obliged to winter in Egypt. Excavated at Thebes and bequeathed collection to National Museum of Antiquities, Edinburgh. Noted for the Mathematical Papyrus (BM10057–8), which was sold to the British Museum, and is considered the oldest manuscript dealing with Egyptian mathematics.
right ascension	The arc along the celestial equator which separates a star from an arbitrary zero point; analogous to longitude around the stellar vault.
sacred triangles	Right triangles with sides in such proportions as 3–4–5 or 2–$\sqrt{5}$–3, which were credited with magic or esthetic properties.
Saqqara	Situated 28 kilometers south of modern Cairo, just west of Memphis and south of Giza. Ancient burial site named after Sokar, the god of measure. Graves date from the First Dynasty. Pyramids attributed to the Fifth and Sixth dynasties. Site of the stepped pyramid built for King Zoser of the Third Dynasty by the architect Imhotep.
Schwaller de Lubicz, R. A. (?–1961)	Philosopher, archeologist, and author who spent twelve years at Luxor reconstructing the philosophical and theological system of the ancient Egyptians. Born in Alsace, he was granted the title Chevalier de Lubicz by O. W. de Lubicz Milosz for his help after World War I in obtaining independence for the Baltic States.
sextant	An instrument for precise measurement of angular distances to determine latitude and longitude.

sidereal year	The time it takes the earth to revolve around the sun so that an observer will see a given star reappear in the same position—about 20 minutes longer than the solar year.
Sneferu (ca. 2700 B.C.)	First king of the Fourth Dynasty. Father of Cheops. Built bent pyramid at Medûm.
solar parallax	The angle formed by the semidiameter of the earth as regarded from the sun, or 8.80″.
solar year	The time between two successive equinoxes 365 days, 5 hours, 8 minutes, 49.7 seconds 365 days, 5 hours, 48 minutes, 46 seconds
solstice	The two points—in summer and winter—when the sun is at its greatest declination north or south of the equator.
Sothic year	365 days, 6 hours—introduced in ancient Egypt to correct the civil calendar year of 365 days. A "Sothic cycle" began when civil and Sothic new year coincided.
Syene	Site of the modern Aswan. The southern limit of Egypt at the First Cataract of the Nile, close to the Tropic of Cancer. Nearby quarries supplied the hard granite monoliths for the King's Chamber in the Great Pyramid and for the tall Egyptian obelisks used for measuring shadows.
Taylor, John (1781–1864)	Devoted his early years to publishing in London, becoming editor of the *London* Magazine. An amateur astronomer and mathematician, he was also a student of Scripture and devoted much time to mastering Old English, Welsh, French, and Italian. His *The Great Pyramid: Why Was It Built & Who Built It?*, published in 1854, established the π proportion in the pyramid, but his theory, that the Great Pyramid had been built under divine guidance, caused his work to be disputed and he was given little recognition.
Thebes	Ancient city in upper Egypt renowned in antiquity for its hundred gates. Became prominent with the Eleventh Dynasty (c. 2160 B.C.) for the worship of Amon. Went into decline when the locus of power shifted to the Nile Delta. There is a nearby large necropolis where kings and nobles were entombed. It was sacked by the Assyrians in 661 B.C. The remains of the temples of Luxor and Karnak are still among the most impressive in the world.
theodolite	A telescopic instrument for precise measurement of horizontal angles, used in land surveying.
Thoth	Lunar god in form of Ibis, patron of scribes and calendars. The Hermes of the Greeks.
triangulation	By carefully measuring a base line and the angles formed by either end of it with a distant point, the distance of the point may be calculated by trigonometry.
vernier	A small moveable scale attached to a large scale for obtaining finer fractions of measurements.
ziggurat	The stepped-pyramid temples of Mesopotamia.

BIBLIOGRAPHY

TEXT

Adams, Walter Marshal	*The Book of the Master.* New York: Putnam, 1898.
Agnew, H. C.	*A Letter from Alexandria.* London: Longmans, 1838.
Aldersmith, Herbert	*Gog, The Final Gentle Power.* London: R. Banks, 1915.
———	*The Great Pyramid, Its Divine Message.* London: Norgate & Williams, 1932.
Amèlineau, Emile	*La géographie de l'Egypte.* Paris: Imprimerie National, 1893.
Antoniadi, Eugene Michel	*L'Astronomie égyptienne depuis les temps les plus reculés.* Paris: Gauthier-Villars, 1934.
Archibald, R. C.	*Notes on Logarithmic Spiral of the Golden Section.* New Haven: Yale University Press, 1920.
Atkinson, R. J. C.	*Stonehenge.* London: H. Hamilton, 1956.
———	*Stonehenge & Avebury.* London: HM Stationery Office, 1959.
———	*Silbury Hill.* London: BBC, 1968.
Bache, Richard M.	*The Latest Phase of the Great Pyramid Discussion.* Philadelphia: Collins, 1885.
Bailly, Jean Sylvain	*Histoire de l'astronomie ancienne.* Paris: Debure, 1775.
———	*Traite de l'astronomie indienne et orientale.* Paris: Debure, 1787.
Ballard, Robert T.	*The Solution of the Pyramid Problem.* New York: J. Wiley & Sons, 1882.
Barbarin, Georges	*L'énigme du Grand Sphinx.* Paris: Adyar, 1946.
———	*Le secret de la Grande Pyramide.* Paris: Adyar, 1945.
Barbé, Jules	*Grande Pyramide, le secret du Sphinx.* Rouen: Darental Press, 1933.
Barber, Francis Morgan	*The Mechanical Triumphs of the Ancient Egyptians.* London: Tribner, 1900.
Barnard, F. A. P.	*The Imaginary Metrological System of the Great Pyramid.* New York: J. Wiley, 1884.
Bell, Edward	*The Architecture of Ancient Egypt.* London: G. Bell, 1915.
Benavides, Rodolfo.	*Dramáticas profecias de la Gran pirámide.* Mexico: Libro Mex, 1961.
Beverini, Luigi	*Le piramidi di Egitto.* La Spezia: Moderna, 1953.
Bindel, Ernst V.	*Die aegyptischen Pyramiden.* Stuttgart: Freie Waldorf-Schule, 1932.
Biot, Jean Baptist	*Recherches sur plusiers points de l'astronomie égyptienne.* Paris: Didot, 1823.
Bissing, Friedrich Wilhelm von	*Der Bericht des Diodor über die Pyramiden.* Berlin: A. Duncker, 1901.
Blavatsky, Helene P.	*The Secret Doctrine.* 2 vols. Los Angeles: Theosophy, 1930.
———	*Isis Unveiled.* Los Angeles: Theosophy, 1931.
Boll, F. J.	*Sternglaube und Sterndeutung.* Berlin: B. G. Teubner, 1919.
Bonwick, James	*Pyramid Facts & Fancies.* London: C. Kegan Paul, 1877.
Borchardt, Ludwig	*Längen und Richtungen der vier Grundakten der Grossen Pyramide bei Gise.* Berlin: J. Springer, 1926.

———	*Beiträge zur aegyptischen Bauforschung und Altertumskunde.* Heft 1. Berlin: J. Springer, 1926.
———	*Das Grabdenkmal des Königs Ne-User-Re.* Leipzig: J. C. Hinrichs, 1907.
———	*Das Pyramidenfeld von Abusir zur Zeit de fünften Dynastie.* Leipzig: J. C. Hinrichs, 1907.
———	*Die Entstehung der Pyramide.* Berlin: J. Springer, 1928.
———	*Die Pyramiden, Ihre Entstehung und Entwicklung.* Berlin: K. Curtins, 1911.
———	*Einiges zur Dritten Bar periode der Grossen Pyramide.* Berlin: J. Springer, 1932.
———	*Gegen die Zahlenmystik an der Grossen Pyramide bei Gise.* Berlin: Behrend, 1922.
Bothwell, A.	*The Magic of the Pyramid.* Goose, 1915.
Breasted, James H.	*A History of Egypt from the Earliest Times to the Persian Conquest.* New York: Scribner, 1909.
Bristowe, E. S. G.	*The Man Who Built the Great Pyramid.* London: William E. Norgate, 1932.
Brooke, M. W. H. L.	*The Great Pyramid of Gizeh.* London: Robert Banks, 1908.
Bruchet, Julien	*Nouvelles recherches sur la Grande Pyramide.* Aix-en-Provence: La Pensée Universitaire, 1965.
Brugsch, Karl H.	*Materiaux pour servir à la reconstruction du calendrier des anciens.* Leipzig: J. C. Hinrichs, 1864.
———	*Egyptiens.* Berlin: F. Schneider, 1856.
Brunés, Tons.	*The Secrets of Ancient Geometry.* Copenhagen: Chronos, 1967.
Brunton, Paul	*A Search in Secret Egypt.* London: Rider, 1936.
Burattini, Tito Livio	*Misura Universale.* Krakow: Nakaladem, 1697.
Capart, J.	*Memphis, à l'ombre des pyramides.* Brussels: Vromant, 1930.
Carré, Jean Marie	*Voyageurs et écrivains français en Egypte.* Le Caire: Institut Français, 1932.
Casey, Charles	*Philitis.* Dublin: Carson, 1880.
Cerny, Jaroslav	"A Note on the Boat of Cheops." *Journal of Egyptian Archaeology.* Vol. 41 (1955), 75.
Chapman, Arthur Wood	*The Prophecy of the Pyramid.* London: L. N. Fowler, 1933.
Chapman, Francis W.	*The Great Pyramid of Ghizeh from the Aspect of Symbolism.* London: Rider, 1931.
Choisy, Auguste	*L'art de bâtir chez les Egyptiens.* Paris: Rouveyre, 1904.
Ciampi, Sebastiano	*Bibliografia critica.* Firenze: L. Allegrini, 1834–42.
Clark, R.	*The Ancients Days.* Cincinnati: Privately printed, 1873.
Clarke, Somers, and Reginald Engelbach	*Ancient Egyptian Masonry: The Building Craft.* London: Oxford University Press, 1930.
Cole, J. H.	*Determination of the Exact Size and Orientation of the Great Pyramid of Giza.* Cairo: Government Press, 1925.
Cole, John	*A Treatise on the Circular Zodiac of Tentyra.* London: Longmans, 1824.
Corats, André Fournier de	*La Proportion egyptienne et les rapports de divine harmonie.* Paris: Vega, 1957.

Corbin, Bruce — *The Great Pyramid, God's Witness in Stone.* Guthrie, Oklahoma: Truth, 1935.

Coryn, G. P. — *The Faith of Ancient Egypt.* Los Angeles: Theosophical, 1913.

Cormack, Maribell — *Imhotep, Builder in Stone.* New York: F. Watts, 1965.

Cotsworth, Moses B. — *The Rational Almanac.* York: Privately printed, 1902.

Cottrell, Leonard — *The Mountains of Pharaoh.* London: J. Hale, 1956.

Crowell, Harold L. — *Time to Tell.* Shelter Island, New York: Privately printed, 1953.

Daninos, A. — *Sepulchral Monuments of Ancient Egypt.* Paris: E. Lerouse, 1908.

Darter, Frances M. — *Our Bible in Stone.* Salt Lake City: Desert View, 1931.

Davidson, David — *The Great Pyramid.* London: Williams & Norgate, 1927.
——— *The Great Pyramid, Its Divine Message.* London: Williams & Norgate, 1932.
——— *The Hidden Truth in Myth and Ritual and in the Common Culture Pattern of Ancient Metrology.* Leeds: Davidson, 1934.
——— *The Judgement of the Nations in the Great Pyramid Prophecy.* London: Covenant, 1910.
——— *The Path to Peace in Our Time Outlined from the Great Pyramid.* London: Covenant, 1943.

Davie, John G. — *The Great Step of the Great Pyramid of Egypt.* Griffin, Georgia: Privately printed, 1937.
——— *Hermes, The Geometer.* Griffin, Georgia: Privately printed, 1935.
——— *The King's Chamber in the Great Pyramid of Egypt.* Griffin, Georgia: Privately printed, 1938.
——— *Pythagoras Takes the Second Step.* Griffin, Georgia: Privately printed, 1935.

Day, Vincent St. John — *Papers on the Great Pyramid.* 1870.

Decourdemanche, Jean Adolphe — *Traité des monaies, mesures et poids anciens et modernes.* Paris: E. Leroux, 1913.

Delambre, Jean Baptiste Joseph — *Histoire de l'astronomie ancienne.* Paris: V. Courcier, 1817.

Denon, Dominique Vivant — *Travels in Upper & Lower Egypt.* London: T. Longman & O. Rees, 1803.

Dickerman, L. — *On the Etymology and Synonyms of the Word Pyramid.* Boston: J. H. Mansfield, 1890.

Dufeu, A. — *Découverte de l'âge.* Paris: Morel, 1873.

Dümichen, Johannes — *Altaegyptische Tempelinschriften.* Leipzig: J. C. Hinrichs, 1867.

Dupuis, Charles F. — *Mémoire explicatif du Zodiac chronologique et mystique.* Paris: Courcier, 1806.

Durville, Henri — *La science secrète.* Paris: H. Durville, 1928.

Edgar, Morton — *The Great Pyramid—Its Scientific Features.* Glasgow: MacLure & MacDonald, 1924.
——— *The Great Pyramid: Its Spiritual Symbolism.* Glasgow: Bone & Hulley, 1924.
——— *The Great Pyramid and Its Time Features.* Glasgow: Bone & Hulley, 1924.

Edwards, I. E. S. — *The Pyramids of Egypt.* Middlesex: Penguin, 1949.

Emery, Walter B. — *Archaic Egypt.* Baltimore: Penguin, 1961.

Engelbach, Reginald and Somers Clarke

Ancient Egyptian Masonry; the Building Craft. London: Oxford University Press, 1930.

Erman, Adolf

Life in Ancient Egypt. New York: Macmillan, 1894.

Eyth, Max

Lebendige Kräfte. Berlin: J. Springer, 1919.

Fakhry, Ahmed

The Monuments of Sneferu at Dashur. Cairo: Government Press, 1959.

——— *The Bent Pyramid at Dashur.* Cairo: Government Press, 1954.

——— *The Pyramids.* Chicago: University of Chicago Press, 1961.

Favaro, A.

Intorno alla vita ed ai lavori di Tito Livio Burattini fisico Agordino del secolo XVII. Real Instituto Veneto.

Firth, Cecil M.

Excavations at Saqqarah. Cairo: Institut Français, 1935.

Fish, Everett W.

The Egyptian Pyramids. Chicago: Privately printed, 1880.

Ford, Samuel Howard

The Great Pyramid of Egypt. St. Louis: Ford's Christian Repertory, 1882.

Fraenzel, K.

Die Chiops Pyramide? Stettin: L. Saunier, 1924.

French Government

Description de l'Egypte—recueil des observations et des recherches qui ont été faîtes en Egypte pendant l'expédition de l'armée française. 21 Vols. Paris: French Government, 1809–22.

Frith, Francis

Lower Egypt, Thebes and the Pyramids. London: Mackenzie, 1862.

Funck-Hellet, Charles

La Bible et la Grande Pyramide d'Egypte, témoignages authentiques du mètre et de pi. Montreal: Hellet Vincent, 1956.

——— *La proportion en architecture, l'équerre des maîtres d'oeuvre.* Paris: Hellet Vincent, 1951.

——— *Composition et nombre d'or dans les oeuvres peintes de la Renaissance.* Paris: Vincent, Freuls, 1950.

Galleani Viacava, E.

El legado de los antiquos. Lima: Privately printed, 1966.

——— *Las pyramides y el universo.* Lima: Privately printed, 1966.

García Cubas, Antonio

Ensayo de un estudio comparativo entre las pyramides. Mexico: I. Escalente, 1871.

Garnier, Col. J.

The Great Pyramid: Its Builder and Its Prophecy. London: Robert Banks, 1912.

Gauquelin, Michel

The Scientific Basis of Astrology. New York: Stein & Day, 1969.

Gelder, Mrs. Jane

The Storehouses of the Kings. London: W. H. Allen & Co., 1885.

Ghunaim, Mohammed Z.

The Buried Pyramid. New York: Longmans Green, 1956.

——— *The Lost Pyramid.* New York: Rinehart, 1956.

Ghyka, Matila C.

Le nombre d'or. Paris: Gallimard, 1931.

Gillain, Olivier

La légende de la Grande Pyramide d'Egypte. Brussels: L'Eglantine, 1926.

Gispen, W. H.

Het Pyramide Geloof. Copenhagen: Kampen, 1953.

Goguet, Antoine

Origin of the Laws, Arts and Sciences. Edinburgh: A. Donaldson & J. Reid, 1761.

Goodsell, Samuel C.

Book of Stubborn Facts. New Haven, Hoggson & Pubmor, 1885.

Goose, A. B.

The Magic of the Pyramids. London: Women's Printing Society, 1915.

Goyon, Georges

Les inscriptions et graffiti des voyageurs sur la Grande Pyramide. Cairo: Société Royal de Géographie, 1944.

Graham, Edwin R.	*The Ancient Days or the Pyramid of Ghizeh in the Light of History.* Chicago: C. Jones, 1888.
Grandjean, Bent Otto	*The Physiological Basis of the Five Arts: A Theory.* Storkens Kvarter: Albertslund, 1967.
––––––	*Pyramiden-Konstructionen Ved Hjaelr Kvadratrod.* Storkens Kvarter: Albertslund, 1967.
Gray, Julian Thorbirn	*The Authorship and Message of the Great Pyramid.* Cincinnati: E. Steinmann, 1953.
Greaves, John	*Pyramidographia, or a Description of the Pyramids of Egypt.* London: J. Brindley, 1736.
––––––	"A Discourse of the Roman Foot and Denarius," In *Churchill: A Collection of Voyages.* London: 1732, Vol. II, p. 675.
Gressmann, Hugo	*The Tower of Babel.* New York: Jewish Institute of Religion Press, 1928.
Grimthorpe, Edmund Beckett	*A Book of Building, Civil & Eccliesiastical.* London: Crosby & Lockwood, 1876.
Grinsell, Leslie V.	*Egyptian Pyramids.* Gloucester: J. Bellows, 1947.
Grobert, Jacques F. L.	*Description des pyramides de Ghize et de la Ville du Kaire.* Paris: Logerot-Pehet, 1801.
Groffier, Jean	*La mathématique de l'histoire et son étique.* Paris: La Colombe, 1957.
Grossi, Vincenzo	*Le leggende delle piramidi.* Genova: A Ciminago, 1890.
Guemard, Gabriel	*Historique de la Commission des Sciences et Arts et de l'Institut d'Egypte.* Cairo: Barbey, 1936.
Haberman, Frederick	*The Great Pyramid's Message to America.* St. Petersburg, Florida: The Kingdom Press, 1932.
Hannay, H. Bruce	*The Secret of Egyptian Chronology.* London: Sampson, Law, Marston, 1736.
Hassan, Selim	*The Sphinx, Its History in the Light of Recent Excavations.* Cairo: Government Press, 1949.
––––––	*The Great Pyramid of Khufu and Its Chapel.* Cairo: Government Press, 1960.
Hein, Heinrich	*Das Geheimnis der Grossen Pyramide.* Zeite Sis Verlag, 1921.
Henry, J. G.	*La voix du Sphinx.* Paris: Editions Jean Meyer, 1926.
Herodotus	*The Histories.* Various editions.
Herschel, Sir John	*Popular Lectures on Scientific Subjects.* London: W. H. Allen, 1880.
Hilaire de Bareton (père)	"Le mystère des pyramides et la chronologie sothiaque égyptienne," in *Etudes Orientales #4.* Paris: Geuttner, 1923.
Holscher	*Uvo das Grabdenkmal des Königs Chephren.* Leipzig: J. C. H. Hinrichs, 1812.
Howard-Vyse, Richard William	*Operations Carried On at the Pyramids of Gizeh in 1837.* III Vols. London: J. Fraser, 1840–42.
Hudd, A. E.	*The Great Pyramid of Ghiza.* Exeter: Proceedings of the Clifton Antiquarian Club, 1888.
Hultsch, Friedrich O.	*Griechische und Römische Metrologie.* Berlin: Wiedmann, 1882.
Ibek, Ferrand	*La Pyramide de Cheops a-t-elle livré son secret?* Malines Celt, 1951.

397

James, Sir Henry — *Notes on the Great Pyramid of Egypt and the Cubits Used in Its Design.* Southampton: T. G. Gutch, 1860.

Jeffers, James A. — *The Great Sphinx Speaks to God's People.* Los Angeles: Alberts, 1942.

Jeffery, Edmond C. — *The Pyramids and the Patriarchs.* New York: Exposition Press, 1952.

Jequier, Gustave — *Fouilles à Saqqarah.* Cairo: Institut Français d'Archeologie, 1935.

Jomard, Edmé François — *Description générale de Memphis et des pyramides.* Paris: Imprimerie Royale, 1829.
——— *Remarque sur les pyramides.* Paris: Imprimerie Royale, 1829.

Kingsland, William — *The Great Pyramid in Fact and in Theory.* London: Rider, 1932.

Kircher, Athanasius — *Obelisci aegyptiaci.* Rome: Varesii, 1666.

Kleppisch, K. — *Willkür oder Mathematische Überlegung beim Bau der Cheops-Pyramide.* Munich: Oldenburg, 1927.

Knight, Charles Spurgeon — *The Mystery and Prophecy of the Great Pyramid.* San Jose, California: Amore, 1933.

Knötel, August — *Cheops der Pyramidenerbauer.* Leipzig: Dyksche, 1861.

Kolosimo, Peter — *Il pianeta sconosciuto.* Milan: Societa Editrice Internet, 1959.

Koudascheef, Vladimir — *It Shall Come to Pass.* New York: Privately printed, 1936.

La Jonquière, C. De — *L'expédition en Egypte.* Paris: H. Lavanzelle, 1899–1907.

Landone, Brown — *Prophecies of Melchi-Zedek in the Great Pyramid.* New York: The Book of Gold, 1940.

Lane, E. W. — *An Account of the Manners & Customs of the Modern Egyptians.* London: C. Knight, 1856.

Lange, Kurt — *Pyramiden, Sphinxe, Pharaonen.* Munich: Hormei Verlag, 1952.

Latif, Abdal — *Relation de l'Egypte.* Paris: Dreutel et Wurtz, 1810.

Latimer, Charles — *The French Metric System or the Battle of the Standards.* Chicago: T. Wilson, 1880.

Lauer, Jean Philippe — *Fouilles à Saqqarah.* Cairo: Institut Français, 1935.
——— *Les Pyramides de Saqqarah.* Cairo: Institut Français, 1961.
——— *Les Pyramides à degrés IIIe dynastie.* Cairo: Institut Français, 1962.
——— *Observations sur les pyramides.* Cairo: Institut Français, 1960.
Le problème des Pyramides d'Egypte. Paris: Payot, 1948.

Le Corbusier (pseud. Charles E. Jeanneret-Gris) — *The Modulor.* London: Faber and Faber, 1954.
——— *The Modulor II.* Cambridge, Mass.: MIT Press, 1968.

Lepsius, Richard — *Uber den Bau der Pyramiden.* Cairo: 1843.

Lewis, Havre Spencer — *The Symbolic Prophecy of the Great Pyramid.* San Jose, California: Amore, 1936.

Libri, G. — *Histoire des sciences mathématiques en Italie.* Paris: Panlon, 1835.

Lindsay, Lord A. W. C. — *Letters from Egypt, Edom & The Holy Land.* London: Henry Colburn, 1839.

Lockyer, Joseph Norman — *The Early Temple and Pyramid Builders.* Washington, D.C.: Smithsonian Institution, 1893.
——— *The Dawn of Astronomy.* London: Macmillan, 1894.
——— *Surveying for Archeologists.* London: Macmillan, 1909.

———— *Stonehenge and Other British Stone Monuments.* London: Macmillan, 1856.

L'Hote, Nestor *Notice historique sur les obelisques Egyptiens.* Paris: Leleux, 1836.

Longh, James Perot *In the Beginning God Created the Heaven and the Earth.* New York: Erudite Book, 1936.

Macnaughton, Duncan *A Scheme of Egyptian Chronology.* London: Luzac, 1932.

Maillet, Benoit de *Description de l'Egypte.* Paris: Chex Genneau et Rollin, 1735.

Maragioglio, Vito, and Celeste A. Rinaldi *L'Architettura delle Piramidi Menfite.* Rapallo: Officine Grafiche Canessa, 1963.

Marks, T. Septimus *The Great Pyramid, Its History and Teachings.* London: S. W. Partridge, 1879.

Martiny, Gunter *Die Kulturichtung in Mesopotamien.* Berlin: Hans Schoetz, 1932.

Maspero, Gaston C. C. *Art in Egypt.* London: William Heinemann, 1901.

McCarty, Louis P. *The Great Pyramid of Jeezeh.* San Francisco: Privately printed, 1907.

McConkey, G. M., and W. C. Rufus "A Construction Substitute for Pi in the Great Pyramid." *Popular Astronomy,* Vol. II (1943), 185.

Mayer, Ludwig *Views of Egypt.* London: R. Bowyer, 1804.

Mencken, August *Designing and Building the Great Pyramid.* Baltimore: Privately printed, 1963.

Mohammed, Bey *L'age et le but des pyramides.* Alexandria: Privately printed, 1885.

Moremans, Victor *Pyramides et gratte-ciels au pays des pharons.* Belgium: A l'Enseigne du Plomb qui Fond, 1951.

Moreux, Theophile *La Science Mysterieuse des Pharaons.* Paris: G. Douin, 1923.
———— *Les énigmes de la science.* Paris: G. Douin, 1949.

Morgan, Jacques de *Fouilles à Dachour.* Vienna: Mars-Juin, 1894.

Morison, Stanley *Fra Luca Pacioli.* New York: Grolier Club, 1933.

Muck, Otto Heinrich *Cheops und die Grosse Pyramide.* Berlin: Olter Walter, 1958.

Munck, Carl V. Valdemar *Pyramiderne Og Sphinxen.* Copenhagen: Forfallern, 1921.

Neikers, Herman *Der Goldene Schnitt und die Geheimnisse der Cheops Pyramide.* Koln: M. Dumont, 1907.

Neugebauer, O. *The Exact Sciences of Antiquity.* Princeton: Princeton University Press, 1951.

Newberry, P. E. *El Bersheh.* London: Egyptian Exploration Fund, 1893–4.

Nicklein, J. Bernard *Testimony in Stone.* Haverhill, Massachusetts: Destiny, 1961.

Noetling, Fritz *Die Kosmischen Zahlen der Cheops Pyramide.* Stuttgart: E. Schenzenburt, 1921.

Norden, F. C. *Travels in Egypt and Nubia.* London: L. Davis & Cheyners, 1757.

Ostrander, S., and L. Schroeder *Psychic Discoveries Behind the Iron Curtain.* Englewood Cliffs, N.J.: Prentice-Hall, 1970.

Pacioli, Luca *De Divina Proportione.* Milano: Fontes Ambrosiani, 1956.

Palmer, Ernest G. *The Secret of Ancient Egypt.* London: W. Rider, 1924.

Parcker, John T. *The Quadrature of the Circle.* London: S. W. Benedict, 1851.

399

Parker, Richard A.   *The Calendars of Ancient Egypt.* Chicago: Chicago University Press, 1950.

Parker, Richard A., and   *Egyptian Astronomical Texts.* London: L. Humphries, 1960–64.
O. Neugebauer

Parrot, André   *Ziggurats et tour de Babel.* Paris: Michel, 1949.
————   *The Tower of Babel.* New York: Philosophical Library, 1955.

Parsons, Albert R.   *New Light on the Great Pyramid.* New York: Metaphysical, 1893.

le Pere, Gratien   "Memoire sur les pyramides d'Egypte," in *Description de l'Egypte.* Paris: 1820.

Perring, John Shae   *The Pyramids of Gizeh from Actual Survey and Measurement on the Spot.* London: J. Fraser, 1839–42.

Persigny, Jean G. V. F.   *De la destination et de l'utilité permanente des pyramides d'Egypte.* Paris: Ponlim, 1845.

Petrie, William Matthew   *The Great Pyramid.* London: Tract Society, 1893.
Flinders

————   *Meidum.* London: David Nutt, 1892.
————   *The Pyramids and Temples of Gizeh.* London: Field & Tuer, 1883.
————   *Ancient Weights & Measures.* London: University College, 1926.
————   *Ten Years Digging in Egypt.* London: Religious Tract Society, 1893.
————   *70 Years in Archeology.* London: S. Low, Marston, 1931.
————   *A History of Egypt.* London: Methuen, 1898–1905.

Platt, Paul T.   *The Secret of Secrets.* New York: Thothmona Book, 1955.
————   *Secret: The Pyramid and the Lisa.* New York: Comet Press Books, 1954.

Philo-Israel (pseudonym)   *The Great Pyramid of Egypt.* London: W. A. Guest, 1879.

Pococke, Richard   *The Travels of Pococke through Egypt.* London: The World Displayed, 1762–90.
————   *A Description of the East.* London: W. Bowyer, 1743.

Polixa, Johann   *Die Sprache der Cheops Pyramide.* Steltin: Fischer und Schmidt, 1922.

Power, Alexander   *An Appeal to the Jewish Nation.* London: Privately printed, 1922.

Proctor, Richard Anthony   *The Great Pyramid: Observatory, Tomb, and Temple.* London: Chatto & Windus, 1883.

Quinby, Watson Fell   *Solomon's Seal.* Wilmington, Delaware: C. P. Johnson, 1880.

Racey, Robert R.   *The Gizeh Sphinx and Middle Egyptian Pyramids.* Winnipeg, Canada: Public Press, 1937.

Rand, Howard B.   *The Challenge of the Great Pyramid.* Haverhill, Massachusetts: Destiny, 1943.

Rawlinson, Georges   *History of Ancient Egypt.* New York: J. W. Lovell, 1880.

Reisner, George Andrew   *Mycerinius, the Temples of the Third Pyramid of Giza.* Cambridge, Massachusetts: Harvard University Press, 1931.

Rey, Abel   *La Science orientale avant les Grecs.* Paris: La Renaissance du Livre, 1930.

Richer, Jean   *Geographie sacrée du monde Grec.* Paris: Hachette, 1966.

Riffert, G. R.   *The Great Pyramid, Proof of God.* Haverhill, Massachusetts: Destiny, 1944.

Rinaldi, C. A., and V. Maragioglio	*L'Architetturo delle piramidi menfite.* Rapallo: Officine Grafiche Canessa, 1963.
Rouchier, Alexandre	*De l'architecture naturelle.* Paris: Vega, 1949.
Rolt-Wheeler, F. W.	*The Pyramid Builder.* New York: Dappleton, 1929.
Rosenberg, Karl	*Das Raetsel der Cheopspyramide.* Vienna: Osterreichische, 1925.
Rougie, Maurice	*La Cle Secrète de la Pyramide.* Paris: Dunod, 1938.
Ruhlmann, Gerhard	*Kleine Geschichte der Pyramiden.* Dresden: Verlag der Kunst, 1962.
Rutherford, Adam	*Pyramidology.* Dunstable, Bedfordshire: Institute of Pyramidology, 1961.
———	*Anglo-Saxon Israel.* Maplewood, New Jersey: J. A. Greaves, 1934.
———	*Behold the Bridegroom.* Glasgow: Privately printed, 1928 (?).
	A New Revelation: The Controversy of the Cubits Settled. London: Institute of Pyramidology, 1957.
———	*Outline of Pyramidology.* London: Institute of Pyramidology, 1957.
Sander, Hansen, Ce	*De Gammelae Egyptiske Pyramidekster.* Copenhagen: Bianco Lonos, 1953.
Sandys, George	*Sandys Travailes.* London: J. Svveeting, 1652.
Schiaparelli, Ernesto	*Il Significato Simbolico delle Piramidi.* Rome: E. Loescher, 1884.
Schmaltz, John B.	*Nuggets from King Solomon's Mines.* Boston: Barton Press, 1908.
———	*Pyramid Symbols.* Boston: Privately printed, 1911.
Schott, Siegfried	*Untersuchungen Zur Schriftgeschichte der Pyramiden.* Heidelberg: F. Hornung, 1926.
Schwaller de Lubicz, R. A.	*Le Roi de la theocratie pharaonique.* Paris: Flammarion, 1961.
———	*Le Miracle Egyptien.* Paris: Flammarion, 1963.
———	*Le Temple de l'homme: Apet du Sud à Louqsor.* Paris: Caractères, 1958.
Seiss, J. A.	*Miracle in Stone, or the Great Pyramid of Egypt.* Philadelphia: Porter & Coates, 1877–8.
Shaw, Robert	*Four Cosmical Lectures.* St. Louis: Beckhold, 1889.
Shealy, Julian B.	*The Key to Our God Given Heritage.* Columbia, South Carolina: South Carolina State, 1967.
Sinnett, Alfred P.	*The Pyramids and Stonehenge.* London: Theosophical, 1958.
Skinner, James Ralston	*Actual Measures of the Great Pyramid.* Toledo, Ohio: Blode, 1880.
———	*The Great Pyramid of Jizeh, the Plan and Object of Its Construction.* Cincinnati: R. Clarke, 1871.
———	*Key to the Hebrew-Egyptian Mystery in the Source of Measures.* Cincinnati: R. Clarke, 1894.
———	*Some Light on the Egyptian Method of Chronology.* Cincinnati: 1876.
Smith, Robert William	*Mysteries of the Ages.* Salt Lake City: Pyramid, 1936.
Smith, William Stevenson	*Art & Architecture of Ancient Egypt.* Middlesex: Penguin, 1958.
Smith, Worth	*Isles of Splendor.* Cleveland: Louis S. Vosburgh, 1942.
———	*The House of Glory.* New York: Wise, 1939.
———	*Miracle of the Ages.* Tarrytown, New York: Book of Gold, 1952.
Smyth, Charles Piazzi	*Life and Work at the Great Pyramid.* Edinburgh: Edmonton & Douglas, 1867.
———	*New Measures of the Great Pyramid.* London: R. Banks, 1884.

———	*On an Equal-Surface Projection for Maps of the World.* Edinburgh: Edmonton & Douglas, 1870.
———	*On the Antiquity of Intellectual Man.* Edinburgh: Edmonton & Douglas, 1868.
———	*Our Inheritance in the Great Pyramid.* London: A. Straham & Co., 1864.
———	*The Great Pyramid & the Royal Society.* London: N. Isbister & Co., 1874.
Stewart, Basil	*The Great Pyramid and Current Events.* Kew Gardens, England: Privately printed, 1929.
———	*The Mystery of the Great Pyramid.* London: Routledge, 1929.
———	*Collected Addresses on the Great Pyramid.* London: J. Bale & Sons, 1935.
———	*The Witness of the Great Pyramid.* London: Convenant, 1927.
———	*History and Significance of the Great Pyramid.* London: Staples & Staples, 194–(?).
———	*The True Purpose of the Great Pyramid.* Exeter: Blarne & Evans, 1935.
Straub, Walter L.	*Anglo-Israel Mysteries Unmasked.* Omaha, Nebraska: Straub, 1937.
Taylor, John	*The Great Pyramid: Why Was It Built? & Who Built It?* London: Longmans, Green, 1864.
Thom, Alexander	*Megalithic Sites in Britain.* London: Oxford University Press, 1967.
Timerding, Heinrich	*Der Goldene Schnitt.* Leipzig: B. G. Teubner, 1919.
Tompkins, Henry	*The Pyramids and the Pentateuch.* London: Privately printed, 1873.
Touchard, Michel C.	*Les Pyramides et leurs mysteres.* Paris: Editions Planète, 1966.
Tracey, Benjamin	*The Pillar of Witness.* London: W. H. Guest, 1876.
Thevenot, Melchisedech	*Relation de divers voyages currieux.* Paris: T. Moelte, 1696.
Tucker, William J.	*Ptolemaic Astrology.* Sidcup, Kent: Pythagorean Publications, 1962.
U.A.R.	*The Nocturnal Magic of the Pyramids.* Cairo: Gaston Bonhien, 1960.
Valeriani, Domenico	*Atlante del Basso ed alto Egitto illustrato.* Florence: P. Fumagalli, 1836–40.
Vecht, C. F. van der	*De Steenen Spreken.* Den Haag: W. P. van Stockum, 1950.
Waddell, L. A.	*Egyptian Civilization, Its Sumerian Origin and Real Chronology.* London: Luzac & Co., 1930.
Ward, John	*Pyramids & Progress.* London & New York: Eyre & Spottiswoode, 1900.
Watkins, Alfred	*The Old Straight Track.* London: Methuen, 1925.
Watson, C. M.	*The Coffer of the Great Pyramid.* Palestine Exploration Fund, 1900.
Weigall, Arthur	*A History of the Pharaohs.* London: Thornton Butterworth, 1925.
Werner, Rudolph	*Le Secret de la Pyramide de Cheops.* Brussels: La Flambée, 1943.
Whitehouse, Fred C.	*The Pyramid-Hill of Gizeh.* New York: Privately printed, 1885.
Wilkinson, Sir Gardner	*The Architecture of Ancient Egypt.* London: John Murray, 1850.
Winckler, Hugo	*History of Babylonia and Assyria.* New York: Scribners, 1907.
Wilson, John	*The Lost Solar System of the Ancients Discovered.* London: Longman Brown Green, 1856.
Wood, Herman Gaylord	*Ideal Metrology.* Dorchester, Massachusetts: Privately printed, 1908.

Wynn, Walter — *The Last and the Next War.* London: Society of Communion, 1927.

Yeats, Thomas — *A Dissertation of the Antiquity, Origin and Design of the Principal Pyramids of Egypt.* London: J. A. Arch, 1833.

Zaba, Zbynek — *L'Orientation astronomique dans l'ancienne Egypte et la precession de l'axe du monde.* Prague: 1953.

APPENDIX

Aldred, Cyril — *Akhenaten, Pharaoh of Egypt; a New Study* (London, 1968).

Borchardt, Ludwig — "Ein weiterer Versuch zur Längebestimmung der ägyptischen Meilen." *Janus: Festischrift zum C. F. Lehmann-Haupt's sechstigstem Geburtstage* (Wien, 1921), I, 119–123.

Brugsch, Karl H. — *Die Geographie Ägyptens nach den ältagyptischen Denkmälern* (Leipzig, 1857).

Decourdemanche, Jean Adolphe — *Traité pratique des poids et mesures des peuples anciens et des Arabes* (Paris, 1909).

Engelbach, Reginald — "Précis of the Survey of Egypt Paper No. 39, by J. H. Cole." *Annales du Service des Antiquités de l'Égypte,* 25 (1925), 167–173.

Gardiner, Alan H. — *Ancient Egyptian Onomastica* (Oxford, 1943).

Griffity, Francis Llewellyn — "An Omphalos from Napata." *Journal of Egyptian Archaeology,* 3 (1916), 255.

Hapgood, Charles H. — *Maps of the Ancient Sea Kings; Evidence of Advanced Civilizations in the Ice Age* (Philadelphia, 1966).

Homolle, Théophile — "Ressemblances de l'omphalos delphique avec quelques représentations égyptiennes." *Revue des études grecques,* 1919, 338–358.

Hultsch, Friedrich — "Beiträge zur ägyptischen Metrologie," *Archiv für Papyruskunde,* 2 (1903), 87–93; 273–295; 521–528.

Kees, Hermann — *Ancient Egypt; a Cultural Topography.* Translated from the German by Ian F. D. Morrow. Edited by T. G. James (Chicago, 1961).

Lauer, Jean Philippe — *Études complementaires sur les monuments du roi Zoser à Saggarah; Reponse à Herbert Ricke (Bemerkungen zur ägyptischen Baukunst des Alten Reiches)* Supplement aux Annales du Service des Antiquités de l'Égupte, Cahier No. 9 (Le Caire, 1948).
"La Géometrie des pyramides," *Chronique d'Égypte,* 19 (1944), 166–171.

Montel, Paul — "Sur la grande pyramide de Guizeh," *Bulletin des Sciences Mathématiques,* 71 (1947), 76–81.

Montet, Pierre — *Géographie de l'Égypte ancienne* (Paris, 1957).

Oxé, August — "Kor und Kab: Antike Hohlmasse und Gewichte in neuer Beleuchtung," *Bonner Jahrbücher,* 147 (1942), 91–216.

Petrie, William Matthew Flinders — *Measures and Weights* (London, 1934).

Santillana, Giorgio de, and Hertha von Dechend — *Hamlet's Mill; an Essay on Myth and the Frame of Time* (Boston, 1969).

Segrè, Angelo — *Metrologia e circolazione monetaria degli antichi* (Bologna, 1928).

Sethe, Kurt Heinrich

Stecchini, Livio C.

––––––

Sutzu (Soutzo), M. C.

Dodekaschoinos, das Zwölfmeilenland an der Grenze von Aegypten und Nubien (Leipzig, 1901).

"The Delphian Column of the Dancers," *American Journal of Archaeology,* 61 (1957), 187.
"A History of Measures," *American Behavioral Scientist,* IV (1961), No. 7, 18–21; "The Origin of the Alphabet," *ibid.,* No. 6, 3–7, 35.

"Les Mérites et les illusions de M. Flinders Petrie," *Arethuse,* VII (1931), 31–35. Cf. *Buletinul Societatei Numismatice Romane,* XXVI (1921), Volum festiv inchinat D-lui M. C. Sutzu, and XXV (1930), 7.

INDEX

Abd-al-Latif: on Cheops'
  Pyramid 2, 21, 383
Abdullah Al Mamun 5–6, 383
  Cheops' Pyramid, exploration
    6–7, 9–13, 15, 17, 25, 243,
    245, 252, 383
  latitude measured by 6, 21,
    22, 206
Abu Abd Allah Mohammed ben
    Abdurakin Alkaisi 7
Abury Hill (Eng.) 129
Abusir: pyramid 28
Abu Zeyd el Balkhy 218
Abydos 269
acre (unit of measurement):
  Egyptian 370
  English 74
  Roman (jugerum) 370
Acropolis 355; see also
    Parthenon
Adams, W. Marshal 259
"Agartha" of Tibet 269
Agatharchides of Cnidus 201,
    371, 372, 373–75, 383
  on Cheops' Pyramid 201, 203,
    209, 371
Ahmosis I 388
Aiton, Mr. 90, 91
Akhnaten (Akhenaten) 201, 202,
    207, 322, 336–38, 340, 341,
    342, 343, 345, 373, 383, 384
Akhtaten (Akhet-Aten) 201,
    337–38, 340, 342, 343, 373,
    383
  "Boundary Stelae" 201, 340–
    41, 342
Akkadian 290, 296
  measurement: gā (pint) 312
    imēru 319
Aldred, Cyril: on Akhnaten
    236, 337
Alexander Polyhistor 2
Alexander the Great 214–15
Alexandria 5, 214
  library 3, 5, 215
Ali Gabri 81, 85, 91, 97, 99,
    383
Alvarez, Luis Walter 383
  Kephren, pyramid of 270–72,
    275
Alvarez Lopez, José: Cheops'
    Pyramid, theory 265, 266,
    267
  Fisica y Creacionismo 264–65
al-Warraq 292–93, 335

Amèlineau, Emile 224, 383
Amenemhet 302, 383
  pyramid, Lisht 226
Amenhotep III 389
Amon (god) 302, 338, 349, 384
  temples, see Napata; Thebes
Anglure, Baron d' 18
Annu see Heliopolis
anomalistic time 111, 384
Antisthenes 2
Antoniadi, Eugene Michel:
    Cheops' Pyramid, theory
    158, 233, 253
Antoninus Pius 354
An-Yang (China) 183
Aper, T. Statilius Vol 23
Apion 2
Apollo (god) 349; see also
    Horus
Arabian Gulf 339
Arbuthnot, Lady Ann 65
Archeological Institute of
    America 356, 358
Arc of the Covenant 278
Aristagoras 2
Aristotle 5
armillary sphere 155
aroura (unit of measurement)
    212
arshin (unit of measurement)
    305
artaba (unit of measurement)
    206, 267, 312–13, 314, 318,
    319, 320, 350, see also
    ounce, artabic
Artemidorus of Ephesus 2
Arya-Bhata 384
Assizes of Weights and
    Measures 314
Assyria 165–66, 216
astrolabe 155
astrology 281–83; see also
    cosmology; Egyptian
    mysteries
astronomy 4, 5–6, 21, 347–48,
    354, 381
  azimuth 155, 384
  Babylonia and Mesopotamia
    174, 176–77
  Britain 127, 129–30, 133, 137–
    38, 139–40, 141
  declination 153, 154, 158, 386
  devices and instruments for
    measurement, see armillary
    sphere; astrolabe;

astronomy, devices (contd.)
    chronometer; lens; rod,
    ring-carrying; telescope;
    tube, direction
  diurnal pattern 156, 387
  Egyptian 150, 155, 159, 161,
    165, 166–67, 168–69, 172–
    78, 180, 181, 182, 210–12,
    215, 216, 285, 326, 327,
    347, 369–70, 378
  equinox 156, 158, 159, 165,
    387
  equinoxes, precession of the
    112–13, 145–46, 165, 166,
    169, 172, 174, 175, 380,
    381, 391
  Greek 5–6, 21, 22, 31, 138,
    215, 285
  heliacal rising or setting 155,
    166, 167, 388
  heliocentric pattern 388
  Ireland 140
  right ascension 154, 158, 391
  solar parallax 266, 392
  solstice 392
  sunspots 155, 281–82
  zenith 183
  see also astrology;
    cosmology; earth; latitude
    and longitude; time; zodiac
Aswan see Syene
Aten (god) 338, 384
Athelstan, King 344–45
Atkinson, R. J. C. 138
atur (unit of measurement)
    178, 303, 321, 327, 333,
    340, 341, 342

Babylon: ziggurat 184, 186–87,
    378
Babylonia: astronomy 174,
    176–77
  cosmology 184
  measurement 214
    cubit 216, 266
  ziggurats 119, 184, 186, 187–
    88, 279, 378, 392
  see also Akkadian; Chaldea;
    Mesopotamia; Sumerians
Baghdad (Dar-al-Salam) 5
Ballard, Robert T. 117, 119–20,
    268, 384
  Cheops' Pyramid, theory 229
  The Solution of the Pyramid
    Problem 120, 121, 384

Barber, F. M.: Cheops'
Pyramid theory 223, 226,
231, 233, 269
*Mechanical Triumphs of the
Ancient Egyptians* 223
Barluk, Sultan 18
Barnard, F. A. P. 107, 141, 384
Barsipki: ziggurat of Nabu 184
basi (mathematics) 372
Bede, Venerable 139–40
Behdet (Hermopolis Parva)
178, 180, 181, 201, 211,
293–94, 299, 315, 317, 333,
334, 338, 339, 340, 342, 343,
384
Belzoni, Giovanni Battista 384
Kephren, pyramid of,
exploration 272, 384
Benjamin ben Jonah 29
Bessel, Friedrich Wilhelm 212
Bible 217, 262–63, 319
Biot, Jean Baptiste 121, 168,
384
Cheops' Pyramid, theory 121
Bird, John 360
bird (as symbol) 298, 349
Blavatsky, Madame H. P.: on
Cheops' Pyramid 256–57, 259
Isis Unveiled 257
The Secret Doctrine 256–57
Blue Nile 339
The Book of the Dead 93, 259–
60, 284, 369, 370, 385
Borchardt, Ludwig 385
Cheops' Pyramid: exploration
202, 366
theory 220, 236, 238–39,
240, 368
on Egyptian measurement
177–78, 332–33
Borst, Lyle B. 138–39
Boscovitch, Father Ruggiero
362–63
Bouchard, Capt. Pierre-
François-Xavier 51, 385
Bovis, M. 275, 277
brasse (fathom; orgyia; unit of
measurement) 203, 206,
209, 212, 213
Britain: megalithic monuments
and astronomical
observations 127, 129–30,
133, 137–38, 139–40, 141,
146; *see also* Maes-Howe;
Stonehenge
Bruchet, J.: Cheops' Pyramid,
theory 251–52
Brugsch, Karl H. 292, 385

Brunés, Tons 385
Cheops' Pyramid, theory 235,
261
*The Secrets of Ancient
Geometry* 256, 257, 261–62,
385
building construction 220, 222–
35
corbeled masonry 153, 386
finding true level 151, 220
"stretching of the cord" 150,
380
stoneworking tools, 103, 222,
228, 229, 323
see also Cheops, Pyramid of,
building construction;
column; mastaba;
Parthenon; pylon; pyramid;
ziggurat
Bull, cult of the 169, 172, 174
Burattini, Tito Livio 30, 31, 96,
304, 305, 385
Butoridas 2

cabala 260–61, 301, 385
Cairo (El Kaherah) 17–18, 317
Smyth's description 78
Campbell, Col. Patrick 65, 385
canne (unit of measurement)
206, 209, 212
Canterbury, Archbishop of 24
Canterbury Cathedral 139
Cape Az Zaytīyah 340
Cardano, Girolamo 22, 317, 385
De Subtilitate 317
cartouche 65, 220, 385
Cassini, Cesare Francesco 386
Cassini, Giacomo 386
Cassini, Giacomo Domenico
386
Cassini, Gian Domenico 385–
86
Cassini family 32, 33, 385–86
Caviglia, Giovanni Battista 56,
61, 386, 389
Cheops' Pyramid, exploration
56–59, 61, 386
Cayce, Edgar 115, 385
chain (unit of measurement)
31, 306
Chaldea 264
Champollion, Jean-François:
Rosetta Stone deciphered 55,
201, 305
Charlemagne 313
Charroux, Robert: *Le Livre des
Secrets Trahis* 269
Chassapis, C. S. 138

Cheops (Khufu) 65, 116, 234,
235, 236
Cheops, Pyramid of 1–3, 4,
141–42, 183, 217, 236, 275
Ascending Passage 10–11, 12,
25, 81, 115, 151–52, 239,
240, 242, 243, 251, 252–53,
255
granite plugs 9–10, 15, 25,
78, 235, 236, 238, 240–41,
243, 244, 245, 246, 251,
252–53, 255
limestone plugs 10, 25, 58,
236, 240–41, 245, 252, 255
bats in 25, 27, 35, 36, 44, 56,
57
building construction 2, 26,
68, 105, 151, 153, 220, 223–
35, 240
cement 105, 247
dates assigned 219–20, 227
granite 1, 9, 10, 15, 17, 25,
26, 27, 36, 63, 78, 103, 220,
235, 236, 240–41, 243, 244,
245, 248, 249, 251, 253,
255, 266, 270, 392
limestone 1, 2, 7, 17–18, 25–
26, 65, 67–68, 220, 229,
230, 236, 240, 241, 242,
245, 248, 249, 255
mortar 105, 229, 230
plaster 247, 249
Campbell's Chamber 63, 65,
385
capstone, *see* pyramidion
below
casing stones 1, 2, 3, 17, 18,
19, 45, 67, 68, 89, 103, 105,
108, 220, 225–26, 228, 229,
230–31, 232, 244, 265–66
commentaries on: Abd-al-
Latif 2, 21, 383
Agatharchides 201, 203,
209, 371
Blavatsky 256–57, 259
Diodorus Siculus 3, 45, 371
Herodotus 2–3, 65, 70, 190,
194, 196, 201, 222, 225–26,
231, 234, 307, 368, 370, 374,
375
Hogben 142
Muck 143, 145, 146
Philon of Byzantium 371
Pliny 3, 208, 231, 371, 373
Strabo 3, 45, 371
corners *see* sockets *below*
Davison's Chamber 36, 38, 44,
56, 63, 244, 249, 386
Descending Passage 3, 9, 19,

Cheops, Descending Passage (contd.)
24, 47, 58, 81–82, 87, 100, 101, 114–15, 150, 151, 153, 238, 239, 241–45 *passim,* 249, 251, 252, 255
entrances 3, 7, 9, 17, 18, 19, 81
exploration of: Abdullah Al Mamun 6–7, 9–13, 15, 17, 25, 243, 245, 252, 383
Borchardt 202, 366
Caviglia 56–59, 61, 386
Davison 35–36, 38, 386
Greaves 24–30 *passim*
Howard-Vyse 59, 61, 63, 65, 67–68, 81, 101, 105, 385, 386, 388
Petrie 97–98, 99, 105, 228, 229, 234, 247–48, 251, 279, 323
Smyth 78, 80–81, 91, 100, 101
graffiti 2, 3, 38, 252
Grand Gallery 12, 25, 27, 35–36, 87, 115, 152–56 *passim,* 158, 211, 236, 239–47 *passim,* 249, 252, 255
grotto, *see* pit *below*
hieroglyphs reported 2, 15
Horizontal Passage 11, 25
"King's Chamber" 15, 17, 26–27, 29, 47, 49–50, 63, 65, 67, 75, 101, 103, 115, 119, 191, 220, 235, 239, 240, 244, 245, 247–48, 252, 253, 255, 264, 270, 275, 279, 312, 322, 363, 392
coffer ("sarcophagus") 15, 26, 27, 47, 75, 83, 103, 257, 266–67, 278, 321–26 *passim*
portcullis 15, 26, 253, 270
ventilating shafts 29–30, 67, 78, 101
Lady Arbuthnot's Chamber 63, 65
legends and superstitions 2, 18, 19, 21, 217–18, 219–20, 268–70, 271
as Masonic symbol 38, 256, 261, 301
measurement 209, 213
angle of slope 45, 47, 67, 68, 70, 89, 189, 231, 366, 368, 379
apothem 45, 46, 47, 108, 203, 206, 208, 209, 213, 262, 264, 368, 370, 372, 373, 374

Cheops, measurement (contd.)
base 1, 28, 31, 44, 46–47, 68, 70, 72, 89–90, 91–92, 106, 108, 111, 112, 113, 189, 197, 202, 203, 206, 208, 209, 210, 213, 365, 368, 373, 374, 378
brasse 206, 209
Burattini 30, 31, 304, 385
canne 206
Cole 202, 203, 207, 208, 220, 323, 362–68 *passim,* 386
Cotsworth 123
cubit 30–31, 47, 74, 75, 77, 81, 92, 103, 106, 112, 145, 206–10 *passim,* 213, 264, 307, 320, 322–23, 363, 365, 368, 370, 372, 373
Davidson 264
decapode 206, 209, 213
Edgar, M. 113
finger 264, 365
foot 206, 209, 210, 213
Golden Section (phi proportion) 190, 191, 194–200 *passim,* 359, 367, 368, 369, 370, 373, 374, 375, 377, 378
Greaves 28, 30, 31, 70, 304, 312, 323, 324, 388
height 28, 44, 47, 68, 70, 72, 89, 94, 112, 189, 190, 197, 307, 368, 369, 370–71, 373
Howard-Vyse and Perring 67, 68, 69, 70, 89, 90, 92
inch 72, 74, 75, 90, 92, 93, 111, 112, 145
Jomard, Coutelle, and Le Père 44–47, 68, 70, 90, 202, 206, 207, 208, 210
latitude 84–85, 206, 213, 293, 372, 375
Newton 30–31, 47, 74, 112, 145, 305, 323
palm 264
parasang 213
Petrie 98–99, 100, 101, 103, 105, 106, 108, 111, 112, 119, 151, 202, 264, 266–67, 323, 324, 362, 363, 366, 368
pi proportion 70–71, 77, 89, 90, 101, 106, 113, 126, 189, 190, 359, 367, 368, 373, 374, 375, 377, 392
plethron 206, 209, 213
remen 206, 209
rod 209
schoenion, long 213

Cheops, measurement (contd.)
schoenion, short 206
Smyth 77, 78, 81–85, 89–91, 94, 106, 107, 108, 112, 145, 323, 324
stadium 206, 209, 213, 364, 372, 373
Taylor 70–71, 72, 74, 75, 89, 94
yard, megalithic 209, 213
Nelson's Chamber 63, 65
painting 2, 265
red ochre 65, 220, 229, 265–66
pavement 68, 90, 106, 123, 124, 145, 220, 229
pit (well, including shaft and grotto) 9, 27, 35, 44, 57–58, 78, 81, 100, 234, 236, 238, 239, 241–47 *passim,* 249, 251–52, 255, 386
pyramidion (capstone) 68, 203, 371, 372, 373, 374
"Queen's Chamber" 11, 12, 25, 62, 130, 239, 240, 247, 252
sockets (corners) 44, 56, 67, 90–91, 106, 202, 357, 359, 363
theories on 275, 277, 278–79
Alvarez Lopez 265, 266, 267
Antoniadi 158, 233, 253
Ballard 229
Barber 223, 226, 231, 233, 269
Biot 121
Borchardt 220, 236, 238–39, 240, 368
Bruchet 251–52
Brunés 235, 261
Caviglia 59
Cotsworth 122–25, 127, 226, 232, 233
Cottrell 239, 240–41
Davidson 108, 111, 113, 114, 116, 125, 245–47, 248–49, 251, 253, 255, 267
Edgar, J. and M. 253
Edwards 220, 227, 229, 235
Funk-Hellet 156, 262–63, 264, 267, 270
Goyon 252–53
Jomard 47, 48, 51, 67, 72, 75, 116, 176, 189, 201, 207, 208, 212, 267
Kingsbury 255
Kingsland 124, 234, 253, 256, 259, 270

Cheops, theories on (contd.)
McCarty 270
Macnaughton 255
Maragiolio and Rinaldi 229,
230, 240, 242–43, 249, 252
Mencken 107, 233, 243–44
Menzies 93, 108, 114
Petrie 103, 105, 106, 219,
226–27, 228, 229, 231, 235,
236, 242, 248, 249
Proctor 147, 149–56 *passim,*
158, 253, 284, 391
Smyth 87, 89, 92, 93, 94, 96,
103, 106, 107, 108, 111,
112, 114, 116, 121, 122,
207, 212, 267, 269–70, 384
Stecchini 206, 267, 322–26,
359, 364–75, 380–81
Steward 218–19
Taylor 70–71, 72, 74, 75–76,
77, 83, 89, 90, 94, 96, 106,
108, 116, 189, 207, 212,
267, 392
see also legends and superstitions *above*
tourists 2, 3, 81, 89, 100–01
well, *see* pit *above*
Wellington's Chamber 63
see also Giza complex
chetverik (unit of measurement) 311, 318
Chichen Itzá (Mex.): ball court
295
China: measurement 304, 312
chronometer 176, 183
Cicero 259
circle: as sacred 260–61
squaring of 197, 198, 199, 200
Clarke, Somers: *Ancient
Egyptian Masonry* 229
Clarke Spheroid 295, 327, 331,
346
clepsydra, *see* water clock
clinkstone 83, 386
clinometer 81–82, 386
Colbert, Jean Baptiste 363
Cole, J. H.: Cheops' Pyramid,
measurement 202, 203,
207, 208, 220, 323, 362–68
passim, 386
Cologne, Baron de 269
column: Egyptian 331
Greek 331, 332
compass (as symbol) 261
Copernicus 156, 175
cosmology: Babylonian 184
Egyptian 292, 299, 301–02
maet 301, 336–37, 343

cosmology (contd.)
Mycenean 353–54
see also Golden Section;
seven; triangle
Cotsworth, Moses B. 121–22,
386
on ancient astronomical
studies 122, 125–27, 129,
141, 142, 146, 386
Cheops' Pyramid: measure-
ment 123
theory 122–25, 127, 226,
232, 233
Cottrell, Leonard 386
Cheops' Pyramid, theory 239,
240–41
Mountains of Pharaoh 239
Coutelle, Jean Marie Joseph:
Cheops' Pyramid, measure-
ment 44, 47, 68, 70, 90, 207
Croon, L. 231
cross (as sacred) 261
cubit 47, 74–75, 206, 210, 212,
300, 305, 307, 310, 315,
319, 320, 365
in Bible 262–63
Chaldean 264
geographic (Greek) 201, 202,
206, 207, 208, 209, 211,
213, 266, 303, 318, 321,
322, 326, 342, 345, 351,
352, 369
great 216, 266
pyk belady 47, 206, 209, 213
Roman 305, 318, 319, 320
royal (Memphis; profane;
septenary) 30–31, 47, 106,
112, 177–78, 209, 213, 216,
262–63, 299–300, 303, 305,
315, 320–21, 322–23, 326,
332–34, 345, 363, 365
sacred 30, 31, 74, 77, 81, 112,
145
see also Cheops, Pyramid of,
measurement, cubit
Cuernavaca (Mex.): Pyramid
of Xochicalco 185
Cush, *see* Nubia
Cyril, St. 4
Cyrus the Great 262

Darius the Great 214, 298
Darwin, Charles 76
Dashur: pyramid of Sneferu
28, 125–26, 133, 137, 217,
226, 243, 268
Daued 63

Davidson, David 208
Cheops' Pyramid: measure-
ment 264
theory 108, 111, 113, 114,
116, 125, 245–47, 248–49,
251, 253, 255, 267
Davison, Nathaniel: Cheops'
Pyramid, exploration 35–36,
38, 386
decagon 261
decans 386
decapode (unit of measurement) 206, 209, 212, 213
Dechend, Hertha von: *Hamlet's
Mill* 174, 289, 297, 381
decimal units of measurement
212; *see also* metric system
de Clifford, Norman Frederick:
*Egypt, The Cradle of
Ancient Masonry* 259
Decourdemanche, Jean
Adolphe 310
degree, *see* latitude and
longitude
Delphi 183, 184, 348–50
omphalos 349, 350
Delphos 349
Delta 180, 292–93, 299, 300,
303, 335, 342, 343
Demetrius of Phaleron 2
Demoteles 2
Dendera 386, 388
temple of Hathor 49, 168–69,
172, 386
zodiac 49, 168, 172–74, 175,
386
temple of Isis 168, 286
Denis-Papin, Maurice 278
Denon, Baron Dominique
Vivant 387
*Voyage dans la basse et la
Haute Egypte* 51, 387
Desaix, Gen. Louis Charles
Antoine 48–49, 168, 172
Description de l'Egypte . . .
50–51, 208
Didoufri 387
Diodorus Siculus 48, 387
on Cheops' Pyramid 3, 45,
371
Dionysius of Halicarnassus 2
Dodekaschoinos 303
Dnieper River: landmarks used
in surveying 346
Dodona 183, 184, 348–49, 350
Drbal, Karel 277–78
Drioton, Etienne 208, 212
Druids 127

Dümichen, Johannes 150, 387
Duris of Samos 2

earth, circumference of 206–
07, 213, 315, 346
Arabs 6, 206
Bessel 212
Egyptian 176, 210, 211, 215,
326, 327, 347, 370
Eratosthenes 22, 31, 215,
285
Galileo 31
Helmert 334
obelisks used in measure-
ment 210, 211
Picard 311
Ptolemy 5–6, 21, 22
earth, flattening of:
Egyptian 369–370, 378
Newton 211, 262
see also Clarke Spheroid;
Helmert; International
Spheroid
earth, latitude and longitude
of, see latitude and
longitude
Edfu 387
Edgar, John: Cheops' Pyramid,
theory 253
Edgar, Morton 115
Cheops' Pyramid: measure-
ment 113
theory 253
Edwards, I. E. S. 387
Cheops' Pyramid, theory 220,
227, 229, 235
Egypt: dynasties 387, 389
Middle Kingdom 201–02, 290
New Kingdom 390
Northern (Lower) 293, 294,
299, 322
red straw as symbol 293,
300
To-Mehu (hieroglyph) 300,
353
Southern (Upper) 293, 294,
299, 322
white wool cap as symbol
293
To-Shemau (hieroglyph)
296, 353
To-Mera (hieroglyph) 290,
292, 377
Egyptian mysteries 256–57,
259–67, 285–86, 387
eight, see octagon
Einstein, Albert 278

Elephantine 387
nilometer 47
observatory 177
"well" 180–81, 186
eleven, see undecimal units of
measurement
Elgin, Thomas Burke, Lord
61, 386
Elizabeth, Queen 311
Emery, W. 220, 222
Engelbach, Reginald L. 220,
366, 387
Ancient Egyptian Masonry
229
England: measurement 304,
305, 309, 343–45
acre 74
chain 31, 306
foot 22, 23, 24, 27, 72, 207,
305, 311–12, 343–45
grain 309, 313
inch 72, 73–74, 75, 77, 90,
106, 111
king's girth 344
measuring rod 27, 82–83
mile 31, 74
ounce avoirdupois 309
ounce Tower 313
ounce troy 313
pound 304
quarter 75
yard 74, 344
Imperial 311, 360
see also Britain
Enoch, see Hermes
Trismegistos
Eratosthenes 22, 31, 45, 183,
215–16, 285, 323
Euclid 5, 377
Euhemerus 2

Fakhry, Ahmed 225, 268
fathom, see brasse
Fibonacci, Leonardo Bigollo
192, 387
Fibonacci series 192, 194, 285,
368, 387
finger (unit of measurement)
209, 212, 264, 305, 318, 365
First Cataract 178, 295, 296,
302–03, 333
Firth, Cecil Mallaby 387
five: five-pointed star 261–62,
377
pentagon 261–62
Flinders, Matthew 96
Flinders Petrie see Petrie,
William Matthew Flinders

foot (unit of measurement) 33,
206, 305
Egyptian 33, 206, 208, 209,
210, 212, 213, 305, 307,
309, 310, 312, 319; see also
geographic below
English 22, 23, 24, 27, 72,
207, 305, 311–12, 343–45
geographic (Greek) 24, 206,
208, 209, 213, 216, 312,
314, 318, 350–51, 352, 356,
359, 360, 361
Mycenean (Oscan; Italic)
352, 355, 358, 360, 361
Persian 206
pied de roi 38, 311, 318, 363
Ptolemaic 207
Roman 22, 23–24, 208, 304,
305, 309, 310, 312, 316,
317, 318, 319, 350–51, 352,
359, 360, 363
cubed (geometric; scientific;
quadrantal; pes
quadrantus) 310–11, 312,
318–19
longer (pes Aebutianus) 310
shorter (pes Statilianus) 310
United States 311
four, see quarter; quaternary
units of measurement
France: measurement 362–63
grain 308–09, 313
livre 308–09, 313
measuring rod 32
ounce 309, 313
pied de roi 38, 311, 318, 363
toise 33, 38
see also meter, French;
metric system, French
Free Masons 256, 259, 261
apron resembling royal
napkin 195
Cheops' Pyramid as symbol
38, 256, 261, 301
straightedge and compass as
symbol 261
Funk-Hellet, Charles 194
La Bible et la Grande
Pyramide d'Egypte 262–66
passim
Cheops' Pyramid, theory 156,
262–63, 264, 267, 270
Furville, Henri
La Science Secrète 260

Galen 5
Galileo (Galileo Galilei) 30, 31,
156, 316

Garnier, Col. J. 116
Gauguelin, Michel: *The Scientific Basis of Astrology* 281, 282
geodesy and geography 5, 21, 176, 177, 180–85, 189, 201, 202, 203, 207, 214, 215, 293–303, 317, 320–21, 326–27, 332–35, 339–43, 345–47, 369–70; *see also* earth; Eratosthenes; land surveying; measurement; Mercator projections; Ptolemy; spheroid
geometry *see* mathematics
Germany: Cologne ounce 313
  mark 313–14
Ghānim 340
Gibbon, Edward 5
Giza complex 1, 35, 59, 80, 268
  legends and building construction 217, 218, 219–20, 222–35
  pyramids as basis for computing triangulation 98–99, 117, 119–20
  see also Cheops, Pyramid of; Kephren, pyramid of; Mykerinos, pyramid of
gnomon, geodetic 387
gnomon, mathematical 372
Golden Chersonnesos 185
Golden Section (phi proportion) 190, 191, 193–200 *passim,* 262, 285, 359, 367, 368, 369, 370, 373, 374, 375, 377, 378, 385, 388
  and pi proportion relation to 194, 377
Goneid, Amr 273, 275
Goths 127
Goyon, Georges 252
  Cheops' Pyramid, theory 252–53
grain (unit of measurement):
  English 309, 313
  French 308–09, 313
gram (unit of measurement) 304, 309, 313, 314, 318, 319, 320
Greaves, John 21, 22–23, 28–29, 96, 304, 388
  Cheops' Pyramid: exploration 24–30 *passim*
  measurement 28, 30, 31, 70, 304, 312, 323, 324, 388
  Pyramidographia 29, 388

Greece: architecture, *see* Acropolis; column, Greek; Parthenon
  astronomy 5–6, 21, 22, 31, 138, 215, 285
  geodesy and geography 183, 185, 215, 302; *see also* Eratosthenes; Ptolemy
  mathematics 195, 261, 262, 331–32, 372, 377; *see also* Euclid; Pythagoras
  measurement 24, 306, 308, 311, 350–51; *see also* cubit, geographic; foot, geographic; stadium
  oracles, *see* Delphi; Dodona
Gregory I, Pope 139–40
Groves, Brig. P. R. C. 108
Guignaud, Maurice: *Falicon* 140–41

Hall, Manly P. 284–85
hand (unit of measurement) 305, 318, 321
Hapy 388
Harun Al-Rashid 5
Harvey, William 29, 67
Hasan, Sultan: mosque, Cairo 18
Hassan, Selim 224
Hathor (goddess) 388; *see also* Dendera, temple of Hathor
Hawkins, Gerald S.: *Stonehenge Decoded* 159
Hayford, John Fillmore 112, 343, 369; *see also* International Spheroid
Heliopolis (Annu; On) 234–35; 388
  temples 167, 168, 388
  university 214, 388
Helmert: circumference of earth calculated 344
  spheroid calculated 322, 327, 329, 369
Heluan 269
Henry I, King 344
Heraclitus 259
Hermes (god) 284; *see also* Thoth
Hermes Trismegistos (Enoch) 218, 389
Hermopolis Parva, *see* Behdet
Herodotus 47, 48, 165, 177, 185, 227, 279, 370, 388
  on Cheops' Pyramid 2–3, 65,

Herodotus (contd.)
  70, 190, 194, 196, 201, 222, 225–26, 231, 234, 307, 368, 370, 374, 375
  History 2, 388
Herschel, Sir John 89, 149, 186, 264, 388
  unit of measurement 72–74
Hetepheres, tomb of 236
hexagesimal units of measurement 187
hexagon 261
hieroglyphs 3, 38, 103, 176, 177, 260, 294, 296, 333
  on Cheops' Pyramid, reports of 2, 15
  determinative 292
  for Egypt (intermediary district) 297, 300
  for Egypt (*To-Mera*) 290, 292, 377
  for Egypt, Northern (*To-Mehu*) 300, 353
  for Egypt, Southern (*To-Shemau*) 296, 353
  for meridians and parallels 298, 349
  Rosetta Stone 51, 55, 65, 385
  "Unity of Egypt" 300–01
Hill, Mr. 67
Hipparchus 45, 145, 215, 285
Hiram Ariff 263
Hogben, Lancelot 158
  on Cheops' Pyramid 142
Holland, Thomas 270
Homer: *Odyssey* 185
"horn of the East" 339
Horus (god) 387, 388; *see also* Apollo
hourglass 152
Howard-Vyse, Richard 59, 61, 388
  Cheops' Pyramid, exploration 59, 61, 63, 65, 67–68, 81, 101, 105, 385, 386, 388
  Dashur, pyramid of Sneferu, exploration 268
  Operations Carried on at the Pyramids of Gizeh in 1837 69, 388
Hultsch, Friedrich 307–08, 309, 315
Hyksos 388, 390
Hypatia 4

ibn-Batuta 218, 389
Ibrahim ben Ebn Wasuff Shah 218

Imhotep 168, 217, 320, 375–
76, 377, 384, 389, 391; *see
also* Saqqara, pyramid
inch (unit of measurement)
305
Egyptian 72, 74, 75, 90, 92,
93, 111, 112, 145
English 72, 73–74, 75, 77, 90,
106, 111
Roman 305
Inglis, Mr. 90, 91
International Spheroid 326,
327, 331, 346, 365, 369
Ireland: "Round Towers" 140
Ismail Pasha 78
Israel: cabalistic symbol of
triangles as emblem 301;
see also Jews
Italic foot, *see* foot, Mycenean

Jefferson, Thomas 316
Jerusalem 183
Tabernacle 262
Temple 31, 263
Jews 302
Arc of the Covenant 278
emblem of Israel cabalistic
symbol 301
legends about Cheops'
Pyramid 31, 217
Lost Tribes of Israel 75
mathematics and measure-
ment 31, 262–63, 306
mile 212
Mount Gerizim as center of
Worship 183
see also cabala; Jerusalem;
Josephus
Jomard, Edmé-François:
Cheops' Pyramid: explora-
tion 44
measurement 44–48, 202, 206,
207, 208, 210
theory 47, 48, 51, 67, 72, 75,
116, 176, 189, 201, 207,
208, 212, 267
Jonas, Dr. Eugen 283–84
Josephus 31, 217
Julius Caesar 3

ka 389
Karnak: temple of Amon-Ra
161, 165
temples 165, 195, 391, 392
Kephren 271
Kephren, pyramid of 1, 224,
272, 320, 325, 378–79, 380,
381, 384

Kephren (contd.)
coffer 321, 325–26
examination by cosmic rays
271–72, 275
Petrie, measurement 325,
378, 381
portcullis 235
see also Giza complex
Kepler, Johannes 156
khe (unit of measurement) 340,
342; *see also* stadium
Kher-aha (Kerkasoros) 335
Khufu, *see* Cheops
kilogram (unit of measurement)
308
Kingsbury, Donald: Cheops'
Pyramid, theory 255
Kingsland, William 284
Cheops' Pyramid, theory 124,
234, 253, 256, 259, 270
Kircher, Father Athanasius 30,
305, 385, 386
Knights Templar 140, 256
Kolosimo, Peter 269
Terra Senza Tempo 219

Lake Moeris: pyramids 268
land surveying 98–99, 117,
119–20, 297
basi 372
iku 297
merkhet 260
theodolite 84, 96, 99, 392
triangulation 392
Dnieper River landmarks
used 346
Nile landmarks used 117,
180, 339–40, 346
Langlois 363
latitude and longitude 6, 21,
22, 32–33, 46, 47, 73, 84–
85, 138, 146, 147, 149, 151,
152, 154, 174, 176, 177,
178, 181, 182, 185, 189,
199–203, 206, 207, 209–15,
293, 314, 315, 321, 322,
323, 326–32, 334, 335, 342,
343, 345–48, 351, 352, 365,
369, 372–73, 375, 390
birds as symbol 298, 349
net as symbol 301, 349
*Smithsonian Geographical
Tables* 178, 315, 317, 321,
322, 327, 334, 345, 346–47,
350
see also sidereal time; solar
time

Lauer, Jean Philippe 194, 208,
221, 376–77
Le problème des Pyramides
208, 376
Lehmann-Haupt, Carl Friedrich:
on ancient measurement
315, 316
lens (for astronomical
computation) 219
Leonardo da Vinci 193
Le Père, Gratien: Cheops'
Pyramid, measurement 47,
68, 70, 90, 207
Lepsius, Karl Richard 389
libra (unit of measurement)
308–13 *passim,* 318
Lieder, Rudolph Theophilus
183, 389
Lindsay, Alexander William
Crawford, Lord 56, 389
linear measurement, *see*
measurement
Lisht: pyramid of Amenemhet
226
livre (unit of measurement)
308–09, 313
Lockyer, Sir Joseph Norman
126, 159, 389
astronomical theories 159,
161, 165–69 *passim,* 172,
174, 234
The Dawn of Astronomy 159,
169
Lost Tribes of Israel 75
Luini, Bernardino 194
Luxor 389; *see also* Thebes

McCarty, Louis P.: *The Great
Pyramid of Jeezeh* 270
Macnaughton, Duncan: *A
Scheme of Egyptian
Chronology* 255
Maes-Howe (Scot.) 130, 133,
137, 146, 255
maet (truth or justice) 301,
336–37, 343
Mamun, Al, *see* Abdullah Al
Mamun
Mandeville, Sir John 21, 389
Manetho 387, 389
Maragioglio, Vito: *L'Archi-
tettura delle Piramidi
Menefite* 228–29
Choeps' Pyramid, theory 229,
230, 240, 242–43, 249, 252
Mariette, Auguste 389
Mark Anthony 3
Martiny, Gunther 165–66

Masons, *see* Free Masons
Maspero, Sir Gaston Camille
 Charles 146, 165, 169, 185,
 383, 385, 389
mastaba 126, 146, 153, 389
Masudi, Al 5
mathematics 4, 5, 177, 264
 Britain 137
 Egyptian 48, 72, 176, 190,
 191, 194–200, 261, 285,
 290, 292, 293, 306, 307,
 328, 377
 Greek 195, 261, 262, 231–32,
 372, 377; *see also* Euclid;
 Pythagoras
 Rhind Papyrus 71–72, 261,
 379, 391
 square root 372
 see also circle; decagon;
 Fibonacci series; Golden
 Section; hexagon;
 measurement; octagon;
 pentagon; pi proportion;
 square; triangle; indivdual
 numbers
Maupertuis, Pierre de 363
Maypole (for measuring time)
 129, 133, 146
measurement 304, 307, 319
 Akkadian 312, 319
 Assizes of Weights and
 Measures 314
 Babylonian and Mesopota-
 mian 214, 216, 266, 304,
 308, 315, 380
 Chinese 304, 312
 decimal units 206, 209, 212,
 213, 261, 286; *see also*
 metric system
 devices and instruments:
 armillary sphere 155
 astrolabe 155
 chronometer 176, 183
 clinometer 81–82, 386
 gnomon 387
 hourglass 152
 lens 219
 as Masonic symbols 261
 Maypole 129, 133, 146
 nilometer 47, 390
 obelisk, *see* obelisk
 rod, measuring, *see* rod,
 measuring
 rod, ring-carrying 155, 156
 sextant 84, 96
 sundial 155
 telescope 162, 156, 159,
 176

measurement (contd.)
 theodolite 84, 96, 99
 tube, direction 155, 156
 vernier 82, 96, 392
 vessels 306
 water clock 152, 158
 Egyptian 30–31, 209, 212,
 304–10 *passim,* 317, 326,
 328
 English, *see* England,
 measurement
 French, *see* France,
 measurement
 German 313
 Greek 24, 306, 308, 311, 350–
 51
 Herschel 72–74
 hexagesimal units 187, 261,
 301
 Jews 31, 262–63, 306
 length, units of 307, 308,
 309–10
 medieval European 305, 308,
 314
 Mycenean 351–53
 quaternary units 75, 212, 352,
 353
 Roman, *see* Roman Empire,
 measurement
 Russian 305, 311, 312, 313,
 318, 344, 346
 septenary units 185, 187, 294,
 302, 305–07, 321, 326; see
 also *atur;* cubit, royal
 sexagesimal units 187, 212
 standards, concern with: in
 antiquity 308, 315, 351
 in Renaissance 301, 304, 308,
 317, 351
 Sumerian 176, 309, 312, 315,
 372
 undecimal units 306–07, 311
 volume, units of 306, 307,
 309, 310
 weight, units of 307, 308, 309,
 310
 see also earth; land surveying; mathematics; time;
 individual numbers and
 units of measure
Mecca 184, 340
 Kaaba 184
Medûm: pyramid 125, 127, 133,
 137, 217, 226, 392
Mela, Pomponius 370–71
Memphis 181–82, 297, 391
 temples 262

Mencken, August 234, 243
 Cheops' Pyramid, theory 107,
 233, 243–44
 *Designing and Building the
 Great Pyramid* 107
Menes 390
Menon, C. P. S.: *Early
 Astronomy and Cosmology*
 184
Menzies, Robert: Cheops'
 Pyramid, theory 93, 108,
 114
Mercator, Gerhardus 285
Mercator projections 184, 186,
 200, 285
Mercury (planet): association
 with god of measurement
 294
meridian, *see* latitude and
 longitude
Meroe 390
Mesmer, Franz 107
Mesopotamia: astronomy 176–
 77
 measurement 315, 380
 cubit 216
 pound 304, 308
 see also foot, geographic
 ziggurats 184, 302
 see also Akkadian; Babylonia
meter: absolute 265, 266
 Burattini 304
 Chaldean 264
 French 38, 73, 264, 311, 318,
 363, 369
metric system, French 304,
 305, 309, 316, 335, 363
 adopted by Russia 305, 311
 adopted by Spain 314
 adoption considered and
 dropped by United States
 316
Meyer, Eduard 321
Middle Ages: measurement
 305, 308, 311
mile (unit of measurement) 213
 Arabic 6
 Egyptian 212, 213
 English 31, 74
 Hebraic 212
 Roman 351, 352
Miletus, Bishop 140
Minutoli, Johann Heinrich Carl
 390
moira (unit of measurement)
 212
Mokattam 28
 quarries 63, 220, 222

Montagu, Edward Wortley 35, 386
Montel, Paul 376
Moses 259, 262
Mount Gerizim 183
Muck, O.: *Cheops and the Great Pyramid* 143, 145, 146
Murad Bey 39
Mycenae 351, 352
  Grave Circle 355
  Lion Gate 353–54, 355
Myceneans 351
  cosmology 353–54
  measurement 351–55, 359, 361
    foot (Oscan; Italic) 353, 355, 358, 360, 361
Mykerinos, pyramid of 1, 224
  sarcophagus 69
  see also Giza complex

Napata: temple of Amon, omphalos 302
Napoleon 38, 50, 55
  in Egypt 38–39, 50, 305
  visit to Cheops' Pyramid 49–50
navel 302; *see also* omphalos
navigation 5, 308, 314, 321, 351
Nefertiti 336
Nelson, Adm. Horatio 65
Neroman, D.: *La Clè Secrète de la Pyramide* 112
net (as symbol) 301, 349
Newton, Sir Isaac: Cheops' Pyramid, interpretation of measurements 30–31, 47, 74, 112, 145, 305, 323
  A Dissertation upon the Sacred Cubit . . . 31
  earth flattened at poles 211, 362
  gravitation, theory of 31–32, 311, 385, 390
  on precession of the equinoxes 146
  Principia 32, 33, 362
  telescope 133
Nile 292, 317, 339
  flooding 117, 142–43, 226, 228, 233, 292
  Hapy 388
  landmarks used in surveying 117, 180, 339–40, 346
  see also Delta; First Cataract
nilometer 47, 390

Nilopolis, *see* Pi-Hapy
Nimrod 183
Norwell, Richard 31
Novgorod (Russia): Church of St. Sophia 312
Noyes, Alfred 32
Nubia (Cush) 390

obelisk 155, 210–11, 390, 392
  Cotsworth on 122, 126, 127, 146
  Maypole as 129, 133, 146
  Muck on 146
  pyramidion 203
  and Sphinx 33
octagon 261
omphalos (navel; as geodetic mark and symbol) 182, 298, 302, 338, 349, 390
On, *see* Heliopolis
orgyia (unit of measurement) 209, 212; *see also* brasse
Oscan foot, *see* foot, Mycenean
Ostrander, S. 283
ounce (unit of measurement):
  artabic (Cologne ounce; ounce Tower) 313, 314
  avoirdupois 309
  French 309, 313
  Roman 318
  troy 313
Oxé, August 309–10

Pacioli, Luca 193
palm (unit of measurement) 209, 212, 264
Paracelsus 107
parallel, *see* latitude and longitude
parasang (unit of measurement) 213
Parembole 180, 297
Parthenon: columns 332, 360, 361
  measurement 24, 206, 355–61, 380
Paul, St. 259
Pelusium 299, 303
Penrose, Francis Cranmer 356
  Parthenon, measurement 355–56, 358, 359, 360
pentagon 261–62
Pepi 390
Pepi I 168, 390
Pepin 313
Perring, John Shae 59, 67, 390
  Dashur, pyramid 268

Perring (contd.)
  The Pyramids of Gizeh from Actual Survey and Measurement on the Spot 69, 390
Persepolis 183, 214, 298
  tomb of Darius 298
Persia: measurement 213, 214, 298
  see also artaba; foot, geographic; parasang
Peter the Great 311
Petrie, William 96, 97
Petrie, Sir William Matthew Flinders 96, 107, 208, 383, 390
  on ancient measurement 315, 317
  Cheops' Pyramid: exploration 97–98, 99, 105, 228, 229, 234, 247–48, 251, 279, 323
  measurement 98–99, 100, 101, 103, 105, 106, 108, 111, 112, 119, 151, 202, 264, 266–67, 323, 324, 362, 363, 366, 368
  theory 103, 105, 106, 219, 226–27, 228, 229, 231, 235, 236, 242, 248, 249
  Kephren, pyramid, measurement 325, 378, 381
  The Pyramids and Temples of Gizeh 106
Pharaoh 281
  cartouche 65, 385
  crowns 293
  napkin (loincloth) 195
  royal cubit as symbol 307, 321
  "Unity of Egypt" as throne decoration 300–01
  see also obelisk
Philon of Byzantium: on Cheops' Pyramid 371
phi proportion, *see* Golden Section
Phoenician (lang.) 302
pi, *see* pi proportion
Piazzi, Father Giuseppe 77
Piazzi Smyth *see* Smyth, Charles Piazzi
Picard, Jean 32, 311, 362, 390
pied de roi (unit of measurement) 38, 311, 318, 363
Pi-Hapy (Nilopolis) 178, 333, 334, 335
Pindar 259

pint (unit of measurement) 312, 318
pi proportion 70–71, 77, 89, 90, 101, 106, 107, 113, 126, 189, 190, 195, 196, 263, 285, 306, 359, 367, 368, 373, 374, 375, 377, 384, 390, 392
and Golden Section, relation to 194, 377
Plato 5, 48, 119, 259, 262
Timaeus 119, 147, 191, 262
plethron (unit of measurement) 206, 209, 212, 213
Pliny: on Cheops' Pyramid 3, 208, 231, 371, 373
Pococke, Richard 390
Poge, A. 149
pole (unit of measurement) 212
pound (unit of measurement) 304
Proclus 147
Proctor, Richard Anthony 281, 391
Cheops' Pyramid, theory 147, 149–56 *passim,* 158, 253, 284, 391
The Great Pyramid, Observatory, Tomb, and Temple 147
Ptah (god), 375, 391
Ptolemy 6, 21, 22, 183, 215
Almagest 5
pyk belady see cubit, *pyk belady*
pylon 159, 165, 391
pyramid 22, 126, 133, 137, 149–50, 177, 184, 217, 236, 302, 317
apothem 384
Cotsworth on 125–27
as geometric shape 277–78
legends about 217
pyramidion 203, 371
Stecchini on 177
Zaba on 149–50
see also building construction; Cheops, Pyramid of; Dashur, pyramid of Sneferu; Kephren, pyramid of; Medûm, pyramid; Mykerinos, pyramid of; Saqqara, pyramid of Zoser
pyramidion 203, 371
Pythagoras 22, 48, 259, 262, 285, 391
followers 262, 377

quadrant *see* latitude and longitude
quadrantal (unit of measurement) 310-11, 312, 318–19
quarter (unit of measurement) 75
quaternary units of measurement 212, 352, 353
qedet (unit of measurement) 308, 309, 310, 312, 318, 320

Ra 284, 391
ram (as symbol of Amon) 302
Ram, cult of the 169, 172, 174
Rameses II 389
Rameses IX, tomb of 194
Ras Alula 339
Rechnitz, Dr. Kurt 283
rectangle (as symbol) 297, 300
Reich, Wilhelm: orgone energy 278, 282
Reisner, George Andrew 391
remen (unit of measurement) 206, 209
Renaissance: concern with measurement standards 301, 304, 308, 317, 351
Revett, Nicholas: Parthenon, measurement 359–60
Rhind, Henry Alexander 72, 391
Rhind Papyrus 71–72, 261, 379, 391
Ricke, Herbert 376
Rinaldi, Celeste: *L'Architettura delle Piramidi Menefite* 228–29
Cheops' Pyramid, theory 229, 230, 240, 242–43, 249, 252
rod (unit of measurement) 209, 378
rod, measuring: Egyptian 177–78, 320, 332–34, 365
English 27, 82–83
French 32
medieval European 305
rod, ring-carrying (for astronomical computation) 155, 156
Roman Empire: measurement 350–51
acre (*jugerum*) 370
cubit 305, 318, 319, 320
foot *see* foot, Roman
inch 305
libra 308–13 *passim,* 318

Roman Empire (contd.)
mile 351, 352
ounce 318
Rosetta Stone 51, 55, 65, 385
Rosicrucians 256
Russia: measurement 305, 311, 312, 313, 344, 346
arshin 305
chetverik 311, 318
French metric system adopted 305, 311
sajen' 305, 311

Sacred Sycamore 303, 322
sajen' (unit of measurement) 305, 311
Santillana, Giorgio de 169, 260
Hamlet's Mill 174, 175, 289, 297, 381
Saqqara 181, 269, 297, 391
pyramid of Zoser 28, 125, 126, 133, 137, 217, 320, 375, 386, 391
Zoser's Complex 375, 376, 377
see also Sokar (place)
Sardis 183, 349
Sarton, George 155
Saurid, *see* Surid
Schliemann, Heinrich 264, 266
Schmaltz, John B.: *Nuggets from King Solomon's Mines* 112
schoenion, long (grand; great Egyptian; unit of measurement) 209, 212, 213
schoenion, short (unit of measurement) 206, 209, 212
Schroeder, L. 283
Schwaller de Lubicz, R. A. 145, 169, 172–73, 181, 191, 194–95, 203, 266, 391
Le Temple de l'homme 145, 264
Second Pyramid, *see* Kephren, pyramid of
Segré, Angelo 287, 310
Sethites 217
seven (septenary units of measurement) 294, 302, 305–07, 321, 326, 370
in ziggurats 185, 187, 302
see also *atur;* cubit, royal; *sajen'*
sexagesimal units of measurement 187, 212

sexagesime (unit of measurement) 212
sextant 84, 96, 391
sheqel (unit of measurement) 312
sidereal time 111, 153, 317, 347–48, 392
Siemens, Sir W. 278–79
Silbury Hill (Eng.) 127, 129, 146
Simpson, Sir James Y. 94
six: hexagesimal units of measurement 187
hexagon 261
six-pointed star 301
sixty, see sexagesimal units of measurement
Skinner, J. Ralston 260–61
Smith, Worth 278
Smith tablet 186
Smyth, Charles Piazzi 76, 77, 92–93, 96, 107, 108, 122, 208, 312
Cheops' Pyramid: exploration 78, 80–81, 91, 100, 101
measurement 77, 78, 81–85, 89–91, 94, 106, 107, 108, 112, 145, 323, 324
theory 87, 89, 92, 93, 94, 96, 103, 106, 107, 108, 111, 112, 114, 116, 121, 122, 207, 212, 267, 269–70, 384
Life and Work at the Great Pyramid of Jeezeh . . . 93
Our Inheritance in the Great Pyramid 96
Sneferu 125–26, 217, 392; see also Dashur, pyramid of Sneferu; Medûm, pyramid
Socrates 262
Sokar (god) 297–98, 302, 391
Sokar (place) 181–82, 297, 298, 299; see also Saqqara
solar time 108, 111, 112, 113, 143, 207, 316–17, 347–48, 352–53, 392
Solomon 263
Solon 48, 259
Sophocles 259
Sothic time 45, 392
Spain: French metric system adopted 314
spheroid 327; see also Clarke Spheroid; Helmert; International Spheroid
Sphinx 33, 268, 270, 386
square: as sacred 260, 261
as symbol 297, 300

square (contd.)
as unit of measurment 305–06, 307
stadium (unit of measurement) 31, 45–46, 47, 206, 209, 212, 213, 294, 315, 326, 351, 364, 365, 369–70, 372, 373; see also khe
star: five-pointed 261–62, 377
six-pointed 301
Stecchini, Livio Catullo 216, 263, 265, 266–67
on ancient measurement 174, 176–77, 178, 180–88 passim, 194, 201, 202, 206, 211, 214–15, 287–392
Cheops' Pyramid, theory 206, 267, 322–26, 359, 364–75, 380–81
Steward, Basil: The Mystery of the Great Pyramid 218–19
Stonehenge (Eng.) 96, 129, 139, 147, 159, 165, 169
stoneworking, see building construction; tools, for stoneworking
Strabo 339
on Cheops' Pyramid 3, 45, 371
History 3
straightedge (as symbol) 261
Stuart, James: Parthenon, measurement 359–60
Sumerians: measurement 176, 309, 315
basi 372
sila (pint) 312
sundial 155
sunspots 155, 281–82
Surid (Saurid) 218
Susa 183
Sutzu, Prince Mihail 308, 318
Syene (mod. Aswan) 178, 201, 211, 333, 334, 387, 392
quarries 220, 392
see also Elephantine
Sykes, Edgerton 268–69

talent (unit of measurement) 319–20
Taylor, John 70, 75, 93, 107, 185, 208, 392
Cheops' Pyramid: measurement 70–71, 72, 74–75, 89, 94
theory 70–71, 72, 74, 75–76, 77, 83, 89, 90, 94, 96, 106, 108, 116, 189, 207, 212, 267, 392

theory (contd.)
The Great Pyramid: Why Was It Built? & Who Built It? 76, 392
telescope 152, 156, 159, 176
Tellefsen, Olaf 231–32
Tell el-Amarna 201, 337; see also Akhtaten
Templars, see Knights Templar
ten, see decans; decagon; decapode; decimal units of measurement; metric system
Tepe Gawra 309
Thales 2
Thebes (Wast; and Luxor) 302, 303, 343, 389, 392
Labyrinth 317
temple of Amon 165, 194–95, 303, 322, 338, 348, 349, 350, 383, 389
measuring rules 177–78, 332–34
omphalos 182, 302, 338, 349
temples 262
theodolite 84, 96, 99, 392
Theodosius 3
Theon 4
Thom, Alexander: Megalithic Sites in Britain 137–38
Thoth (god) 260, 392; see also Hermes
Thothmes III 168
time: anomalistic 111, 384
devices and instruments for measurement of, see gnomon; hourglass; Maypole; obelisk; sundial; water clock
sidereal 111, 153, 317, 347–48, 392
solar, see solar time
Sothic 145, 392
Titian 194
toise (unit of measurement) 33, 38
tools: for measuring, see measurement, devices and instruments
for stoneworking 103, 222, 228, 229, 323
triangle (as sacred) 103, 119, 139, 194, 261, 290, 292, 301, 377–78, 379, 391
triangulation 392; see also land surveying
Troy 264
tube, direction (for

Tube (contd.)
    astronomical computation)
    155, 156
Tunstall, John 273, 275
Turenne, L. 278
Tyre: temple 165

Udimu 369
undecimal units of
    measurement 306–07, 311
United States: Cheops'
    Pyramid on seal 38, 301
 foot 311
 French metric system
    considered and dropped
    316
United States Naval
    Observatory (Washington,
    D.C.) 153
"Unity of Egypt" 300–01

Ur: ziggurat 184
Uruk: ziggurat 184

Varro 371
  Argonautica 185
Verdi, Giuseppe: *Aïda* 78
vernier 82, 96, 392
Veronese, Paolo 194
Voltaire 363
volume, *see* measurement

Wadi Magharah: quarries 65
Wast, *see* Thebes
water clock (clepsydra) 152,
    158
Watkins, Alfred: *The Old
    Straight Track* 139–40
weight, *see* measurement
Wellington, Arthur Wellesley,
    Duke of 56, 59, 63

White Nile 339
Wood, H. G.: *Ideal Metrology*
    140, 183

yard (unit of measurement):
    English 74, 311, 344, 360
  megalithic 137, 139, 209, 213
Yazolino, Lauren 273, 275

Zaba, Zybnek 149–50, 174
ziggurat 119, 177, 184–85, 186–
    88, 189, 279, 302, 378, 392
zodiac 145, 156, 174, 294–95
 in Dendera 49, 168, 172–74,
    175, 386
Zoser 168, 217, 320, 375, 384,
    386, 391; *see also* Saqqara,
    pyramid of Zoser; Saqqara,
    Zoser's Complex

416